Edward Irving Reconsidered

EDWARD IRVING

Reconsidered

The Man, His Controversies,
and the Pentecostal Movement

DAVID MALCOLM BENNETT

WIPF & STOCK · Eugene, Oregon

EDWARD IRVING RECONSIDERED
The Man, His Controversies, and the Pentecostal Movement

Wipf and Stock
An Imprint of Wipf and Stock Publishers
199 W. 8th Ave., Suite 3
Eugene, OR 97401

www.wipfandstock.com

ISBN 13: 978-1-62564-865-5

Manufactured in the U.S.A.   10/21/2014

Contents

Preface

Edward Irving possesses more of the spirit and purposes of the first Reformers . . . than any man now alive; yes, than any man of this and the last century. I see in Edward Irving, a minister of Christ, after the order of Paul.

—SAMUEL TAYLOR COLERIDGE[1]

It is a strange fact of history that this "minister of Christ, after the order of Paul," was eventually removed from the church he had made famous, expelled from his denomination for heresy, and at the end of his brief life, was demoted in the very sect that emerged from his ministry. He is not well known in today's church. Those that do know him either reject him as a pariah or cautiously praise him as a prophet. The story of Edward Irving is, indeed, a strange one. It is time that his extraordinary life was reconsidered and his teachings reassessed.

To do this, we will draw on many sources. The most important of these is *The Life of Edward Irving* by Mrs. Margaret Oliphant, which in its two-volume edition runs to nearly nine hundred pages. It is cautiously sympathetic. However, Mrs. Oliphant did not understand Irving's theology, which limits her book's usefulness. She saw his greatness, but was uneasy about his later ventures into the charismata. Thomas Carlyle called it "a loyal and clear, but feeble kind of book" and argued that it did not capture the real Irving until towards its end.[2] The book is, in fact, not quite as clear as Carlyle seems to have thought, and it is also rather wordy.

Another very important source is *The Diary and Letters of Edward Irving*, edited by Barbara Waddington and published in 2012. Irving's diary is

---

1. Coleridge, *On the Constitution*, 168.
2. Carlyle, *Reminiscences* (Norton), 1:73, 2:216–17.

very brief. Irving kept it for only one short period in 1810. By contrast, there
are many letters, some of which are very long, spanning virtually his entire
adult life. The letters in this collection, for the most part, do not appear in
Oliphant and other older sources. They were written to a host of people,
both famous and unknown, and present the very heart of Irving. Viewed
collectively, they are both warm and loving, theological and Romantic (in
the philosophical sense). The letters show more than a trace of dogmatism
and, especially towards the end of his troubled life, are at times critical, but
more of groups and ideas than of individuals. It is also striking that many of
the letters written in the last few years of Irving's life are very different from
those written in earlier periods, both in mood and content.

Two other major sources are from the pen of Thomas Carlyle: his *Reminiscences* and *The Carlyle Letters Online (CLO)*. The *CLO* archive contains
many useful letters by Carlyle and his wife Jane, who both knew Irving well.
The lengthy chapter on Irving in Carlyle's *Reminiscences* is a warm-hearted
treasure chest of information, particularly concerning Irving's early life,
even though Carlyle confessed that the chapter was at least as much about
himself as it was about Irving.[3] The Carlyle letters, which relate mainly to
the later period of Irving's life, are more critical of Irving. Considering Carlyle's tendency to exaggerate, his writings, particularly his letters, have been
used with care.

The past twenty years or so have shown a renewed academic interest
in Irving, especially in his theology, and several scholars are attempting to
reinstate him as a preacher and theologian of merit and depth. There have,
in fact, been a large number of learned articles about his theology, plus a
few lengthier works. As one writer put it in 2004, "All at once Irving approaches respectability."[4] He approaches it, but he is, perhaps, still not quite
there. However, as the same writer advises, "Irving must be taken seriously."
Gordon Strachan observed back in the 1970s, "Because of the Pentecostal
analogy and comparison that now exists and which must be the basis of any
future assessment of his person and work, almost everything he wrote and
everything already written about him must be reconsidered,"[5] and this is
what has been happening.

This book is first and foremost a biography of Edward Irving, and it
will take him very seriously. Its main task, then, will be to reconsider his life,
and to do so in depth. However, due attention will be paid to his theology,

---

3. Thomas Carlyle, journal entry, September 26 and December 3, 1866, quoted in
ibid., *Reminiscences* (Norton), 2:220. Please note that both the Froude and Norton editions of Carlyle's *Reminiscences* have been used in research for this book.

4. Sutherland, "Preaching," 4.

5. Strachan, *Pentecostal*, 21.

at least the controversial aspects such as his Christology, his teaching on the Holy Spirit, and his millennialism. To omit Irving's theology would be almost as absurd as telling the story of Houdini and ignoring his escapology. Irving was a theological being, so due attention must be paid to his beliefs.

This volume will not examine the Catholic Apostolic Church (CAC) as such. For although the members of the CAC were often called Irvingites, he was not the leader of that church, nor in the strictest sense its founder, and he died a few years after it began, before it took on some of its distinctive characteristics. We will look at that body only as it connects with Irving's life. That church's later history, for the most part, will not concern us.

We will, however, look at Irving in relationship to the modern Pentecostal Movement in an appendix. Some of today's Pentecostals and Charismatics see Irving as a man after their own hearts. Others, a little nervous of what they have heard of his Christology, show interest in him, but not enthusiasm. Today's Presbyterians—and he was a Presbyterian minister—usually keep him at arm's length, often regarding him as an embarrassment.

So, then, who was Edward Irving? How did he live? With whom did he relate? What made him outstanding? What made him so controversial? What is his legacy? These will be the considerations of this book. It is a compelling story—powerful, yet very sad.

Acknowledgments

I would like to thank the following people and institutions for their help, which was given in a variety of ways. Their assistance has helped make this book possible.

Individuals: Barry Chant, William Faupel, Keith Griffin, Mark Hutchinson, Annette McGrath, Phil Strong, Timothy Stunt, Barbara Waddington, and Helen Weller.

Libraries: Brisbane School of Theology (formerly Crossway College); Creek Road Presbyterian Church; the Lumen Archives; Malyon College; Queensland Theological College; Social Sciences and Humanities and Fryer Libraries, University of Queensland; and the State Library of Queensland.

Wipf and Stock: For granting permission to quote extracts from *The Diary and Letters of Edward Irving*, edited by Barbara Waddington, www.wipfandstock.com

The Banner of Truth Trust, Edinburgh: For giving permission to quote from a letter by John Tizard held by that Trust.

Flower Pentecostal Heritage Center: For permission to quote extracts from John Alexander Dowie's *Leaves of Healing (1894–1906)*, on the *Healing Evangelists, 1881–1957* CD.

Special thanks go to Rev. Ian Richards and Michael Madden for critiquing the manuscript, to Pickwick Publications for access to Irving's diary before publication, and to Peter Elliott for early access to his book and permission to quote from it. As always, thanks also go to my wife, Claire, who so graciously tolerates my wild schemes. Most of them, anyway!

Abbreviations

CAC	The Catholic Apostolic Church
CLO	*The Carlyle Letters Online*
CLSTC	*The Collected Letters of Samuel Taylor Coleridge*
CMA	The Christian and Missionary Alliance
COB	*The Christian Observer*
CS	*The Christian Spectator*
CW	*The Collected Writings of Edward Irving*
GM	*The Gospel Magazine and Theological Review*
DL	*The Diary and Letters of Edward Irving*
LMS	The London Missionary Society
LSPCJ	The London Society for Promoting Christianity Amongst the Jews
NIDPCM	*The New International Dictionary of Pentecostal and Charismatic Movements*
OCEL	*The Oxford Companion to English Literature*
TMW	*The Morning Watch*

Use of Terms

PRESBYTERIAN TERMS

Session: The ruling body of a local Presbyterian church, comprising teaching elders (ministers) and ruling elders (laymen).

Presbytery: A presbytery is made up of an equal number of ministers and ruling elders drawn from each church in a particular district.

General Assembly: The governing body of the Presbyterian Church of Scotland.

OTHER TERMS

Charismatic(s): Churches or people, not in the strictest sense Pentecostal (see below), who claim that they experience or teach about miraculous gifts given by the Holy Spirit.

charismatic: Forms of behavior that are assumed to be miraculous and initiated by the Holy Spirit.

charismata: Assumed manifestations of the miraculous, in line with the gifts of the Spirit in such Bible passages as 1 Cor 12.

Pentecostal(s): Twentieth- and twenty-first-century Pentecostal denominations, churches, or people noted for experiencing the charismata, who usually regard the gift of tongues as the "initial evidence" of the baptism of the Spirit.

pentecostal: Related to the Spirit's coming on the Day of Pentecost.

Author's Note

How any writer records Edward Irving's charismatic phase is inevitably going to be influenced by the author's biases concerning the gifts of the Spirit. I, therefore, feel it is necessary that I state mine. I am not a cessationist. I believe that the gifts of the Spirit *are* still available today, with the exception of the gift of Apostle. However, I suspect that the miraculous gifts are not as common today as many people claim. I think that some of the modern manifestations are genuine, though others I fear are psychological rather than spiritual, still others may be demonic, and I suspect that some are fraudulent. My assessment of Irving's experiences in this area comes from that perspective.

Please also note that emphasis made in quotations is given as in the originals unless otherwise stated.

1

His Family and Childhood

Edward Irving "was the freest, brotherliest, bravest human soul mine ever came in contact with. I call him, on the whole, the best man I have ever . . . found in this world, or now hope to find.

—THOMAS CARLYLE[1]

Two important but highly controversial Christian figures were born in the year 1792: Charles Finney and Edward Irving. They were born into an age of revolution, and each in his own way created spiritual revolution in his respective sphere. In America Finney quite deliberately carved out a new, revolutionary, and dubious theology of evangelism and conversion, while Irving's revolution in Scotland and London seems to have been no less deliberate, but over a wider range of issues. This book is the sad story of this Scottish revolutionary, Edward Irving—free, brotherly and brave, and in some respects, foolish, imprudent, and misunderstood.

Edward Irving was born in Annan, Scotland, on August 4, 1792. He was the fourth of nine children—three boys and six girls—born to Gavin and Mary Irving.[2] The "sandy-blond" Gavin (pronounced "Ga-yin") was "tallish" and "of rugged countenance, which broke out oftenest into some

1. Carlyle, *Carlyle Reader*, 116.

2. Oliphant, *Life*, 1:9–10; Grass, *Edward Irving*, 2, 304, appendix 1. Oliphant says that they had eight children, Grass reports nine. Grass is correct. Oliphant's miscount was presumably caused by the first two children, who both died in infancy, having the same name.

1

innocent fleer of merriment, or readiness to be merry." Gavin Irving was a tanner by trade, though in later life was prosperous enough to be able to supervise that work "from afar," though "afar" is probably metaphoric, for the tanning yard was just across the street from their home. He even served for a time as bailie, or magistrate, in Annan. Thomas Carlyle, the eminent writer, knew the wider Irving family and called them "cheerfully quiet, rational and honest people, of a good-natured and prudent turn."[3]

Mary Lowther Irving, originally from neighboring Dornoch, was "a tall, black-eyed handsome woman . . . thrifty, assiduous, wise, if somewhat fussy" and "full of affection and tender anxiety for her children and husband."[4] Her brother George was famous as the local giant. George was placid and even-tempered, yet when roused to anger on one occasion was said to have bent a poker around an antagonist's neck.[5] Edward Irving seems to have inherited his physical characteristics, including his height and strength, mainly from the Lowther side of the family, and his emotional traits, such as his even temper, from both sides.

According to *The Christian Observer* of September 1823, Irving is said to have claimed in an address to be descended from the Albigenses, a dualistic Middle Ages sect, while Andrew Landale Drummond and Oliphant state that he had Huguenot ancestors on the Lowther side. The latter is more likely than the former. The report about the Albigenses may have appeared because of a scribal error.[6]

Irving's mother's great-grandfather was Rev. Thomas Howy, the minister at the Annan Kirk for much of the first half of the eighteenth century. Irving's grandparents on his father's side were also dedicated Christians. Irving claimed that they rose an hour before the rest of the family to pray for their children, even at harvest time.[7]

Edward's brothers John and George both reached adulthood, but died young and unmarried. John, a doctor, died in India on Edward's birthday, a date Edward later observed as a fast day. Four of his sisters married.[8]

---

3. Carlyle, *Reminiscences* (Norton), 2:2–6.

4. Ibid.

5. Oliphant, *Life*, 1:2–3.

6. "Rev. of—Irving's Orations," 563; Drummond, *Edward Irving*, 15; Oliphant, *Life*, 1:1. Tim Grass doubts that Irving had Albigensian ancestry (Grass, *Edward Irving*, 2 n. 9), though this is what Irving himself claimed in an address, according to the review in *COB* cited above. However, it is possible, perhaps likely, that his words, presumably taken down in shorthand, have been transcribed incorrectly. That is, should "Albigenses" read "Huguenot"?

7. Irving, *CW*, 3:484; Oliphant, *Life*, 1:1.

8. Oliphant, *Life*, 1:4–5; Grass, *Edward Irving*, 304.

The Irvings were regulars at the Kirk in Annan, though were unfortunate in that their minister had a fondness for drink that marred, even destroyed, his ministry. Partly because of this, some in his parish often walked the six miles to a Burgher seceding church in Ecclefechan, where the life and preaching of its minister, Rev. John Johnston, were not so impaired. From about the age of ten Edward Irving became part of this dissenting group, regularly hiking the distance and joining in the spiritual conversations with his older companions. Fit, strong, and healthy, the long trek was not a great difficulty for him. This venture, which seems to have continued until he went to university, was not entirely approved by his parents. It was, perhaps, made more acceptable to them in that Edward's schoolteacher was usually in the traveling party and because one of Edward's uncles lived in Ecclefechan and attended that church.[9] It could have been at this church that Irving first learned his particular understanding of the humanity of Christ.

It appears to have been these experiences that stirred in Irving a love for the Scottish Covenanters, those men and women who had remained loyal to the Presbyterian faith during the persecutions in the late seventeenth century. Irving claimed "with unwearied foot" to have visited "almost every one" of the graves of those martyred at that time.[10] As he once said, "The blood of [these] martyrs mingled with our running brooks; their hallowed bones now moulder in peace within their silent tombs."[11] Their heroic story greatly appealed to his developing Romantic thinking. To Irving, they were not just a part of Scottish history, they were an essential part of his ideal, romanticized Scotland.

It has proven impossible to identify a conversion experience in Irving's life. Perhaps conversions in traditional Presbyterian circles are often perceived to be gradual rather than sudden and are thus less identifiable, or perhaps, in the course of time, it has just slipped under the radar. In fact, as shall be seen, there are those who have charged Irving with placing little emphasis on conversion, which, though an exaggeration, may be partly to blame for this loss. But Irving's life makes it very clear that Christ had made his mark upon him and that Irving was early his dedicated follower.

Annan is a small town in the south of Scotland, near Dumfries and even closer to Gretna Green, where many underage lovers, unable to get married in England, fulfilled their dreams of matrimony. Close by is the Solway, a waterway that divides Scotland from England and which was

9. Carlyle, *Reminiscences* (Norton), 2:2, 11–14; Oliphant, *Life*, 1:18–20. For details of the church at Ecclefechan, see Ian Campbell, "Carlyle and the Secession," in Brown and Newlands, *Scottish Christianity*, 18–36.

10. Irving, "Preliminary Discourse," in Ben-Ezra, *Coming*, 1:cxciii.

11. Irving, *Oracles*, 238.

fordable at low tide. On one occasion Edward came close to disaster when he and his brother John went to meet their uncle George at Solway when the tide was out. Their uncle took longer than expected to appear, and while the boys amused themselves amongst the rock pools, the tide, unobserved by them, began to come in. They were close to becoming trapped when a man on horseback suddenly burst upon them, hoisted the boys up on his horse, and whisked them away to safety. This man was the giant George Lowther.[12]

Gavin Irving did his best to assure that his children, including the girls, received a good education.[13] Edward Irving's first formal schooling was at the hand of the elderly Peggy Paine. Oliphant believed that she was a relative of Thomas Paine, the author of *Rights of Man*, and thus may have been sympathetic towards both the American and the French Revolutions. However, Oliphant gave no evidence to support that belief, and it is probably no more than a local myth.[14]

But Irving's childhood education did not end there. He soon left Paine's school and went to another run by Adam Hope, who had a considerable influence on him. Then in 1802 a school of some distinction was established in the town, Annan Academy. It was a fee-paying institution and a step or two up from both Peggy Paine's and Adam Hope's establishments. Hope closed his own school the following year and joined the teaching staff of Annan Academy, taking Edward Irving with him.[15]

The Reverend William Dalgliesh was the principal at the Academy, but it seems to have been Hope who made the biggest impression upon Irving's inquiring mind. Irving kept a diary for a short while on either side of his eighteenth birthday, and in it he mentioned both men, but it was Hope that he would "remember while [he had] the remembrance of anything." For if Irving was to "rise to any eminence in the world," which he does not seem to have expected, "it shall, [sic] be attributed totally to Mr. Hope." It was from Hope's teaching that he "derived [his] activity of Mind."[16]

Adam Hope was also in the group that made the long weekly trek to Ecclefechan. Hope was said by Carlyle to have been "a bony, strong-built, but lean kind of man," with a "quietly-severe face," whose "humanely-contemptuous grin" seemed to say, "Nothing *good* to be expected from *you*, or from those you come of . . . but we must get from you the *best* you have."

12. Oliphant, *Life*, 1:15–16.

13. Irving to Henry Drummond, July 7, 1829, in Irving, *DL*, 262.

14. Oliphant, *Life*, 1:11. See also Drummond, *Edward Irving*, 16; Grass, *Edward Irving*, 3 n.15.

15. Drummond, *Edward Irving*, 16; Annan Academy, "Our History."

16. Irving, *DL*, 27.

Carlyle, a slightly later scholar than Irving at the Academy, was presumably taking his view from very high standards when he claimed that Hope "did not know very much," but what he did know "he knew in every fibre and to the very bottom."[17]

Amongst Edward's neighbors and schoolmates were the children of the local surgeon, George Clapperton. There were, in fact, plenty of Clapperton children to choose from—twenty-one in all—though not many were around Irving's age. One of the Clappertons, Hugh, who was five years older than Irving, but nonetheless a childhood friend, later became a daring explorer in Africa. In fact, their friendship went beyond childhood. Oliphant says that the last letter Hugh Clapperton wrote was to Irving.[18]

Irving's generosity, a quality he was well-known for in his later years, seems to have manifested itself at an early age. One day when his mother was visiting a friend, Edward, with his younger brother George in tow, went to the neighbor's home to find his mother. When Mary Irving saw her two youngest boys standing rather solemnly at the door, she must have thought it was a household emergency, but no. Instead, Edward told her about another neighboring family that was in want and asked if he could give them some clothes from their own supply.[19] Mary, who "was kind to the poor," granted the request, and the boys hurried off to do their good deed.[20]

17. Carlyle, *Reminiscences* (Norton), 2:7.

18. Bruce-Lockhart, *Sailor*, 4–5; Hibbert, *Africa Explored*, 81; Oliphant, *Life*, 1:21–22. Edward Irving also makes a veiled reference to Clapperton in Irving, *Babylon*, 2:259.

19. Oliphant, *Life*, 1:17.

20. Irving to Henry Drummond, July 7, 1829, in Irving, *DL*, 263.

2

Student and Teacher

He was vain, there is no denying it. But it was a vanity proceeding out of what was best and most lovable in him—his childlike simplicity and his desire to be loved—his crystal transparency of character.

—One of Irving's "dear friend[s]"[1]

FROM EDINBURGH TO HADDINGTON

Irving did sufficiently well at school to leave at the age of thirteen to begin studying for an Arts degree at the University of Edinburgh. This was made possible by a recent inheritance his mother had received following the death of a clergyman relative. Five years later, Edward remembered that he traveled to Edinburgh on November 7, 1805, with his cousin William, who presumably was also to attend the university. Edward's father also went with them for part of the way. Both boys were to come under the care of Mr. John M'Whir, who may have been a relative of the Clappertons.

Yet, according to Oliphant, Irving was accompanied on this trip by his older brother John, who was to study medicine. It would seem unlikely that Irving's recollection would be wrong so soon after the event, so his version is more credible than Oliphant's, though it is of course possible that

---

1. Oliphant, *Life*, 1:122.

both John and William went with him. Whichever is true here, he later confessed in his diary that he found the parting from his parents, other siblings, friends, and the scenes he loved very difficult. And at so young an age, that was to be expected.

At school Edward had proven especially able at mathematics. His tutors at university included John Leslie (later Sir John), the mathematician and physicist, and Alexander Christison, Professor of Humanity. His subjects included Latin, Greek, mathematics, and philosophy. He graduated AM in April 1809, when he was only sixteen, and began a course of theological study with the intention of later entering the Presbyterian ministry.[2] He continued in this course while he earned his living as a schoolteacher.

His first position as a teacher was at Haddington, a town on the south coast of the Firth of Forth with a population of four-to-five thousand. This was on the recommendation of Professor Leslie, who had described him as "a lad of good character and superior abilities." Irving was to teach primarily mathematics and geography, and receive a salary of £20 a year.[3]

Haddington was also the probable birthplace of the Reformer John Knox. Yet, one of that town's most famous daughters later called it "the dim[m]est deadest spot . . . in the creator's universe" and the most "uninteresting place on the face of God's earth."[4] But it would be foolish to suppose that there were not many dimmer and less interesting spots, even in Scotland, and certainly elsewhere. Haddington had been the scene of the labors of pastor and academic John Brown (1722–1787). His ministry in that town had stretched from 1751 to 1787, and in the later years had been combined with the post of Professor of Divinity. In fact, Brown often taught his students in the Haddington Kirk,[5] so the town had not been academically "dead." During that period, John Wesley also passed through twice (in May 1761 and May 1764), staying just long enough to preach a single sermon on each occasion on the property of Provost Dickson.[6] Early in the nineteenth century, a seven hundred-strong regiment of militia was stationed there.

2. Irving's journal, August 4, 1810, in Irving, *DL*, 27–28, 31; Oliphant, *Life*, 1:25–26, 30. Oliphant reports that he was seventeen when he graduated. However, as he was born in August 1792, he would have been only sixteen, assuming the graduation date is correct. In a letter dated 1828, Irving gave the date as 1809, but was not more precise (Oliphant, *Life*, 2:67).

3. Miller, *Lamp of Lothian*, 455, 528.

4. Jane Baillie Welsh to Eliza Stodart, March 8, 1823, *CLO*; Jane Baillie Welsh to Thomas Carlyle, November 26, 1823, *CLO*.

5. Mackenzie, *John Brown*, 83, 135, 147, 260–61. Note that, not surprisingly, there is more than one John Brown in Scottish ecclesiastic history.

6. Wesley, *Works*, 3:54, 178. A later Provost Dickson was Irving's brother-in-law, who frequently played host to Carlyle (Carlyle, *Reminiscences* [Norton], 2:94–95).

Dressed in "scarlet, with yellow facings, and gray trousers,"[7] they would have assured that Haddington was not dim, dead, or uninteresting.

After he had been in Haddington a year, Irving reflected upon its people. He described them as "Possessed normally of a happy mediocrity," and noted that they seemed "to pride themselves in their happiness." But they were "apt to throw of[f] all allegiance to God as the giver of every good, and to believe that their present comfortable circumstances arise solely from their prudence and carefulness . . . Their external conduct [was] not glaringly bad, but yet inconsistent."[8] This, however, might say more about Irving than it does about the inhabitants of Haddington.

Often on Saturdays Irving and a friend, Robert Story, walked to the manse in Bolton to spend time with the local minister, Andrew Stewart. Stewart had been a doctor and his wife was a great lover of music,[9] so no doubt the conversations they enjoyed would have been wide-ranging. Irving seems to have regarded Stewart as a very able preacher.[10] This is striking because Irving had a rather low opinion of the preaching of most Scottish ministers of his time.

He was not always abstemious. One Saturday night he and three friends drank "three bottles of Port," and the next day he arose too late to attend the morning service. So he stayed home and read the *Westminster Confession* instead. The following Tuesday he drank "three bottles of ale" with two friends, though whether that was one bottle each or three each is not clear.[11] He also played lawn bowls and quoits with his friend, Mr. Reddoch.[12]

Irving was generally a kind-hearted man, but he was not one to be trodden down. On one occasion he visited Edinburgh with some of his pupils to hear Thomas Chalmers, a leading Scottish preacher of the day. When he arrived the church was packed, though not quite. One pew in the gallery was clearly vacant, but an usher blocked access to it with his arm. Irving asked the man to move his arm to let him and his companions sit in the vacant seats. The man refused. Irving roared in response, "Remove your arm, sir, or I will shatter it to pieces." The man took a good look at Irving,

---

7. Miller, *Lamp of Lothian*, 344.

8. Irving, *DL*, 46.

9. Drummond, *Edward Irving*, 21–22.

10. Irving called one of Stewart's sermons "very excellent" (Irving, *DL*, 22).

11. Ibid., 18, 23.

12. Ibid., 16–17, 34, 39.

decided that that was indeed possible, and quickly disappeared.[13] This was not to be the last incident of that kind.

Irving seems to have been well accepted and popular in Haddington during the just over three years he spent there (1809–1812). Apart from teaching at the school, he also tutored a number of the children from some of the wealthier families. These included the children of Lord Cathcart,[14] who had fought in the wars in America and against Napoleon.

The most significant of the children Irving tutored was Jane (also known as Jean or Jeannie) Welsh, who was born on July 14, 1801, the only child of the local doctor, John Welsh. In fact, Irving became "an intimate of the family," teaching Jane from six to eight in the morning each weekday and again after school. He was very impressed by this highly intelligent child and pushed her to excel. She went on to write a novel at the age of thirteen, a five-act play a year later, and eventually became famous for her very colorful letters.[15] Jane, it is also claimed, was a descendant of John Knox.[16] According to Oliphant, Dr. Welsh, who admired and liked Irving, predicted, "This youth will scrape a hole in everything he is called on to believe,"[17] as indeed Irving went on to do. Irving, for his part, was captivated by the intelligent and precocious Jane.

KIRKCALDY

In August 1812 Irving moved to a newly established subscription school at Kirkcaldy, a town on the north shore of the Firth of Forth with a population of around four thousand. The picturesque beach at Kirkcaldy had "a mile of the smoothest sand, with one long wave coming on, gently, steadily, and breaking in gradual *explosion*." This beach and the nearby woods, which Irving loved to roam, satisfied his love of the natural world.[18]

In a letter written during his time there, Irving described the people of Kirkcaldy as wearing "the same faces as when you left" with "their manners . . . nearly as stationary."[19] The school was called Kirkcaldy Academy, and

13. Oliphant, *Life*, 1:43.

14. Irving, *DL*, 5–6.

15. Carlyle, *Reminiscences* (Froude), 2:79; Miller, *Lamp of Lothian*, 455–56; Oliphant, *Life*, 1:36–39; Surtees, *Jane*, 5, 8–10, 12.

16. Carlyle, *Reminiscences* (Froude), 2:102.

17. Oliphant, *Life*, 1:41.

18. Carlyle, *Reminiscences* (Norton), 2:29–30; Surtees, *Jane*, 12.

19. Irving to one of the Martin sisters (not Isabella), n.d., quoted in Oliphant, *Life*, 1:64. Many years later, Gordon Brown, who had been a schoolboy in Kirkcaldy, went on

Irving's younger brother, George, appears to have been one of his students for a time.[20] It was large enough for Irving to have an assistant, and, in 1814, projected increases caused him to ask the committee for another. By the end of 1815, the school had "almost a hundred" scholars.[21]

By this time it was evident that Edward Irving was a man of considerable intelligence with a wide range of interests. At Kirkcaldy Academy, he taught mathematics, English, Latin, French (this he had learned with a little help from a French governess at Lord Cathcart's home) and even some Italian. He had, in fact, a gift for languages. Yet, ironically, he did not know Gaelic. Amongst his favorite lessons was reading from John Milton's *Paradise Lost*, many verses of which his pupils were expected to learn by heart.[22] On one occasion, a girl arrived early for a lesson only to encounter Irving reciting one of Satan's speeches from *Paradise Lost* so vividly that she ran away in terror.[23]

He seems to have been a fairly strict disciplinarian. Towards the end of 1815 he pulled the ears of one of the boys, and in so doing incurred the wrath of a Mr. Greig, who was presumably the boy's father. Greig asked for an apology, but Irving refused to give it because he "judged it unnecessary" and because he objected to the "unbecoming tone" of the request. Greig proceeded to do the school and Irving "all the ill in his power" by broadcasting his accusations throughout the town.[24]

It is presumably this incident that causes Sheridan Gilley to call Irving "something of a bully."[25] Gilley may also have in mind some other happenings when Irving made threats in non-school environments. But is that charge fair? Certainly Irving's act of discipline would not be approved today, but it was probably mild by the standards of the day, depending on the strength of the pull.

Irving remained in Kirkcaldy for seven years, and in spite of the above conflict, seems to have become a popular and respected figure in that town. During the first three years of this period he also had to make occasional

---

to become Prime Minister of Great Britain.

20. Carlyle, *Reminiscences* (Norton), 2:27.

21. Irving to the Kirkcaldy Subscription School Committee, January 1814, in Irving, *DL*, 61–63; Irving to Rev. John Martin, December 25, 1815, in Irving, *DL*, 65.

22. Oliphant, *Life*, 1:50–58; Irving, *DL*, 5, 40–41, 43.

23. Drummond, *Edward Irving*, 25.

24. Irving to Rev. Martin, December 25–26, 1815, in Irving, *DL*, 64–67.

25. Gilley, "Edward Irving: Prophet," 95.

visits to the Divinity Hall in Edinburgh to maintain his standing as a theological student.[26]

At that time Kirkcaldy was sufficiently large as to have two schools, and in the late summer of 1816 Thomas Carlyle was appointed as the teacher in the rival parish school, a job Carlyle loathed.[27] Irving and Carlyle had both studied at Annan Academy, but Carlyle, who was a few years younger than Irving, began there at about the time that Irving left, so they were not childhood companions. They were, however, aware of each other's families, and both also attended the Ecclefechan Seceder Church. Carlyle, in fact, said that Irving "must have sat, often enough, in Ecclefechan Meeting-house along with me, but I never noticed or knew."[28]

However, they briefly met on three later occasions. In 1808 the "scrupulously dressed" Irving had been invited to speak to Carlyle's class at the Annan Academy.[29] They met again in Edinburgh in the home of a mutual acquaintance just before the close of 1815. On this occasion Irving, pleased to come across someone from his hometown, plied Carlyle with a long string of questions about the people in Annan, including asking about any children recently born to folks he knew. Carlyle's answers did not satisfy Irving, who responded, "You seem to know nothing!"

That was the wrong thing to say to Carlyle, and he became very defensive. "Sir, by what right do you try my knowledge in this way?" he asked. "Are you grand inquisitor, or have you authority to question people, and cross-question, at discretion? I have had no interest to inform myself about the births in Annan; and care not if the process of birth and generation there should cease . . . altogether." The resulting tension was broken by another companion, also a schoolteacher, who joked, "That would never do for me," and they all laughed the incident off.[30]

They met again in July 1816, when they went to offer sympathy to Adam Hope, whose wife had just died. Irving was "kindly taking a sort of lead in the little managements," leading the small group of mourners in worship "in a free-flowing, modest and altogether appropriate manner," acting as precentor for the singing in his "melodiously strong" voice.

A month or two later, Carlyle arrived in Kirkcaldy to take up his teaching position. The two men quickly became close friends. As Carlyle

26. Drummond, *Edward Irving*, 25; Oliphant, *Life*, 1:57–58.

27. Oliphant, *Life*, 1:75; Carlyle, *Reminiscences* (Norton), 2:19.

28. Carlyle, *Reminiscences* (Norton), 1:40–41, 2:15. For Carlyle's attendance at the Ecclefechan Church, see Campbell, "Carlyle," in Brown and Newlands, *Scottish Christianity*, 17, 22–24.

29. Carlyle, *Reminiscences* (Norton), 2:17. See also 2:20.

30. Ibid., 2:22–23.

put it, "From the first, we honestly liked each other, and grew intimate." Carlyle found that Irving's "wide just sympathies, his native sagacities, honest-heartedness and good humour, made him the most delightful of companions."[31] No one that Carlyle knew (and he knew many) "had a sunnier type of character, or *so* little of hatred towards any man or thing."[32] In fact, Carlyle wrote, "The excellent Irving delights in making all about him happy: a miserable creature in his neighbourhood is to him like a disease of his own."[33] Oliphant likewise described Irving's temper as being "eminently social. He could not live without having people around him to love."[34] Carlyle was a key figure in Irving's early inner circle, and he loved him.

They frequently went on long walks together through the countryside, sometimes in company with others. In this group "Irving . . . was the natural King."[35] On one occasion, Irving and Carlyle heard that a geographical survey was being carried out on the Lomond Hills, so they walked to that spot to investigate the procedures being used. When they arrived, the two friends approached the only man on duty, who at first was most uncooperative. However, according to Carlyle, Irving's warmth quickly melted the man's indifference and he then freely answered the questions put to him. He also showed the visitors the theodolite being used, a device with which Irving was already familiar.[36]

Eventually the two men were to travel in quite different directions. Irving went into the ministry of the Presbyterian Church, while Carlyle, at best an unorthodox Christian, became a wide-ranging, highly regarded, and influential writer. It has been said that Carlyle's "religious faith" dominated his writing, but "it is not easy to say with confidence what [that faith] was."[37] It at times sounded Christian, but at other times sounded, for example, pantheistic. Certainly it was not Christian orthodoxy. It appears to have been largely, but not entirely, the Christian ethic without the dogma. But in spite of these differences, Irving and Carlyle never forgot their friendship. Indeed, their letters reveal an ongoing association of considerable warmth. As Carlyle told Irving in 1820, "widely as we differ on many points" he

---

31. Ibid., 2:24–25, 27, 29.

32. Ibid., 2:98.

33. Thomas Carlyle to William Graham, June 12, 1821, *CLO*.

34. Oliphant, *Life*, 1:162.

35. Carlyle, *Reminiscences* (Norton), 2:51.

36. Ibid., 2:30–31.

37. Schlossberg, *Silent Revolution*, 137–38, 146–48, 153–54. See also Carlyle, *Reminiscences* (Norton), 2:90, 92, 206–207; Elliott, *Edward Irving*, 115.

participated "more deeply in my feelings than any other I have met with."[38] Irving even recommended Carlyle for various positions as a tutor.[39] When Carlyle wrote his *Reminiscences*, over two hundred pages were dedicated to his relationship with Irving and their mutual associates, even though the preacher had by then been dead for more than thirty years.

By the time of Irving's sojourn in Kirkcaldy, he was a man of remarkable and attractive appearance; in fact, his countenance was "exceedingly picturesque."[40] He was not less than six feet three inches in height and probably stood higher, which was very tall indeed in the early years of the nineteenth century. He was said to be physically well-proportioned, and "His strength was prodigious and agility surprising."[41] Indeed, "He was an athlete, as well as a Hercules."[42] He was also "decidedly handsome," with wavy, "coal-black" hair, and he had a "melodious," easy-to-listen-to voice and flamboyant dress. In later years he walked the streets dressed in a black cloak and a fedora. In addition to all that, he had a gentle and natural charm. The only thing that marred this ideal figure was a squint.[43] In later years, the fashionable ladies were divided over whether his squint "was a grace or a deformity."[44]

William Hazlitt vividly summed up Irving's appearance when he said, "his very unusual size and height are carried off and moulded into elegance by the most admirable symmetry of form and ease of gesture; his sable locks, his clear iron-grey complexion, and firm-set features, turn the raw, uncouth Scotchman into the likeness of a noble Italian picture; and even his distortion of sight only redeems the otherwise 'faultless monster' within the bounds of humanity."[45] Sir Walter Scott thought similarly. While apparently intimidated by Irving's squint, Sir Walter described him as "resembling . . . our Saviour" as portrayed in Italian paintings, with his "hair carefully arranged in the same way."[46]

Irving's library at this stage contained books by David Hume, twelve volumes of Edward Gibbon's *The Decline and Fall of the Roman Empire*,

38. Thomas Carlyle to Edward Irving, June 3, 1820, *CLO*.

39. See, for example, Thomas Carlyle to John A. Carlyle, January 30, 1822, *CLO*; Carlyle, *Reminiscences* (Norton), 2:102–104.

40. *An Examination and Defence of the Writings and Preaching of the Rev. Edward Irving, M. A.*, quoted in Oliphant, *Life*, 1:173.

41. Isaac Taylor quoted in Irving, *CW*, 1:vi.

42. Wilks, *Edward Irving*, 6.

43. Carlyle, *Reminiscences* (Norton), 2:17, 41, 113.

44. Anna Montagu, quoted in Robinson, *Diary, Reminiscences*, 2:252.

45. Hazlitt, *Spirit*, 84.

46. Scott, "Journal of Sir Walter Scott: May 23, 1829."

Virgil's *Aeneid*, a range of French classics and works by Richard Baxter, Richard Hooker (at least his *On the Laws of Ecclesiastical Polity*), John Milton, and Isaac Newton, plus James Macpherson's *Ossian* poems.[47] Hooker, an Anglican, was a major influence on Irving's developing sacramental theology and probably his Christology. Ossian fired his Romanticism.

Carlyle implied that Irving rarely read a book right through. Rather, according to Carlyle, he developed the skill of drawing out the essential elements of a book without reading the whole.[48] However, there can be little doubt that later Irving displayed an in-depth understanding of theology, amongst other subjects, which was unlikely to have developed by just piecemeal reading. It is also apparent that at some stage Irving became well acquainted with the writings of the early church fathers.

In fact, Irving did record an example of how he, on at least one occasion, read and absorbed a book. In the summer of 1810, when he was reading "Natural Philosophy," Irving notes that he made sure he thoroughly understood a paragraph before writing in the back of the book, "such words and notes as will enable [him] to recollect the substance of it." When he returned to the book, Irving first looked at his notes and then reread the passage he had last read. He was aware that this procedure could eventually "become troublesome,"[49] so he may not have done it often, but it does indicate a much more thorough approach to reading than Carlyle suggested.

In August 1810 Irving expressed in his short-lived diary the desire to possess "the affections & esteem of some religious, well informed, well disposed & good tempered Girl." In fact, to meet such a young lady "should be deemed the happiest circumstance of [his] life."[50] It was to be several years before he was to find such happiness.

But towards the end of his time in Kirkcaldy he told a friend that "in this town or neighbourhood dwells a fair damsel" of whom he could say, "Were I to enter into an enumeration of those charms which challenge the world, I might find the low, equal, and unrhyming lines of prose too feeble a vehicle to support my flights." This "peerless" young woman, who honors *"this part of the world with her presence,"* had earlier been one of Irving's "much respected pupils" in Kirkcaldy: Isabella Martin.[51]

---

47. Carlyle, *Reminiscences* (Norton), 2:28–29; Elliott, *Edward Irving*, 33; Oliphant, *Life*, 1:31; Irving, *DL*, 26, 30–31, 39.

48. Carlyle, *Reminiscences* (Norton), 2:29.

49. Irving, *DL*, 8, 16.

50. Ibid., 45–46.

51. Oliphant, *Life*, 1:59.

Isabella's father and grandfather were both ministers of the Church of Scotland. Her father, Rev. John Martin, was in fact the minister at the Kirk in Kirkcaldy and was associated with Irving's school. Irving had often been a visitor to their manse. Carlyle described him as "a clear-minded, brotherly, well-intentioned man . . . altogether honest, wholesome as Scotch oatmeal."[52] Irving was certainly well received into the family. He later called Mrs. Martin "her to whom, of matrons, I owe the most after her who gave me birth."[53] Isabella was one of several daughters. In fact, Irving's letters give the impression that he had a fondness for more than one of the Martin girls, but it was Isabella to whom he eventually became engaged.

In 1815, when he had concluded his theological studies, Irving, as with other ministerial candidates, had to undergo the trials for license to preach. First, notices were sent out to the presbyters in the region to see if anyone had any objection to him becoming a minister of the gospel. Once the positive responses had been received, he underwent a series of varied examinations that included a discourse in Latin, a test on the Greek New Testament, the exposition of a psalm in Hebrew, and a couple of sermons, at least one of which was delivered to assembled ministers, to test his preaching gifts. He passed, which gave him the right to preach and made him eligible for ordination, though that event would not occur until he had been appointed to a church, as was the custom.[54]

The Reverend Martin invited him to preach in the Kirkcaldy Church, and Irving also had opportunities to preach in Annan. It is said that the whole town turned out for Irving's first sermon in his birthplace. It would seem unlikely that the whole town would fit into the Annan Kirk, but that term presumably meant that the place was packed. Included in the congregation, no doubt, was a good number of the Irving clan. As Irving warmed to his task on this occasion, his arm happened to bump the Bible, sending his sermon notes fluttering to the desk beneath the pulpit. A low murmur arose from the congregation, but Irving calmly bent down and picked up the fallen sheets. He thought for a moment, then crushed the pieces of paper into a ball, put them in his pocket, and fluently continued his sermon as if nothing had happened.

On another occasion in Kirkcaldy, with the congregation "dead-silent under Irving's grand voice," a man near the front of the church rose from his seat, burst through the door of his pew, marched down the aisle to the exit with his "face and big eyes all in wrath," and then "vanished out of doors

---

52. Carlyle, *Reminiscences* (Norton), 2:40.

53. Irving to Mrs. Martin, n.d., quoted in Oliphant, *Life*, 1:89.

54. Oliphant, *Life*, 1:61–66; Grass, *Edward Irving*, 21–22.

with a slam." Irving continued on with his sermon, "victoriously disregarding" the interruption. It would appear that some in Kirkcaldy regarded Irving as having "ower muckle gran'ner" (too much grandeur).[55] Clearly, he was already not loved by everyone.

But in spite of these preaching opportunities, during the next three or four years Irving failed to receive a call from a parish, so he continued teaching. One can only imagine what it must have been like for him during this period in the wilderness. He was keen to serve God, had obvious gifts in preaching, and had a genuine concern for people. It frankly must have been very difficult for him to listen to ministers whose preaching skills were inferior to his own and whose theological understanding was also, almost certainly, not as keen. Indeed, a few years later, Irving is said to have called the preaching of most of the contemporary Scottish clergy "dry theological arguing and disputing, lifeless, pulseless."[56]

Yet the call did not come. Vacancies generally only occurred when the incumbent minister died, and while some ministers were reportedly dead in the pulpit, they still clung to life and their appointed charges and thus barred the way for this man of very special gifts. The system of patronage operating in many Scottish parishes also hindered his advancement. Under this system, a patron decided whom to call to a particular church, but Irving wanted to be called by a church, not one man.[57]

It was all very sad, but sadness was to mark the life of this remarkable man. Yet, these pauses in the lives of the great are often useful and constructive, and it seems he at least had time for further study and reflection upon the truths of Scripture. And it is amazing how much a preacher can learn about preaching from listening to other preachers, even bad ones. In the worst cases, one at least learns what not to do.

Irving's size and imposing manner served him well in a number of incidents in this period of his life, as it had done before. On one of these occasions, Irving escorted some young ladies to a meeting and was accompanying them into the building when an official accosted the group and ordered them all to step aside. When Irving refused to comply, the official

---

55. Carlyle, *Reminiscences* (Norton), 2:42–43; Oliphant, *Life*, 1:66–67. Carlyle and Oliphant present different accounts of the second incident, but Carlyle seems to have been present, so I subscribe to his.

56. Samuel Taylor Coleridge to Edward Coleridge, December 8, 1825, in Coleridge, *CLSTC*, 5:522. However, some of Irving's comments on preachers that he had heard, which, though critical, were not by any means all negative (Irving, *DL*, 10–12, 19–22, 36–38, 41–45, 50). His main criticism was a lack of "connection" in the sermons, one part with another, which he believed was usually caused by extempore preaching (ibid., especially 43–44).

57. See, for example, Irving to Thomas Carlyle, September 21, 1820, in ibid., *DL*, 95.

repeated his order, giving Irving a bit of a push for emphasis. Irving looked down at the offender and raised his cane, saying, "Be quiet, sir, or I will annihilate you." The ladies giggled, knowing that such a blow was unlikely to fall. However, the man was not so sure and made a quick exit.[58]

On another occasion around this time, Irving was hiking with a friend when they came upon an inn. The two companions entered and ordered their evening meal. While it was being prepared, they left their bags and went out for a brief while to examine the area more closely. When they returned, a large group of travelers had commandeered the hostelry, the bags Irving and his friend had left behind had been pushed to one side, and the only meals being prepared were for the newcomers. Irving put it to them that he and his friend had arrived and ordered first and therefore had the right to be served first. Aware of their numerical superiority, the members of this group insisted that would not happen, nor would they share the eating facilities.

But this proved to be another situation where Irving's stature came in useful. He moved over to a window, opened it, and said to his companion, "Will you toss out or knock down?" The members of the larger group looked at each other and then at the towering figure of Irving. That was enough. They compromised and decided to share the meal and the facilities.

In June 1815, Britain and her allies had defeated Napoleon at the Battle of Waterloo. The next year, when Irving was visiting Edinburgh, he saw the forty-second regiment of the Black Watch of that triumphant army lining the streets on guard duty while a carriage took the Royal Commissioner to St. Giles' Cathedral for the General Assembly. Irving looked at the soldiers and noticed that one stood head and shoulders above all the others. He said to a companion, "Do you see that fellow? I should like to meet him in a dark entry." The friend looked at the massive soldier and quickly decided that this was the last person he would like to meet in such circumstances, then proceeded to ask Irving why he would like to take such a dangerous course. Irving replied, "Just that I might find out what amount of drubbing I could bear."[59]

58. Oliphant, *Life*, 1:86.
59. Ibid., 1:70–71.

3

The Scottish Church

It will be helpful at this point to take a brief look at the Presbyterian Church of Scotland, for it is within that church that the story of Edward Irving buds, blossoms, and withers before dying outside it. It is not necessary to sketch a detailed history, but rather to give a quick overview and to look at the structures of that church, for those structures play an important part in what follows.

The Protestant Reformation in Scotland began in a rather piecemeal fashion, and for a time looked unlikely to succeed. Two of the major early figures were Patrick Hamilton and George Wishart, who were both martyred—Hamilton in 1528 and Wishart in 1546.

Without doubt, though, the leading figure in the Scottish Reformation was the fiery John Knox (ca. 1524–1572), who had been influenced by Wishart. He had spent some time in England and on the Continent absorbing Reformation teaching, particularly in Geneva, and in 1559 Knox returned to Scotland intent on reforming the Scottish Church and indeed, Scotland itself. He debated religious issues with the staunchly Catholic Mary Stuart. Blood was spilled on battlefields, and Protestantism emerged triumphant. Mary was eventually deposed in 1567, and later executed by Elizabeth 1.[1]

Knox played a major role in drafting the *Scots Confession* (1560), which plays a key role in Irving's story,[2] and the *Book of Discipline* (1561), which failed to be approved by Parliament. A second *Book of Discipline* was compiled in 1581 and was for the most part ratified in Parliament in

---

1. Macleod, *Scottish Theology*, 4–6, 13; Renwick, *Scottish Reformation*, 26–30, 56–67, 71–87, 91–93, 155–56.

2. See Presbyterian Church, "Scots Confession."

1592, after Knox had died. The method of church government that eventually emerged after the considerable struggle was Presbyterian, that is, ruled by elders, rather than Episcopalian, ruled by bishops. In 1647 the Scottish Church adopted the *Westminster Confession* (1643–1647) as its statement of faith, replacing the *Scots Confession*. (The *Westminster Confession* was originally produced for the English Church.)

Presbyterianism became the established Church of Scotland from 1692, which was confirmed in the Act of Union in 1707. Not everyone accepted this new state of affairs, and opposition and controversy on various points continued on, even to the time of Irving, with some clergy seceding or being deposed.[3]

During Irving's life, the Scottish Church had two factions, the moderates and the evangelicals. The moderates "emphasised learning and morality"[4] but were casual on doctrine, benefitted from patronage, and, as their name suggests, sought to avoid extremes. The evangelicals objected to patronage and stressed traditional Presbyterian confessional beliefs and, ideally, the outflow of that teaching. One writer described the two groups at the time as "two parties drawn up like hostile armies, for incessant warfare,"[5] though the division may not have always been that sharp. In 1843 this culminated in most of the evangelicals, including more than a third of the denomination's clergy, leaving the church and forming a separate Free Church of Scotland (the "Wee Frees"), but Irving had died by then.[6]

The foundation of the Presbyterian Church's structure is the local session, which consists of a specific church's elders, who are men[7] that have been elected by the communicant members of the local congregation. The leader of the session is the minister or teaching elder. All or most other elders in each session are laymen, known as ruling elders. In Irving's London church, the session also had deacons to assist them, though they were not part of the session.

---

3. Macleod, *Scottish Theology*, 14, 25–27, 115; Renwick, *Scottish Reformation*, 105–19; Reid, "Presbyterianism," 800–802; Keay and Keay, *Collins Encyclopaedia of Scotland*, s.v. "Presbyterians," 787–88; Torrance, *Scottish Theology*, 127–28; Drummond and Bulloch, *Scottish Church*, 45–63, 155–56, 211–14. For the origins of the *Westminster Confession*, see Letham, *Westminster Assembly*, 6, 41, 47–48, 50–51.

4. Piggin and Roxborogh, *St. Andrews Seven*, 1.

5. "Letters to a Student in Divinity on the Parties in the Church," *Edinburgh Christian Instructor* 20 (1821) 73, quoted in Lee, "Christ's Sinful Flesh," 62.

6. Macleod, *Scottish Theology*, 189–205, 210–12; Torrance, *Scottish Theology*, 246–51; Keay and Keay, *Collins Encyclopaedia of Scotland*, s.vv. "Church of Scotland," "Free Church of Scotland," and "Presbyterians," 158, 399, 787–88.

7. Women are also eligible for election as elders in some Presbyterian churches, but this was not the case in Scotland at the time.

Though the local congregation elects the minister, the minister is inducted by the relevant presbytery, the church's legislative and judicial body. The presbytery is made up of an equal number of ministers and ruling elders drawn from each church in a particular district. While the local session governs the affairs of a specific church, it is the relevant presbytery that ordains and inducts ministers and settles disputed issues that arise within session, and it is the presbytery that also acts as the go-between linking the various sessions and the General Assembly, the denomination's overarching body.[8] This means—and this is highly relevant to our story—that no local congregation can sack its minister, nor can it retain him if the relevant presbytery has dismissed him, at least not unless it wishes to sever contact with the wider Presbyterian Church. Those issues are the duties of the relevant presbytery.

In addition, each local church, as with other institutions, has trustees to make sure that the affairs of the church are conducted in a proper and legal manner. Sometimes individuals in a particular church might serve as both elders and trustees, as was the case in Edward Irving's church. A session, two presbyteries, and a board of trustees all play crucial parts in the story of Edward Irving.

Crucial in Presbyterianism is the biblical concept of covenant. The signs of the covenant in the Old Testament were circumcision and the Passover. These had been replaced in the New Testament by baptism and the Lord's Supper. Baptism, which was most often performed on the children of Presbyterian families, was a sign that those baptized belonged to the family of God through the covenant, though the act in itself did not regenerate.[9]

Presbyterianism has traditionally also been very strict on doctrine, in theory if not always in practice. Divergence from the *Westminster Confession*, its doctrinal standard, was discouraged. Offending ministers were often called before a church court for their case to be heard, and if found guilty, dismissed from the ministry of the church. It is essential to note this point, for Edward Irving's later life was shrouded in doctrinal controversy and he was to experience the censure of ecclesiastical courts.

8. Reid, "Presbyterianism," 801–802.

9. See Presbyterian Church, "Scots Confession," chs. 21–23, and *Westminster Confession*, chs. 27–29.

4

Heart and Soul

When virtually betrothed to another I would consider myself as her own, and my passions would all be made subservient to this consideration.

—EDWARD IRVING, AUGUST 20, 1810[1]

BACK TO EDINBURGH

By the late summer of 1818 Irving seems to have tired of teaching, so he gave up his job and returned to Edinburgh. It is astonishing that a man with his training, theological understanding, and great preaching ability could still be languishing without a church on his twenty-sixth birthday, but so he was. Certainly, many less gifted mortals have led churches at a more youthful age. A generation later, C. H. Spurgeon, a man of similar knowledge and gifts to Irving's own, was pastoring a country church at seventeen and a major church in London by the age of twenty.

While in Edinburgh, Irving continued his education at the university and helped found, along with Carlyle, a small group named the Philosophical Association. It was also during this period that he took the bold step of jettisoning all his old sermons and began preparing new ones.[2] Without knowing the precise nature and content of the early sermons, it is impos-

1. Irving, *DL*, 46.
2. Oliphant, *Life*, 1:77–83.

sible to know how the new differed from the old or what improvements were made. But this says a great deal about Irving's earnestness and his desire to get it just right. According to Thomas Chalmers, in 1822 Irving was speculating "as much as before on the modes of preaching," so even then he was still planning and molding his pulpit ministry.[3] Oliphant suggests that his long time spent sitting in the pews, rather than standing in the pulpit, gave Irving a deep understanding of how to preach, or, often, how not to preach, and this no doubt stood him in good stead in the years ahead.[4]

Still no call came, but Irving did not seem to lack opportunities to preach. In the summer of 1819 he told Carlyle "I have been preaching at such a rate as to excite no small speculation in this Mighty City."[5] Clearly he was busy, and he was being noticed. A Dr. Grierson called his preaching at this time "very fearless, original, striking, and solemn."[6] It was, perhaps, these qualities that delayed his call to a charge. Not all Christians like originality, and fearless preachers can be loved or hated—or both.

JANE

Irving's relationships with young ladies also took a new and unexpected course at this time. Indeed, the adage that the path of true love never runs smoothly was never proven truer than in Irving's case. As has been noted, he had fallen in love with Isabella Martin and appears to have become formally engaged to her, perhaps in 1818, just before his return to Edinburgh.

But in Edinburgh Irving renewed his acquaintance with Jane Welsh of Haddington, who had been living there for about a year. She was now a vivacious woman of seventeen years, with dazzling eyes and long black hair. Carlyle called her "the most enchanting creature I have ever seen."[7] She had "large black eyes" which were "full of fire and softness" and crowned with "long, curved lashes."[8] Witty and charming, it was said that she was born "for the destruction of mankind." One relative claimed that "every man who spoke to her for five minutes felt impelled" to propose marriage.[9] Edward

---

3. Hanna, *Memoirs* (Edinburgh), 2:351.

4. Oliphant, *Life*, 1:82–83.

5. Irving to Thomas Carlyle, July 16, 1819, in Irving, *DL*, 73.

6. Grierson, quoted in Oliphant, *Life*, 1:83.

7. Thomas Carlyle to Jane Baillie Welsh, August 31, 1823, *CLO*.

8. Hitchcock, *Unhappy Loves*, 184.

9. Quoted in Carlyle, *Reminiscences* (Froude), 2:76. See also Hitchcock, *Unhappy Loves*, 185.

Irving spoke to her and for much longer than five minutes, and if he did not feel impelled to propose, he certainly was tempted to do so.

Back in 1810 he had written, "Women are fascinating and young men are apt to be inflamed; I may hope however that upon that score I have my passions under complete subjugation."[10] In 1810 that may have been so, but meeting the lovely Jane eight years later made those passions rise to the surface. He wrote letters to her and even sent her poetry.

Jane once gave him a lock of her hair. In response, he sent her a sonnet he had composed, possibly called "sonnet *to a lock of my Lady's hair which reached me thro' hair-breadth* 'scrapes.'"[11] That title, if such it was, suggests a degree of secrecy in their relationship, as there may well have been. The poem ran in part:

> Thou raven lock! on which my eyes do rest
> Unwearied. Thou dear emblem of my Jane
> Whose hand did crop thee from her head, fit test
> Of her affection ever to remain.
> The journey as a voyage o'er the Main
> Hath been advent'rous; thou wert cast away
> 'Mongst vulgar hinds; and there unknown hadst lain,
> But that the Queen of Love who watched thy way
> Did pity me and safely thee convey
> Here to my bosom.[12]

These are the words of a lovesick man. Indeed, there can be little doubt that Edward Irving had fallen in love with Jane Welsh. But he was already engaged to Isabella Martin.

Or was he? Carlyle said that at this time Irving had only "some vague understanding" with Isabella, "not a definite engagement."[13] But Jane made it very clear in a later letter to Carlyle that she believed Irving was engaged to Isabella at the time of her romantic dalliance with the preacher.[14] Whether Jane was more likely to know than Carlyle is debatable. The evidence would seem to favor that Edward and Isabella were formally engaged at this time. It certainly points to something stronger than a "vague understanding." Yet, even if there were no formal engagement at this stage, one suspects that

10. Irving, *DL*, 41.
11. Jane Baillie Welsh to Thomas Carlyle, December 19, 1824, *CLO*.
12. Surtees, *Jane*, 14–15.
13. Carlyle, *Reminiscences* (Froude), 2:81.
14. Jane Baillie Welsh to Thomas Carlyle, July 24, 1825, *CLO*.

Isabella would not have viewed any understanding she may have shared with Irving as vague, though he may have done. Edward and Isabella were certainly engaged by September 1820.[15]

That Irving sent Jane letters *and* poetry of that nature leaves little doubt that he had fallen in love with her. Jane, for her part, later said that she "*once* passionately loved him."[16] But it was a love doomed to fail.

Jane cut the above poem out of the letter that contained it. On the back of this fragment are the only remaining words of the rest of Irving's missive, which run, "I have resolved neither to see Isabella nor her father before I . . . cannot brook the sight of either until we have explained and until . . ."[17]

Quite what that means is far from clear. However, according to Thomas Carlyle, at one stage Irving paid a visit to the Martin family to seek "release" from the engagement, but if he did so, the release was not granted, and Irving, being a man of great principle, was unwilling to break the engagement without it.[18] Assuming this is correct, we naturally ask, why did the Martins not accede to Irving's quite reasonable, if difficult, request? The answer lies in the different understanding of such engagements in the early nineteenth century compared with later practice. An engagement to be married at that time was considered more binding than in recent times, and any woman so jilted would have had to cope with a degree of shame. In addition, a Presbyterian minister had broken off an engagement around that time and it had caused a scandal.[19] Irving was not prepared to break his vow and submit Isabella to such humiliation.

Jean Christie Root seems to suggest that Irving, being an honorable man, probably told Isabella of the change in his affections even before his visit to the manse.[20] While this is possible, it is rather difficult to imagine what he could have said to her. "I'm sorry. I think I am falling in love with someone else, so I may not be able to marry you" does not sound especially likely. Certainly Irving's mind at this time was in turmoil. So severe was

---

15. Irving to Thomas Carlyle, September 21, 1820, in Irving, *DL*, 94.

16. Jane Baillie Welsh to Thomas Carlyle, July 24, 1825, *CLO*. Drummond argues that Jane's use of the word "passionately" here should not be taken at face value (Drummond, *Edward Irving*, 94–95). Alexander Carlyle, a nephew of Thomas,' also seems to have regarded it as an exaggeration. However, there seems to be no good reason to agree with them. Jane was making a rather humiliating confession to the man she was to marry the following year, so she was unlikely to have made it sound worse than it was.

17. Surtees, *Jane*, 15.

18. Carlyle, *Reminiscences* (Norton), 2:86.

19. Carlyle, *Reminiscences* (Froude), 2:81.

20. Root, *Edward Irving*, 28–29.

this stress that he confessed that it almost made his "faith and principles to totter."[21]

To make the issue even more complicated, in the summer of 1820 Irving had gone on a two-week hiking tour with three or four friends. One of these friends was Margaret Gordon, who had also been one of his former pupils. Upon returning home, Irving wrote to Carlyle confessing that he had felt strongly attracted to her, though there "was no love" between them. Carlyle later described her as "fair-complexioned, softly elegant, softly grave, witty and comely." It was probably as well that she moved to London soon after Irving's feelings had begun to stir so that no love could develop. Though they did exchange occasional letters, it was eighteen months before Irving saw her again, and then only briefly. Margaret Gordon would later become Lady Bannerman[22] and for Irving was, at most, a brief attraction. Jane was in his very soul.

Back in July 1810, Irving had written in his diary, "I have *almost* formed the resolution never to mar[r]y except I can find a woman of wholly religious principles and a Consistent practice, as well as a sound judgement, who is willing to join her fortune to mine."[23] If he was still so resolved, even just "almost" resolved, then Isabella was undoubtedly the better option. But he was in love with Jane. No wonder his "faith and principles" were shaking.

Jane later confessed that she "showed weakness in loving one whom I knew to be engaged to another," but she also claimed that she "made amends in persuading him to marry that other and preserve his honour from reproach."[24] Irving's feelings are shown in a letter he wrote to Jane at around the time that they decided their love was hopeless, possibly as late as March 1822. He told her,

> When I think of you my mind is overspread with the most af-
> fectionate and tender regard, which I neither know how to
> name nor how to describe. One thing I know it long ago would
> have taken the form of the most devoted attachment, but for an
> intervening circumstance, and showed itself and pleaded itself
> before your heart by a thousand actions from which I must now
> restrain myself . . . When I am in your company my whole soul
> would rush to serve you, and my tongue trembles to speak my
> heart's fullness. But I am enabled to forebear, and have to find

21. Edward Irving, quoted in Hitchcock, *Unhappy Loves*, 200.

22. Irving to Thomas Carlyle, July 10, 1820, in Irving, *DL*, 85–86; ibid., August 1820, 93; ibid., September 21, 1820, 94–95; ibid., September 26, 1820, 98; ibid., December 26, 1821, 122; Grass, *Edward Irving*, 35; Carlyle, *Reminiscences* (Norton), 2:57–59.

23. Irving, *DL*, 10.

24. Jane Baillie Welsh to Thomas Carlyle, July 24, 1825, *CLO*.

other avenues than the natural ones for the overflowing of an
affection which would hardly have been able to confine itself
within the avenues of nature if they had all been opened.

But I feel within me the power to prevail, and at once satisfy
duty to another and affection to you. I stand, truly, upon ground
which seems to shake and give way beneath me, but my help is
in Heaven . . .

It is very extraordinary that this weak nature of mine can
have two affections, both of so intense a kind, and yet I feel it
can. It shall feed the one with faith and duty and chaste affection; the other with paternal and friendly love, no less pure, no
less assiduous, no less constant. In return seeking nothing but
permission and indulgence.[25]

Thomas Carlyle, Jane's eventual husband (they married in 1826), said
that it was "highly probable that if *flirting* were a capital crime, she would
have been in danger of being hanged many times over." Yet he also argued
that the claims about her flirtations were "much exaggerated." One suspects
this was a very sensitive issue for him.

Carlyle also confirmed that at that time "a few young fools . . . made
offers to her."[26] Though he would not have included Irving in the company
of fools, Carlyle was certainly by then well aware of Irving's past romantic interest in Jane. However, Carlyle's own relationship with her appears
to have been well developed before he knew of it.[27] In fact, in the middle
of December 1824, Jane actually quoted a small part of Irving's sonnet to
Carlyle and asked him if he had ever seen it. She omitted, of course, the line
that gave her own name and the fact that it had been written to her. Oddly,
and seemingly deceptively, she told Carlyle "there is not one word of Isabella
in [the poem] from beginning to end."[28] Indeed, how could there be? It was
written to her, not Isabella. It was not until July of the following year that
Jane told Carlyle how serious her relationship with Irving had been.

However, even though Irving believed that his duty lay with Isabella,
in a letter as late as February 1822, he could still address Jane as "My dear
and lovely pupil," though he did also express his desire to be a brother to
her. Seven months after his eventual marriage to Isabella, he said that he was
reluctant to meet with Jane because though his "dear Isabella had succeeded

25. Irving to Jane Baillie Welsh, in Irving, *DL*, 139. Waddington notes that Carlyle
"deduced" that the date of this letter was March 6, 1822.

26. Carlyle, *Reminiscences* (Froude), 2:79, 91–92.

27. Elliott, *Edward Irving*, 132–33.

28. Jane Baillie Welsh to Thomas Carlyle, December 19, 1824, *CLO*. Carlyle does
not seem to have responded to Jane's question about the sonnet, at least not in writing.

in healing the wounds of [his] heart by her unexampled affection and tenderness," he was still "hardly in a condition to expose" those wounds.[29]

Strangely, a month after the Irving wedding, Jane complained to Carlyle that Irving was "telling all people" that she, Jane, "was the Love of his intellect" and that Isabella was "the Love of his youth." This led Jane to respond, "confound his intellect[,] I shall never hear the last of it."[30] While it is impossible to imagine that Irving was "telling *all* people" about his love life (it is hardly something he would have announced from the pulpit), one suspects that there was some foundation in Jane's charge and that it was not just an expression of her mischievous humor. Certainly Irving could speak inappropriately at times.

Nearly eighteen months later, Anna Montagu, a prominent London woman, wrote a letter to Jane at Carlyle's request,[31] to which she seems to have received at least one response. About ten days after she had written, Mrs. Montagu penned a letter to Carlyle in which she said Jane's "heart is in England, her heart is not there." The comment itself might mean anything or nothing, but Irving was by then in England, so it was presumably a reference to him. This is confirmed by Mrs. Montagu, for she continued, "I feared to be the means of stirring an old flame, the embers of which are still glowing on both sides—I am at once a link between persons separated by duty, rather than inclination, and there is a third party still more difficult to deal with, Mrs. Irving herself." In Anna Montagu's judgment, then, Edward Irving and Jane Welsh still had strong feelings for each other, even after the Irving wedding. While Mrs. Montagu's acquaintance with Jane Welsh at that time was limited to these letters, she knew Irving very well. Therefore, her opinion is not easily dismissed.

Anna Montagu concluded that for Jane Welsh to have been married to Irving would have been "entire and unmixed misery" for her, for they were "not the least fitted to each other."[32] It would most likely have been just as much misery for him. It was as well that the romance between Edward and Jane went no further than it did.

One can only speculate what it was like for Isabella to live with a man whom she knew once loved and might still love someone else. The answer

29. Irving to Jane Baillie Welsh, February 9, 1822, in Irving, *DL*, 133–34; and Irving to Jane Baillie Welsh, May 10, 1824, in ibid., 196.

30. Jane Baillie Welsh to Thomas Carlyle, November 26, 1823, *CLO*. Irving did refer to Jane as "the child of my intellect" in a letter to her dated May 10, 1824, in Irving, *DL*, 196.

31. Thomas Carlyle to Anna D. B. Montagu, May 20, 1825, *CLO*.

32. Mrs. Montagu to Thomas Carlyle, May 30, 1825, quoted in Thomas Carlyle to Jane Baillie Welsh, June 24, 1825, n. 6, *CLO*.

was probably that she hoped Irving's love for her would grow, and, no doubt, so did Irving. And that is what seems to have happened. In his letters to Isabella in the following years, Irving frequently expressed his love for her. For example, in one he closed the missive with "Beloved, I desire you to love me as I love you, and let us love one another as one self, not as one another, but one—the same."[33] It would be churlish to accuse Irving of hypocrisy in this: expressing a love he did not feel. Whatever his faults, hypocrisy was not one of them.

Yet it would seem that Isabella did harbor some doubts about his love. In one letter Irving, looking forward to an evening alone with his wife, complained to her "nothing afflicts me so much as to see you incapable of enjoying the society and love for which you do not always give me credit, but which I trust I always feel."[34] One senses in this missive that even if Edward could get Jane Welsh out of his mind, Isabella could not dismiss that rival from hers.

Many years later, Margaret Oliphant interviewed Jane and asked her about this romantic triangle. While Jane let nothing specific slip, Oliphant reported that she detected that Jane had a distinct dislike of Isabella.[35] Such feelings can also be sensed in her letters to Carlyle.

Eventually, Jane married Thomas Carlyle. Their marriage was a stormy one. It has been said that their relationship is proof that not all marriages are made in heaven. It is also claimed that Samuel Butler remarked, "It was very good of God to let Carlyle and Mrs. Carlyle marry one another, and so make only two people miserable instead of four."[36]

It needs to be noted, as Peter Elliott points out, that Carlyle and Jane frequently used contradictory language in reference to Irving.[37] They each had genuine affection and respect for him, but disagreed with his direction and many of his Christian beliefs, about which they could be very critical. And Jane's earlier romantic attachment to Irving seems to have made her, at times, critical even of his character. This may have been because she was trying to cover her true feelings for him.

33. Oliphant, *Life*, 2:45, Irving to Isabella Irving, July 25, 1828. Grass states that the correct date for this letter is July 28 (Grass, *Edward Irving*, 171 n. 102). This is presumably correct, as Oliphant quotes another letter dated July 25 (Oliphant, *Life*, 2:43).

34. Edward Irving, quoted in Oliphant, *Life*, 2:61.

35. Oliphant, *MacMillan's Magazine*, n.d., quoted in Root, *Edward Irving*, 29–30.

36. Blackburn, *Oxford Dictionary of Philosophy*, s.v. "Carlyle, Thomas," 53.

37. Elliott, *Edward Irving*, 130–31, 142–43.

THE CALL

Confused in love and frustrated in calling, Irving's world had become rather dark and uncertain. He seems to have considered offering himself as a missionary, but he made no concrete move in that direction. It is not surprising that he found Edinburgh in this period his "Patmos," and felt himself alone as John the Apostle in exile, particularly when Carlyle left.[38]

Yet, at times Irving's letters portray the spiritual and temperamental ability to rise above his troubles, even to treat them lightly, which was as well, for his life was to have many of them. In one letter he said, "And for myself, here I am to remain for further orders—if from the east I am ready, if from the west I am ready, and if from the folk of Fife I am not the less ready."[39]

Early in 1819 he planned a year-long study trip to Europe, beginning that May, which would possibly include some tutoring. He intended to visit France, Switzerland, Italy, and perhaps Germany. This seems to have emerged from his great sense of frustration at still not having received a call.[40] However, the trip never eventuated.

Amidst all this uncertainty and darkness, suddenly a ray of hope shone, as it were, from the heavens: an answer to prayer. He received an invitation from a friend, Dr. Andrew Thomson, one of the leading figures in the Presbyterian Church, to preach at St. George's Church.

His visit to St. George's took place towards the end of July 1819. In the congregation was a visitor, Dr. Thomas Chalmers. Chalmers was highly regarded, indeed, many thought of him as the top man in the Scottish Church at the time. He had originally been a moderate, but was now firmly in the evangelical camp of that church.[41]

Carlyle called him "truly lovable, truly loved," genial, and good, with "honest eyes and face," which in later life displayed "a serene sadness."[42] Chalmers had been minister of the Tron Church in Glasgow, where he had exercised a highly successful and wide-ranging ministry and extended that church's influence to minister more effectively to the poor of Glasgow. A year before he heard Irving, Chalmers had left Tron and gone to serve in the newer and poorer parish church of St. John's, which had been especially

---

38. Oliphant, *Life*, 1:87–88, 90.
39. Quoted in Oliphant, *Life*, 1:91.
40. Irving to Rev. Martin, March 31, 1819, in Irving, *DL*, 68–69.
41. Macleod, *Scottish Theology*, 256.
42. Carlyle, *Reminiscences* (Norton), 2:61, 72–74.

established for him.[43] Chalmers was on the lookout for a ministerial assistant at St. John's, and he viewed Irving as a possibility.

After the service in St. George's, Irving knew that he had made an impression. On August 2, he wrote to Rev. John Martin, saying,

> I preached Sunday week at St. George's before Andrew Thomson and Dr. Chalmers, with general, indeed, so far as I have heard, universal approbation. Andrew said for certain "It was the production of no ordinary mind;" and how Dr. Chalmers expressed his approbation I do not know, for I never put myself about to learn these things, as you know . . . I believe it was a sort of pious and charitable plot to let Dr. C. hear me previous to his making inquiries about me as fit for his assistant. Whether he is making them now he *has* heard me, and where he is making them, I do not know.[44]

At last there was hope: a call was possible, even likely. Irving waited and waited for the expected letter, but it did not come. Once more disappointment and frustration overwhelmed him. It is a standard joke in Presbyterian circles (not appreciated by all) that that church's wheels move very slowly, and slow they were in this instance. Grass argues that the specific reason for the delay was a crisis at St. John's caused by Chalmers considering a position at Edinburgh University and his elders protesting.[45] But Irving knew nothing of what may have been going on behind the scenes, and each day that passed without a call added to his frustration.

Even through these delays, Irving never seems to have lost confidence in his ability. The letter to John Martin indicates that he was not particularly modest, nor did he downplay his remarkable gifts. He felt quite free to use such phrases as "universal approbation" and "no ordinary mind" in connection with himself.

Nearly five months later, and thus after he had accepted a call, he advised Carlyle,

> Known you must be before you can be employed. Known you will not be for a winning, attaching accomodating [*sic*] man, but for an original, commanding & rather self-willed man. Now establish this last character and you will take a far higher grade than any other. How are you to establish it? Just by bringing yourself before the public as you are. Find vent for your notions.

43. Drummond and Bulloch, *Scottish Church*, 172; Newble, "Thomas Chalmers: Biography."

44. Oliphant, *Life*, 1:91–93.

45. Grass, *Edward Irving*, 29 n. 17.

Get them tongue. Upon every subject get them tongue . . . Now what way is to be sought for—I know no other than the press. You have not the pulpit as I have. [46]

Irving went on to direct Carlyle to various journals to which he could send his writings and thus "gain money & favour & opinion." Clearly Irving was not against a bit of self-promotion. He was himself "an original, commanding," and "self-willed man," with, as shall be seen, a great willingness to proclaim his "notions."[47] In fact, reading his letters, one becomes aware that he not only had considerable confidence in his own ability, but also at times seemed to consider himself above most other mortals.

But the delay continued. When he could not bear to wait any longer, he decided to leave Edinburgh and return home to Annan. At Greenock Quay, after some frustration waiting for the right vessel, he decided to board the next one due to depart and ended up in Belfast, Ireland. However, this may not have been as impulsive as it sounds, for back in July he had been considering a trip to Ireland.

His arrival in Belfast was poorly timed. A major crime had just been committed, and strangers were being viewed with suspicion. With Irving's striking height and build, it was impossible for him to escape attention. Irving was questioned by the authorities and only released after he had contacted a Presbyterian minister, the Reverend Hanna, who identified him, spoke for him, and took him into his home. He spent about two weeks "among the ragged sons of St. Patrick," enjoying the company of the Hanna family, exploring the region, and spending time in contemplation.[48]

Then, on a visit to the Coleraine Post Office, Irving found a package addressed to him. It was from his father, and inside it was a letter from Dr. Chalmers inviting the young preacher to come to meet him. Unfortunately, the letter was dated about the time he had arrived in Ireland, so it was quite likely that Chalmers would be wondering why he had not received a reply. Though the letter was not a formal call to the position of assistant, it did invite Irving to meet Chalmers either in Edinburgh on August 30, or in Glasgow the following day. It was cutting it fine to make the Edinburgh deadline, so Irving hastily made his way to Glasgow. Upon his arrival there, he discovered that Chalmers had been delayed and was still away.

---

46. Irving to Thomas Carlyle, December 26, 1819, in Irving, *DL*, 78–79.

47. Ibid.

48. Irving to the Martin family, September 1, 1819, quoted in Drummond, *Edward Irving*, 32. See also Hanna, *Memoirs* (Edinburgh), 2:282–84; Oliphant, *Life*, 1:93–94, 97; Irving to Thomas Carlyle, July 16, 1819, in Irving, *DL*, 75.

It is strange how at each step in this story there seemed to be something blocking Irving's way, another hurdle to leap, or another delay. But God overrules. Eventually, Chalmers returned and offered the position to Irving, initially on a month's probation, and Irving accepted. At last he had received the call that he had so long desired.

As Irving departed for Glasgow, Thomas Carlyle told a friend, "if . . . his fervid genius do not prompt him into extravagancies, from which more stupid and less honest preachers are exempted, his success, I doubt not, will be brilliant."[49] Carlyle clearly knew him well.

49. Thomas Carlyle to John Fergusson, September 25, 1819, *CLO*; Oliphant, *Life*, 1:95–97.

5

Glasgow: "This Overgrown City"[1]

GLASGOW AND THOMAS CHALMERS

Once Irving had received this call, there was little delay. He began his ministry at St. John's in Glasgow at the end of September 1819.[2]

The Glasgow of that time was a fast-growing city. Like London and many other cities in Britain, it was rapidly expanding and swallowing the villages that surrounded it. Its people were generally literate, or at least more so than in similar towns in England. Its main industry was weaving, both by mill and handloom. However, in this second decade of the nineteenth century, many of Glasgow's handloom weavers were living in poverty as the mills gradually superseded their work, and a spirit of radicalism was fermenting, encouraged by earlier events in America and France. As Irving later put it, this was "the scantiest, and perhaps sorest time" that Glasgow had experienced.[3]

In fact, a couple of weeks before Irving was to take up his position in Glasgow, nearby Paisley became the scene of a riot of about five thousand people protesting their condition and the deaths of those slain in the Peterloo Massacre in Manchester a month earlier. This unrest was to lead to

1. Irving to Rev. Martin, n.d., quoted in Oliphant, *Life*, 1:107.

2. According to Oliphant, *Life*, 1:99, he began there in October, but a letter Irving wrote to Carlyle seems to indicate that it was at the end of September (Irving to Thomas Carlyle, September 25, 1819, in Irving, *DL*, 76).

3. Irving, "Farewell Discourse," in Irving, *CW*, 3:354.

the 1820 Rising, which culminated in the Battle of Bonnymuir, though as a battle it was little more than a skirmish. Some of the leaders of this protest were executed, while others were transported to Australia.[4] With the French Revolution still haunting the living memory of many, such movements and events, however justified, made the nation's leaders very nervous. As Irving, who was sympathetic to the poor, said, "Nobody knows a whit and everybody fears a deal. The common ignorance is only surpassed by the common alarm."[5]

Dr. Thomas Chalmers was only twelve years older than Irving, but a man of great ministerial experience and very wide knowledge. Chalmers had taken a census of the St. John's parish in 1819, which showed that it contained over ten thousand inhabitants—a large parish even for two men. To make it more manageable, Chalmers had divided it into twenty-five "groups" or "proportions," each with sixty to one hundred families, and had appointed an elder and a deacon to each area to care for the people's spiritual and temporal needs.[6]

Soon after his arrival Irving told Carlyle, "I never saw or heard of a parish[,] much less a town parish, organised and attended to in such a way before. He visits from house to house, and by acts of duty purely religious has contrived to establish himself in the affections of many of the very outcasts of human society whom I have visited along with him."[7]

Chalmers, in fact, had intense sympathy for the poor and had previously carried out an early sociological study of poverty and ways to deal with it. He had written, "If you wish to extinguish poverty, combat with it in its first elements. If you confine your beneficence to the relief of actual poverty, you do nothing."[8] He believed that poverty had to be dealt with at its source, through education and by enabling the poor to be independent and provide for their own needs by labor, rather than by charity. Consistent with those beliefs, Chalmers had established a number of schools for the poor children of Glasgow.[9]

One of his later students, John Urquhart, said that when he was walking with Chalmers on one occasion to visit the sick and poor, Chalmers said, "This is what I call preaching the gospel to every creature; that cannot

---

4. Halliday, "1820 Rising."

5. Irving to his brother-in-law, Mr. Fergusson, n.d., quoted in Oliphant, *Life*, 1:104–105.

6. Irving to Rev. Martin, n.d., quoted in ibid., 1:107; Hanna, *Memoirs* (Edinburgh), 2:287. See also ibid., 2:230.

7. Irving to Thomas Carlyle, September 25, 1819, in Irving, *DL*, 76.

8. Newble, "Thomas Chalmers: Poverty."

9. Oliphant, *Life*, 1:108–109; Root, *Edward Irving*, 19.

be done by setting yourself up in a pulpit, as a centre of attraction, but by going forth and making aggressive movements upon the community, and by preaching from house to house."[10] This is not to say that Chalmers was against preaching from the pulpit, just that many of the people he visited were not usually in the pews to hear him, and by entering the world of his parishioners, he was showing the love of Christ.

Nor was the gospel of Christ lost in the midst of social theory. Chalmers, though originally a moderate, was by this time firmly in the evangelical wing of the church and was held in high regard as a preacher of that gospel. One person who had sat regularly under his ministry at Kilmany, his earlier parish, recalled, "He would bend over his pulpit and press us to take the gift as if he held it at that moment in his hand and could not be satisfied till every one of us got possession of it."[11] Carlyle said, "no preacher ever went so into one's heart" as did Chalmers.[12]

Chalmers was not to be at St. John's for long. Late in 1823 he was appointed Professor of Moral Philosophy at St. Andrews University.[13] By then, Irving had already moved on.

IRVING'S MINISTRY IN GLASGOW

Oliphant claimed that Irving's position at St. John's "was completely secondary" to Chalmers. Secondary it was, but not quite completely so. Yet Irving did live and work in the shadow of that great man. Nevertheless, Irving was happy to be serving in the ministry at last, even if his role was subordinate to another.[14] Indeed, not only did he serve, but he also learned. He later described St. John's as "the cradle of [his] clerical character."[15]

Carlyle indicated that Irving's status in Glasgow might not have been as lowly as Oliphant suggested. In one letter, Carlyle told a friend that Irving's "popularity in Glasgow is said to be great beyond example. Chalmers even is thought to look with some anxiety at the pillars of his throne." And this was just two months after the young assistant's arrival. A few months later, Carlyle could report that Irving "succeeds wonderfully."[16] But one has to

10. Orme, *Memoirs*, 39, quoted in Newble, "Thomas Chalmers: Quotes."

11. Quoted in Pearce, *Life-Changing*, 44–45.

12. Carlyle, *Reminiscences* (Norton), 2:75.

13. Drummond and Bulloch, *Scottish Church*, 175; Piggin and Roxborogh, *St. Andrews Seven*, 1.

14. Oliphant, *Life*, 1:101, 124–25.

15. Irving, "Farewell Discourse," in Irving, *CW*, 3:353.

16. Thomas Carlyle to Robert Mitchell, December 30, 1819, *CLO*; Thomas Carlyle

ask, are these merely Carlyle's characteristic exaggerations? Quite possibly they are, though they do suggest that Irving had more success in Glasgow than is usually reported.

An important aspect of Irving's work was sharing the visitation with Chalmers. Indeed, he visited about three hundred families in his first few months in Glasgow, most of them very poor, and he "met the kindest welcome and entertainments and invitations."[17] As he entered each home, Irving pronounced, "Peace be to this house" (Luke 10:5), which often seemed to have a calming effect upon those who otherwise might not have welcomed him.[18] He claimed that "Churchmen, Dissenters, Catholics and Protestants, received [him] with equal graciousness."[19] Irving also found himself in great sympathy with these poor people, and his opinion of them was "so favourable" that he wondered if he might be labeled a "radical" if he were to voice it.[20]

It is, perhaps, not surprising that after five months he told Carlyle that he had been "wrought almost to death, by labour and kindness." It was the latter he found most difficult to cope with, for his hosts kept favoring him with "roast beef and Glasgow punch."[21]

In this visitation, Irving made an impression upon the people in a number of ways. One woman thought that he looked like "a brigand chief," while another described him as having the appearance of "a highland chief," and one man thought that he was "a cavalry officer."[22] His great size and bearing made him very noticeable. A woman from his church reported that she was about her household duties one day, with her servants given strict instructions not to interrupt her, when a maid burst in upon her. "Mem!" the maid blustered. "There's a wonderful grand gentleman called. I couldna say you were engaged to him."[23] Irving's imposing figure was a passport in many instances.

However, households with servants were not common in the part of Glasgow where Irving was working. Oliphant said that the investigations carried out by Chalmers showed that only about 3 percent of homes

---

to James Johnston, May 6, 1820, *CLO*.

17. Irving to his brother-in-law, Mr. Fergusson, n.d., quoted in Oliphant, *Life*, 1:104.

18. Ibid., 1:112.

19. Irving, "Farewell Discourse," in Irving, *CW*, 3:355–56.

20. Irving to his brother-in-law, Mr. Fergusson, n.d., quoted in Oliphant, *Life*, 1:104.

21. Irving to Thomas Carlyle, March 14, 1820, in Irving, *DL*, 81.

22. Dallimore, *Life*, 23.

23. Oliphant, *Life*, 1:99.

employed servants in that area,[24] and this in an age when maids, house-keepers, and other servants were very common, and were not just the province of the rich.

While in Glasgow, Irving inherited thirty pounds, or perhaps a little more. He quickly turned the money into single pound notes and took one with him each day on his visitation to give to a needy family until the money was exhausted. As Oliphant observed, this practice was hardly in line with the philosophy of Chalmers,[25] but it is unlikely that he knew about it at the time.

Yet, Irving was not well received by all he visited. On one visit to a weaving shop Irving uttered his "Peace be with you," only to hear one weaver respond in an "angry and fiery" outburst, "Ay, Sir, if there's *plenty* w'it" before starting in to lecture Irving about his grievances. But by the time Irving was ready to leave, the man had calmed down, and they parted on "soft terms."[26]

Irving also went on a number of occasions to the home of a cobbler who held radical views, but while the man's wife entertained Irving, the shoemaker always continued his work with his back to the minister. It is said that on one visit, Irving commented on the quality of the leather that the man was using. The cobbler bristled and snorted, "What do ye ken [know] about leather?" Irving, the son of a tanner, happened to know a lot about leather and the making of shoes, and he was able to engage the man in conversation on the subject and impressed him with his understanding and sympathy. The cobbler was so taken by the preacher's knowledge that he turned up at church the following Sunday and then began to attend regularly. He later described Irving as "a sensible man. He kens about leather."[27] While there were probably also other homes where he was not well received and where there was no change of heart, they seem to have remained unrecorded. These families, presumably, would remain outside the church and generally off the printed page.

Dallimore may well have a point when he observed that "Chalmers knew and loved" these people "*en masse* but Irving knew them individually."[28] No doubt Chalmers did know individuals in his parish and took an interest in them, for he, like Irving, cared deeply about people and not just about social theory. But the very different natures of these two men

24. Ibid., 1:109.

25. Ibid., 1:114.

26. Carlyle, *Reminiscences* (Norton), 2:70.

27. Oliphant, *Life*, 1:110–11.

28. Dallimore, *Life*, 26.

led them to demonstrate their concern for others in different ways and to different degrees.

Another part of Irving's work in Glasgow was visiting the local prison. Irving had a very trusting nature. One of the prisoners he met, who was awaiting execution for murder, protested his innocence. Irving took him at his word and in the following days searched, with the help of others, to try to find evidence to establish the man's innocence. Sadly everything they discovered rather confirmed the man's guilt.[29] As this story suggests, Irving could at times be very gullible, and that trait would rise disastrously to the fore towards the end of his life. However, looking at this story from a more positive perspective, he was always sympathetic with those who suffered and had an innocence that would rather choose to believe than disbelieve what he was told, even by a man in prison.

Of course, Irving had many opportunities to preach at St. John's. There were generally three services held in the church each Sunday, and one in a nearby schoolhouse. The two ministers each led two of the Sunday services, taking turns so that they did not normally take the same service on successive Sundays.[30]

If some in the congregation were impressed by Irving's preaching, there were certainly others who were not. There are even accounts of people walking out of the church when they discovered that Irving was in the pulpit rather than Chalmers. This may have been a case of people being comfortable with the familiar and suspicious of the new, though it may just as likely have been because of the length of Irving's sermons. Later, he would sometimes preach for an hour-and-a-half or more, and though he does not seem to have done this in Glasgow, it is probable that his sermons there were still unusually long, even in an age of long sermons. In addition, his addresses were often strongly doctrinal and very profound, and they may not have effectively carried his message to his listeners, many of whom were not well educated.

Chalmers himself said, "Irving's preaching is like Italian music. It is only appreciated by connoisseurs,"[31] and it would seem that this particular part of Glasgow had few "connoisseurs" at that time. In fact, Chalmers was not usually complimentary about his assistant's preaching. Irving complained to Carlyle that sometimes when "Dr. C." spoke of the people's

---

29. Oliphant, *Life*, 1:124.

30. Hanna, *Memoirs* (Edinburgh), 2:284–85.

31. Oliphant, *Life*, 1:115–16. See also ibid., 1:124–26.

opinion of his young associate, he did it in such a way that it made him "feel all black in [his] prospects."[32]

Irving, for his part, was full of appreciation and admiration for Chalmers. So, if in any respect Irving was put down by his senior, he does not seem to have been greatly aggrieved by it. He later said to Chalmers that he thanked God for the "dispensation [that] brought me acquainted with your good and tender-hearted nature, whose splendid accomplishments I knew already; and you now live in the memory of my heart, more than in my admiration. While I laboured as your assistant, my labours were never weary."[33] Irving also called him a "man of transcendent genius," whom he both loved and admired.[34]

Though Irving had certainly been impressed by Chalmers as a man, he appears to have been less moved by his social theory. In fact, Peter Elliott has suggested that "the harsh reality of Glasgow's poverty may have convinced Irving that the self-seeking competitiveness of urban life was not to be routed by social and economic theory" such as Chalmers' taught, "and that the cure was far more likely to be found through a more profound Christianity that touched the heart."[35] In his ministry after his time in Glasgow, Irving certainly emphasized the religion of the heart, and, while not usually naming names, he became strongly critical of existing evangelicalism.

In the spring of 1821 Irving's sister, Elizabeth, was taken ill, and he quickly went to Annan to visit her. In a letter to Chalmers reporting on her condition, Irving said that he found "her conscience in considerable disquietude and longing for the peace of the Gospel." This, Irving hinted, she was unlikely to find under the incumbent minister at Annan. Irving ministered the gospel to her and noticed that not only her soul, but her body also seemed to revive. As her spiritual condition improved, so did her health. This showed to him "that Christ is the physician of the body as well as the soul."[36]

Irving's understanding of this incident could be taken as an early stage of his movement towards acceptance of the charismata. However, it is likely too early for that. He probably had in mind that some ailments of the body seemed to be directly caused by mental stress or spiritual disorder. Thus, if the mental and spiritual causes were removed, physical health would automatically improve.

32. Irving to Thomas Carlyle, December 26, 1821, in Irving, *DL*, 122.

33. Irving, *Oracles*, xi.

34. Irving, "Farewell Discourse," in Irving, *CW*, 3:361.

35. Elliott, *Edward Irving*, 150.

36. Irving to Thomas Chalmers, April 6, 1821, in Irving, *DL*, 105–106.

During this period Irving and Chalmers also visited Rosneath, where Irving's old friend Robert Story (1790–1859) was the minister. While there, Irving is said to have danced the Highland fling with his host's children. He also rekindled his love for the Scottish countryside when the party climbed Tamnaharra, the highest spot in the locality.[37]

At about this time, Irving also made a short return visit to Ireland. While there, upon entering the house of one poor woman, Irving noticed three roughly drawn portraits and asked whom the figures represented. The woman replied, "Sure that's St. Paul on the right. An' sure, isn't that St. Peter?" pointing to the one on the left. Irving then asked the identity of the man in the middle. The woman, aghast at his ignorance, answered, "Don't you know Pat Donnelly, the bruiser? Sure, everybody knows him."[38]

ANOTHER CALL

After two years at St. John's and approaching the age of thirty, it was time for Irving to move on. He was clearly a man too talented to remain long in any position where he was subordinate to another. It is easy to imagine that he yearned for his own church and an avenue of service in which he could fully use the remarkable gifts that God had given him. To a considerable degree, in Glasgow he was stifled by another man of extraordinary ability. It is said that at about this time Irving received a call from a Presbyterian church in Kingston, Jamaica, and he gave it careful and prayerful consideration before finally rejecting it.[39]

But hot on the heels of that call, another came. This time it was from a little nearer to home. Early in November 1821 Irving received a call from the Caledonian Church in Hatton Garden, London. Hatton Garden was the center of London's flourishing jewelry business, and still is. By contrast, this church at that time had been "reduced to great and almost hopeless straits."[40] The church building was owned by the Gaelic Fund, a Scottish charitable society that also operated an associated orphanage.

Seven years later, Irving wrote an account of that call. It said that one morning as he was sitting in his apartment, "meditating the uncertainties of a preacher's calling, and revolving in my mind purposes of missionary work, [a] stranger stepped in upon my musing, and opened to me the commission with which he had been charged." The stranger was James Laurie, and his

37. Story, *Memoir*, 61–62.
38. Hanna, *Memoirs* (Edinburgh), 2:290.
39. Oliphant, *Life*, 1:129.
40. Irving, "Dedication," July 8, 1828, in Irving, *Last Days*, xxxiv.

commission was to invite Irving to become the minister of the Caledonian Chapel in London.

Irving gives the impression in his record of this event that his response was immediate, or at least almost so: "The answer which I made to him . . . was to this effect: 'If the times permitted, and your necessities required that I should not only preach the Gospel without being burdensome to you, but also by the labour of my hands minister to your wants, this would I esteem a more honourable degree than to be Archbishop of Canterbury.'"[41] This, one might say, was spoken like a true minister of the Scottish Church. The call may have been to London, but it was to Scots in exile, and thus esteemed "more honourable" than to lead the Church of England.

The call outlined the forsaken nature of the work, and Irving later said that he consequently expressed his willingness to labor "without being burdensome" to the congregation if necessary; thus, presumably, without stipend.[42] However, a letter Irving wrote to William Dinwiddie, a member of the Caledonian session, immediately after the invitation indicates that he was more hesitant about accepting the call than the above account suggests, and one of the reasons was to do with money. He was receiving £150 per annum in Glasgow, plus generous expenses, and he stated that he would expect £200 in London, for he did not want to fall into debt. But he realized that the Caledonian Church was unlikely to be able to offer such a sum.[43]

Dinwiddie responded promptly to Irving's letter, offering him £150 plus a half-share in the pew rents. This assured Edward Irving that he would be financially secure if he said yes to the call. He accepted and offered to go to London for a few weeks on trial.[44] The arrangements were quickly made, and he arrived in London no later than December 23 "to make trial and proof" of his gifts over three Sundays before the congregation.[45]

The first Sunday passed off splendidly. The congregation was larger than expected and comprised "almost entirely young Scotsmen." And afterwards "the compliments . . . burst upon" him, which was a new experience for Irving. Whenever he was praised in Scotland, he felt that it was "with

---

41. Ibid., xxxiv–xxxv.

42. Ibid.

43. Irving to William Dinwiddie, November 6, 1821, in ibid., *DL*, 116–17.

44. Draft of a letter from William Dinwiddie to Edward Irving, November 12, 1821, in Grass, *Edward Irving*, 43–44; Irving to William Dinwiddie, November 16, 1821, in Irving, *DL*, 117–18.

45. According to Irving, *Last Days*, xxxvi, he arrived the day before Christmas, so presumably December 24. However, in a letter written on that date, he said that he had preached at the Caledonian Church "yesterday," (Irving to Thomas Chalmers, December 24, 1821, in ibid., *DL*, 119).

reservation often with cold and unprofitable admonition," but in London he was "hailed with the warmest reception" and the people made it clear that "they anticipate great things." On the third Sunday, he preached a "Charity sermon," at which the Duke of York, a son of King George III, was present. His Lordship was the president of the orphanage attached to the Caledonian Church, hence his presence.[46]

Towards the end of this trial period Irving told Carlyle that he found these few weeks of preaching in London had changed his attitude to pulpit ministry. "The pulpit I am now beginning to study as a means of power," he said, whereas "formerly I arose no higher than to contemplate it as means of livelihood, or rather[,] for I never was mercenary, as a prison house of fruitless exertion."[47] The change may have been caused by the different responses he had received from his two groups of listeners. In Scotland he had rarely been praised. In London, even in just a few weeks, a positive response to his preaching was common. In that great city, Irving knew he was being listened to and understood.

Once seen and heard, it would appear that the Caledonian Chapel congregation desired to call him. Amongst those who issued the call to Irving was William Hamilton from Dumfriesshire, who would later become the husband of Elizabeth Martin, a sister of Isabella, Irving's future wife.[48] However, two impediments stood in the way of the call. First, perhaps oddly for a church in London, even a Scottish one, the church's Trust Deed declared that any minister employed had to be able to preach in Gaelic. Irving could not speak Gaelic. On hearing of this problem, he quickly offered to learn that language in six months, though he later thought that he would be unable to do so in that time frame. Yet in the end, such a step did not prove necessary. To maneuver around the Gaelic stipulation, the church's leaders considered acquiring another building, but in the end they rented the Caledonian Chapel from the Gaelic Fund, which made them no longer subject to that rule.[49]

The second problem concerned a declaration of the Church of Scotland that stated that any church calling a minister had to be able to pay him

46. Irving to Thomas Carlyle, December 26, 1821, in ibid., 122. See also Irving to Thomas Chalmers, December 24, 1821, in ibid., 119–20.

47. Irving to Thomas Carlyle, January 22, 1822, in ibid., 129.

48. Oliphant, *Life*, 1:64–65.

49. Irving, *Last Days*, xxxvi; Hair, *Regent*, 20–21 (note that the page numbers in this edition of Hair's book differ from the original edition published by James Nisbet in 1899); Irving to William Dinwiddie, January 26, 1822 in Irving, *DL*, 130; Irving to the Elders of the Caledonian Chapel, February 21 and March 12, 1822, in ibid., 136, 140–41.

an adequate salary. It would seem that at that time the chapel had a congregation of fifty families[50] and the relevant presbytery expressed doubts that such a small number could provide the proposed financial support for him. Irving's ordination could not proceed without the presbytery's approval.

When Irving heard this, his warm blood must have risen to boiling point. However, he seemed calm enough in a letter dealing with that problem addressed to William Hamilton, though his frustration is obvious. "I am doing my utmost," he told Hamilton, "to get the Presbytery to consent to my ordination without a bond, and I hope to succeed. But if they will not, I come in June, ordination or no ordination; and if they are not content with the security I am content with, then I shall be content to do without their ordination and seek it elsewhere, or apply for it after."[51] Those are bold words, and words that one suspects rattled a few cages.

In the end he was guaranteed £500 a year, including pew rents, which was certainly an adequate salary. Quite how the Caledonian Church could pay so much is unclear, but its membership, small though it may have been, was probably not poor. In addition, they must have been pretty certain that once Irving was amongst them their congregation would quickly increase.[52]

In addition, as so often happens, after that frustrating period waiting for a call to a church, once one offer arrived, others soon followed. While the Caledonian Chapel was still going through the processes, he received a call to Dundee as well as inquiries from a major church in New York. The Dundee call he declined, and the American situation seems not to have materialized, probably because by the time a definite call could be framed he was already committed to London, where it would seem his heart now lay.[53]

The Reverend Thomas Fleming gave a testimonial for Irving at this time that tells us much about the person he had become, though his qualities were clearly not recognized by everyone. Fleming's comments are also quite notable on a point that will later prove highly significant. He wrote that Irving's

50. Some seem to have assumed that the whole congregation at that time totalled fifty. However, the church was full within a few weeks of Irving's eventual arrival, and it seems highly unlikely that the congregation would have risen from fifty to 500 to 600 people in just three or four Sundays. Grass says that "fifty heads of families signed the call" (Grass, *Edward Irving*, 43), which, if true, would mean that the original congregation was probably nearer two hundred.

51. Irving to William Hamilton, April 24, 1822, in Irving, *DL*, 143.

52. Irving to Thomas Carlyle, April 29, 1822, in ibid., 144.

53. Irving to the Elders of the Caledonian Chapel, February 21, 1822, in ibid., 135–36.

mind is . . . gigantic. There is scarcely a branch of human science which he does not grasp, and in some degree make his own. As a scholar, and as a man of science, he is eminently distinguished. His great talents he has applied to the acquisition of professional knowledge, and both his talents and acquisitions he is, I believe, sincerely resolved to consecrate to the services of his great Master. His views of Scripture truth, while they are comprehensive, are, in my judgment, sound.

Fleming also stated that Irving's preaching had undergone a change, probably due to contact with Chalmers, from being "too refined and abstract for ordinary hearers [to] plain, sound preaching,"[54] though how plain was "plain" may be argued. Certainly Irving's preaching at this time still carried a very lofty tone. However, Fleming's view was that Irving was a remarkable man. But few yet saw it. That would soon change, and many would become greatly attracted by him and to him.

With regard to Fleming's comments about doctrinal issues, a few years later there were those who would say that Irving's "views of Scripture truth" were decidedly *unsound*, even heretical, but at this point nothing had emerged in his teaching that worried Dr. Fleming or, seemingly, anyone else.

FAREWELL TO GLASGOW

Before Irving concluded his ministry in Glasgow he visited his old haunts and caused quite a stir. In Carlyle's brief report on the visit he said, "Nothing since the days of Knox or the Erskines has excited so much speculation in the theological world as his appearance here. They think him the cleverest and strangest person they have ever fallen in with."[55] Clever and strange! There was no doubt that Irving was very clever, but he also had an air of mystery about him that made him seem strange to many. Clearly, Irving's reputation was beginning to build.

The practicalities of Irving's call to London eventually went through. He was ordained in Annan on June 19,[56] and he then prepared to leave his beloved Scotland. Ordination by the Annan presbytery, though his church was in London, became significant in his later troubles. After that was completed, nothing remained to stop him moving to his new area of service in London.

54. Quoted in Oliphant, *Life*, 1:132–33.

55. Thomas Carlyle to David Hope, March 23, 1822, *CLO*.

56. Irving to the Elders (and the Congregation) of the Caledonian Church, June 14 and 20, 1822, in Irving, *DL*, 151–52.

In his farewell "discourse" to the St. John's congregation, Irving departed "from the approved custom of preaching on some useful topic"[57] and
instead, in an address of farewell rather than a sermon, began by gently wip-
ing away any conflicts that may have existed between him and any member
of the congregation, for as we have seen, there had been a few. This farewell
address was the first item by Irving that ever appeared in printed form, and
William Collins published it.[58] However, William Hanna claimed that before this sermon went to press, Mrs. Chalmers heavily edited it, and Irving
did not become aware of that until months after it was published. He was
not impressed.[59]

In the address, Irving declared:

> When friends part, they part in peace, making mention of the
> kind passages which have occurred between them, and giving
> assurance of the good-will and tender attachment which these
> passages of kindness have wrought within their hearts. At such
> a time, to remember aught but affection, or to utter aught but
> blessing, were an indecency to revolt the common heart of na-
> ture, and draw down the visitation of God . . . Religion . . . com-
> mands . . . "Have ye not broken of the same bread of blessing,
> and drunk from the same cup of blessing and supped around
> the holy table of Christ? Therefore, part as the sworn brothers
> of Christ."
>
> When there exist feelings of gratitude and affection towards
> the people of his charge, and longing desires after their present
> and everlasting welfare, the pastor is doing both the manly and
> a Christian part to bring these feelings forth, and to seal with
> the strong impression of love, all the passages of love which have
> occurred between him and his flock.[60]

Though this was not strictly a sermon, preachers tend to preach even
when they are trying not to, and Irving did at times slip into the sermonic
style in this address. In the following passage, God is the focus:

> We will not be silent in this congregation of His people, to
> meditate and speak His praise, and make mention of His loving-
> kindness to the most unworthy of His ministering servants . . .

---

57. Irving, *CW*, 3:345.

58. Oliphant, *Life*, 1:127; Irving to David Hope, May 28, 1822, in Irving, *DL*, 149.

59. Hanna, *Memoirs* (Edinburgh), 2:402. Whether the text of this address used
here is as edited by Mrs. Chalmers is unclear. It is rather long and very wordy, so it
might be a later Irving revision.

60. Irving, *CW*, 3:343-45.

He is the best of patrons, He who casteth down the proud and exalteth those of low degree. He is the best of friends, He who hath the hearts of men in His hands and turns them at His pleasure. He is the best of masters, He who doth not chide nor keep anger still, but waiteth to be gracious, and sendeth down every good and every perfect gift. Ye people, put your trust in Him continually.[61]

In this address Irving also gave a warning to those young men "destined for the holy ministry." He urged them to

stand aloof from the unholy influences under which the Church hath fallen; from the seats of power and patronage let them stand aloof; from the boards of ecclesiastical intrigue on both sides of the Church let them stand aloof; from glozing the public ear, and pampering the popular taste . . . let them stand aloof; and while thus dissevered from fawning intriguing and pandering, let them draw near to God, and draw inspiration from the milk of His word."[62]

Perhaps such sentiments, which Irving had presumably held throughout his Glasgow ministry, were a reason for his rejection by some of his congregation, for Irving was well aware that his ministry had "alienated" some. Nevertheless, Irving also knew that throughout his Glasgow ministry others had given him a "patient and willing ear."[63] But Irving was never a man to avoid tough issues. Nor was he one to pamper to the popular taste. Such uncompromising preaching does tend to divide its hearers.

Peter Elliott says that in this address Irving was "romanticising his own journey as the obscure but dedicated youth on a valiant quest towards an apostolic ministry."[64] His urging others to "stand aloof from the unholy influences under which the Church hath fallen" was encouraging others to do as he had done.

At one point, Irving paraphrased Shakespeare in a way that seemed to show that he knew that there would be trouble ahead for him. "There is a tide in public favour," he said,

which some ride on prosperously, which others work against and weather amain. Those who take it fair at the outset, and will have the patience to observe its veerings, and to shift and hold

61. Irving, CW, 3:347.
62. Irving, CW, 3:347–48.
63. Irving, CW, 3:349.
64. Elliott, Edward Irving, 69.

their course accordingly, shall fetch their port with prosperous and easy sail; those again, who are careless of ease, and court danger in a noble cause, confiding also in their patient endurance, and the protection of Heaven, launch fearlessly into the wide and open deep, resolved to explore all they can reach, and to benefit all they explore, shall chance to have hard encounters and reach safely through perils and dangers. But while they risk much, they discover much; they come to know the extremities of fate, and grow familiar with the gracious interpositions of heaven. So it is with the preachers of the gospel. Some are traders from port to port, following the customary and approved course, others adventure over the whole oceans of human concern . . . of the latter class of preachers was Paul the apostle . . . Luther . . . and . . . Calvin.[65]

In the future Edward Irving was to "launch fearlessly into the wide and open deep" and "adventure over the whole oceans of human concern," in some respects like Luther and Calvin, but sometimes quite differently from them. In so doing, he was to "risk much" and "discover much," but in the end, the deep swallowed him.

In closing he said,

And now brethren, I thank you, in fine, for the patience with which you have heard me, on this and on all other occasions . . . I can speak of your kindness and of the Almighty's grace, but of my own performances I cannot speak. Imperfections beset me round, which it is not my part to confess, save to the God of mercy. All these imperfections I crave you to forgive. Forget your injuries, real or imagined. Lay asleep your suspicions. My failings forget. For fain would I have a place in your esteem, as you have in mine. And beside this I have no favour to ask—your kind remembrance that is all . . .

Finally, then, brethren, farewell. The Lord of heaven and earth prosper you in your various conditions of wealth and poverty, good fortune or evil fortune. May your spirits prosper in the way of peace and holiness, through the word of the Gospel of Christ and the supply of His ministering Spirit. May your families rejoice in unity . . . May you see your children's children . . . May your affairs prosper . . . Pray for us and the ministry of the gospel in the city we are bound to.[66]

65. Irving, CW, 3:350.
66. Ibid., 3:361–62.

When the whole discourse is considered, one cannot help but wonder what Irving's less educated listeners, of whom there must have been many, made of such words as "cozenage" (to cheat or deceive), "glozing" (to fawn or flatter), and "simony" (the traffic in sacred things), not to mention "execrable," "indefatigable," "phalanx," "amain," "polity," and many more, though along the way he still felt himself free to plead for "a more natural style of preaching."[67] In his comments on this address, William Hanna matched Irving in saying that it contained "magniloquent phraseology" (lofty expression).[68] Probably Irving's eruditeness was another reason that some listeners found his preaching unacceptable.

Yet some had found a place for him in their hearts. As one of his early biographers said, "Glasgow did not forget *him* . . . The poor in particular" had cause to cherish his memory.[69]

While Irving was preparing to end his ministry in Glasgow, he told Jane Welsh "from being a poor desolate creature, melancholy of success, yet steel against misfortune, I have become all at once full of hope and activity. My hours of study have doubled themselves—my intellect, long unused to expand itself, is now awakening again, and truth is revealing itself to my mind."[70] Ten days later he told Robert Gordon, "My devotion to study [is] three times as intense, my desire of excellence [is] quite consuming."[71]

Irving had also become more serious. In a letter written to Jane seven months later he wrote, "ten years agone I had a little humour, which has now nearly deceased from neglect. My mind was then light and airy, and loved to utter its conceptions, and to look at them and laugh at them when uttered." But now he was "aiming from morning till night to be a serious and wise man, though," he admitted, "God knows how little I succeed."[72] It was probably as well that he never did entirely succeed in deleting his humor, for there are numerous later reports of him laughing in the company of others.

But with humor or without it, at last he was "full of hope." The way ahead looked very bright.

Carlyle was also confident about Irving's future, for he regarded him as "likely . . . to earn a vast renown for himself and do much good among the religious inhabitants of the Metropolis."[73]

67. Ibid., 3:347–50, 352.

68. Hanna, *Memoirs* (Edinburgh), 2:402.

69. Wilks, *Edward Irving*, 26.

70. Irving to Jane Baillie Welsh, February 9, 1822, in Irving, *DL*, 134.

71. Irving to Robert Gordon, February 19, 1822, in ibid., 137.

72. Irving to Jane Baillie Welsh, September 9, 1822, in ibid., 159.

73. Thomas Carlyle to his mother, January 12, 1822, *CLO*.

6

London: "This Dazzling Moment"[1]

"[Edward Irving] proclaimed himself the peer of [London's] intellectual aristocracy; and avowed a mission to the irreligious great, talented, and influential."

—WASHINGTON WILKS[2]

LONDON BEGINNINGS

It is vain of me to think of conveying to you any idea of London, [for] one's wits are lost in the magnitude of the objects, which solicit one on every hand. [And] between anxiety to know, and difficulty to find out, I feel myself rent in twain.

—EDWARD IRVING[3]

Irving's departure from Glasgow was delayed because Chalmers became sick and Irving did not feel that he could leave St. John's unattended. However,

1. Oliphant, *Life*, 1:166.
2. Wilks, *Edward Irving*, 62.
3. Irving to Thomas Carlyle, December 26, 1821, in Irving, *DL*, 121.

49

in the middle of July 1822 Irving boarded the James Watt Steamboat[4] and traveled south to London to become the minister of the Scotch Caledonian Church in Hatton Garden. Though the congregation of that church was fairly small, the expectations were now much greater. To meet those expectations, the Caledonian Chapel needed some action.

The chapel had, in fact, been built in 1796 for the Swedenborg sect, but when they vacated it, it quickly passed through the hands of several groups, including at least one assembly of Baptists and some seceders from the Church of England. It was then purchased by and for Scots in exile in 1812 and became associated with the Caledonian orphanage for Scottish children from 1816. The new church was quite successful under its first minister, but when he left it went into decline. Its membership appears to have sunk to about fifty families just before Irving arrived, though the building could seat around six hundred people.[5] It also needs to be understood that at this time the Caledonian Church was not a major place of worship. In addition, it was a Scottish outpost in England's main city, a Presbyterian interloper in staunch Church of England territory.

Irving first lodged in Queen Square, Bloomsbury, not far from his church, in "three very good rather elegant apartments, a sitting-room, a bed-room and dressing-room," with an attic to accommodate visitors. He spent each weekday morning after breakfast in study.[6]

His first sermon at his new church was from Peter's words to the household of Cornelius: "Therefore came I unto you without gainsaying, as soon as I was sent for: I ask therefore for what intent you have sent for me?" (Acts 10:29). There appears to have been no detailed record taken of this address,[7] but one suspects that Irving answered the question for them. This sermon proved to be the first in a series of Sunday morning addresses about Peter's meeting with Cornelius.[8]

A few weeks after his arrival, in a letter to William Graham, an old friend from Burnswark in Scotland, Irving wrote, "You cannot conceive how happy I am here in the possession of my own thoughts, in the liberty of my own conduct, and in the favour of the Lord. The people have received me with open arms; the church is already regularly filled; my preaching, though of the average of an hour and a quarter, listened to with the most serious

4. Irving to William Dinwiddie, July 8, 1822, in ibid., 153.

5. Hair, Regent, 9–10, 17–19.

6. Irving to William Graham, August 5, 1822, in Irving, DL, 157–58.

7. Oliphant, Life, 1:151.

8. Irving, "Last Sermon in the Caledonian Church," in Irving, CW, 3:504.

attention."[9] His church was, then, "already regularly filled," which, since it seated six hundred, presumably meant the congregation was by then not less than five hundred, probably more. That this should be the case so soon after his arrival indicates that Irving's ministry quickly made a major impact upon that church and the Christian circle surrounding it. The congregation had risen from about fifty families—say, a little more than two hundred people—to presumably over five hundred in three or four Sundays. Early in December, after a little more than four months of London ministry, he told Mrs. Welsh, "my church overflows."[10] This all seems in stark contrast to Irving's work in Glasgow, where he was always subordinate to Chalmers and seemingly not appreciated by everybody. In London, if he had not exploded like a bombshell, he had still cast a dazzling ray of light and hope upon a struggling ministry.

In the phrase, "in the liberty of my own conduct" one senses Irving's relief that now he was, under God, the master of his own destiny. If as a Presbyterian minister he was to some degree subject to the local presbytery, one senses that the men of that presbytery already had a pretty good idea of the caliber of man that had been called and were not likely—at that stage at least—to place too many restrictions upon him.

Not that he was satisfied in every respect. In the letter to Graham he also reflected,

> My thoughts . . . have of late turned almost entirely inward upon myself; and I am beginning dimly to discover what a mighty change I have yet to undergo before I be satisfied with myself. I see how much of my mind's very limited powers have been wasted upon thoughts of vanity and pride; how little devoted to the study of truth and excellency upon their own account. As I advance in this self-examination, I see farther, until, in short, this life seems already consumed in endeavours after excellence, and nothing attained; and I long after the world where we shall know as we are known, and be free to follow the course we approve, with an unimpeded foot. At the same time I see a life full of usefulness, and from my fellow creatures, full of glory, which I regard not; and of all places this is the place for one of my spirit to dwell in. Here there are no limitations to my mind's highest powers . . . Oh, that God would keep me, refine me and make me an example to this generation of what His grace can produce upon one of the worst of His children![11]

9. Irving to William Graham, August 5, 1822, in ibid., *DL*, 157.

10. Irving to Mrs. Welsh, December 6, 1822, in ibid., 166.

11. Irving to William Graham, August 5, 1822, in ibid., 157.

Towards the end of September Thomas Chalmers went to London to do some research. He met with Irving several times. On the first occasion, Irving and three of his elders approached Chalmers about inducting Irving into his church. Chalmers protested that he did not have the time, and the induction was eventually carried out by the London Presbytery.

Two days later they met again, and Chalmers recorded in his diary that Irving "is happy and free, and withal making his way to good acceptance and a very good congregation," sentiments that noticeably echo those written by Irving in his own letter to Graham. But Chalmers was still uneasy. A week later, he wrote, "I hope that he will not hurt his usefulness by any kind of eccentricity or imprudence."[12] This statement can be viewed as tentatively prophetic, and it does suggest that Chalmers, during their association in Glasgow, had seen signs that Irving might be led towards extremes. Certainly the closing stages of Irving's ministry in London were and are regarded by many as both eccentric and imprudent.

In fact, Irving had earlier expressed to a leader in his new church,

> There is a sea of troubles, for my notions of a clergyman's office
> are not common, nor likely to be in everything approved. There
> is a restlessness in my mind after a state of life less customary,
> more enterprising, more heroical . . . certainly more apostolical.
> My notions of pulpit eloquence differ from many of my worthy
> brethren. In truth I am an adventurer on ground untried, and
> therefore am full of anxieties.[13]

These "notions," or some of them at least, had probably been detected by Chalmers when they had worked together, which gave him a little unease about Irving's future.

Irving's ministry in London was even more demanding than he had expected. Before the end of September he told Carlyle, "My business has grown upon my hands into the double of what I had calculated on." Each week he had to produce two sermons, and he found himself taking greater care than ever before in preparing them. Whether this was because his mind had "taken more important views of the questions [he] handled," or whether it was because he was responding to the needs of his "young and thoughtful audience," he was unsure. But every week he had to write the equivalent of

---

12. Thomas Chalmers, quoted in Hanna, *Memoirs* (Edinburgh), 2:348–51, 355.

13. Letter from Edward Irving, quoted in Hair, *Regent*, 22. According to Drummond, this was written to an office bearer of the Caledonian Chapel (Drummond, *Edward Irving*, 46).

"three or four ordinary discourses, and to refresh [his] mind with reading," as well as to attend to other ministerial duties.[14]

A LOFTY CROWD

By early November, four months after his arrival, Irving could say, "The church overflows every day."[15] The main reason his church filled so quickly seems to have been because of word-of-mouth invitation. For example, the jurist Sir James Macintosh heard Irving preach soon after his arrival in London. Sir James was so deeply moved by Irving's public prayers that he recommended Irving to no less a person than George Canning, the nation's Foreign Minister (1822–1827) and later Prime Minister (1827). Canning paid the Caledonian Church a visit, liked what he heard, told others, and, it is claimed, mentioned Irving in a debate on church revenues in the House of Commons.[16]

From then on, everybody who was anybody wanted to hear this new Scottish preacher. In fact, Canning's estimate of Irving was very high. He "repeatedly declared that Edward Irving was the most powerful orator, in or out of the pulpit, he had ever heard."[17] That, coming from a Member of Parliament, was praise indeed. The poet Samuel Taylor Coleridge also called him "certainly the greatest orator, I ever heard."[18]

Amongst the people at his services in the early years were Sir David Wilkie (Scottish artist), Allan Cunningham (Scottish poet), Sir Peter Lawrie (later Lord Mayor of London), James Gilliland Simpson (merchant), Zachary Macaulay (slavery abolitionist), Basil Montagu (judge and legal reformer, later made Sir Basil), Sir James Mackintosh (judge and author), William Hone (satirist), Lord Liverpool, Lord Jersey, the Duke of Sussex, the Earl of Aberdeen, the Duke of York, and "other members of the royal family." Even critic William Hazlitt, who had "forgot what the inside of a church was like," went to listen to this new phenomenon, and was less critical than one might expect. Indeed, he described Irving as having an intellect

---

14. Irving to Thomas Carlyle, September 23, 1822, in Irving, *DL*, 162.

15. Irving to David Hope, November 5, 1822, in ibid., 164.

16. Oliphant, *Life*, 1:158–59; Drummond, *Edward Irving*, 48–49. Liam Upton, in an unpublished work, argues that no evidence of this can be found in *Hansard* (Grass, *Edward Irving*, 54).

17. Gilfillan, *Third Gallery*, 55.

18. Samuel Taylor Coleridge to Edward Coleridge, July 23, 1823, in Coleridge, *CLSTC*, 5:286.

"of a superior order."[19] Irving's congregation, then, included "every rank and degree of men, from the lowest, basest of our press hirelings, up to the right hand of royalty itself."[20] It was a motley crew. But it was a rich motley crew, and more importantly, a very influential one.

Another future Prime Minister, W. E. Gladstone, then a boy at Eton College, went to hear Irving with his father, another parliamentarian. As Gladstone later recalled,

> It required careful previous arrangements to secure comfortable accommodation. The preacher was solemn, majestic (notwithstanding the squint), and impressive; carrying all the appearance of devoted earnestness. My father had on a certain occasion, when I was still a small Eton boy, taken time by the forelock, and secured the use of a convenient pew in the first rank of the gallery. From this elevated situation we surveyed at ease and leisure the struggling crowds below. The crush was everywhere great, but greatest of all in the centre aisle. Here the mass of human beings, mercilessly compressed, swayed continually backwards and forwards. There was I, looking down with infinite complacency and satisfaction from this honourable vantage ground upon the floor of the church, filled and packed as one of our public meetings is, with people standing and pushing.

As Gladstone looked down at the swarming mass below him, he spotted a figure he recognized, Dr. John Keate, the headmaster of his school, who was a strict disciplinarian. Gladstone went on, "What was my emotion, my joy, my exultation when I espied among this humiliated mass, struggling and buffeted—whom but Keate! Keate, the master of our existence, the tyrant of our days! . . . Never, never, have I forgotten that moment."[21] It is clear that Gladstone's attention was not entirely upon the preacher, but he was nonetheless impressed by him, and it seems to have been Irving that impressed him rather than what he said. Irving was "solemn" and "majestic (notwithstanding the squint)."

Frances Williams-Wynn, "A Lady of Quality" and the daughter of a baronet, had mixed feelings when she first heard Irving. She recorded in her diary entry of June 29, 1823, that she did not like his Scottish accent and that when he began to preach he spoke for over twenty minutes before he said what his subject would be. In that introduction she found him "vulgarly enthusiastic, self-sufficient, [and] dogmatical." Her brother seated next to her

---

19. Gilfillan, *Third Gallery*, 54; Hazlitt, *Spirit*, 82; Wilks, *Edward Irving*, 31–32.

20. Irving, *Last Days*, xxxvii.

21. Morley, *Life*, 1:44.

leaned over and said, "We have been twenty-three minutes at it and now the sermon is to *begin*." However, she wrote, "the hour which followed appeared to me very short, though my attention was on the full stretch during the whole time." To her, the sermon had both "great faults"—including a lack of simplicity—and "transcendent beauties," but she "admired it extremely, at least in parts." In fact, she "never knew what eloquence was until [she] had heard Irving" and she eagerly desired "to hear him again."[22]

Yet Williams-Wynn disliked his accent. This was not to say that she had difficulty understanding him; it was just that she found the Scottish brogue irritating. Judging by the way crowds flocked to hear him, Irving's English listeners must have generally found him easy to understand, though Williams-Wynn said that his pronunciations included "high-sup" (hyssop), "crucifeed," and "scorged."[23]

When Dorothy Wordsworth read some of Irving's sermons, she thought one of them "worse than a Methodist rant."[24] However, on a visit to London in 1824 she heard Irving preach, and her opinion of him greatly improved. She described his person as "very fine . . . his action often grace-ful," though at times "far otherwise," his reading "excellent," and remarked that "while he keeps his feelings under, nothing can be finer than his man-ner of preaching." However, she still thought that "he wholly wants taste and good judgment," which was presumably because at times Irving did give full rein to his feelings.[25]

She also seems to have preferred Irving to the Mexican curiosities on exhibition at that time in Piccadilly and to the Swiss giantess. Irving, it appears, had become one of the sights to be seen by visitors to London, with some of those visitors viewing the Caledonian Chapel and its preacher as little more than tourist attractions. While this may not have been the case with Ms. Wordsworth, for she gave him "full credit" for his obvious sincerity,[26] it was probably the case with an increasing number of listeners. Such a visit appears to have become to some an early nineteenth-century equivalent of tourists going to see *The Mousetrap* in the second half of the twentieth century or the London Eye in the twenty-first. In other words, Irving was a must-see, or perhaps more accurately, a must-hear.

22. Williams-Wynn, *Lady of Quality*, 117–22.

23. Ibid.

24. Dorothy Wordsworth to a "friend," August 20, 1823, in Wordsworth and Wordsworth, *Later Years*, 212.

25. Dorothy Wordsworth to John Monkhouse, April 16, 1824, in ibid., 260, 262.

26. Ibid.

Henry Crabb Robinson, a journalist and friend of many literary figures, found one Irving sermon "very impressive," even though it "lacked
a master-feeling running through the whole." He described Irving as being "very vehement, both in gesticulation and declamation." Robinson also
praised Irving's reading of the Scriptures, which he regarded as beautiful
and said, "gave a new sense to them." He heard Irving again the following
week and found this sermon more to his liking, even though Irving exposed
the dangers that intellectuals can fall into.[27]

A graphic and detailed description of a service at the Caledonian Chapel was penned by George Gilfillan, a Scottish preacher and poet. Gilfillan
said, "You go a full hour before eleven, and find that you are not too early.
Having forced your way with difficulty into the interior, you find yourself in
a nest of celebrities. The chapel is small, but almost every person of note or
notoriety in London has squeezed him or herself into one part or another
of it." Gilfillan then reeled off a list of these celebrities (Is the celebrity cult
older than we think?), noting that George Canning, William Wilberforce,
Robert Peel, William Plunket and Henry Brougham (both later to become
barons), Jeremy Bentham, William Godwin, William Hazlitt, Zachary Macaulay, and Samuel Taylor Coleridge were among those present. The time
for the service drew close, then:

> Eleven o'clock strikes, and an official appears, bearing the Bible
> . . . [There is] a rustle, which is instantly succeeded by deep
> silence, as, slowly and majestically, Edward Irving advances,
> mounts [—] with a measured and dignified pace, as if to some
> solemn music heard by his ear alone—the pulpit, and, lifting
> the Psalm-book, calmly confronts that splendid multitude. The
> expression of his bearing while he does this is very peculiar; it
> is not that of fear, nor that of deference, still less is it that of
> impertinence, anger or contempt. It is simply the look of a man
> who says internally, "I am equal to this occasion and to this as-
> sembly, in the dignity and power of my own intellect and nature,
> and more than equal to it, in the might of my Master, and in the
> grandeur and truth of my message . . ."
>
> He is a son of Anak in height, and his symmetry and ap-
> parent strength are worthy of his stature . . . his whole aspect is
> spiritual, earnest, Titanic; yea that of a Titan among Titans—a
> Boanerges among the sons of thunder. He gives out the psalm—
> perhaps it is his favourite psalm, the twenty-ninth—and as he
> reads it, his voice seems the echo of the "Lord's voice upon the
> waters," so deep and far-rolling are the crashes of its sound. It

---

27. Robinson, *Diary, Reminiscences*, 2:253–54.

sinks, too, ever and anon into soft and solemn cadences, so that you hear in it alike the moan and the roar, and feel both the pathos and the majesty of the thunderstorm. Then he reads a portion of Scripture, selecting probably, from a fine instinctive sense of contrast, the twenty-third psalm . . . to give relief to the grandeurs that have passed or that are at hand. Then he says, "Let us pray," not as a mere formal preliminary, but because he really wishes to gather up all the devotional feeling of his hearers along with his own, and to present it as a whole burnt-offering to Heaven. Then his voice, "Like a steam of rich distilled perfumes," rises to God, and you feel as if God had blotted out the Church around, and the Universe above, that the voice might obtain immediate entrance to his ear.

The prayer over, he announces his text, and enters upon his theme. The sermon is upon the days of the Puritans and the Covenanters, and his blood boils as he describes the earnest spirit of their times. He fights over again the battles of Drumclog and Bothwell; he paints the dark muirlands, whither the Woman of the Church retired for a season to be nourished with blood, and you seem to be listening to that wild eloquence that pealed through the wilderness and shook the throne of Charles II. Then he turns to the contrast between that earnest period and what he thinks our light, empty and profane era, and opens with fearless hand the vials of apocalyptic vengeance against it. He denounces our "political expediences," and Canning smiles across to Peel. He speaks of our "godless system of ethics and economics," and Bentham and Godwin shrug their shoulders in unison. He attacks the poetry and criticism of the age, inserting a fierce diatribe against the patrician Byron in the heart of an apology for the hapless ploughman Burns; knocking Southey down into the same kennel into which he had plunged Byron; and striking next at the very heart of Cobbett; and Hazlitt bends his brow into a frown, and you see a sarcasm . . . crossing the dusky disc of his face . . . [W]axing bolder, and eyeing the peers and peeresses, the orator denounces the "wickedness in high places" which abounds, and his voice swells into its deepest thunder, and his eye assumes its most portentous glare, as he characterises the falsehood of courtiers, the hypocrisy of statesmen, the hollowness, the licentiousness and levity of fashionable life . . . It is Isaiah and Ezekiel over again, uttering their stern yet musical and poetical burdens. The language is worthy of the message it conveys, not polished, indeed, or smooth, rather rough and diffuse withal, but vehement, figurative and bedropt with terrible or tender extracts from the Bible. The manner is as

graceful as may well co-exist with deep impetuous force, and as
solemn as may evade the charge of cant. The voice seems meant
for an "orator of the human race," and fitted to fill vaster build-
ings than earth contains, and to plead in mightier causes and
controversies than can even be conceived of in our degenerate
days.[28]

Gilfillan's is a stunning description that might at first be considered
full of hyperbole. Yet, it so coincides with the reports of others and gives
such bountiful explanation of why so many educated people went to hear
him, that it would seem foolish to regard it as exaggeration, though Gilfillan's descriptions of the responses of Irving's listeners may be imagined. So,
taking this account as generally true, it is clear that Irving was playing with
fire. Criticisms of the cultural and ruling elites were bound to have repercussions, and they eventually did, as shall be seen.

However, Hazlitt suggested that Irving had "found out the secret of
attracting by repelling." That is, "Those whom he is likely to attack are curious to hear what he says of them; they go again, to show they do not mind
it," while "He keeps the public in awe by insulting all their favorite idols,"
including politicians, rulers, moralists, poets, critics, and magazine-writ-
ers.[29] There may well be some truth in Hazlitt's observation, but it is highly
unlikely that this was Irving's intention. He proclaimed what he believed
to be the truth, knowing that some would be offended by it, but with the
firm conviction that it was the preacher's job to speak that truth regardless
of its consequences. Hazlitt also said that in his preaching, Irving "mixed
the sacred and the profane together, the carnal and the spiritual man, the
petulance of the bar with the dogmatism of the pulpit, the theatrical and
theological, the modern and the obsolete."[30] In Hazlitt's view it was this,
allied with his eloquence, that captured Irving's listeners.

Washington Wilks believed that "the secret of Irving's attraction lay
in the tenderness with which he bound up the wounds of poor humanity,
rather than in the skill with which he probed them."[31] And this, no doubt,
did encourage some of his listeners to come back to hear him again.

Oliphant noted that the many descriptions of Irving's eloquent preaching seem to have been accompanied by descriptions of his appearance. She
said that it was as if "His person, his aspect, his height, and presence have all
a share in his eloquence. There is no dividing him into sections, or making

28. Gilfillan, *Third Gallery*, 54–58.
29. Hazlitt, *Spirit*, 86.
30. Ibid., 81.
31. Wilks, *Edward Irving*, 34.

an abstract creature of this living man."[32] Hazlitt put it less kindly and suggested that if Irving had been only "five feet high" he would not have been nearly so successful, for "people would have laughed at his monkey tricks."[33] It seems, then, that Irving's eloquence was inseparably linked to his remarkable presence. He preached not just with his voice, but with his whole, magnificent being.

On some occasions Irving stood on tiptoe in the pulpit and raised his arm vertically above his head. In this way his great height was further extended, which, in one writer's opinion, "gave him the aspect of supernatural majesty." From this position, he "sent down his burning words, like so many thunderbolts, upon the heads of his breathless hearers."[34]

Irving had once written that there were two kinds of preaching. One kind "draws the attention from the speaker to the Subject and keeps it steadily to this one object." The other type "tends to lead your mind from the matter of the discourse to the person who delivers it."[35] Somehow he seems to have combined both, though probably not intentionally. Some of his listeners concentrated on his message and were captured by it. Others were only interested in fine words eloquently expressed, for it is clear that many of his hearers were more interested in the man than his message.

Not surprisingly, some strongly disapproved of Irving and the following he attracted. Lord Eldon complained, "All the world here is running on Sundays to the Caledonian Chapel in Hatton Garden, where they hear a Presbyterian orator from Scotland, preaching, as some ladies term it, *charming* matter, though downright nonsense. To the shame of the King's ministers be it said, many of them have gone to this schism-shop with itching ears."[36] One writer called the furor surrounding Irving "one of the most extraordinary and extensive infatuations that ever seized upon a community calling itself intelligent."[37] The publication *John Bull* described the bustle surrounding Irving as "so degrading, so theatrical, so laughable, and so contemptible." As to Irving himself, he was "a great brawny Scotchman," with "a vulgar and abominable" accent, talking "the most detestable nonsense."[38]

---

32. Oliphant, *Life*, 1:174. See also Brown, "Personal Reminiscences," 217.

33. Hazlitt, *Spirit*, 83.

34. [Bonar?], "Edward Irving," 232.

35. Irving, *DL*, 45.

36. Lord Eldon to Lady M. Banks, July 1823, quoted in Williams-Wynn, *Lady of Quality*, 116.

37. Quoted in Wilks, *Edward Irving*, 31.

38. *John Bull*, July 20, 1823, 228, quoted in Grass, *Edward Irving*, 66–67.

It would seem unlikely that Irving, on his move to London, had deliberately planned to minister to the nation's movers and shakers. In Glasgow he had worked mainly amongst the poor, and he must have known that the congregation at the Caledonian Church would be wealthier and better educated. Yet when he was first called to London he could have had little idea about the types of people he would draw to that church and the popularity he would experience. It must have come as a surprise even to him.

It is striking that Carlyle did not consider Irving's preaching in London "superior to his [earlier] performances" in Scotland.[39] While this is just one man's opinion, it is tempting to ask why there was such a great difference in response between the two places, if there was little difference in Irving's preaching. Perhaps it was because, as Chalmers had claimed, Irving's preaching was only "appreciated by connoisseurs," and in London there were simply more "connoisseurs." It is only to be expected that Irving's erudite sermons, such as his farewell address in Glasgow, would appeal to a more educated people, and that is exactly what Irving encountered in that part of London. He went from preaching to a mainly working-class congregation to a highly educated one, and there he found his mission field. Yet there still remains an element of mystery about the extent of Irving's appeal in the English capital. It seems to have been far above what anyone expected, even beyond what anyone could have expected.

If it were thought that Irving's pulpit ministry at this time was conducted just to appeal to the desires of London's intellectuals, it needs to be noted that some of the criticisms he made from the pulpit, as we have seen, are clearly not the comments of a man seeking praise. In this regard it is also well to take note of the words of others who heard him. Fellow Presbyterian Dr. James Hamilton stated that "his presence was like Elijah's in the land of Israel, a protest against prevailing sins; and, like every protest in Jehovah's name, it carried a sanction and diffused an awe."[40] Wilks claimed, "Never were the pretentions of rank more ruthlessly spurned—never the vices of the rich more sternly denounced" than by Irving.[41] Hazlitt said that Irving preached with "sledge-hammer blows."[42] Thomas De Quincy called him "a very demon of power."[43] In addition, ironically, Irving also criticized

39. Carlyle, *Reminiscences* (Norton), 2:134.
40. Root, *Edward Irving*, 131.
41. Wilks, *Edward Irving*, 33.
42. Hazlitt, *Spirit*, 81.
43. Drummond, *Edward Irving*, 52.

"Dawdlers and mere lookers-on,"[44] and he must have known that there were plenty of such in his congregation.

An aged man who had heard Irving in his youth said, "He read the Scriptures as one reading a direct message from God. He prayed as one who speaks with God. When he began to preach one forgot everything but the message he was listening to. Absolute silence reigned and one was unconscious of the flight of time."[45] And bearing in mind that Irving's sermons usually lasted an hour-and-a-quarter or longer, that says a great deal for his compelling power as a preacher. One Church of England clergyman said, "From [Irving's] instruction I learned more of Christian truth, and from his example more of the Christian life, than from any other man."[46] Irving's primary aim was not to promote himself, but the word of God and the God of the word, no matter whom it would offend.

Yet Gilfillan argued that Irving's pulpit efforts, "while exciting general admiration in London, were not productive of commensurate good. They rather dazzled and stupified, than convinced and converted. They sent men away wondering at the power of the orator, not mourning over their own evils, and striving after amendment."[47] While it cannot be denied that this happened, it would be foolish to suppose that was the whole story. The evidence shows that, while many listeners soon left him, many more remained loyal to Irving and to the gospel.

By the middle of 1823, Irving's level of fame was such that Rudolph Ackermann did a portrait of him and reproduced it for sale at two shillings. Notification of this appeared on the famed first page of *The Times* that August, sandwiched between an advertisement for "Superior Accommodation" for a gentleman and one for "Oates and Harper's Livery Stables."[48]

It had also become clear by that time that a larger church needed to be built to hold all those wishing to hear Irving preach. On May 19 of that year a meeting was held to discuss the matter. It decided first, that a larger church be built, and secondly, and very importantly, that it retain its "connection with the Church of Scotland, and that the doctrines, forms of worship and mode of discipline of that Church shall be taught, observed and practised therein." Thirdly, that Irving should remain its minister and that any eventual replacement should be a minister of the Church of Scotland. Fourthly, it declared that the required money for the building should be raised by

44. Wilks, *Edward Irving*, 36.
45. Root, *Edward Irving*, 26.
46. Ibid., 129.
47. Gilfillan, *Third Gallery*, 58.
48. "At a Meeting of the Congregation," *The Times*, August 22, 1823, 1.

subscription. Six of the church's laymen were appointed as treasurers to administer the fund.

The July 29 edition of *The New Times* printed a lengthy list of those who had made one-off gifts or had agreed to make a donation annually for the next five years. The list included a number of the aristocracy, which suggests that at least some of the titled fraternity saw genuine value in Irving and did not just regard him as an interesting freak. The publisher James Nisbet was also on the list, and in addition, he promised to donate a pulpit Bible.[49]

But what was Irving's rationale in the early stages of his London ministry? At that time, Irving believed that the Christian religion "doth not denounce the rational or intellectual man, but addeth thereto the spiritual man, and that the latter flourishes the more nobly under the fostering hand of the former."[50] Hence, he seems to have begun specifically to teach "imaginative men and political men, and legal men, and scientific men, who bear the world in hand," and thus influence the nation and indeed, the world for Christ.[51] As Oliphant said, "At this dazzling moment he had access to the highest intelligences in the country."[52]

With such a following, it would have been no surprise if Irving had shed all traces of humility and become full of his own importance. Indeed, Jane Welsh feared that "these London flatteries" might affect him.[53] But he was well aware of such dangers. In one of his sermons a little later he said, "As we grow great, we generally grow proud; as we grow in favour with men, we grow vain and ostentatious."[54] In one of his books' dedication to Basil Montagu, Irving said more specifically that on the one hand, he was afraid that the circles he now moved in would either engulf him "by their enormous attractions" or repel his "simple affections," leaving him to "the mockery and contempt of every envious and disappointed railer."[55]

When he returned to Scotland in September 1823 to get married, Irving met an old friend, the Reverend Robert Gordon of Edinburgh. Gordon soon afterwards described Irving as being "The same noble fellow—and in spite of all his *alleged* egotism, a man of great simplicity and

49. *New Times*, July 29, 1823, 1. The list also includes the name John Murray, who may be the second person of that name in the John Murray publishing dynasty.

50. Irving, *Oracles*, 379.

51. Ibid., vii. "Medical men" seems to have been substituted for "scientific men" in some records.

52. Oliphant, *Life*, 1:166.

53. Jane Baillie Welsh to Eliza Stodart, July 22, 1823, *CLO*.

54. Irving, "On Prayer," in Irving, *CW*, 3:123.

55. Ibid., *Sermons*, 2:333.

straightforwardness."[56] But it must have been very difficult for a man experiencing such adulation to remain humble. Ironically, criticism from some quarters, it would seem, helped him keep his feet on the ground.

Carlyle was concerned that Irving might incur "the risk of many vagaries and disasters, and at best the certainty of much disquietude." Carlyle was on the mark, for the beginning of that disquietude was not far away and the disasters would soon follow. Yet Carlyle imagined that at that time, "Happy Irving" entertained "no doubt that he is battering to its base the fortress of the Alien, and lies down every night to dream of planting the old true blue Presbyterian flag upon the summit of the ruins."[57]

ORACLES OF GOD

Irving had his first book published in London on July 2, 1823. "Two large impressions"[58] sold out that year, and an American edition was also soon published, which demonstrates that his fame had already spread well outside London's boundaries. This book was, in fact, two collections of his expanded addresses in one volume: *For the Oracles of God, Four Orations* and *For Judgment to Come, an Argument, in Nine Parts.*[59] Before its publication, Irving told Mrs. Welsh, "I intend introducing the volume with a discourse on the preparation for reading the Scriptures, and concluding it with a discourse on the advantage of obeying them." He also called it "a curious book, a kind of defiance rather than defence,"[60] and that is how many seem to have seen it.

The *Orations* in the first, much shorter part of the book were deliberately "after the manner of the antient oration, the best vehicle for addressing the minds of men, which the world hath seen." The *Argument* was written in the style of the "antient Apologies" as a defense of Christian teaching on the judgment, and in that mode brought this teaching "before the tribunal of the human mind."[61] So, one assumes, these two works were intended for the intellectuals in the community, not the masses, and not even the literate

56. Oliphant, *Life*, 1:178.

57. Thomas Carlyle to Jane Baillie Welsh, August 10, 1823, *CLO.*

58. *The British Press*, June 30, 1823, 1; Wilks, *Edward Irving*, 126.

59. A third part was intended, on "The Incarnation of Christ" (Irving to Thomas Chalmers, January 21, 1822 [1823], in Irving, *DL*, 169). This appeared later in another series.

60. Irving to Mrs. Welsh, December 6, 1822, in Irving, *DL*, 167; Irving to Jane Baillie Welsh, February 23, 1823, in ibid., 174.

61. Ibid., *Oracles*, viii.

portion of the general population. In fact, Hazlitt criticized Irving's writing for being governed by "an obsolete style and mode of thinking."[62] A century later, A. L. Drummond complained that this book, and Irving's writings generally, affected "the diction of a bygone age [which] revealed both lack of historic sense and lack of taste."[63] Irving's language, in this style, only increased the difficulty of making his ideas understood and widely accepted.

Irving was well aware that with this book he was putting his head in the hornet's nest. In the preface he wrote, "For criticism I have given most plentiful occasion, and I deprecate it not; for it is the free agitation of questions that brings the truth to light." Criticism, then, he expected, and criticism he received. And while he did not claim divine inspiration for the book, he did indicate that much prayer had gone into the writing of it.[64]

The preface to the book began with a series of statements that were bound to ruffle feathers. Irving claimed that after "more than ten years' meditation upon the subject" it appeared to him "that the chief obstacle to the progress of divine truth over the minds of men is the want of it being properly presented to them." In fact, Irving estimated that 90 percent of the population had a most inadequate understanding of the revealed truths of Christianity, and that this was not because the people were uninterested, but mainly because of a lack of "a sedulous and skilful ministry on the part of those to whom" those truths were "entrusted." In other words, the clergy were largely to blame for Christian Britain's ignorance of the Bible and the God of the Bible. Yet Irving went on to state that though what he had said might seem "to convey a reflection upon the clerical order," that was not his intention. Rather, he was just trying to get the clergy to pay attention to the issue he was raising.[65]

The *Orations* was arranged under three headings, with the third having two parts, and was based on John 5:39: "Search the scriptures" (AV). The three sections were "The Preparation for Consulting the Oracles of God," "The Manner of Consulting the Oracles of God," and "The Obeying of the Oracles of God." Clearly, if this book was aimed at intellectuals, its aims were not purely intellectual, considering that roughly half of the whole was given over to the practical outworking of the subject.

Bearing in mind events of a charismatic nature in Irving's last years, there are some comments that are most striking in the book's second paragraph. Irving wrote, "But now the miracles of God have ceased, and Nature,

62. Hazlitt, *Spirit*, 80.

63. Drummond, *Edward Irving*, 60.

64. Irving, *Oracles*, ix–x.

65. Ibid., v–vi.

secure and unmolested, is no longer called on for testimonies to her Creator's voice." In fact, with regard to the Scriptures, "The vision is shut up, and the testimony is sealed, and the Word of the Lord is ended."[66] In his later ministry, Irving was involved in a movement that claimed to experience the miraculous, including ongoing divine revelation, but at this stage that was not part of either his theology or his practice.

To Irving, the Bible was "the offspring of the divine mind, and the perfection of heavenly wisdom," which came "from the love and embrace of God" to disclose "the mysteries of hereafter, and the secrets of the throne of God."[67] He urged his readers to "Let the Word be appealed to, in order to justify [y]our opinions and resolve [y]our doubts," for "it is a duty to peruse the Word of God," but it is also "something infinitely higher . . . When my Maker speaks, I am called to listen by a higher authority . . . Out of duty, out of love, out of adoration, out of joy, out of fear, out of my whole consenting soul, I must obey my Maker's call."[68]

Indeed, this word was delivered "to speak welfare to you and your children" and to "set up" its throne "in the hearts of men."[69] In spite of the profound, intellectual nature of his sermons and writings, he saw Christianity as essentially a religion of the heart. To Irving, the "Doctrines" of the faith "should be like the mighty rivers which fertilize our island." They should "carry health and vitality to the whole soul and surface of Christian life."[70] He complained about:

> the logical and metaphysical aspect with which Religion looks out from the temples of this land, playing about the head, but starving the well-springs of the heart, and drying up the fertile streams of a holy and charitable life! . . . It is high intolerance of the far greater number, whose heart and whose affections may be their master faculty, to present nothing but intellectual food, or that chiefly: and moreover, it is a religious spoliation of the heavenly wisdom, which hath a strain fitted to every mood; and it is an unfeeling, unfaithful, dealing between God and the creatures whom he hath been at such charges to save.[71]

Whereas the first part of the book ran to a little less than a hundred pages, the second, containing sermons preached in the spring of 1823,

66. Ibid., 1–2.
67. Ibid., 4–5.
68. Ibid., 33–34.
69. Ibid., 5.
70. Ibid., 41–42.
71. Ibid., 44–45.

extended to over four hundred. It was "Addressed to such heads" as Carlyle's.[72] Its aim was to take the subject of God's judgment away from "poetical visionaries" and "religious rhapsodists" (he had in mind particularly the
"Vision of Judgment" poems by Robert Southey and Lord Byron) and "to
place it upon the foundation of divine revelation, human understanding,
and the common good." To this end, Irving sought "to argue" the subject
"like a *man*, not a *theologian*; like a *Christian*, not a *Churchman*."[73] But,
whether he liked it or not, he was both a theologian and a churchman, and
this inevitably came through.

Irving's understanding of God's judgment in the last days appears for
the most part to have been a common, traditional view. This was to change
somewhat in later years, as shall be seen. But at this moment he seems to
have envisaged just one divine judgment at the end of Earth's history. And
this judgment was to be a magnificent, "ideal scene," with "the great white
throne descending out of heaven, guarded and begirt with the principalities
and powers thereof," with God seated "on his blazing throne." At this sight,
"the heavens and earth flee away" as the dead are raised. So amazing is this
scene that "Imagination cowers her wing, unable to fetch" its compass.[74]

The Judge pronounces "blessing for ever and ever upon the heads of his
disciples, and dispenseth to them a kingdom prepared by God from the first
of time . . . Their trials are ended, their course is finished, the prize is won."
But then, "Again the Judge lifteth up his voice, his countenance clothed in
that frown which kindled hell, and he pronounceth eternal perdition with
the devil and his angels, upon the wretched people who despised and rejected him on earth . . . the age of necessity has begun its reign; all change
is forever sealed."[75] And the only way in which one can enter that blessing
and escape that wrath is through Jesus Christ.[76] Indeed, the "revelation of
hell is . . . the vantage ground on which the genius of the Gospel [of Christ]
stands, and from which she points aloft to heaven."[77] He also argued against
the prevailing view that the judgment was "far off." He pointed out that to
the Apostles it was "close at hand," and argued that is how we should also
see it.[78]

72. Irving to Thomas Carlyle, February 23, 1823, in Irving, *DL*, 176.

73. Irving, *Oracles*, 101–3; Wordsworth and Wordsworth, *Later Years*, 212 n.

74. Irving, *Oracles*, 321.

75. Ibid., 323–24.

76. Ibid., 351–52.

77. Ibid., 426.

78. Ibid., 317–20.

THE CRITICS

The book quickly caused a stir. A number of publications took exception to it, or in some cases, to parts of it, and sought to expose Irving "to general ridicule and contempt" and so subjected him to "fierce" criticism.[79] Yet the controversy, as so often happens, increased the demand, and further editions were published.

Soon after publication, *The Times* called the book "poor thought wrapped up in tinsel" and dubbed Irving "this turgid and shallow declaimer."[80] *The Quarterly* agreed, calling Irving "a declaimer turgid and unintelligible," his writing "coarse and incorrect," and his reasoning "vague and inconsistent."[81]

In August and September of that year a lengthy review of Irving's book appeared in *The Christian Observer*, a Church of England publication. This review noted the popularity of the author, but also observed that he was also already the object of considerable hostility. The reviewer expected this hostility to increase, for "The infidel will hate him . . . The formalist will show him no reverence . . . Even among the ministers of religion he must expect very few cordial friends." In fact, "there is gathering in a certain quarter, to which Mr. Irving has directed very pointed attention, a dark thunder cloud, destined ere long to burst upon his head."[82] In addition, *The Christian Observer* noted that Irving had already become the object of "disgusting abuse" from some unnamed journals.[83]

This reviewer also reported that there had also been suggestions from different quarters that Irving was not quite orthodox, though the reviewer rejected those claims. These misunderstandings, the reviewer argued, may have been caused by Irving's "love of paradox" and his practice of "saying strong things in strong terms."[84] In fact, in the reviewer's opinion, in this book Irving firmly maintained "The great truths of Christianity."[85]

The *Observer* reviewer also noted that this "man of commanding intellect" clearly possessed "very considerable powers" and that he was also "evidently conscious" that he possessed them, adding, "his impassioned appeals are almost irresistible." However, "In the high and commanding tone

79. "Rev. of—Irving's Orations," 493, 578.

80. Quoted in Drummond, *Edward Irving*, 62.

81. Quoted in Wilks, *Edward Irving*, 116.

82. "Rev. of—Irving's Orations," 492–93.

83. Ibid., 564. There is a hint in the context that these were secular "journals," not religious publications.

84. Ibid., 500–501.

85. Ibid., 578.

which [Irving] so frequently assumes, he does not appear to seek to magnify himself, but to set forth the mighty interests of religion."[86] The reviewer closed by saying that he was cautiously optimistic about Irving's future.[87]

The following year, *The Westminster Review* admitted that Irving's sermons "are full of earnestness, and certainly contain most of those qualities in which he asserts the discourses of others are deficient." This reviewer also praised Irving's "boldness," but lamented his lack of "discretion." In addition, the reviewer doubted that the methods Irving was employing in this volume would achieve the hoped-for results. For example, "He is a Quixote, who holds all parley in scorn; and rides, with lance couched, not only against ravishers and giants, but also against fulling-mills and flocks of sheep." In addition, "had he contented himself in expounding St. Peter and St. Paul, without interweaving a running commentary upon Byron, Southey, and Moore; his talents and his earnestness would have made more converts and fewer enemies."[88]

Also that year, a reviewer in *The Christian Spectator* of New Haven said that he had a high "estimate of [Irving's] genius."[89] He also noted Irving's quick rise to fame and stated that while Irving "has great power, much originality and often a pathetic, and sometimes a sublime eloquence," yet he often left "important points unguarded . . . sometimes speaks unadvisedly" and at times was "much wanting in the good taste which would invite the attention of his readers."[90]

The August 1823 edition of *Blackwood's Edinburgh Magazine*, which one might have expected to be sympathetic, mocked the book's title and called Irving, "one of the most absurdly self-conceited persons of our time." In an earlier edition it had also criticized the "epidemic frenzy" surrounding the Caledonian Chapel, which had afflicted "All London."[91]

Even Carlyle was critical, though this was presumably at least partly because of his different religious views. He wrote, "There is strong talent in it, true eloquence, and vigorous thought but the foundation is rotten, and the building itself is a kind of monster in architecture—beautiful in parts— vast in dimensions—but on the whole decidedly a monster . . . Sometimes

---

86. Ibid., 493. See also ibid., 578.
87. Ibid., 587.
88. Review of *Oracles*, by Edward Irving, *Westminster Review* 1 (1824) 29–30.
89. Review of *Oracles*, by Edward Irving, CS 6 (1824) 155.
90. Ibid., 150–51.
91. "Rev. Mr. Irving's Orations," 14:147; ibid., 13:214.

I burst right out o' laughing, when reading it; at other times I admired it sincerely."[92]

From within Irving's own denomination, Dr. James Hamilton later said of *Orations*, "seldom have bigger thoughts and loftier sentiments struggled for expression in modern speech . . . and though his practical wisdom did not keep pace with his discursive prowess, the might of his genius, and the grandeur of his views, and the prevailing solemnity of his spirit gave a temporary lift to an earthly age."[93]

Both Hamilton and *The Christian Spectator* referred to Irving's "genius," and it is unlikely that either used that word lightly. Indeed, more than 150 years later Arnold Dallimore, who was often critical of Irving, used the same word of him when considering this book.[94] It was no ordinary literary tome. Yet the *Spectator* reviewer found that though Irving's writing was generally of a "good quality," at times it was "cumbersome from superabundance or obsoleteness."[95] Even his writing, it seems, held too much grandeur for some. In fact, Dallimore argues that in this book Irving was "straining after grandeur."[96]

Wilks summarized the opinions of the sterner critics of his time. He said they accused Irving of "Theological obscurity and unsoundness—groundless aspersion of his contemporaries—frequency of inconclusive reasoning—indulgence in coarse, and even irreverent, expressions [and] disjointed imagery."[97]

Leading from that, it has been argued of this book and his later writings that Irving was at times rather careless in his use of language and lacking in clarity. In this case, it has been suggested that this was because the process of preparing the book for publication was rushed,[98] as it probably was, but that is the lot of most busy people.

With regard to his lack of clarity, in *Judgment* Irving criticized "The evangelical preachers," without specifically indicating how he was using the term or clarifying to whom it referred. After all, surely he himself was an evangelical preacher. Many then and now would have considered him so, at least in his early years, but he clearly regarded himself as outside the group

---

92. Thomas Carlyle to Margaret Carlyle, September 28, 1823, *CLO*. See also Thomas Carlyle to Alexander Carlyle, January 13, 1824, *CLO*.

93. Root, *Edward Irving*, 131.

94. Dallimore, *Life*, 40.

95. Review of *Oracles*, by Edward Irving, *CS* 6 (1824) 200.

96. Dallimore, *Life*, 40.

97. Wilks, *Edward Irving*, 125.

98. Cuthbertson, "Edward Irving," 8.

he was criticizing. Indeed, he did not want "to go to war" with them. It was also "*The* evangelical preachers" (used three times), not *some* evangelical preachers, so this was a criticism of a whole group, not of certain individuals within it. This term could potentially refer to the evangelical wing in the Scottish Church as a group distinct from that church's moderates,[99] but Irving's target seems to have been wider than that. Four years later, he seemed to equate "the Evangelical people" with the dissenters,[100] which may be what he meant here.

Irving claimed that to the evangelical preachers, "the word of God [is] a dead inefficient letter until the Spirit of God put meaning into its passages." This would seem to have been a misunderstanding of those he was criticizing. Certainly, it has been a common Christian belief for centuries that it was necessary for the Holy Spirit to awaken the individual conscience to the saving truth of the Scriptures. This idea was based on such passages as "The man without the Spirit does not accept the things that come from the Spirit of God, for they are foolishness to him, and he cannot understand them, because they are spiritually discerned" (1 Cor 2:14). Yet that does not mean that the text in itself was "dead," "inefficient," or without meaning.[101] As Michael Madden has observed, "the deadness is in the sinner, not the word."[102]

The reviewer in the *Observer* noted these problems and asked who these evangelical preachers were. Does the term, he questioned, refer to men "who preach the same great truths of the Gospel" as Irving? And do these people really "disparage the word of God by declaring it to be unintelligible?"[103] The *Spectator* reviewer went as far as to say that Irving was actually "head in the school of those who have sought to render 'evangelical religion' 'acceptable to men of cultivated taste.'"[104] The problem was Irving had not presented his point clearly or fairly, and this was not the last time that he would do that.

Yet, if Irving did not think of himself as an evangelical preacher, then it is clear that others did, and a major one at that. However, even this early on, a gulf was opening between Irving and other evangelicals. In the dedication

---

99. Chambers, "Doctrinal Attitudes," 160–61.

100. Irving to Thomas Chalmers, March 26, 1827, in Irving, *DL*, 239.

101. Irving, *Oracles*, 464–65.

102. Michael Madden, e-mail message to author, April 21, 2013.

103. "Rev. of—Irving's Orations," 582.

104. Review of *Oracles*, by Edward Irving, *CS* 6 (1824) 151.

to one of his later books, Irving referred to "the distance at which I was held from the affections of my Evangelical brethren."[105]

THE "COURT'S" JUDGMENT

Such language as Irving used in *Orations* was bound to make enemies of some who would otherwise have been friends. For the first time, in print at least, but by no means the last, Edward Irving was angering those from whom he could have gained most support. It is clear that he could have made the same points just as boldly in language that was less critical, but he did not. He almost seems to have taken this course deliberately, knowing the consequences.

Irving also knew well that the congregation at his chapel expected, probably even needed, a highly intellectual approach to the preaching of the Word, so he supplied it. This strategy would not have worked in most other evangelical churches and chapels. This difference in method unintentionally set Irving apart from many of his evangelical colleagues, and later the gulf was widened by his criticisms of his fellow preachers in such works as *Orations*. Some preachers, no doubt, were also jealous of his success. It is hard to rejoice in the successful work of others if one's own work is not going too well. In addition, though some of the new members at the Caledonian Chapel may not have been regular attendees at any church prior to Irving's arrival in London, many more must have defected from other churches. This would have caused suspicion of Irving's work and, perhaps, jealousy.

The most colorful criticism of Irving at this time came in an anonymous satirical book called the *Trial of the Rev. Edward Irving M.A., A Cento of Criticism*, which ran to five editions in the space of six months.[106] This volume began with a series of none too complimentary caricatures of Irving in the pulpit, drawn, it appears, by Robert Cruikshank, brother of George. Indeed, it has been argued that he also wrote the text.

The book was a transcription of a mock trial of Irving before "The High Court of Commonsense," which, strikingly, was as critical of the critics as it was of Irving. In it a "Mr. Jacob Oldstyle" (the eldest of the Oldstyles) brought seven charges against the defendant:

> First, For being ugly.
> Second, For being a merry-andrew [a buffoon or clown].

---

105. Irving, *Sermons*, 2:333. The issue of whether Irving was an evangelical or not is examined on my Edward Irving website, www.edwardirving.org.

106. Oliphant, *Life*, 1:169.

Third, For being a common quack.

Fourth, For being a common brawler.

Fifth, For being a common swearer.

Sixth, For being of very common understanding.

And, Seventh, For following divisive courses, subversive of the discipline of the order to which he belongs, and contrary to the principles of Christian fellowship and charity.[107]

The imagined witnesses were the editors of various leading publications, and their actual words were quoted. First was the editor of *The Times*. He testified "that Mr. Irving is a man of very ordinary talents; that his understanding is weak in its grasp, and limited in its observation; and that his taste is of the very lowest order of badly-instructed schoolboys."[108]

The editor of the *Literary Chronicle* complained about Irving preaching only to the rich and famous and neglecting, for example, those who spoke Gaelic. He also said that Irving's "reasoning is superficial; his judgment indiscreet; his taste bad; his conceit overwhelming; his assurance unblushing."[109] Then the editor of the *British Press* argued that Irving "professes to address himself to a blind and senseless generation, but he seems to have caught the distemper he came to cure." The editor of *John Bull* described Irving's popularity as "one of the most flagrant and disgusting pieces of humbug ever foisted upon the people of this metropolis."[110]

The *Trial*'s greatest complaints were against Irving's claim in *Orations* that "*nine-tenths* of every class . . . know *nothing at all* about the truths of revelation" and his accompanying criticism of the nation's preachers, describing Irving's claim as "nonsense."[111] His teaching on judgment and hell also came in for repeated criticism.[112] And Irving's claim that his book was written in the style of the ancient orations and apologies was "after the manner of the Fudge Family," for his addresses were not significantly different in style from the sermons of many other preachers.[113]

Inevitably, Irving's squint did not go unnoticed by the author of *Trial*. The book contained a nine-verse song called "Doctor Squintum." It ran in part:

107. *Trial*, 1, 3–4.

108. Ibid., 6–7.

109. Ibid., 22–25.

110. Ibid., 34, 50–51.

111. Ibid., 19, 35.

112. For example, ibid., 8–9, 18, 23–24.

113. Ibid., 37–38.

Come, Beaux and Belles, attend my song,
Come, join with me the motley throng,
The time is apt, the tide runs strong,
Your heart no longer hardens.
The world at once is pious grown,
And vice a thing no longer known;
For *Doctor Squintum*'s come to town
To preach in Hatton Garden.

The Doctor is a charming man,
A good deal on the Whitefield plan,[114]
Men's vices he doth plainly scan,
Not delicately hint'em.
A fire upon his flock he'll keep,
And treats them more like wolves than sheep,
Til some go mad—but more to sleep:
Oh, charming Doctor Squintum . . .

My Lord, the Duchess, and his Grace,
All join the scrambling melting race,
And Ministers in pow'r and place,
Whose names—we scorn to print 'em:
These leaving their pastors in the lurch,
And much it grieves us in the search,
To find the *State* desert the *Church*,
For such a thing as Squintum.

It was not very kind, but not entirely inaccurate either.

As one would expect, in this trial, satirical though it may have been, Irving conducted his own defense. Also, as one would expect, his defense was long, wordy, and quoted from his book.

After the "jury" had deliberated, it found Irving not guilty of the first six charges and guilty only of the last, that of "following divisive courses . . . contrary to the principles of Christian fellowship and charity."

According to Carlyle, when he met with Irving in October 1823, the preacher seemed to accept all this "with jocund mockery, as something

114. George Whitefield, the great evangelist of the previous century, also had a squint.

harmless and beneath him."[115] But it was not all as harmless as Irving seems to have supposed. It was the early stages of opposition to him that would, in the next few years, rise in intensity and destructiveness.

In his first year in London, then, Irving had been subjected to both much praise and much condemnation and abuse. Through it all, one thing was clear: love him or hate him, Edward Irving had arrived. In addition, one question arose: How long would he last?

115. Carlyle, *Reminiscences* (Norton), 2:111.

7

Peace and War

"Edward Irving [was] one of the greatest actors on the theological stage."

—JEAN CHRISTIE ROOT[1]

HE MARRIES ISABELLA

Irving's romantic life had not run smoothly. He seems to have fallen in love with one woman while engaged to another, but could not wriggle out of the earlier commitment. However, whatever his doubts and problems with regard to affairs of the heart, Irving remained loyal to Isabella Martin. Their wedding was set for Tuesday, October 14, 1823, in her father's manse in Kirkcaldy. It seems probable that Isabella had not seen Irving during the fifteen months of his London ministry and may well have been wondering whether his success had changed him. She need not have worried. Any changes that may have taken place were not in his character.

Upon his return to Scotland, Irving's first port of call was Haddington, where he had had his first teaching post. When he had previously left Haddington, he was a schoolteacher of no great reputation. Once he eventually left Scotland he had become a preacher, but of hardly any more fame. But on

1. Root, *Edward Irving*, 4.

75

his return he was, in modern parlance, a celebrity. Many of his former pupils delighted to shake hands with the Scot who had taken London by storm.[2]

The wedding ceremony was conducted by the bride's grandfather. What Irving's feelings were for Isabella at that stage one can only guess, but there is little doubt that later he genuinely loved her. This love, however, may not have been stirred by physical beauty. Carlyle, probably in a mischievous mood, described her as "*dead ugly*," though "otherwise a very decent, serviceable person."[3] In a further description of Isabella to Jane Welsh, Carlyle told her, Irving's "wife you will hardly like, but neither can you well dislike her. She *is* unbeautiful; has no enthusiasm, and few ideas that are not prosaic or conceited: but she possesses I believe many household virtues; she loves her husband and will love his friends."[4] That seems to be as close as Carlyle ever got to paying Isabella a compliment. It would appear that he did not have a high opinion of her intelligence and regarded her as too compliant.

The Irvings spent their honeymoon roaming the Scottish countryside, with Irving, on at least one occasion, carrying a packed suitcase on his shoulder. Perhaps strangely, they met up with Thomas Carlyle, and he accompanied them on their travels for a couple of days. He described Irving as being at this time "superlatively happy . . . as if at the top of Fortune's wheel," with Isabella "demure and quiet," though, he thought, "*not* less happy."[5]

Irving seems to have taken a complete rest from preaching during this time and, for the most part, enjoyed a refreshing break from crowds. After more than a year's energetic labor in London, he had been feeling rather unwell, but this rest did much to restore his health. Their honeymoon ended with a brief visit to Glasgow just in time to hear Thomas Chalmers preach his final sermon at St. John's before taking up his professorial chair at St. Andrew's University. Irving was given the task of leading the congregation in prayer at the end of the service, in which he asked God's blessing upon Chalmers' future work.

---

2. Oliphant, *Life*, 1:177–78; Grass, *Edward Irving*, 82. Oliphant gives the date as October 13 on page 178, but as the 14th of that month in a footnote on page 302. Irving said it would be Tuesday, October 14 in a letter to Thomas Carlyle dated October 7, 1823 in Irving, *DL*, 189. According to Grass, there was "no entry in the relevant register for Kirkcaldy," which is surprising, but *The Times* also gave October 14 (Grass, *Edward Irving*, 82 n. 12).

3. Thomas Carlyle to John A. Carlyle, October 20, 1823, *CLO*.

4. Thomas Carlyle to Jane Baillie Welsh, October 22, 1823, *CLO*.

5. Thomas Carlyle to John A. Carlyle, October 20, 1823, *CLO*; Carlyle, *Reminiscences* (Norton), 2:109–10.

After that it was back to London, where the Irvings settled into a house in Myddelton Terrace, Pentonville (now Islington), which had been furnished by two friends while they were away.[6]

It must have been quite a challenge for Isabella to settle into not just a marriage, but a very different way of life. True, she was moving from one manse to another, but the situations were a world apart. Kirkcaldy was a small, quiet town where Isabella's father had been a leading figure. But the people who attended their kirk were, for the most part, folks of little worldly distinction. London was a vast metropolis, ever extending its dimensions and influence, and her husband had the ear, and in some cases even the friendship, of many of the most famous people in the kingdom. And he was very busy. In fact, their house was "never empty of idle or half-earnest wondering people."[7] Mrs. Montagu said that Isabella, "but for her great piety, must be wretched, for [her husband] cannot (with every desire to do so) give her any part of his time except in the hours of refreshment & sleep—and she must live among persons whom you could not endure for a moment."[8]

Isabella also looked after their financial arrangements. She was Irving's "good chancellor" of the exchequer.[9] This may have been because, as she was running the household, she was more aware of how their finances should be spent, though it may also have been because her husband thought he already had enough to do without that responsibility. It may also have been partly because of Irving's very generous nature. If, when he was out, someone asked him for money, he was inclined to give whatever he had. If he had little in his pocket to begin with, then that generosity would do little harm to the family's budget. It is unlikely to have been because Irving lacked financial sense, for after all, he had proven very able at mathematics.

Dallimore argued that Isabella was not strong-minded or wise enough to keep Irving from his later excesses. If he had married a wiser woman with a more resolute will, she might have been able to steer him on a more

6. Carlyle, *Reminiscences* (Norton), 2:118–19; Oliphant, *Life*, 1:179–83. Myddleton Terrace was later named Claremont Square (Irving, *DL*, 193 n. 155). Interestingly, in the 1820s and 1830s, George Cruikshank, who illustrated the books of Charles Dickens, also lived in that Terrace, just a few houses away.

7. Thomas Carlyle to Margaret A. Carlyle, December 24, 1834, *CLO*.

8. Mrs. Montagu to Jane Baillie Welsh, May 30, 1825, quoted in Jane Baillie Welsh to Thomas Carlyle, June 12, 1825, n. 3, *CLO*. Irving called Mrs. Montagu "The Noble Lady" (Carlyle, *Reminiscences* [Norton], 2:112).

9. Drummond, *Edward Irving*, 82; Irving to Isabella Irving, July 25, 1828, quoted in Oliphant, *Life*, 2:43.

moderate course.[10] It could be regarded as certain that had he married Jane Welsh, she would have tried to keep him clear of the things that later destroyed him. But Jane would just as surely have wrecked his ministry in other ways. Yet Irving, though at times surprisingly easily influenced, was not one to be persuaded against his will by anybody. A stronger wife would have increased the conflict in the home without reducing it in the church and the world.

Two months after the wedding, Isabella told her mother that there had been numerous conversions through her husband's ministry.[11] Thus Irving's preaching was not just appealing to the intellect, it was also striking the heart.

It comes as no great surprise that by February of the next year Irving was nearing exhaustion. Apart from his normal ministerial duties, he was writing a preface to *The Life of Bernard Gilpin*, clergyman, artist, and educationalist, for the publisher William Collins. Collins appears to have been concerned that Irving was taking a long time about it and thus was delaying publication. Irving assured the publisher that he would fulfill his commitment, but complained, "I am at present worked beyond my strength and you know that is not inconsiderable. My head! My head! . . . If you saw me many a night unable to pray with my wife, and forced to have recourse to forms of prayer, you would at once discover what has caused my delay."[12] In the end his condition improved, and the preface became an "Introductory Essay" that ran to nearly fifty pages, but it does not seem to have been completed until that December.[13] Irving did not know how to keep things short, and this assured an excessive workload. As Andrew Landale Drummond said, with Irving "Every speech must be an oration,"[14] and a prolonged one at that.

On July 22, 1824, Edward Irving wrote to his father-in-law to tell him that "Isabella was safely delivered of a boy (whom may the Lord bless) at half-past-eleven this forenoon, and is, with her child, doing well." Isabella's mother and one of her sisters were on hand to assist her during the delivery. The child was called Edward and later baptized by his great-grandfather.[15]

---

10. Dallimore, *Life*, 55.

11. Isabella Irving to Mrs. Martin, December 24, 1823, quoted in Grass, *Edward Irving*, 58.

12. Irving to William Collins, February 24, 1824, in Irving, *DL*, 194.

13. Gilpin, *Bernard Gilpin*, liv.

14. Drummond, *Edward Irving*, 273.

15. Irving to Rev. Martin, July 22, 1824, in Irving, *DL*, 200; Oliphant, *Life*, 1:211.

It would appear, however, that Irving wanted to name him John after his deceased brother, but "the higher power" (Isabella) objected.[16]

A few months later Carlyle joined them on holiday at Dover. In a letter to Jane Welsh, Carlyle rather mocked the fact that Irving bathed the little boy himself, and also recorded, "Oh that you saw the giant with his broad-brimmed hat, his sallow visage, and sable matted fleece of hair, carrying the little pepper-box of a creature, folded in his monstrous palms, along the beach; tick-ticking to it, and dandling it."[17]

In fact, Irving seems to have been more attentive to his son than many other fathers in nineteenth-century Britain. Again according to Carlyle, "the worthy preacher dandles and fondles and dry-nurses and talks about" the little boy "in a way that is piteous to behold. He speculates on the progressive development of *his* senses, on the state of his bowels, on his hours of rest, his pap-spoons and his *hippings* [diapers]; he asks you twenty times a-day (me he dare not ask any longer) if *he* is not a pretty boy; he even at times attempts a hideous chaunt to the creature by way of lullaby."[18] When the Irvings went for their regular afternoon walk, the father carried the son in his arms, to the amusement of many a passer-by.[19] Seen through modern eyes, Irving's treatment of his son seems more to be applauded than mocked. But to Carlyle, while the baby was a source of "many blessings," he was still "a squeaking brat."[20]

It is the common lot of Christian ministers to be subjected to people with a wide variety of problems, begging for money and other favors. Irving was consistently kind and generous to these people in London, as he had been in Glasgow. It did not matter to him whether the beggar belonged to the so-called deserving poor or not. If a person was in need, Irving endeavored to supply that need. Fifty years later, William and Catherine Booth of The Salvation Army would also refuse to make this distinction between the deserving and undeserving poor. A person in need was a person in need.

During this early period in Irving's London ministry, John Macbeth, a ministerial probationer of the Church of Scotland, came knocking. This man had been unable to gain a call to a church, and Irving, knowing what that was like, gladly helped him. Macbeth had written a book on the

16. Irving to Jane Baillie Welsh, October 12, 1824, in Irving, *DL*, 203.

17. Thomas Carlyle to Jane Baillie Welsh, October 5, 1824, *CLO*.

18. Thomas Carlyle to Margaret A. Carlyle, November 12, 1824, *CLO*. See also Thomas Carlyle to Jane Baillie Welsh, November 15, 1824, *CLO*.

19. Oliphant, *Life*, 1:233.

20. Thomas Carlyle to John A. Carlyle, September 27, 1824, *CLO*. Thomas and Jane Carlyle never had any children, which was probably as well, since they both disliked infants.

Sabbath, and Irving not only bought a copy, but also made sure that some of his friends did so too. This way, Irving presumably thought, he could assist the man without making him feel he was receiving charity. However, Macbeth proved only too happy to receive any amount of charity. Carlyle, who was more inclined to be cynical and was in a position to be so, did not like Macbeth. He "thought ill of him from the first" and said that he had "a sharp, sarcastic, clever kind of tongue" and that "envy, spite and bitterness, looked through every part of him."

One wintry evening Irving received a letter from Macbeth, delivered by the landlord of "a low public house" where the unfortunate man had been residing for several days. Inevitably, he had run up a bill that he could not pay, and he had told the landlord that Mr. Irving of the Caledonian Church would pay it. The note was advising Irving of his unfortunate predicament. Irving went to the pub, paid the bill ("some £2.10s or so," according to Carlyle), and brought Macbeth back to the manse. He stayed with the Irvings for some time and then disappeared. It was not long before another note arrived from him, again asking for help. Oliphant told this story but failed to record how it ended, though she hinted that it did not end favorably and with the Irvings well out of pocket.[21] But Irving's generosity here stemmed from a naturally kind heart, and one that sincerely sought to follow the example and teachings of Jesus Christ.

Understandably, Irving has at times been charged with looking after the rich while neglecting the poor, but however far that was true, it had more to do with circumstances than intent. Yet at about this time, some women who had set up a school in the Billingsgate area of London were having trouble getting the children of the poor to attend, so they enlisted Irving's help. Irving, pleased to be able to minister to the underprivileged for once, accompanied the women as they went from house to house inviting the parents to send their children to the school. Irving did most of the talking, and with his gentle manner, melted the hearts of the previously suspicious mothers.[22] It was, in fact, one of Irving's strong points that he could feel comfortable in the presence of the great as well as in the company of the lowly, rather like John Wesley in the previous century.

During this period Irving's old friends Jane Welsh and Thomas Carlyle complained that he hardly ever wrote to them. They wondered whether he had dropped them for grander folk. In fact, sarcastic nicknames for Irving such as "his Reverence," "the Arch-Apostle," "the good priest," and, most

---

21. Oliphant, *Life*, 1:212–15. Thomas Carlyle supplies the man's surname, though his Christian name is in doubt. See Thomas Carlyle to Alexander Carlyle, December 14, 1824, *CLO*; Carlyle, *Reminiscences* (Norton), 2:137–39.

22. Oliphant, *Life*, 1:229–31.

frequently, "the Orator" appear in their letters to each other, and Jane on one occasion even called him "the Hero of Hatton Garden."[23] In a letter to Carlyle, Jane acknowledged Irving's loving friendship and then turned right around to say, "'speaking of Swine' what is become of our gigantic friend?"[24] She was, no doubt, not being serious, but her humor often presented a sharp cutting edge.

It is noticeable that at times when Carlyle had little contact with Irving he became rather cynical about him, seemingly stirred up by the formidable Jane, but when they met again he distinctly softened. Carlyle even stayed with Irving in July 1824, and during that time they grew "very intimate again" and had "great talking-matches."[25] Elliott suggests that "Jane and Carlyle were dealing with a mixture of envy, bitterness and regret where Irving was concerned."[26] Envy and regret there certainly was on both their parts, and from Jane perhaps a little bitterness, but Carlyle showed no trace of bitterness towards his long-term friend. In fact, it would appear that during these times of separation Irving had not forgotten them; rather he was hindered in making contact by his heavy workload and the large circle of new friends all calling for his attention.

THE MISSIONARY ADDRESS

In 1824, Irving's standing in the worldwide church was to be severely tested. The London Missionary Society (LMS), which was by then run by the Congregationalists, invited him to speak at its anniversary that May. Irving had previously told Chalmers that he was not impressed by the leadership of that Society, but in spite of that he accepted the invitation, though "without much thought of what [he] was undertaking."[27]

Irving was very conscientious and never favored giving anything short of his best. Nor was he prepared to avoid controversy at any cost. Indeed, as has been seen, he at times seems to have courted trouble. When he sat down to consider the task, he soon became aware of "the duty full of peril

23. For example, see Thomas Carlyle to Jane Baillie Welsh, October 22, 1823, September 27, 1824, November 15, 1824, and January 31, 1825, *CLO*; Jane Baillie Welsh to Thomas Carlyle, July 15, 1823, *CLO*.

24. Jane Baillie Welsh to Thomas Carlyle, July 21, 1823, *CLO*.

25. Thomas Carlyle to Margaret A. Carlyle, July 6, 1824, *CLO*. Just before Irving went to London he wrote Carlyle a lengthy letter, which is probably best described as an astute and warm-hearted criticism of Carlyle (Irving to Thomas Carlyle, April 29, 1822, in Irving, *DL*, 145–47).

26. Elliott, *Edward Irving*, 120.

27. Irving to Thomas Chalmers, December 24, 1821, in Irving, *DL*, 120.

and responsibility" that lay before him. Many other speakers would doubt-lessly have felt burdened by the responsibility before them. But "peril"?[28] Yes, peril. Irving's great problem was that he had "the double curse of origi-nality and independence,"[29] and, one might add, a dangerous willingness to express himself in ways that he knew would bring severe criticism down upon him.

Irving realized that if he were to speak on a missionary topic, he would be unable to toe the party line. He was well aware that he thought differently from most Christians on an increasing number of topics, including mission-ary matters, and if he was to be true to his sincerely held beliefs, his address would have to be carefully thought through and, when delivered, would upset many in his audience, including his hosts. He seems to have taken a little time out from his duties at the Caledonian Chapel in preparation for the LMS anniversary, "retiring into the quiet and peaceful country among a society of men devoted to every good and charitable work," apparently at Sydenham in Kent. In this new situation he "searched the Scriptures in secret" and with his hosts, "conversed of the convictions which were secretly brought to [his] mind concerning the missionary work."[30]

The anniversary meeting was held in Whitefield's Tabernacle in Lon-don's Tottenham Court Road on May 14. The Tabernacle was full long before the time appointed, and the organizers took the unusual step of beginning the meeting an hour early. Irving's address was so long—more than three hours—that he stopped twice while the congregation sang hymns. His ad-dress advocated the use of the "apostolic" method of missionary work as ini-tiated by Christ, and he argued that most nineteenth-century missionaries and missionary societies had drifted from that by using methods different from those taught by Jesus, particularly with regard to material support.[31]

This lecture was published the following year as *For Missionaries after the Apostolical School*. This book was intended as the first of a four-part work, but the other three were never published. The planned four sections were: "The Doctrine" (which was published), "The Experiment," "The Argu-ment," and "The Duty."[32] Characteristically, Irving arranged for the royal-ties from this book to be given to the widow of a missionary by the name of

28. Irving, *Missionaries*, xi.

29. Wilks, *Edward Irving*, 8.

30. Irving, *Missionaries*, xi–xii. See also ibid, 11–12; Oliphant, *Life*, 1:208.

31. Oliphant, *Life*, 1:196–97; Wilks, *Edward Irving*, 134–35. It was presumably this address that Thomas Carlyle called his "four-hours sermon" (Thomas Carlyle to Jane Baillie Welsh, May 27, 1824, *CLO*).

32. Irving, *Missionaries*, iv, vi; Oliphant, *Life*, 1:204; Wilks, *Edward Irving*, 135, 149.

John Smith, who had died while imprisoned in Demerara (Guyana) for his supposed support of a slave uprising.[33]

How much the book corresponds with the lecture is not entirely clear, though the printed form does bear some hallmarks of a spoken work rather than a written one. The main part of the book is in "three orations," but not one of them seems complete in itself. While it is possible that the first oration was delivered at the LMS anniversary and the other two on later occasions, it seems more likely that these three orations are the three parts of the original lecture. If the latter is correct, then it must indeed have been a very long meeting. The book also contains some introductory and supplementary material. The following assessment is of the book, and assumes that its core, the three orations, faithfully reflected the original lecture.

The book was introduced by what Irving called the "Missionary Charter," that is, Christ's sending out the Twelve as recorded in Matt 10:5–42.[34] The first full chapter began in a respectful tone that acknowledged the value of missionary societies. It then announced the seven points to be dealt with. (With Irving, there were rarely just the traditional three points.) They were:

1. an exposition of Christ's instructions to his Apostles;

2. an examination of whether those instructions were temporary or permanent;

3. an assessment of whether the apostolic success was due to following these principles;

4. an examination of how the success and failure in the history of the Church related to the following or departing from these principles;

5. a working out of how Christ's instructions could be successfully applied to the nineteenth-century situation;

6. an explanation of how a missionary society could implement them; and

7. a mandate to "private Christians" to support missionary societies.

And all this was "an argument founded upon our Lord's words" in Matthew 10.[35]

Irving's understanding at this time was that missionaries were the successors of the Apostles. That is, that it was their role, like the Apostles, to preach the gospel to "the people who know it not . . . When there are no heathen, the apostolic office will cease." In other words, a missionary was one who took the gospel to the unconverted, not one who taught Christians,

33. Irving, *Missionaries*, xii; Oliphant, *Life*, 1:201; Ishmael, "Demerara Slave."

34. Irving, *Missionaries*, 1–2.

35. Ibid., 12–13.

though some missionaries in certain situations might also have a teaching ministry. Therefore, "the Missionary" had to be brought back "to the Apostolical office," by preaching to non-Christians, not nursing those already converted.[36]

Crucially, Irving proclaimed that these instructions given to the first-century Apostles and recorded in Matt 10 had, with the exception of "two clauses which are local and temporary," ongoing authority for missionaries of all eras. The two exceptions were the instruction to go only to the house of Israel and not to the Samaritans and Gentiles (vv. 5–6) and the statement, "Ye shall not have gone over the cities of Israel until the Son of Man be come" (v. 23). That coming of the Son of Man, in this instance, Irving understood as referring to when Jesus "would openly announce himself to the nation" during Christ's time on earth.[37] But for the remainder, these "glorious words of Christ" on missionary work "were not for one occasion, but for all occasions; not for one race of men, but for all races of men; not for one age, but for all ages of the world."[38] Central to this was the idea that the missionary was to be supported by his or her mission field, not the people back home.

As an example of the ongoing nature of this "Charter," Irving argued that after Christ's death and resurrection, the Apostles were still following the teachings of Matt 10. In one place, Paul says that the other Apostles were taking their families with them on their missionary journeys and being provided for by those to whom they ministered (2 Cor 9:4–14), in keeping with Matt 10:9–11 and Matt 10:41–42. Paul and Barnabas were the exceptions to this practice, in that they provided for their own needs, "out of . . . the high prerogative of an inspired Apostle," because they believed that the gospel could be advanced by providing for themselves.[39] But the first-century norm was that the needs of the missionaries would be met by the recipients of the message. By contrast, in common nineteenth-century practice the needs of the missionaries were supplied mainly by the sending agencies and their supporters.

Yet, while in this book Irving was clearly criticizing the modern missionary movement, he insisted that he was not against the modern mission agencies. Indeed, he pointed out that in his Glasgow ministry he had been the secretary to the two major missionary societies in Scotland and that he

36. Ibid., xiii–xiv, xx–xxii, xxiv.
37. Ibid., 46–48.
38. Ibid., 75.
39. Ibid., 61–62.

wished that he still had time to fulfill such duties.[40] In addition, Irving's seventh point urged Christians to support these societies. Nor did he wish to discourage people offering for missionary service. Rather, by remaining true to what he believed to be a correct understanding of the passage, he hoped to challenge others to respond to its message.[41]

It is not our purpose here to discuss whether Irving was right or wrong in his interpretation of Matt 10. But we do need to note the contemporary response to the address and to the book.

Oliphant said that after the address, "The wildest hubbub rose," and indeed, "the vexation and wrath of the 'religious world'" fell upon Irving.[42] Not surprisingly, one of the major criticisms came from the secretary of the LMS, William Orme, who wrote an "Expostulatory Letter" to Irving, which in its published form ran seventy-six pages long.[43] Bearing in mind that one of the main purposes of the lecture was to raise funds for LMS missionary work, one can understand Orme being aggrieved. After all, Irving was effectively saying, "Don't give money to missionary societies."

Orme stated that Irving's missionary address was "charged with invective and misrepresentation." He also pointedly observed, "It ill becomes any individual who wishes well to the cause—who enjoys the 'fat and convenient things' of the metropolis of England, to use the language of disparagement concerning the labours and sacrifices of men, whose work is with the Lord, and the recompense of that work with their God." He argued that Irving made modern missionaries sound like "mercenary hired servants, mere stipendiaries, who engage in the work rather from love of the reward, than from love to the work itself."[44]

According to a reviewer in the *Congregational Magazine*, Orme exposed "the absurdities" of Irving's missionary orations in "a judicious and able" manner. This reviewer called Irving's book "a leafy farrago" (a hodgepodge) and regarded it as "lamentable" that Irving had "deemed it necessary to direct his assault" against the way in which missionaries were provided for, particularly as the required funds were always in short supply.[45]

On the strength of the address alone the *Evangelical Magazine* charged Irving with regarding missionaries as "men of sordid purpose, upon whom

40. Ibid., xxv. One was the Bible Society (Edward Irving, quoted in Wilks, *Edward Irving*, 177).

41. Irving, *Missionaries*, 114–15.

42. Oliphant, *Life*, 1:198, 200.

43. Ibid., 1:206–207.

44. "Irving's *Missionary Orations*," 346–47.

45. Review of "Expostulatory Letter," by William Orme, *Congregational Magazine*, July 1825, 384.

are conferred the luxuries of an easy and recreative existence."[46] Yet such ideas cannot be found in Irving's book, which suggests that they were unlikely to have been heard in the address, except with the liberal use of the listener's imagination.

The Eclectic Review, however, made the quite reasonable comment that the modern missionary was often in a very different situation from the Apostles when Christ first sent them out. Whereas the Twelve were ministering to their own people, and thus might reasonably expect hospitality, "the very circumstance" that the nineteenth-century missionary was "a foreigner among men of a strange tongue, must make an incalculable difference." Contemporary missionaries were "not precisely in the predicament of the twelve Apostles." The *Review* conceded "that Mr. Irving's meaning is good, and his intentions upright," but it also lamented that "his imagination sadly misgoverns his judgment." In fact, it concluded, his "estimate of some of the individuals who have engaged in the Missionary service" was "contemptuous."[47]

Whether these criticisms were fair might be argued. They probably were in some cases and not in others. It was certainly unfair to criticize the very generous Irving for living off that fat of the land. But Irving wholeheartedly believed in his message, so he had to proclaim it knowing that he would encounter "peril" by so doing.

Irving's personality gave him the happy knack of making friends easily. But the controversial nature of his ideas and the way he expressed them made him enemies just as readily. It was already seemingly inevitable that those enemies would eventually catch up with him. Yet Irving seemed to have lacked the sense to see how far he was sailing into troubled waters. Some time after the publication of this book, he considered sending copies "to all the Mission Houses."[48] Whether he did this or not seems to have gone unrecorded, but one suspects that such gifts would not have been well received.

In this missionary address, Irving had criticized another speaker for saying that the main quality a missionary needed was prudence. Irving boldly and clearly said that was nonsense. Rather, the main need for a missionary was faith.[49] While Irving was most certainly right in his elevation of faith over prudence, it still can be fairly argued that prudence is a valuable Christian virtue. And one of Irving's great problems was that he lacked this

---

46. *Evangelical Magazine*, June 1824, quoted in Wilks, *Edward Irving*, 146–47.

47. "Irving's *Missionary Orations*," 344–45, 347.

48. Irving's journal, November 10, 1825, quoted in Oliphant, *Life*, 1:310.

49. Irving, *Missionaries*, xiv–xv.

prudence, this practical wisdom. It was a quality that he desperately needed. Yet, as Elliott argues, he strongly opposed the concept, seeing it as in opposition to faith.[50]

However, while many disagreed with Irving's interpretation of the "Missionary Charter," others viewed it more positively. Late in 1825 Irving proudly noted that some German missionaries were "fast recurring to the primitive method" of propagating the gospel in Persia.[51] Timothy Richard, a Welsh Baptist missionary to China, adopted at least some of Irving's ideas and in 1887 arranged for copies of Irving's book to be sent to missions in China, India, and Japan.[52] Frederick Booth-Tucker, the pioneering Salvation Army missionary to India from 1882, applied similar principles in his work, though no evidence has been discovered that this was influenced by either Irving or Richard. Booth-Tucker dressed in the robes of a *fakir* and traveled with a begging bowl, preaching Christ and asking for food as he went.[53]

In addition, A. N. Groves, an early Plymouth Brethren missionary to Baghdad and India, adopted practices very similar to those advocated by Irving. In 1825 Groves published a book called *Christian Devotedness*, which espoused these ideas. The publication of Groves' book came a year after Irving's lecture was delivered and the same year it was published. Timothy Stunt sees "an obvious parallel" between the two works, but argues that this does not mean that Irving influenced Groves. Indeed, these ideas seem to have been developing in Groves' mind for some time. However, Stunt does suggest that Irving may have influenced a later edition of Groves' work published in 1829.[54] Groves became very influential in Brethren circles.

In 1888–1889 E. F. Baldwin, an American missionary, also urged the adoption of Matt 10 as the missionary charter. Whether Baldwin got this idea from Irving is unclear, but some of his opponents noticed the similarity of thought and pounced upon it, linking Baldwin with a "heretic."[55]

Then in 1912 Roland Allen wrote *Missionary Methods: St. Paul's or Ours?*, which took a similar stand to Irving, though Allen contrasted Paul's method (rather than Christ's) with "Ours" and favored Paul's. Allen argued that by the early twentieth century the church had been "long accustomed . . . to accept it as an axiom of missionary work that converts in a new

50. Elliott, *Edward Irving*, 161–63.

51. Irving's journal, November 10, 1825, quoted in Oliphant, *Life*, 1:310.

52. Bohr, "Legacy," 75–80.

53. McKenzie, *Booth-Tucker*, 100–101, 132–37.

54. Stunt, *Awakening*, 128. See also Lang, *Anthony Norris Groves*, 53–99.

55. McGee, "Taking the Logic," 106–109.

country must be submitted to a very long probation and training, extending over generations before they can be expected to be able stand alone." Paul, by contrast, established numerous churches in four Roman Provinces, but "When he left them he left them because his work was fully accomplished."[56] In other words, Paul established these churches and then moved on, leaving them to manage their own affairs in line with what he had taught. It is true that Paul made a few repeat visits and sent letters and some of his companions to further assist them, but he trusted these churches to be true to what they had been taught and to determine their own way under the direction of the Spirit of God.

Whether Allen had read Irving's book is unknown.[57] Allen's thesis contains some of the same ideas as Irving's but is sufficiently different from it to suggest neither dependence nor total independence. He first went as a missionary to China in 1895 eight years after the free copies of Irving's book had been distributed, so he may have read it. By the time Allen's book was published, the church was more ready for a review of missionary policy and his book became very influential. His slant, too, was probably regarded as more practicable.

THE NEW BUILDING

While in Sydenham preparing for his missionary address, another matter also occupied Irving's mind. The congregation at the Caledonian Chapel had grown very quickly, and he knew it was necessary to appoint more elders to watch over its welfare, so Irving wrote to William Hamilton, his brother-in-law, and four others asking them to consider such an appointment. With his customary thoroughness, Irving carefully set out the biblical and ecclesiastical requirements for such a role and advised Hamilton that he would visit him on his return to London to discuss the matter further.[58] William Hamilton, described by Carlyle as "very honest" and "shrewd," eventually proved to be an ideal elder, giving great comfort and support to Irving in his ministry and delivering him "of all secular cares."[59]

---

56. Allen, *Missionary*, 3–4.

57. I could find no evidence of it in Allen, *Roland Allen*.

58. Irving to William Hamilton, June 2, 1824, quoted in Oliphant, *Life*, 1:208–10; Irving to James Gilliland Simpson, June 2, 1824, in Irving, *DL*, 197–98. These two letters are very similar, and it is probable that Irving also sent the same message to Mr. Horn, Mr. Whytt, and Mr. Blyth. Isabella assisted him in the task of writing these five fairly long letters, which presumably had more or less the same wording.

59. Irving's journal, November 11, 1825, quoted in Oliphant, *Life*, 1:311; Carlyle, *Reminiscences* (Norton), 2:121.

By April 1827 the chapel's office-bearers were seven elders and seven deacons.[60] Irving said that the Caledonian elders had "a nice idea of things being rightly managed," though he regretted that they did not always have "the spirit of it."[61]

It had been apparent from some time, too, that the Caledonian Chapel was too small to hold all those wishing to attend. Soon after Irving had arrived in London, not only was every seat regularly occupied, but in addition, some members of the congregation were standing in the aisles while others were unable to gain admittance. Such was the chaos outside the church as the crowds arrived for the service that ropes were erected in the street, with the carriages arriving traveling along one lane while those departing ran along another. Eventually, one had to have a ticket to gain admittance.[62]

In the middle of 1823, Coleridge called Irving "the present idol of the world of fashion."[63] But fashions change. A year later, according to Carlyle, "The fashionable tumult about him [was] subsiding." It went instead "to gaze on Egyptian Crocodiles [and] Iroquois Hunters."[64] Carlyle said that Irving appeared disappointed and ill at ease after the departure of many of his more aristocratic listeners because this had "Cruelly blasted" his hopes. He stressed that Irving was still very popular and the crowds kept coming, but it was clear that many of those leading figures that he had hoped to influence for Christ had now deserted him.[65]

Irving knew that he could not please everyone. Indeed, it was not his job even to try to do so. In one very perceptive passage in a sermon on the Parable of the Sower, he stated that one type of person:

> will not have a moral duty inculcated, another will not hear a prophecy explained; one is impatient of instruction, and will rise and go away if you do not excite his feelings, which excitement another decries as enthusiasm; another cannot receive the matter if it be read, and another dislikes that it should be spoken. You may not tell masters their duties lest ye should offend them; and if you preach of duties to rulers, you are political; and if you show the errors of the times, you are setting yourself up

60. Hair, *Regent*, 39–40; Oliphant, *Life*, 1:400.

61. Irving's journal, November 25, 1825, quoted in Oliphant, *Life*, 1:356.

62. Root, *Edward Irving*, 26; Carlyle, *Reminiscences* (Norton), 2:135.

63. Samuel Taylor Coleridge to Charlotte Brent, July 7, 1823, in Coleridge, *CLSTC*, 5:280.

64. Thomas Carlyle to Alexander Carlyle, August 11, 1824, *CLO*; Carlyle, "Death of Edward Irving," 102. See also Thomas Carlyle to John A. Carlyle, November 30, 1824, *CLO*.

65. Carlyle, *Reminiscences* (Norton), 2:135–37.

for a judge of others; and if you bring forth the former times in the experience of the church, you go beyond the knowledge of the people; and unless you harp upon every man's single string, you do not preach Christ. These things I do not imagine, but have sadly experienced, to my own personal wounding.[66]

Throughout his London ministry Irving had received much wide-ranging criticism, both spoken and in print, and this criticism hurt. But balanced preaching will always engender such criticism. It does not necessarily mean that he was on the wrong track.

In spite of the desertions, the congregation was still too large to fit into the existing chapel. Indeed, even when the fashionable element departed, there were plenty of others wishing to take their place. Just prior to one quarter's communion service in 1825 Irving spoke to about thirty-five people wishing to be received into membership.[67] (Even as late as 1831, nearly one hundred people joined his church in six months, though that was a time of much controversy and many others were leaving.)[68]

Moves to build a larger church began soon after Irving had arrived, and £3,000 had been subscribed for that purpose before the end of 1822. Irving even expected it to be built within a year.[69] Plans were drawn up, but it was not until the following May that the congregation approved them and gave the go-ahead. The new church's foundation stone was laid by the Earl of Breadalbane at a site in Regent's Square on July 1, 1824, two years after Irving's arrival in London.[70] But progress was slow, and by the end of November the following year the building had still not been completed.[71]

In 1824 Irving also gave a lecture on human labor, later produced as a book. This demonstrated that his mind encompassed more than the purely religious, though this work was clearly influenced by his theology. "Our notion of human nature," he argued,

is that it is fashioned and furnished for more excellent purposes that to turn the clod, or handle machines; to transport the produce of the earth from place to place, or work in the mines of gold and silver; or to eat, drink and make merry . . .

66. Irving, *CW*, 1:123.

67. Irving's journal, November 30, 1825, quoted in Oliphant, *Life*, 1:370.

68. Irving to Mr. Mcdonald, November 7, 1831, quoted in ibid., 2:204.

69. Irving to Mrs. Welsh, December 6, 1822, in Irving, *DL*, 166.

70. Hair, *Regent*, 28, 30. See the undated report from *The Times* found in appendix A in ibid., 175. The Duke of Clarence, the future King William IV, was to have laid the foundation stone, but he was indisposed.

71. Irving's journal, November 25, 1825, quoted in Oliphant, *Life*, 1:358.

And, therefore, those systems of education whose chief aim is to teach the nature of the physical productions of the earth, and the mechanical arts by which they are to be transported from place to place . . . and the science of economy . . . are to me no systems of education whatever, unless I could persuade myself that man was merely king of the animals, head-labourer and master-workman of the earth.

In fact, "Such education will depress a people out of manliness, out of liberty, out of poetry, and religion and whatever else hath been the crown of glory around the brows of mankind." Yet Irving could still see "great use and value in these physical sciences, to enable a man to maintain himself with less brutal labour, to the end he may have more leisure upon his hands for higher and nobler occupations."[72]

Early in the summer of 1825 a deputation from St. Cuthbert's Church, the largest church in Edinburgh, came to visit Irving to sound him out with regard to a call to the recently opened Hope Park Chapel. He gave the matter considerable thought, but in the end he declined. In a written response to the call, Irving said that one day he did hope to return to his native land, even Edinburgh, but the time for that was not yet.[73] London, it seems, would have him for at least a little longer. Frankly, after such wonderful success in London, the great metropolis, with its access to so many important people, it is hard to imagine Irving wishing to live and minister anywhere else on a permanent basis. London was the center of Britain's affairs, and Irving was in the thick of it.

EDWARD AND ISABELLA

Life for the Irvings, however, had become very stressful. Edward was idolized by many and crowds still flocked to his church, yet others were suspicious of him, disagreed with some of his teachings, and questioned his motives. He was by this time a highly controversial figure. (And that has not changed. He still is.) Inevitably, Isabella was caught up in the tension of it all. For example, their breakfasts were rarely family affairs. Inviting people to the breakfast table became one of Irving's main ways of communicating with those who wanted to speak to him. The day usually started with family worship followed by breakfast at eight o'clock with whoever had come to see him. But by ten in the morning the talk usually ceased, and Irving would

72. Irving, "The Curse as to Bodily Labour," in ibid., *Sermons*, 3:809–10.

73. Irving to the Elders of St. Cuthbert's, July 16, 1825, in Irving, *DL*, 213–14; Irving to the Congregation of the Caledonian Church, July 16, 1825, in ibid., 214–16.

retreat to the study.[74] At other times, however, he would spend much of the day counseling those troubled about spiritual matters.

In the first two years or so of their marriage Isabella does not appear to have assisted her husband at all in the preparation of his sermons and books. Indeed, when he was working on them "he could bear no one in the room with him." But by the middle of 1826, after a bout of ill health, he decided to enlist his wife as an amanuensis, a task she gladly accepted. In fact, he even gave ear to her "observations" during the transcription process. By this time he could "bear no one" in the room with him but her.[75] Yet at a later date, a Miss McDonald took up that role on occasion.[76] Isabella also wrote a lot of his letters for him, no doubt with some dictation.

If one were to ask about the nature of his affections for Isabella at this time, the answer seems to be that he genuinely loved her. He may have earlier been thwarted in love over his infatuation with Jane Welsh, but all the evidence points to the fact that he had by this time developed a deep and sincere love for his wife, his "better and dearer half." Indeed, he told her that he sought "to love her as Christ loved the Church."[77] She was his "beloved Isabella," his "best beloved," and his "dearest love."[78] He told one correspondent that "my dear wife . . . I love as myself,"[79] which suggests a deep union between them. Yet, while his letters to Isabella breathe strong affection and devotion, they do seem to lack passion. Perhaps the letters of nineteenth-century clergymen to their wives were rarely passionate.

One of Irving's letters to Isabella hints that there were some tensions between them. In this letter, he referred to "the discords and divisions of their souls."[80] Quite what those "discords and divisions" were is unknown, but they seem to have been within their relationship rather than something external to it. Whatever the nature of their love, the events of the following year were to test and prove its strength.

If they were not experiencing enough difficulty already, more was to come in 1825. The trouble first centered on their son, Irving's "greatest earthly hope and joy."[81] Isabella was pregnant again, and she returned to

---

74. Oliphant, *Life*, 1:233; Brown, "Personal Reminiscences," 227.

75. A letter from Isabella Irving to her sister, quoted in Oliphant, *Life*, 1:387.

76. Ibid., 2:39–42, 49.

77. Irving to Isabella Irving, November 30, 1824, in Irving, *DL*, 208; Irving's journal, November 21, 1825, quoted in Oliphant, *Life*, 1:338.

78. Irving's journal, October 26 and 28, 1825, quoted in Oliphant, *Life*, 1:259–61.

79. Irving to "An Unknown Recipient," February 1827, in Irving, *DL*, 234.

80. Irving's journal, November 27, 1825, quoted in Oliphant, *Life*, 1:302.

81. Irving to Isabella Irving, November 30, 1824, in Irving, *DL*, 207–208.

Scotland at the end of June to prepare for the birth, taking little Edward with her. Irving joined them in July for a short period.

Sometime that summer the boy caught whooping cough. By September he had greatly improved, and there ceased to be any great concern for him. Irving went north again, and on October 2 a daughter, Margaret (called Maggy), was born. Soon afterwards, little Edward began to deteriorate to the great distress of his parents. He died nine days after the birth of his sister, as his father watched on helplessly. The lad was less than fifteen months old. He was buried on the second anniversary of the Irvings' wedding.[82]

It comes as no surprise that Irving later recalled that he was "stunned and staggered" by this devastating event.[83] It was a terrible blow to both Edward and Isabella. Yet, as Irving said on the day of the boy's death, "the stroke of death [was] subdued by faith, and the strength of the grave [was] overcome."[84]

Carlyle went to visit Irving soon afterwards. "Yesterday, I went . . . to meet the Orator," he told Jane Welsh:

> I found him sitting in his Father's little parlour, among a crowd of cousins and admirers, of whom he soon shook himself loose, to go and stroll among the fields with me. The sight of the poor Orator mollified my heart, and his cordial welcome awoke in me some old feelings which late events have been doing much to extinguish. He is sallow and care-worn; his boy died of hooping-cough [sic] about a week ago, a few days after his wife (who was not once allowed to see the little sufferer!) had brought him a daughter. Yet he bears these things wonderfully; his vivacity has not forsaken him; he talks with undiminished eagerness about the "spirit of the Gospel" and "the mind of man"; now and then as our dialogue proceeded he even laughed with all his ancient vehemence. I will not judge harshly of this strange man. He has a heart with many virtues; and tho' overgrown with still ranker weeds than formerly of what in another I should call cant and affectation, it ill becomes me to forget the noble plants that flourish in the midst of them. I was sad to the very heart when I saw him step out of his Father's little quiet room, to dash once more into the great billowy sea of life.[85]

A week later Carlyle told a friend,

82. Oliphant, *Life*, 1:234–35, 243–46, 302 n.

83. Irving, *CW*, 4:382.

84. Irving to William Hamilton, October 11, 1825, in Irving, *DL*, 224.

85. Thomas Carlyle to Jane Baillie Welsh, October 19, 1825, *CLO*.

> Edward Irving was in Annan last week for a little while; and I passed half a day with him. He is of a green hue, solemn, sad, and in bad bodily condition. The worthy man (for so he is, when every say is said) has lost his boy at Kirkcaldy, and left his wife there, who had brought him a daughter only ten days before that event. He bears it well; for his heart is full of other wondrous things, from which he draws peculiar consolation. He seems, as his enemies would say, still madder than before. But it is not madness: would to Heaven we were all thus mad![86]

In fact, the Irvings were truly distraught, but they found real comfort in their faith. Isabella's father said that they "both bear the stroke, though sore, with wonderful resignation." Soon after the death, a friend asked Edward how his wife was. He answered, "She is bearing it as well as one saint could wish to see another do," which presumably meant with sadness, but also hope.[87]

The death of infants in nineteenth-century England was sadly very common, and many parents experienced the trauma of it, some several times. Forty years later, William Booth of Salvation Army fame expressed relief and gratitude that he and his wife Catherine had been spared "those gloomy visits to the churchyard which so many other families have to pay."[88] Their eight children all lived to adulthood in spite of whooping cough, small pox, and other illnesses. But that family was a fortunate exception. The Irvings, by contrast, were to lose five of their eight children in infancy, and only two outlived their mother.

Oliphant says that little Edward's brief life and death "sent echoes through all the strong man's life,"[89] and so it did. The boy's death was a pivotal moment in Irving's life. It would seem that he was not quite the same man afterwards.

Inevitably, there was a great sense of loss and grief for both parents and the wider family. Irving found some alleviation from that grief one night when he felt a deep sense of his departed son's presence in heaven, which greatly "uplifted" his soul.[90] A few days later he had a similar experience while out walking in a garden that he, Isabella, and young Edward had often

---

86. Thomas Carlyle to James Johnston, October 26, 1825, *CLO*. (Although Carlyle reports that ten days passed between the birth of Irving's daughter and the death of his son, it was in fact nine.)

87. Oliphant, *Life*, 1:243–44.

88. William Booth to Catherine Booth, November 1864, WB145, in Booth, *Letters*, 351.

89. Oliphant, *Life*, 2:211.

90. Irving to Isabella Irving, October 25, 1825, quoted in ibid., 1:254.

visited.[91] Such experiences often haunted him. More than five years later he reflected that one of the things that he learned from the death of his firstborn was "how little of human existence is on this side [of] the grave, and by how much the better and nobler portion of it is in eternity." From this he drew great comfort.[92]

But the boy's death had wider repercussions than one might expect. Little Edward's death turned Irving's mind to again investigate what the Bible said about death, resurrection, and related matters, this time in even greater depth. Later he reflected that "it was in the season" of his son's sickness and death that God "did reveal in me the knowledge and hope and desire of his Son from heaven."[93] This was to result in Irving becoming a key figure in the revival of old ideas about the return of Christ and the emergence of new ideas, which, combined, eventually led to a new Christian eschatology. And those ideas would begin to filter through to the rest of his theology.

At the end of October Irving returned to London, leaving Isabella, "the sharer and partner of [his] very soul,"[94] and the baby Margaret in Scotland. He arrived late on a Saturday evening but preached the following morning at his church "with a full heart" and was given "great liberty of utterance."[95]

Irving's letters to Isabella during this separation were written in the form of a journal "intended for [her] comfort,"[96] that began on October 26 and ended on December 3, just prior to their being reunited. Amongst the entries is an account of his Sunday ministrations, which clearly demonstrates Irving's deep spirituality and his intense commitment to God and to the people God had given him. He told Isabella,

> This has been to me a day to be held in remembrance, my dearest wife, for the strength with which the Lord hath endowed me to manifest his truth. I pray it may be a day to be remembered for the strength with which He hath endowed many of my people to conceive truth and to bring forth its fruitfulness.
>
> In the morning I arose before eight, and having sought to purify myself by prayer for the sanctification of the Sabbath, I

91. Irving's journal, October 28, 1825, quoted in ibid., 1:258. See also Irving's journal, November 3, 1825, quoted in ibid., 1:290–91.

92. Irving to Mrs. Fergusson (his sister), January 17, 1831, quoted in ibid., 2:169–70.

93. Irving, "Preliminary Discourse," in Ben-Ezra, *Coming*, 1:lxxiv. See also ibid., 1:clxxii.

94. Irving's journal, November 2, 1825, quoted in Oliphant, *Life*, 1:287.

95. Irving to Isabella Irving, October 25, 1825, quoted in ibid., 1:254–55.

96. Irving's journal, November 4, 1825, quoted in ibid., 1:296.

came down to the duties of my family[97]—but before passing
out of my bedchamber, let me take warning, and admonish
my dear Isabella how necessary it is for the first opening of the
eyelids upon the sweet light of the morning to open the eye of
our soul upon its blessed light, which is Christ, otherwise the
tempter will carry us away to look upon some vanity or folly
in the kingdom of this world, and so divert our souls, as that,
when they come to lift themselves up to God, they shall find no
concentration of spirit upon God, no sweet flow of holy desires
. . . so that we shall have complainings of absence instead of
consolations of His holy presence, barrenness and leanness for
faithfulness and beauty. So, alas, I found it in the morning, but
the Lord heard the voice of my crying and sent me this instruction, which may He enable me and my dear wife to profit from
in the time to come.

After our family worship, in which I read the first Chapter
of the Hebrews, as preparatory to reading it in the church, Mr.
Dinwiddie, our worthy and venerable elder, came in as usual,
and we joined in prayer for the blessing of the Lord upon the
ministry of the Word this day throughout all the churches, and
especially in the church and congregation given into our hand
. . .

[At church] we began by singing the first six verses of the
forty-fifth Psalm, whose reference to Messiah I shortly instructed the people to bear in mind. In prayer I found much
liberty, especially in confession of sin and humiliation of soul,
for the people seemed bowed down, very still and silent, and
full of solemnity—then, having read the first of Hebrews, I told
them that it was the epistle for instructing them in the person of
Christ as our mediator, both priest and king . . . It throws much
light upon His eternal Sonship and divinity . . . in passing; that
the purpose of the epistle was to satisfy the believing Hebrews,
who were terribly assailed and tempted by their unbelieving
brethren, and confirm them in the superiority of Christ to Mo-
ses as a law-giver, to Aaron and the Levitical priesthood as a
priest, and to angels, through whose ministry they believed that
the law was given, as the Apostle himself teacheth in his Epistle
to the Galatians. And therefore he opens with great dignity the
solemn discourse by connecting Christ with all the prophets
and exalts Him above all rank and comparison by declaring His

97. That is, presumably, the members of his household. In other words, his house-
keeper, Mrs. Hall, her husband, and at least one guest (Irving to Margaret Martin, November 12, 1825, in Irving, *DL*, 226).

inheritance, His workmanship, His prerogative of representing God, of upholding the universe, of purging sins by Himself, and sitting at the right hand of the majesty on high.[98]

Irving then drew his congregation's attention to Ps 102 and "took occasion to rebuke them very sharply for going after idolatries of profane poets, and fictitious novelists, and meagre sentimentalists, who are Satan's prophets, and wear his livery of malice, and falsehood, and mocking merriment, while they forsook the prophets of the Lord, and their sublime, pathetic, true, wise and everlasting forms of discourse."[99] Note that this was not the sermon. That was still to come. These were just some well-thought-out and none-too-brief comments on the reading. After that he prayed, and then, in good Presbyterian fashion, they sang the last verses of Ps 102.

Only then did Irving preach. His text was Phil 1:21, "For to me to live is Christ, and to die is gain," a passage that he had been meditating upon much during the preceding days. He then proceeded to join "earnest battle with the subject," showing that "the life that was Christ" consisted "in a total loss of personality and self, and surrender of all our being unto Him who had purchased us with His blood." To this end he urged his people to love God with all their hearts, for only by so doing could they experience "the same grace at death, which Christ, the man Christ, the Messiah, by His resurrection, attained to." He then closed his sermon by warning them of the dangers of death without Christ.[100]

Yet the sermon was not, in one sense, completely finished. He recorded in his journal that he still had "a good deal of matter . . . remaining," which he no doubt presented on another occasion. The service closed with an infant baptism, an offering, and the singing of the first verses of Ps 23. After walking home to take a meal and some rest, he went out to the evening meeting, in which he preached from Gen 22.[101] It was not unusual for Irving to leave much of the material he had prepared for a service unused. The next week he was only able to deliver about half of what he had prepared, even though that morning service did not conclude until 1:45 p.m.,[102] probably two-and-three-quarters hours after it had started.

It comes as no surprise that the next meeting of the church's session "proceeded with good harmony and unity, till they came to speak of time," specifically the time it took Irving to conduct the church's services. It would

98. Irving's journal, October 30, 1825, quoted in Oliphant, *Life*, 1:271–73.

99. Ibid., 1:274.

100. Ibid., 1:275–76.

101. Ibid., 1:276–77.

102. Irving's journal, November 6, 1825, quoted in ibid., 1:300–301.

seem that some did not like having their Sunday lunch so long delayed. But Irving was adamant. He made it clear that he would submit to no authority on that matter but "the church" (presumably the presbytery, or perhaps higher), and even then he would appeal. He was "resolved" that he would "have the privilege" of "two hours and a half."[103] That is, the time for the whole service, not just the sermon. Three weeks later, the morning service ran to thee hours and the evening to two-and-a-half.[104]

Considering Irving's own account of a morning service at the Caledonian Chapel, one can understand why many of his listeners came but soon drifted away, even though he was such a great preacher. His words did not please those who came seeking entertainment. They did not encourage the fashion-chasers. He was biblical, confrontational, and pulled no punches. Nor were his sermons brief or trivial; indeed, they were profound and often over-long. Such preaching always divides. Jesus himself preached, and some believed even while others strongly rejected his message. It was the same with the preaching of the Apostles. It has always been that way. Listeners looking for a good time did not find it for long under Edward Irving. They heard the challenge of Jesus Christ, and that has always been a stumbling block to many.

Irving also spent much time in counseling, both in his own home and in the homes of others. Different parts of his days were often dedicated to it. Amongst his visitors one evening was a young widow who had recently lost her son after a prolonged illness. "She wanted to know," Irving told his wife, "whether she would know her son in heaven." Irving said that he "could have wept for her." Yet he saw that "she needed another treatment . . . and [he] showed her the way to the spiritual world," to which he prayed "the Lord to lead her."[105] He knew what it felt like to lose a beloved child, but he recognized that the woman's needs went even deeper than the loss of her child.

At the close of some days Irving put pen to paper to write to his "dear Isabella," even though he was exhausted. On October 27 he told her that he was "so worn out with work." Less than a week later, after two days in which he counseled a number of people, his head was so "weary" that not even "The command of King George" could have made him "take a pen in [his] hand," but he did so, if only for a few lines. Three weeks later he was "so

---

103. Irving's journal, November 7, 1825, quoted in ibid., 1:305.

104. Irving's journal, November 27, 1825, quoted in ibid., 1:365.

105. Irving's journal, November 15, 1825, quoted in ibid., 1:325.

fatigued" he barely wrote more than her name before retiring to bed. The next day he woke at six, but was "too weary to rise till eight."[106]

This journal/letter, written for Isabella's comfort during the couple's five-week separation after their son's death, extends to 120 pages in the two-volume edition of Oliphant's biography, and even then it was incomplete. Isabella returned to London early in December, at which point the journal ended.[107]

106. Irving's journal, October 27, November 1, 19, and 20, 1825, quoted in ibid., 1:260, 284, 334, and 336, respectively.

107. Irving's journal, November 26, 1825, ibid., 1:362.

8

Irving the Romantic[1]

[Edward Irving] was a puritan with the temperament of a cavalier . . . an irreconcilable mix of passion and brilliance, wisdom and foolishness, humility and pride.

—MARK RAYBURN PATTERSON[2]

Of all the people that Irving knew well, perhaps the most remarkable was poet and philosopher Samuel Taylor Coleridge (1772–1834). Charles Lamb called him "an archangel slightly damaged."[3]

On Thursday, May 10, 1827, Irving took Thomas Chalmers to visit Coleridge while he was in London. Chalmers kept a record of the encounter, which is very illuminating:

> Mr. and Mrs. Montague [*sic*] took us out in their carriage to Highgate, where we spent three hours with the great Coleridge. He lives with Dr. and Mrs. Gillman[4] on the same footing that Cowper did with the Unwins. His conversation, which flowed in a mighty unremitting stream, is most astonishing, but, I must

1. Peter Elliott's *Edward Irving: Romantic Theology in Crisis* has been very helpful in writing this chapter.

2. Patterson, "Designing," 16.

3. Charles Lamb, quoted in Clej, "Coleridge, Samuel Taylor," 1:162.

4. Interestingly, the Gillmans' house was built by William Blake and was bought by model Kate Moss in 2011.

confess, to me still unintelligible. I caught occasional glimpses of what he would be at, but mainly he was very far out of all sight and all sympathy. I hold it, however, a great acquisition to have become acquainted with him. You know that Irving sits at his feet, and drinks in the inspiration of every syllable that falls from him. There is a secret and to me as yet unintelligible communion of spirit betwixt them, on the ground of a certain German mysticism and transcendental lake-poetry which I am not yet up to. Gordon[5] says it is all unintelligible nonsense, and I am sure a plain Fife man as uncle "Tammas," had he been alive, would have pronounced it the greatest *buff* he had ever heard in his life.[6]

On their way back to Irving's home, Chalmers called Coleridge's conversation obscure and stated that he preferred to engage in conversation where one could see "all sides of an idea" before accepting it. "Ha!" laughed Irving in reply, "You Scotchmen would handle an idea as a butcher handles an ox. For my part, I love to see an idea looming through the mist."[7] Though Chalmers was unable to name the mode of thought in which Coleridge and Irving engaged, it was, in fact, known as Romanticism.

Samuel Taylor Coleridge was twenty years Irving's senior. His father had been a Church of England clergyman in Devon who had died while Samuel was still a child. The young Coleridge later adopted Unitarian views and became a preacher for that church. He studied at Cambridge from 1792 to 1794, and at the end of that period he began a friendship with the writer Robert Southey, whom he had met at Oxford, and the two teamed to write a play titled *The Fall of Robespierre*. In 1797 Coleridge moved to Nether Stowey in Somerset, and he met William Wordsworth and his sister Dorothy in nearby Dorset. They became so close that Coleridge described them as "three persons with one soul."[8] The next year they published *Lyrical Ballads*, which opened with Coleridge's "Ancient Mariner" and closed with William Wordsworth's "Tintern Abbey." Before the end of that century, Coleridge traveled to Germany with the Wordsworths to follow their interest in German philosophy. He later translated two works by Johann Schiller, the playwright and philosopher.

5. Presumably Rev. Robert Gordon.

6. Hanna, *Memoirs* (New York), 3:168. Although "buff" has many possible meanings, it is likely that Chalmers intended it in the sense of "to say nothing" (Partridge and Simpson, *Dictionary of Historical Slang*, s.v. "buff," 124).

7. Ibid.

8. Drabble, "Wordsworth, Dorothy," and "Wordsworth, William," 1095; Elliott, *Edward Irving*, 62–64.

The lengthy friendship between Coleridge and the Wordsworths has been described as "one of the most creative partnerships in English Romanticism."[9] The Romantic Movement (or Movements) was for the most part a reaction against the Enlightenment in that it exposed the limits of human reason and was partly inspired by the revolutions in America and France as well as by French philosophers such as Rousseau. Romanticism stressed the importance of the individual and the role of the imagination, recognized the value of the natural environment and delighted in it, and was involved in social issues. It influenced, among other things, the emergence of feminism. It did, however, lean towards pessimism, particularly when matters did not go as hoped. Romanticism was a philosophical movement rather than a formal organization and included both Christians as well as those opposed to religion, influencing literature, music, art, and, as shall be seen, theology.

One of Wordsworth's most popular poems runs:

> I wandered lonely as a cloud
> That floats on high o'er vales and hills,
> When all at once I saw a crowd,
> A host, of golden daffodils;
> Beside the lake, beneath the trees,
> Fluttering and dancing in the breeze.[10]

This verse expresses well certain aspects of Romanticism, particularly lonely wandering, both mental and physical, and the love of nature.

The Wordsworths moved to the Lake District in the north of England in 1799, and Coleridge joined them a year later. That region shortly became the center of British Romanticism. Over the next few years Coleridge became addicted to opium and alcohol, which led to a decline in health, and he separated from his wife. He even argued with the Wordsworths. Coleridge renewed his interest in Christianity, adopted Trinitarian beliefs, and in 1816 moved into the home of James Gillman, a surgeon in Highgate, which was then one of north London's satellite villages. Gillman helped him deal with his addictions.[11]

Carlyle, another Romantic, described Coleridge in terms that are vivid but none too complimentary:

---

9. Drabble, "Samuel Taylor Coleridge," 214.

10. Wordsworth, "I Wandered Lonely as a Cloud," stanza 1, in Bloom, *Wordsworth*, 54.

11. Elliott, *Edward Irving*, 65–67; Lee, "Christ's Sinful Flesh," 102–103.

Figure a fat flabby incurvated personage, at once short, rotund and relaxed, with a watery mouth, a snuffy nose, a pair of strange brown, timid, yet earnest looking eyes, a high tapering brow, and a great bush of grey hair—you will have some faint idea of Coleridge. He is a kind, good soul, full of religion and affection, and poetry and animal magnetism. His cardinal sin is that he wants *will*; he has no resolution, he shrinks from pain or labour in any of its shapes.[12]

Indeed, Carlyle thought Coleridge spent too much time "tawlking [*sic*] and taking snuff" rather than getting on with his writing.[13] However, this graphic picture of Coleridge does not seem entirely fair, for his literary output was considerable, and it must be recognized as coming from one who did not have "much esteem" for him.[14] In fact, one gets the impression that Carlyle found Coleridge rather irritating.

As suggested by Chalmers, Coleridge had a considerable influence upon Edward Irving. Coleridge first went to hear Irving preach early in July 1823. They first met at around that time, or perhaps earlier that year, and were introduced by Basil Montagu, a legal reformer and expert on bankruptcy law. Montagu was a close friend of a number of leading figures in the Romantic Movement. In fact, when Montagu's first wife died, the Wordsworths raised their son, and Coleridge had even stayed for a while with Montagu after moving to London and before joining the Gillmans.[15]

Coleridge called Irving "the super-Ciceronian, ultra-Demosthenic Pulpiteer." Soon after they had met he said that Irving's preaching was marred by "high and passionate Rhetoric not introduced & pioneered by calm and clear Logic," so that what he said tended to miss the mark.[16] But the poet's view of the preacher improved on further acquaintance. The following year in a letter to a friend, he called Irving "interesting and highly gifted," which was a real compliment coming from Coleridge, even though he failed to spell Irving's name correctly ("Irvine").[17]

12. Thomas Carlyle to John A. Carlyle, June 24, 1824, *CLO*.

13. Thomas Carlyle to Anna D. B. Montagu, July 18, 1825, *CLO*. For Coleridge's procrastination, see Elliott, *Edward Irving*, 63–64.

14. Carlyle, *Reminiscences* (Norton), 2:131.

15. Elliott, *Edward Irving*, 66; Montague, "Basil Montagu." In a letter to Jane Baillie Welsh dated September 9, 1822, Irving stated, "I have made no acquaintance in London [of] any literary eminence," which must mean that he first met Coleridge after that (Irving, *DL*, 161).

16. Samuel Taylor Coleridge to Charlotte Brent, July 7, 1823, in Coleridge, *CLSTC*, 5:280; Coleridge, *Text*, 4963.

17. Samuel Taylor Coleridge to Henry Taylor, May 18, 1824, in Coleridge, *CLSTC*,

In another letter Coleridge spoke favorably of the evenings that he spent with Irving and Basil Montagu, particularly of "the friendly Sympathies and Collisions between Mr. I. and myself." Coleridge went on to say that he found Irving in these drawing room conversations to be even "more delightful" than when he was in the pulpit. Clearly Irving did not visit Coleridge just to listen to him.[18]

Irving greatly enjoyed his visits to Highgate and went there weekly when he could. Oliphant spoke of Irving as having a "reverential respect" for the poet.[19] But if it be thought that Irving was a little gullible in his acceptance of Coleridge's ideas, perhaps overawed to be a friend of such a great man, this does not seem to have been the case. Irving is unlikely to have adopted anything Coleridge said simply because he said it; he was too smart for that. As Graham McFarlane said, "The influence of Coleridge upon Irving was a strong but distilled one, for Irving took nothing from Coleridge unless it would serve his own ends."[20] As an example of that, it has been argued that Coleridge was seeking to "fuse the intellectual, volitional, and emotional elements in religious experience into one harmonious whole,"[21] and if this was so, then it melded beautifully with Irving's own developing ideas. Thus, for the most part, Coleridge was not persuading Irving to adopt new beliefs, but was assisting him in deepening existing ones.

Irving dedicated his book on mission to Coleridge, which added to the controversy surrounding it. When Anna Montagu told Irving that such a dedication would do him no good, he replied, "That shall be a reason for doing it."[22] Part of this tribute stated that the poet had been "more profitable to my faith in orthodox doctrine, to my spiritual understanding of the Word of God, and to my right conception of the Christian Church than any or all of the men with whom I have entertained friendship and conversation."[23] This suggests that Irving was well aware of a considerable degree of help from Coleridge in developing his own ideas. It was also an astonishing, even dangerous, statement for Irving to have made when one considers that Irving's theology must have already been well developed long before he met Coleridge and that Coleridge's views were not considered entirely consistent

---

5:362–63.

18. Samuel Taylor Coleridge to Mrs. Charles Aders, June 3, 1824, in ibid., 5:368.

19. Oliphant, *Life*, 1:189; Elliott, *Edward Irving*, 76–77.

20. McFarlane, *Christology*, 206, quoted in Elliott, *Edward Irving*, 56. For more on Coleridge's influence on Irving, see McFarlane, *Christ and the Spirit*, 165–72.

21. J. D. Boulger, *Coleridge as Religious Thinker*, 92, quoted in Elliott, *Edward Irving*, 67.

22. Oliphant, *Life*, 1:206, n.

23. Irving, *Missionaries*, vii–viii.

with Christian orthodoxy. It also indicates that Irving did not hold the contemporary crop of Scottish preachers and theologians in high regard.

Yet Peter Elliott argues that "in the three areas of Irving's greatest theological distinctiveness—Christology, the charismata, and millennialism—Coleridge had very little influence on him at all." Indeed, with regard to the charismata, Coleridge was very uneasy about Irving's beliefs, as he was initially with his millennialism. However, Elliott concedes that in other areas, including his understanding of the Trinity, Coleridge's influence is more evident.[24] Strikingly, Elliott offers evidence that Irving actually influenced Coleridge in the area of millennial studies, rather than the other way around.[25]

Yet Coleridge did influence Irving, and there can be little doubt that part of that influence was along Romantic lines. Irving's Romanticism evidenced itself in his spirit of adventure and danger, in his desire to be original, and in his hope to experience Christ—not just to believe in him, but to *feel* him, as it were, not just to know about him.

A. L. Drummond said, "far from anticipating Coleridge's teaching, Irving embraced it with the enthusiasm and imperfect apprehension of a late learner."[26] However, Elliott points out that Irving was well along the Romantic road during his ministry in Glasgow before he had met Coleridge and possibly even before he had read him, though he was already well aware of William Wordsworth's works.[27]

Indeed, in a letter to Carlyle in June 1819 Irving confessed "I have a turn for the romantic."[28] In another letter penned in 1822, before he had met Coleridge, Irving expressed clear Romantic sentiments. In it he said, "There is a restlessness in my mind after a state of life less customary, more enterprising, more heroical . . . certainly more apostolical . . . In truth I am an adventurer on ground untried."[29] He even referred to himself as "a

24. Elliott, *Edward Irving*, 106–107. See also Grass, *Edward Irving*, 100. Dallimore claimed that Coleridge influenced Irving in all these three areas (Dallimore, *Life*, 46–47), but Coleridge's influence on these issues, such as it was, does not seem to have been great. For an assessment of Dallimore's views on this, see Martindale, "Edward Irving's," 23–25.

25. Elliott, *Edward Irving*, 90–91. Here Elliott quotes from Coleridge's marginal notes on Irving's translation of Lacunza, vol. 2.

26. Drummond, *Edward Irving*, 66.

27. Elliott, *Edward Irving*, 70–71, 106–107; Robinson, *Diary, Reminiscences*, 2:253.

28. Irving to Thomas Carlyle, June 4, 1819, in Irving, *DL*, 70.

29. Letter to an office bearer of the Caledonian Chapel, in Drummond, *Edward Irving*, 46.

renegado" (renegade),[30] someone who thought and desired to act differently. In addition, some of his ideas in *Orations*, which Irving preached and
probably published before he had met Coleridge, were also along Romantic
lines, placing a great emphasis on feelings and the spiritual dimension of
the faith.[31] The *Orations* also included calls to adventure and the heroic.
Irving argued that the Scriptures teach us to live lives "of heavenly enter-
prise." Indeed, "Such adventurers should all men become. What to us are
the established rules of life that they should blindly overrule us? . . . Is there
nought noble, nought heroical, to be undertaken and achieved? . . . Adventurers above your sphere I would have you all to become; brave designs, not
antiquated customs, should move your life. A path heroical you should trace
out and follow to glory and immortality."[32]

In fact, Elliott argues that a strain of Scottish Romanticism influenced Irving before his sojourn in London.[33] As that seems to be the case;
Coleridge was not pointing Irving in a new direction, but for the most part
confirming him in a journey already begun.

Irving's Romanticism may be one of the reasons he preferred the *Scots
Confession* to the later *Westminster Confession*. Thomas F. Torrance argues
that the *Westminster Confession*, though a great statement of the faith, "does
not manifest the spiritual freshness and freedom, or the evangelical joy"
of the *Scots Confession*.[34] If this is so, one would expect Irving, with his
Romantic disposition, to have favored the earlier confession, as he did.

As early as 1825 Anna Montagu could say, "Mr. Irving feels more than
he reasons"[35] (a Romantic leaning), which was a tendency that increased
as the years went by and led Irving into even more trouble. That same year
William Wordsworth called Irving "a poet in spirit,"[36] which suggests that
he also saw something of that quality in the preacher.

This aspect of Irving's thinking was also evident in his remarkable ordination sermon for Hugh McLean. He charged McLean "thou must preach
Christ in a mystery, and show the very great mysteries of godliness, especially of the . . . two sacraments. Get thee out of the bright sunshine of the
intellect, and meditate the deep mysteries of the Spirit, which the natural

30. Irving to Thomas Chalmers, January 21, 1822 [1823], in Irving, *DL*, 170.

31. For example, ibid., *Oracles*, 40–46.

32. Ibid., 82–84.

33. Elliott, *Edward Irving*, 14–16, 71–72.

34. Torrance, *Scottish Theology*, 127. Other reasons will become apparent later.

35. Mrs. Montague, quoted in Thomas Carlyle to Anna D. B. Montague, May 20,
1825, n. 6, *CLO*.

36. William Wordsworth to Allan Cunningham, November 23, 1825, in Wordsworth and Wordsworth, *Later Years*, 402.

man perceiveth not . . . try the depths, sound with thy deepest line, my brother. Oh, I charge thee, enter into the mysteries of these two sacraments; if I hear of thee setting them forth as mere naked signs, I will be the first to charge thee with a most dangerous error."[37]

Yet, the stars of the Romantic Movement did not escape Irving's criticism. On one occasion he told his wife that Coleridge desired "the idolatry of himself."[38] After he had met William Wordsworth, he is supposed to have said that he did not regard these literary people "so highly" as he once did.[39] But Irving loved ideas, and to see them "looming through the mist" stirred him to think through the specific issue and to adapt it according to his understanding of Scripture.

Oliphant argued that "Despite [Irving's] own strong individuality, he never seems to have come in contact with any mind of respectable powers without taking something from it,"[40] and this was particularly so with the very respectable powers of Coleridge. In his "Preliminary Discourse" to Immanuel Lacunza's commentary on the book of Revelation, Irving called Coleridge his "kind and honoured instructor" and said that the poet had given him some clues that had helped him understand the prophetic portions of the Bible.[41] In fact, this form of apocalyptic writing was not alien to the Romantic Movement.[42]

One way in which Coleridge's influence actually changed Irving's belief was in the latter's shift from a general optimism about the future of mankind to a very pessimistic one.[43] When Irving sent Coleridge a copy of his *Oracles of God*, Coleridge wrote in it, "Let this young man know that the world is not to be converted, but judged."[44]

Irving's pessimism, as shall be seen, was most evident in his later theology, particularly his eschatology. Another cause of this later pessimism may have been that so many of the nation's leading figures who had attended

---

37. Irving, *CW*, 1:532.

38. Irving's journal, October 29, 1825, quoted in Oliphant, *Life*, 1:270.

39. Jane Welsh Carlyle to Mary Welsh, December 27, 1831, *CLO*.

40. Oliphant, *Life*, 1:23. John Hair had a similar view to Oliphant (Hair, *Regent*, 57–58).

41. Irving, "Preliminary Discourse," in Ben-Ezra, *Coming*, 1:lxxv. See also Oliphant, *Life*, 1:190.

42. Elliott, *Edward Irving*, 10.

43. Irving seems to present an optimistic, postmillennial view in 1825 in his preface to *Missionaries*, xxi–xxii, which was a very common opinion in his time. He was clearly pessimistic and premillennial later, as shall be seen.

44. W. W. Andrews, *Edward Irving: A Review*, 60, quoted in Grass, *Edward Irving*, 78.

his church had now deserted it. He had hoped to influence these important people with the gospel of Christ such that they might influence the world in turn. But that now looked to be a vain hope.

By the end of 1825, Irving suspected that the seven churches in chapters 2 and 3 of the book of Revelation referred to the different ages in church history. The age in which he was living would be the final period, the lukewarm Laodicean age, consistent with, as he now saw it, the church in decline.[45]

Though it is clear, then, that Irving was influenced by Coleridge and had a very high regard for him, Coleridge also greatly respected Irving. In fact, he called him "my valued and affectionately respected friend" and described him as having a "high heart and vehement intellect."[46] Coleridge regarded him as having "a vigorous" and *growing* mind" and a "*manly*" character, and he also believed that Irving had "fewer prejudices, national or sectarian" than just about any other person he knew.[47] In addition, Coleridge said that while he had "no faith in [Irving's] prophesying" and disagreed with "certain peculiarities of his theological system," he held that "Edward Irving possesses more of the spirit and purposes of the first Reformers, that he has more of the Head and Heart, the Life, the Unction, and the genial power of Martin Luther, than any man now alive: yea, than any man of this and the last century. I see in Edward Irving a minister of Christ after the order of Paul."[48]

It also appears that Coleridge even turned to the study of the book of Revelation and probably Daniel through Irving's influence, though the poet found the preacher's views on these books "Aberrations . . . into the Cloud-land of prophecies."[49] In fact, Coleridge said that he went through Revelation chapter by chapter with Irving early in 1826,[50] but that does not seem to have changed Irving's views.

Coleridge even penned a verse to his "honored" friend in a debate with him on infant baptism in which he called Irving "Friend pure of heart and fervent!"[51]

45. Irving's journal, November 25, 1825, quoted in Oliphant, *Life*, 1:357.

46. Coleridge, *On the Constitution*, 166; Coleridge, *Collected Works*, 12, pt. 3:11. Some other occasions in which Coleridge called Irving "my friend," with or without complimentary adjectives, are to be found in Coleridge, *Text*, 5293, 5323, 5402.

47. Samuel Taylor Coleridge to Daniel Stuart, [July 8?], 1825, in Coleridge, *CLSTC*, 5:474; Samuel Taylor Coleridge and J. Blanco White, July 12, 1825, in ibid., 476.

48. Coleridge, *On the Constitution*, 168.

49. Ibid., *Text*, 5323; ibid., *Notes*, 5439 n.

50. Coleridge to Mrs. C. Aders, March 8, 1826, in Coleridge, *CLSTC*, 6:570.

51. Ibid., *Aids*, 290.

Elliott points out that both Coleridge and Thomas Carlyle desired Irving's help in their causes. He concludes from that, "It is no small compliment to Irving that two of the greatest minds of nineteenth-century Britain wanted him as an ally in the struggle to change and improve the world."[52] Even as late as 1830, Carlyle's respect for Irving's powers were so great that in one letter to his brother Carlyle said that if he had such a man as Irving on his side, he felt that he "could defy the Earth."[53] And Carlyle has been called "the most influential of Victorian sages."[54]

52. Elliott, *Edward Irving*, 136.
53. Thomas Carlyle to John A. Carlyle, August 21, 1830, *CLO*.
54. Inwood, *History of London*, 497.

9

Babylon and Infidelity Foredoomed of God

Every day I feel more and more alone, and more and more rooted and
grounded in the truth.

—EDWARD IRVING[1]

THE FRENCH REVOLUTION

The French Revolution and the Napoleonic Wars had a major impact upon
the study of biblical prophecy in Europe and America in the early years of
the nineteenth century. Their influence in this regard was as great as the
foundation of the modern state of Israel in the twentieth century. In fact,
the French Revolution, which "burst like a thunderclap upon the startled
world"[2] in 1789, and the rise of Napoleon Bonaparte (who became Em-
peror in 1804) caused a strong resurgence in the belief that the last days had
arrived.[3]

---

1. Irving's journal, November 23, 1825, quoted in Oliphant, *Life*, 1:351.

2. Elliott, *Horae Apocalypticae*, 4:529.

3. For more details of the impact of the French Revolution on the study of prophecy, see Bennett, *Origins*, 201–206.

In the years 1686 and 1687, Pierre Jurieu, a French Protestant pastor, had predicted that France would experience a Revolution in the 1780s that would overthrow Rome.[4] The Revolution and the following wars had, in fact, clipped papal Rome's wings, though they had not overthrown it. Perhaps more significantly, in 1708, Increase Mather, a leading American Congregationalist, stated that the Scriptures taught that one of the ten Roman Kingdoms, probably France, "shall undergo a marvellous Revolution."[5] And eighty years later, it did.

Ruth Bloch argues that that Revolution and its associated war "provided the greatest single stimulus for the growth of eschatological speculation."[6] Many came to believe that these events were the fulfillment of biblical prophecy. And if some of the Bible's prophecies were now being fulfilled, then there was good reason to believe that others would soon be fulfilled as well, including the return of Christ. Ernest Sandeen notes that "the apparently complete and precise fulfillment of biblical prophecies during the French Revolution had a direct impact upon the biblical interpretation generally. It became a hallmark of the millenarian party that literal rather than figurative or spiritualized fulfillments should be sought for every biblical prophecy."[7] This influence had an impact upon Edward Irving and his circle. In fact, Irving came to believe that in this Revolution, "a prophetic period of great prominence in the book of God" had been "accomplished."[8]

DRUMMOND, WAY, AND FRERE

Notwithstanding the controversy surrounding his LMS lecture, Irving still received requests to speak at a variety of functions. One of these came from Henry Drummond, who asked Irving to give an address for the Continental Society for the Diffusion of Religious Knowledge. Drummond (1786–1860), later a member of Irving's church, was the grandson of a viscount and was a banker and politician with a keen interest in biblical prophecy. He was one of the founders of the Continental Society, which had commenced in 1817.

Oliphant described Drummond as "impatient, fastidious, and arbitrary, a master of contemptuous expression, acting and speaking with all the suddenness of an irresponsible agent," while Carlyle called him "a

4. Vereté, "Restoration," 5–6; Jurieu, *Accomplishment*, vi.

5. Mather, *Dissertation*, 101–102.

6. Bloch, *Visionary Republic*, 152. See also Patterson, "Designing," 44–45; Oliver, *Prophets*, 41; Sandeen, *Roots*, 5.

7. Sandeen, *Roots*, 13. See also ibid., 6–7; Stunt, *Awakening*, 21–22.

8. Irving, *Babylon*, 1:40.

sharp, elastic haughty kind of man" with "an insatiable love of shining and figuring."[9] Reporting on a meeting of another society, Irving said, "Henry Drummond was in the chair; he is in all chairs—–I fear for him. His words are more witty than spiritual; his manner is *spirituel* [refined and lively], not grave."[10] In fact, in Carlyle's view, Drummond did Irving "a great deal of ill."[11] However, Drummond did on one occasion help Irving's parents out of a difficult financial problem, so he was not without kindness.[12]

It has also been said of Drummond that he inspired "controversy wherever he landed."[13] If that was so, he and Irving must have been made for each other, and their association did indeed continue until Irving's death. In fact, "Drummond appears to have exercised a certain degree of influence, varying, but always increasing, over the career of Irving,"[14] and, as Carlyle said, that influence was not always beneficial.

Henry Drummond and other British evangelicals also spent time on the Continent, particularly in Switzerland, meeting with like-minded Europeans, discovering their needs, and learning from them as well. Some of these Europeans also visited Britain. While there can be little doubt that there was a sharing of ideas, it appears debatable who most influenced whom, and in what ways and to what degree, but Scottish Presbyterianism certainly was involved in this exchange.[15]

The Continental Society was established to assist European evangelicals and their churches "in preaching the gospel and in distributing Bibles, Testaments and Religious publications over the Continent of Europe, but without the design of establishing any distinct sect or party."[16] It drew support from most major denominations in Britain.

Theoretically, the Continental Society sought to fulfill its mandate while avoiding controversy. However, with Drummond a leading figure and Irving enrolled as a speaker, controversy was bound to arise. Kenneth Stewart, in fact, notes four controversies that hit the Society in the 1820s. Two of them involved Edward Irving. One of these did not take place until near the end of that decade, after Irving had become a member of the Society's

9. Oliphant, *Life*, 1:390; Carlyle, *Reminiscences* (Norton), 2:187.

10. Irving's journal, November 21, 1825, quoted in Oliphant, *Life*, 1:343–44.

11. Carlyle, *Reminiscences* (Norton), 2:199.

12. Irving to Henry Drummond, July 7, 1829, in Irving, *DL*, 261–64; Irving to Henry Drummond, July 9, 1829, in ibid., 264–65.

13. Carter, *Anglican Evangelicals*, 159.

14. Oliphant, *Life*, 1:391.

15. Stunt, *Awakening*, 31–36, 102–107, 110–16, 225–37.

16. For the Continental Society, see Kenneth J. Stewart, "Millennial Maelstrom," in Gribben and Stunt, *Prisoners*, 122–49. The quotation is from the society's 1819 report.

committee. By that time Irving was close to achieving his maximum notoriety, and almost anything he said or did was controversial simply because it was associated with him. He appears to have been dropped from the Society's committee in 1829. The other controversy was associated with Irving's lecture and book, *Babylon and Infidelity Foredoomed of God*, but was wider than just that. It centered on the nature and timing of the return of Jesus Christ.[17]

Henry Drummond was one of three key men who began to influence Irving's eschatology during this period. The other two were Lewis Way (1772–1840)[18] and James Hatley Frere (1779–1866). Lewis Way was one of the first Protestants to encounter Immanuel Lacunza's book on Revelation, a work that was to have a profound influence upon Irving, as shall be seen. Way was a wealthy Anglican who had an intense interest in the welfare of the Jews, which included a staunch belief in the restoration of the Kingdom of Israel.[19] He became associated with the London Society for Promoting Christianity Amongst the Jews (LSPCJ), which had been founded as an inter-denominational mission in 1808 or 1809, but was adopted by the Church of England in 1815.[20]

Hatley Frere began studying the prophetic Scriptures seriously in 1798. According to Coleridge, he was "a pious and well-meaning, but gloomy and enthusiastic Calvinist."[21] Frere published his *Combined View of the Prophecies of Daniel, Esdras and St. John* in 1815.[22] In is noteworthy that Frere, a Protestant, included 2 Esdras from the Apocrypha in his book on prophecy. In fact, in this work he "propounded a new scheme of interpretation."[23] Included in it was the restoration of Israel,[24] though he did not have as strong an emphasis on this as Lewis Way. Frere's book was later frowned upon by C. H. Spurgeon, the Baptist preacher.[25]

According to Oliphant, Frere had by 1825 "been unable to secure the ear of the religious public" for his ideas.[26] However, Frere secured Irving's

17. Stewart, "Millennial Maelstrom," in Gribben and Stunt, *Prisoners*, 127–34.

18. Irving, "Preliminary Discourse," in Ben-Ezra, *Coming*, 1:xix–xx.

19. Basilicus, "Thoughts," 102–108.

20. Lewis, *Lighten*, 131, 207; Sandeen, *Roots*, 10.

21. Samuel Taylor Coleridge to Edward Coleridge, February 8, 1826, in Coleridge, *CLSTC*, 6:557.

22. Froom, *Prophetic Faith*, 3:386; Oliver, *Prophets*, 132; Sandeen, *Roots*, 8–9. Frere's brother John was a friend of Coleridge's (Elliott, *Edward Irving*, 25 n. 73).

23. Oliphant, *Life*, 1:221.

24. Oliver, *Prophets*, 133.

25. Spurgeon, *Commenting*, 127.

26. Oliphant, *Life*, 1:221. Irving mentioned "Mr. Frere's Scheme" in his "Preliminary

ear that same year and influenced him significantly. In fact, Isabella Irving called Frere her husband's "instructor in the Prophecies." Indeed, he was "the John of the present age."[27]

Oliphant had a point when she noted, "Despite [Irving's] own strong individuality, he never seems to have come in contact with any mind of respectable powers without taking something from it."[28] But it could also be argued that at times he garnered something from less powerful minds, which no doubt showed his humility, though it also at times demonstrated a gullible streak.

FOREDOOMED

Irving absorbed the influences of these men, and at the end of 1825 he presented some "new" teachings in his address in London to the Continental Society. This presentation was later enlarged and published the next year in two volumes in typical Irving fashion as *Babylon and Infidelity Foredoomed of God*.[29] The book was long—very long—and repetitious.

It is perhaps not surprising that when he delivered the lecture, some of his listeners did not stay to the end. Edward Irving, once more, had offended at least some of his audience.[30] Irving was becoming a master at that, but it did not seem to bother him. When the book was published, it was dedicated to the man who had first turned his thoughts to the in-depth study of Christ's return, Hatley Frere. In this dedication Irving said that he was so impressed by Frere's scheme that he had offered himself as Frere's "pupil, to be instructed in prophecy, according to" his ideas.[31] In fact, Irving went further and claimed that he learned "*all*" of his "knowledge of the divine prophecy" from Frere.[32] This was doubtlessly an exaggeration, but clearly Frere had a major influence upon him in this regard.

So what did Irving say in *Babylon*? Indeed, to what did the terms "Babylon" and "Infidelity" refer? That is, the two identities that he pronounced were "Foredoomed" in this work. "Babylon" was the Roman Catholic

Discourse," in Ben-Ezra, *Coming*, 1:xxxvi, xli–xlii.

27. Isabella Irving to Mrs. Martin, June 3, 1825, quoted in Grass, *Edward Irving*, 102. Isabella's letter appears to have been sent with one written by her husband on the same day, but hers is now lost (Irving, *DL*, 211–12).

28. Oliphant, *Life*, 1:23.

29. Grass, "Edward Irving," in *Prisoners*, 97–98; Oliphant, *Life*, 1:220–23.

30. Oliphant, *Life*, 1:226–27.

31. Dedication to Frere in Irving, *Babylon*, 1:vi.

32. Ibid., 2:23–24 n., emphasis added.

Church, which would not be converted or reformed, but would instead be judged by God.[33] "Infidelity" was atheism and "the worship of reason," that was then dominant in France and had been spreading abroad since the Revolution.[34]

Though Irving was strongly opposed to Catholicism, he was not a bigot. True he regarded most Catholics as "gross idolaters," but he also acknowledged that some Catholic priests were "singular saints" and that God "preserveth a seed" within the Catholic Church.[35]

By this time, Irving believed that there were two kinds of biblical prophecy: the "discursive" (for example, Isaiah, Jeremiah, and Ezekiel) and the "historical" (primarily Daniel and Revelation). He seems to have viewed both kinds as predictive in nature, but while the discursive books did not predict events in chronological order, the historical books did, and at times with specific dates. In fact, the historical prophecies have an "exact order," even "a complete system of prophetic chronology."[36] Daniel, for example, "carries us as upon a voyage of discovery, down the stream of time, noting the various powers which should have the ascendant, and the duration of their times, until the time of the end, when the saints shall possess the kingdom." And Revelation is "the book of Daniel unfolded."[37] Irving slotted the prophecies of the other books into the scheme that he had drawn from Daniel and Revelation.[38]

Babylon was for the most part an examination of "historical" biblical prophecy, mainly Daniel and Revelation, and of how, in Irving's opinion, it was being fulfilled in his time and would be further fulfilled in the immediate future. In other words, these biblical books told what would happen in the future, some of which had been fulfilled by the 1820s, but much more was still to come and soon to come. Irving argued that this form of scriptural prophecy is "the most important part of the revelation of God"—that is, if one can say that one part is more important than another—and an integral part of the orthodox faith. He charged the church's "chief and leading men [of] ploughing with other oxen"; that is, of ignoring, even rejecting, the study and proclamation of the predictive aspects of prophesy. In fact, Irving

33. Ibid., 1:153–56, 202–203; 2:15–16, 228, 430. It should be noted that others before Irving had called Roman Catholicism "Babylon," usually because of the use of that name in Rev 16–18; thus he was using the term in an already established way.

34. Ibid., 1:132–37; 2:23–24.

35. Irving's journal, October 30 and November 14, 1825, quoted in Oliphant, *Life*, 1:277, 318.

36. Irving, *Babylon*, 1:42–50, 67.

37. Ibid., 1:53, 2:199.

38. Ibid., 2:241–43.

claimed that by ignoring this part of the Bible's teaching, the church "doth herself most grievous wrong."[39]

Irving's understanding of the book of Revelation at this time was a form of historicism based on the teachings of Hatley Frere and the seventeenth-century scholar Joseph Mede.[40] That is, he believed that Revelation predicted events in different periods of church history beginning from the first century AD and culminating in the return of Christ, though they did not do so in strict chronological order. In best historicist fashion, Irving's scheme taught that the 1,260 days and forty-two months of Daniel and Revelation stood for 1,260 *years*.[41] Later he was to interpret Revelation from a futurist perspective, with chapter 4 onwards referring to the end of time. Then 1,260 days would mean 1,260 *days*. But he had not arrived at those beliefs yet.

Irving also included some comments upon the Apocryphal book, 2 Esdras in this study. However, he placed them mainly in a "Digression" so that he would not "give encouragement to the providential advocates of the Apocrypha."[42] Yet, he believed that the passage in 2 Esdras 11–12 was "a true and marvellous prophecy"[43] and "so very exact" that he did not know how to "refuse it the character of being divinely inspired." He also referred to it favorably in his final chapter.[44] As Elliott says, Irving was willing "to see some parts of the Apocrypha as inspired,"[45] though those parts seem to have been only these two chapters of 2 Esdras. That he should consider Esdras at all was no doubt because of Frere's influence on him.

In Irving's "Digression" and the introduction to it, one senses his deep struggle in regarding 2 Esdras or any part of the Apocrypha as being inspired by God. Of another Apocryphal book, Ecclesiasticus, he said, "It is rather shrewd than divine; and . . . has little heavenward drift in it to the soul."[46] This suggests that he may have considered, but ultimately rejected, the divine inspiration of the remaining parts of the Apocrypha.

In 1827 he argued against the Bible Society's practice of including the Apocrypha in certain editions of the Bible for use mainly in Catholic

39. Ibid., 1:23–27, 39.

40. Irving regarded Frere as having "perfected" Joseph Mede's "method of synchronism" (Irving, "Preliminary Discourse," in Ben-Ezra, *Coming*, 1:xli–xlii).

41. Irving, *Babylon*, 1:53–54, 74–76, 88–115, 126–34, 173–206, 213–15; 2:206–223.

42. Irving's journal, November 23, 1825, quoted in Oliphant, *Life*, 1:350–51; Irving, *Babylon*, 2:35–57.

43. Ibid., 2:397.

44. Ibid., 1:265, 2:397–99.

45. Elliott, *Edward Irving*, 185.

46. Irving's journal, November 4, 1825, quoted in Oliphant, *Life*, 1:296.

countries. There had, in fact, been very strong opposition from the Scottish Church to this use of the Apocrypha by the Bible Society, so Irving was one amongst many who were against it.[47] (Yet Irving regarded the Bible Society as "that most noble instrument"; indeed, it was the angel taking "the everlasting gospel . . . to every nation" referred to in Rev 14:6.[48])

Irving proclaimed that the recent events in France and beyond were clearly predicted in the book of Revelation and in Daniel.[49] In addition, he dubbed the papacy the beast of Revelation, a common belief throughout Protestant history that Irving feared was being watered down.[50] In fact, throughout this book Irving was highly negative about Catholicism, for as we have seen, he viewed it as Babylon.

He also expected that Christ would return soon and set up an earthly Millennium.[51] Indeed, he even went as far as to say that he expected the Jews to return to Palestine by 1847[52] and that Christ would come back by 1868.[53] Yet he still argued against speculative interpretation and claimed that he "refrained from theories."[54]

However, Irving did express some doubts as to whether Christ would return and reign in a "personal or corporeal" sense.[55] In other words, he was unsure whether Christ would reign from heaven or on earth during the Millennium. But he did not seem to have any doubts about the last possible commencement date. This conviction was to cause him considerable trouble later.

A common belief at that time was that the gospel would be preached throughout the world and the nations would be gradually Christianized. This was a core belief of postmillennialism, with which Irving was originally sympathetic. But in *Babylon* Irving strongly rejected that view. "Convert the nations!" ministers and mission agencies proclaimed. Irving argued that that would not happen, for "The Lord, and his twelve, and his seventy, the Holy Ghost, and his thousands of converts, could not convert the Jewish

---

47. Drummond, *Edward Irving*, 108–109; Macleod, *Scottish Theology*, 226–27, 260; Wilks, *Edward Irving*, 174–77. The controversy about the Bible Society's use of the Apocrypha had been going on for some years; see Browne, *History*, 1:94–109, especially 102 and 106; Standish and Standish, "Trinitarian Bible Society."

48. Irving, *Babylon*, 2:290, 435.

49. Ibid., 1:191–93, 218–26, 233–34, 240–41; 2:11–35.

50. Ibid., 1:26, 206–208.

51. Ibid., 1:32, 192, 205–206; 2:8, 138–47, 155–56.

52. Ibid., 2:225–28.

53. Ibid., 1:173–75, 2:152, 218–19.

54. Ibid., 2:167, 220.

55. Ibid., 2:168–69. Also see 2:150.

people," because their hearts were ossified "and their consciences seared with a red hot iron." Nor would the Gentiles be converted. In fact, "The deaf world! The reprobate—the infatuated world!" would not be converted. "It must be destroyed."[56] Here can be seen the influence of two unlikely bedfellows, Coleridge and Frere.

For the most part, *Babylon* was written in the very confident tone frequently used by people predicting the return of Christ. Irving seems to have had little doubt that his scheme was right. This forces us to ask, why did so intelligent and spiritual a man have such confidence in this shaky system and even take the foolish step of dating, even approximately, the return of Christ? He must have known that so many before him had done the same and been proven wrong, and he must have been aware of the biblical teaching that Christ's return would be unexpected, "as a thief in the night" (2 Pet 3:10).

The answer seems to be in the impact that the French Revolution had upon Europe, allied with the supposition shared by many that these events were the fulfillment of Scripture. It is noteworthy that the Revolution and the Napoleonic Wars feature prominently in most early nineteenth-century discussion about the return of Christ, not only in Irving's. This assumed fulfillment of Scripture gave Irving and many other interpreters confidence that they could plot future events from such books as Daniel and Revelation, and plot them they did. In fact, a surprising number at this time believed, like Irving, that Christ would return in the 1860s.[57]

That Irving made some major revisions to his scheme in the next few years, added to the failure of his prediction about Christ's return, warns us that dogmatism in this area is ill-advised. Jesus Christ will return in his time, not ours.

It must be remembered, however, that the belief that the return of Christ was close at hand was by no means a new idea, but it was not held by all Christians in any era and not by very many in the 1820s. As we have noted, the dominant belief at the beginning of the century was that Christ's kingdom would be brought in gradually through the church, as in postmillennialism. However, through the work of Irving and others, this understanding was beginning to be placed in the shade by the idea that Christ would dramatically break into this sinful world and suddenly set up his kingdom, an understanding known as premillennialism.

56. Ibid., 2:89–91.

57. Francis Gumerlock names eleven people in this period, including Irving and Frere, who expected Christ's return in the 1860s, and this is probably only the tip of the iceberg (Gumerlock, *Day*, 246–48).

Two printings of *Babylon* sold out very quickly,[58] but it does not seem to have received as many attacks as *Oracles* and *Missionaries,* or at least such criticisms have not been easy to find. Either the matter was too obscure for most reviewers or people were beginning to get tired of Irving. Yet one suspects that accusing the church's "chief and leading men [of] ploughing with other oxen" did not go down well. At the very least, this sounded as though Irving was again setting himself above the other clergy.

In fact, a review of *Babylon* in the *Baptist Magazine* of July 1826 concentrated more on criticizing Irving's methods and tone rather than the specific predictions made. The reviewer seemed content to let time decide the prophetic issues. But he wrote that Irving "assumes . . . the demeanour and authority of one commissioned from above, and scatters abroad his denunciations and announces his predictions, as if he were, indeed, a prophet." The reviewer criticized Irving's use of 2 Esdras and asked, "What will his friends at Edinburgh say of this?" He also described the book as Hatley Frere's ideas "dressed and prepared in the Irving style," which was at least partly true.[59]

The review closed by saying, "Whether he is, or not, a good interpreter of prophecy, is a question that will ere long be set at rest: twenty years hence, it *may be* admitted, even by himself, that he was rash—uncharitable—conceited—fonder of positive assertion than calm inquiry—more fanciful than wise." Once more, Irving's lack of prudence was evident, as the reviewer plainly noted.[60]

C. H. Spurgeon much later described the book as "More of rolling sound than anything else."[61] However, if *Babylon* did not cause quite the stir of his earlier works, major controversy was later to center on Irving's understanding of the return of Christ. But by then it had undergone a degree of change and development. The confident theories in *Babylon* had been modified, and in some cases, replaced by other ideas.

AT THE LONDON HIBERNIAN SOCIETY

In 1800 the British government passed the Act of Union, which joined Ireland with Britain and gave the British Parliament power over the Irish people. From that time on, Catholic emancipation—that is, allowing Catholics

58. Wilks, *Edward Irving,* 184.

59. Review of *Babylon,* by Edward Irving, in *Baptist Magazine and Literary Review,* 317–20.

60. Ibid.

61. Spurgeon, *Commenting,* 128.

to sit in Parliament and hold political office—became a major issue. But it was not until April 1829 that the government passed an Act that permitted this.[62] In between those two dates, a heated debate raged over that subject and over Irish affairs generally.

In April 1826[63] Irving played his part in that debate when he spoke at a London Hibernian Society meeting held to discuss Ireland and Catholic Emancipation. According to Oliphant, Irving was taken to the meeting by "An English clergyman of high standing" who, it seems, tried to urge the Scot to adopt a peaceful approach in the deliberations. Whether or not Irving was in a peaceful mood when he arrived, which is probably unlikely, he certainly was not by the time it was his turn to speak. In the audience were a number of ardent supporters of Catholic Emancipation. When one man spoke against it, he was so frequently interrupted that he had to sit down with his address unfinished. A few other speakers had their say, but they only "amused the audience with sentiment and mild description."[64]

By the time it was Irving's turn to speak, he was furious. He got up from his seat, and, rising to his full height, strode to the front of the platform, a heavy stick in his hand. "I have been put to shame this day," he began, striking his cane repeatedly on the floor to emphasize his words. "I have had to sit still and see a servant of God put down in a so-called Christian assembly for speaking the simple truth. Ichabod! Ichabod! The glory is departed." The audience went silent.[65]

His address in its published form was called "The Cause and the Remedy of Ireland's Evil Condition." He had used as his text Rev 9:20–21, which spoke of those who refused to repent in spite of the plagues inflicted upon them. He sympathized with the Irish people in their sad state. Their condition was caused, he believed, not by governments, but by "some disordered state of the inward organs of spiritual life, and the continual administration of unwholesome food to the soul's necessities, rather than by the operation of any outward cause." Thus the Catholic Church was the real cause of the problems, for "the root of the evil is in the [people's] religion." His solution to Ireland's ills was threefold: the "preaching of the living Word," the distribution of "the written Word," and genuine, uncompromised Christian

---

62. Beales, *From Castlereagh*, 22, 25; Blake, *Conservative Party*, 10–11.

63. Irving, *CW*, 3:430 dates this meeting as May 1825, which Oliphant follows (Oliphant, *Life*, 1:220, 227). However, the press response to it was in May 1826. Grass dates the meeting to April 12, 1826 (Grass, *Edward Irving*, 143).

64. Oliphant, *Life*, 1:227–28.

65. Ibid., 1:228–29.

education in the schools.[66] While this proposal contained some truth, it can be fairly said that it was a simplistic answer to a complex problem.

In spite of its explosive start, or perhaps because of it, Irving continued his address uninterrupted and at the end "was surrounded by a crowd of excited and applauding hearers."[67] Irving was not a friend of Catholic emancipation or democracy.[68] Indeed, according to Carlyle, Irving "found *Democracy* a thing forbidden, leading down to outer darkness."[69] This was really because he believed that all government ultimately should be under the kingship of Jesus Christ. Indeed, it is noticeable that his emerging beliefs about the last days kept peeking through in this address. Those beliefs, including Christ's soon-to-arrive earthly millennial reign, were to become dominant in his thought.

A little later, a sarcastic report on Irving's Hibernian address appeared in *The Examiner* ("A Sunday paper on Politics, Domestic Economy, and Theatricals"), under the heading: "Irving the Rhapsodist and his Gold Repeater." The brief review sounded more like an account of a theatrical performance than of a serious address. Indeed, the writer did refer to Irving's "theatrical display," stating that Irving "vehemently reprobated the report of the Irish Education Commissioners," which recommended that while Catholic and Protestant children should be taught in the same schools, each child should be taught the faith of their respective parents. "Out upon such driveling," he cried. *The Examiner* claimed that Irving called one such hybrid school "a poor mongrel, a spawn of the thirty years of the French Revolution."[70]

Also, according to the writer, at the close of his address Irving condemned the worship of money, which he believed was "the besetting sin" in British society, and said that he grieved that "the love of money should have found its way into our Societies" (presumably here he meant missionary societies). According to *The Examiner*, Irving continued,

> I can say for myself, "Silver and gold I have none: but what I have, I give unto thee." I have no money but from two sources: from my church, and by that I must live, "for they that partake of the altar should live by the altar"; and I make it a principle not to lay by a farthing of my receipts from that source. The other

66. Irving, "Cause and the Remedy," in Irving, *CW*, 3:430–34, 468.

67. Oliphant, *Life*, 1:229.

68. Irving's journal, October 26, 1825, quoted in ibid., 1:258. By this time, Irving frowned upon his old literary hero John Milton, regarding him as "the archangel of Radicalism" (Irving's journal, November 3, 1825, quoted in ibid., 1:294).

69. Carlyle, *Reminiscences* (Norton), 2:197. In his later life, Carlyle was not fond of democracy either.

70. "Irving the Rhapsodist," 314.

is from my books, and the produce of these I devote conscien-
tiously to religious charities. I give you now (having no money)
the dying gift of a dear brother [John Irving], who breathed his
last in India, and who died, I hope, in the faith of Christ," (Here
Mr. Irving handed to the Secretary a Gold Watch.) "And I pledge
myself to redeem that, to me, precious gift, out of the first produce of the sale of my last book."

Lord Gambier [the meeting's chairman] endeavoured to prevail on Mr. Irving to keep the watch; but Mr. Irving strenuously
refused, saying he had done this solely for *example's* sake . . .
Mr. Irving, however, observing Lord Gambier's hand stretched
out, as if in earnest entreaty, eagerly grasped and shook it with
vehemence, and retired amidst the loud plaudits of the assembly. *Loud plaudits!* If this be not a splendid example of Sectarian
vanity and quackery, then there is nothing of the sort in this
most enlightened of lands . . . Out upon such *examples!*[71]

These concluding comments reported by the *Examiner* do not appear
in the *Collected Writings* record of this address. This may simply be because
they were not seen as an essential part of it rather than because of false reporting by the *Examiner*. However, the exchange regarding the watch seems
to have been true.[72] But whatever Irving said and did at this meeting, he
did receive "Loud plaudits," which indicates that many in the audience were
very pleased with his performance.

In 1831 Irving preached a sermon in which he advocated giving aid
to the Irish poor. At the end of the service his congregation raised £350
for Irish relief, a remarkable amount at the time.[73] This demonstrates that
Irving was not by any means anti-Irish.

Back in November 1825 Irving had told his wife,

I have been much exercised this last week with the possibility
of some trial coming to me from the resolute stand which I
have taken, and will maintain, upon the subject of the liberty of
my ministry. For the spirit of authority and rule in the church

71. Ibid. See Irving, "Cause and the Remedy," in Irving, *CW*, 3:454–55, 464–66, for
his comments on the schooling issue. The system of education that Irving was criticizing here proposed to have Irish primary school children of all denominations brought
together for secular subjects, but taught religious education according to the faith of
their families. None of the denominations were completely happy about this proposal.
See Coolahan, *Irish Education*, 5.

72. According to Grass, *Edward Irving*, 143 n. 43, it was also reported in *The Pulpit*
160 (May 11, 1826) 238–39.

73. Mrs. Montagu to Jane Carlyle, June 23, 1831, quoted in Grass, *Edward Irving*,
228.

begins to grow upon me, and I fear much there is not enough of the spirit of obedience in our city churches to obey it . . . but I am prepared, if the Lord should see it meet to try me here also, and I sometimes think I shall be tried here at some time or other . . . there are too many open rivets in my armour.[74]

This was a prediction full of foreboding. The trial was coming. Indeed, the *trials* were coming.

74. Irving's journal, November 13, 1825, quoted in Oliphant, *Life*, 1:316–17.

10

The Coming of Messiah in Majesty and Glory

The second coming of the Lord is the '*point de vue*', the vantage ground . . . from which, and from which alone, the whole purpose of God can be contemplated and understood.

—EDWARD IRVING[1]

HIS DEVELOPING ESCHATOLOGY

It seems to have been early in 1826 that a friend introduced Irving to a book called *The Coming of Messiah in Glory and Majesty*, a commentary on the book of Revelation. This work, written in Spanish, was supposedly by a Christian Jew called Juan Josafat Ben-Ezra, who in fact was a Chilean Jesuit named Manuel (also known as Emanuel) Lacunza. As we have seen, Irving was not sympathetic to Catholicism, but he would not condemn a book simply because it was written by a Catholic. In his mind, such a book must stand or fall on its own merit or lack of it. As it happened, *The Coming of Messiah* had, Irving thought, great merit, and he read it with increasing

---

1. Edward Irving to Thomas Chalmers, December 1828, quoted in Oliphant, *Life*, 2:68.

interest. Perhaps the fact that the Vatican had condemned Lacunza's book also made it easier for Irving to accept.[2]

Irving had already entered the field of millennial studies with his lecture and book, *Babylon and Infidelity Foredoomed of God*. Soon after that, late in 1825 Irving also began to preach about the last days in his church, in which he "opened and defended" three main points "out of the Scriptures from sabbath to sabbath." Those points were first, that the existing church—Catholic, Orthodox, *and* Protestant—"standeth threatened in the Holy Scriptures because of its hypocrisies, idolatries, superstitions, infidelity and enormous wickedness . . . with such a terrible judgment" as had never been seen before. And that judgment was "close at hand."[3]

Presbyterians and other Protestants were used to hearing such pronouncements being made with regard to the Catholic Church, and perhaps occasionally the Orthodox Churches, or even some specific Protestant denominations. But here Irving was leveling these accusations and threat of judgment against Protestant Churches generally, amongst which he certainly included Presbyterianism, though he acknowledged that the faithful were to be found within those churches.

Secondly, Irving argued that God would "bring unto" the Jews "those days of refreshing spoken of by all the holy prophets since the world began." That refreshing would be in the form of a revival that would stir both Jews and Gentiles, which in turn would awaken "those persecutions of the Antichrist, which the faithful are taught to expect immediately before the coming of the Lord."[4] Here he was probably on safer ground. Certainly there were others before and during Irving's time who expected a Jewish restoration and return to Palestine as a forerunner of the second coming. Indeed, as far back as 1810, Irving himself had said that he expected "the speedy" conversion of the Jews, and Dr. Robert Lorimer, his minister at Haddington, appears to have agreed with him.

Irving's third point was that Christ would then return in judgment, "taking vengeance on those who know not God . . . and raising those who sleep in Jesus." Christ would then set up his kingdom on earth, reigning for a thousand years. Here, Irving was again teaching premillennialism as he had done in his Babylon address. While premillennialism was certainly not new (it had been taught by some even in the early church and had been accepted by others in different eras), in Protestant circles at that time,

---

2. Bennett, *Origins*, 206, 213; Irving, "Preliminary Discourse," in Ben-Ezra, *Coming*, 1:xv–xvii, xxiii–xxv.

3. Irving, "Preliminary Discourse," in Ben-Ezra, *Coming*, 1:iv–vii.

4. Ibid., 1:v–vi.

postmillennialism dominated. That is, it was generally believed that Christ would not return until after an earthly Millennium.

Irving stated that at that time he did not know "one brother in the ministry" who agreed with him "in these matters."[5] It is, in fact, unlikely that any of his Presbyterian brother-ministers would have agreed with him on all three points, though some would have accepted the second and the third. But there was about to begin a movement that was to emphasize all three of these points, as shall be seen, and Irving was to be one of the leaders in that movement, though only for a short time.

The members of Irving's congregation seem to have reacted to these sermons in different ways. Many continued to attend the Caledonian Church and thus displayed either acceptance or indifference to these teachings. However, these sermons appear to have been one of the reasons why some congregants became disillusioned with Irving at around this time.

Lacunza's book fanned Irving's growing interest in the return of Christ to a white heat. For him it was now a major issue, seemingly *the* major issue. In fact, as Irving later told Thomas Chalmers, "The second coming of the Lord is the '*point de vue*,' the vantage ground, as one of my friends [probably Frere] is wont to word it, from which, and from which alone, the whole purpose of God can be contemplated and understood."[6]

By the summer of 1826, Irving was exhausted. That May, Mrs. Montagu told Carlyle that "Mr. Irving is a mere shadow, he will soon be nothing but a voice:—he is more fervent, more zealous, more mystical and more prophetical every day."[7] Later that year she told Jane Welsh, "I saw Mr. Irving yesterday, and either I have lost the habit of looking at the sunshine rather than the shade, or he gave me the impression that his own little girl was very unwell, and in that same terrible complaint of which the Boy died—something is wrong in the lungs of the Children, and their Father looks as if he

5. Ibid., 1:vi–vii, xiv. For Lorimer, see also Irving, *DL*, 32. For the restoration of the Jews in Protestant thought, see Bennett, *Origins*, 123–30, 184–85, 204–206. For premillennialism in the early church and in Protestant circles prior to Edward Irving, see ibid., 86–98, 145–52, 175–78, 202–203.

6. Irving to Thomas Chalmers, December 1828, quoted in Oliphant, *Life*, 2:68. Lee argues that "The reconciliation of God and humanity through Christ [that] was attainable mainly through the work of the Holy Spirit . . . was a key to his theological framework" (Lee, "Christ's Sinful Flesh," 16). That certainly was "a key," but his eschatology seems to have been *the* key.

7. Mrs. Montagu to Thomas Carlyle, May 13, 1826, *CLO*; see Thomas Carlyle to Jane Baillie Welsh, [May 31 ?], 1826, n. 1, *CLO*.

was consumptive."[8] Coleridge, too, feared that Irving's excessive exertions would "shorten his life" and thus "rob Mankind of his future Self."[9]

The leaders of his church, also concerned about Irving's health, urged him to take time off and gave him access to a country home in Beckenham, Kent, to rest. Irving took the opportunity, but resting to Irving always involved some kind of work. He decided to make good use of the time by translating Lacunza's book from the Spanish into English. In November the previous year Irving had made contact with the Sottomayor brothers, two Spanish Catholics who had become Protestants. One had been a Catholic priest, the other a soldier. Irving began to take daily lessons in Spanish from Giuseppe Sottomayor, the soldier. Their textbooks were the Spanish Bible and *Don Quixote*.[10] These lessons now stood him in good stead.

Irving's rest, then, was translation during the week, with a return to London to attend to at least some of his ministerial duties each weekend. But however imperfect this rest may have been, it did seem to restore his health and energy. Isabella was able to tell one of her sisters, "I rejoice to tell you that Edward is very much better."[11] Perhaps being removed from the incessant calls of his normal ministerial life for five days each week took the pressure off his wearied mind and body. The English translation of the book was eventually published in 1827 with a "Preliminary Discourse" by Irving that ran to over 180 pages.

Interpretation of the book of Revelation has always been a battlefield and, one might add, a minefield. Since the Reformation, the vast majority of Protestants had a historicist understanding of Revelation, regarding it as prophesying the history of the church. In this scheme, the 1,260 days (or 42 months: 42 x 30 = 1,260 days) of Rev 11–13 stood for 1,260 *years* of the beast's reign, and that beast was nearly always identified with the pope or the Catholic Church. Thus the pope was usually seen as the Antichrist, and the rule of this Antichrist had already been going on for centuries. As time passed, interpreters tended to move forward the commencement date of the 1,260-year period, thus advancing the closing date, which was usually thought to signal the return of Christ. A number of interpreters settled on the year 606 as the date the Antichrist emerged. Add 1,260 to 606, and you arrive at 1866, a year that seemed very close to those interpreting the

8. Mrs. Montagu to Jane Baillie Welsh, August 7, 1826, *CLO*; see Jane Baillie Welsh to Thomas Carlyle, August 31, 1826, n. 4, *CLO*.

9. Samuel Taylor Coleridge to Basil Montagu, February 1, 1826, in Coleridge, *CLSTC*, 5:550.

10. Irving's journal, October 31 and November 28, 1825, quoted in Oliphant, *Life*, 1:254 n., 278–79, 365–66.

11. Ibid., 1:384–87.

prophetic Scriptures in the late 1820s, which inevitably filled them with great excitement.

The Catholics had countered this historicism by giving Revelation a futurist interpretation, mainly through the work of the sixteenth-century scholars Francisco Ribera and Robert Bellarmine. Futurism argued that the book of Revelation from chapter 4 prophesied events that are still in the future, and that the 1,260 days of Antichrist's reign were, indeed, 1,260 *days*. A tiny handful of Protestant interpreters had also adopted a futurist understanding in the seventeenth and eighteenth centuries, but by far the majority was historicist until well into the nineteenth century.[12]

Lacunza's book taught futurism. It also taught premillennialism, though Lacunza did not claim certainty about the duration of Christ's reign on earth. He also taught that the Jews would return to Palestine and that there would be a period of tribulation immediately before Christ's return.[13]

Reading Lacunza confirmed Irving in his recently adopted premillennial beliefs. In fact, he regarded Lacunza's book as "the finest demonstration of the orthodoxy of the ancient system of the millenarians which can be imagined; indeed, I may say perfect and irrefragable." It was also, in fact, "the finest specimen of Logic."[14] Yet he initially rejected Lacunza's futurism. He continued to hold to the historicist interpretation until at least 1828 before finally accepting futurism.[15]

Irving's sentiments on the importance of these issues were dramatically expressed in his dedication to Lacunza's book, which begins:

> My soul is greatly afflicted because of the present unawakened and even dead condition of all the churches, with respect to the coming of our Lord Jesus Christ, which draweth nigh, and which, as I believe, is close at hand: and having, by God's especial providence, been brought to the knowledge of a book, written in the Spanish tongue, which clearly sets forth, and demonstrates from Holy Scripture, the erroneousness of the opinion, almost universally entertained amongst us, that He is not to come till the end of the millennium, and what you call the *last day* . . . I have thought it my duty to translate the same into the English tongue for your sake, that you may be able to disabuse yourselves of that great error.

12. Bennett, *Origins*, 118–22, 176–77, 180, 219.

13. Ben-Ezra, *Coming*, 1:67–69, 80–83, 92, 106–107; Bennett, *Origins*, 207–209.

14. Irving, "Preliminary Discourse," in Ben-Ezra, *Coming*, 1:xxvi; Irving to Thomas Chalmers, May 31, 1827, in Irving, *DL*, 241.

15. Bennett, *Origins*, 214–16.

Irving continued by urging his readers to "diligently apply" themselves "to the Holy Scriptures . . . upon this subject of Messiah's advent" to gain what he considered to be a better understanding of it. In this dedication, then, Irving clearly and dogmatically rejected the postmillennialism of many of his fellow ministers. He was sure that the days in which they lived were "the last time, because it is written [2 Pet 3:3–4], 'there shall come in the last days scoffers saying, "Where is the hope of his coming?"'"[16]

Irving knew that by translating this work and stating his own similar views in the lengthy "Preliminary Discourse," he was once more putting his head in the hornet's nest. Never one to moderate in his language when a battle was to be waged, he said that he believed that the book "bore hard against the stream of common opinion" and he had considered how he might best defend himself "from the storm which would be raised against it on all hands by the British Inquisition, whose ignorance of truth I knew to be equaled only by their malice against everything which touched the infallibility of their idol Public Opinion." British Inquisition? Surely Britain was tolerant. It no longer burned heretics at the stake or tortured those of dubious views.

But this Inquisition was:

> that court whose ministers and agents carry on their operations in secret; who drag every man's most private affairs before the sight of thousands and seek to mangle and destroy his life as an instructor trying him without a witness, condemning him without hearing, nor suffering him to speak for himself, intermeddling in things of which they have no knowledge, and cannot on any principle have a jurisdiction; and defacing and deforming the finest beauty and the profoundest wisdom by the rancor of their malice. I mean those who set principle, who set truth, who set feeling, who set justice, who set every thing sacred up to sale. I mean the ignorant, unprincipled, unhallowed spirit of criticism, which in this Protestant country is producing as foul effects against truth, and by as dishonest means, as ever did the Inquisition of Rome.[17]

What had stirred Irving to this invective? He hints at one answer to that question a little later in the "Preliminary Discourse," where he argued that the church had "become review-ridden to a most alarming degree." His earlier books had not generally received good reviews, and some of the

---

16. Irving, "Dedication," in Ben-Ezra, *Coming*, 1:i–ii.
17. Ibid., 1:xxi–xxiii.

arguments used against him in those articles must have hurt more than he had previously indicated. But one senses that there was more to it than that.

A little later Henry Drummond was to publish a book that was a report on some conversations with Irving and others about Christ's second coming. Drummond claimed that "all" the religious magazines "of every creed, party, and denomination" attacked the ideas in this book, regarding them as "novel" and of "modern invention."[18] This suggests that Irving's camp was very sensitive to reviews and articles criticizing their books and ideas.

Strikingly, however, Irving stated that he had sent a "goodly portion" of the translation of Lacunza's book before publication to "ministers and members of the Church of Christ, who should seem to be the most honourable, simple-minded, and single-eyed before the Lord." These included Irving's father-in-law, Rev. John Martin; Thomas Chalmers and Dr. Robert Gordon of the Scottish Church; Hon. J. J. Strutt, an Anglican layman who attended at least one Albury Conference; and Samuel Taylor Coleridge.

Irving asked them to send him "any observations which might occur to them as likely to improve the work, that I might embody them in the notes . . . And the result was, that, though they were taken from all denominations of the Church, I received nothing but the highest approbation of the spirit of the writer and the power of his argument."[19] Such general approbation, if such there was, he knew would not greet the book upon publication. His list of readers had been carefully selected. Even then, it seems that Chalmers did not respond (he often avoided controversy), and Coleridge and John Martin each later expressed strong reservations about Irving's eschatology. Irving did at times see agreement where agreement did not exist or was, at best, qualified.

In addition, Irving must have known that his negative comments in this "Preliminary Discourse" would further enflame his enemies. Irving was not to be disappointed. He had lit a torch, and he would get burned. He had become the master of losing friends, but he could still influence people in the process.

The *Congregational Magazine* justly criticized Irving and his associates for "making the adoption of their interpretation a matter of *sacred duty*, and in insisting that to deny the Millenarian scheme is to deny the glory of God, and prove ourselves wanting in faith." It described Irving's teachings about the Millennium and the return of the Jews as speculation.[20]

18. Drummond, *Dialogues*, 1:iv.

19. Irving, "Dedication," in Ben-Ezra, *Coming*, 1:xxii; Irving to J. J. Strutt and Thomas Chalmers, September 12, 1826, in Irving, *DL*, 229–30; Irving to Thomas Chalmers, April 27, 1827, in ibid., 240.

20. "Review of Books—Works on Prophecy," in *Congregational Magazine*, July

However, Lacunza's book became influential in Protestant circles, though more indirectly than directly. Some clergy and leading members of the laity were influenced by its teachings, which they then passed on to those in their charge. In fact, the publication of Irving's translation of Lacunza (in early 1827) marks the beginning of the major rise of futurism in Protestant circles, and it also promoted a significant increase in the acceptance of premillennialism.

Jane Carlyle received a copy of the book in the middle of September. She told a relative, "Edward Irvings [sic] book out of the Spanish came last night and also a copy for his father with a great bundle of preliminary discourses 'to be *distributed among his kindred and addressed to them with his own hand.*'"[21] It is clear from this that Irving intended his "Preliminary Discourse" to have a life of its own, and it is essentially a book in its own right.

A little later, Jane's husband said,

> I have heard several times from the Caledonian Orator of late. He does *not* seem in the least millenniary in his letters: but the same old friendly man we have long known him to be. And yet his printed works are enough to strike one blank with amazement . . . To the last, there is and will be a bee in his bonnet, which only in every new generation buzzes with a new note![22]

Indeed, Irving's future course was to further distance him from the Carlyles.

HIS GREATEST SERMON?

On March 15, 1827, Irving preached what is often considered to be his best sermon. It was the ordination address for the Reverend Hugh McLean, who had been called to the Scots Church at London Wall. A. L. Drummond regarded the published address as "without a peer in theological literature." H. C. Whitley described it as "a magnificent piece of oratory," while Arnold Dallimore called it "Edward Irving at his best," and he seems to have meant at his best not just as a speaker or as one who understood the life and role of the minister, but at his best as a man. What Irving was charging McLean to be was what he hoped and tried to be himself.[23] In fact, the sermon offers wonderful insight into Irving's philosophy of ministry.

1827, 377.

21. Jane Welsh Carlyle to John A. Carlyle, September 13, 1827, *CLO.*

22. Thomas Carlyle to David Hope, December 12, 1827.

23. Drummond, *Edward Irving,* 71; Whitley, *Blinded Eagle,* 23; Dallimore, *Life,* 73.

This sermon contained "five heads: first, the student or scholar, secondly, the preacher or minister, thirdly, the pastor, fourthly, the churchman, and fifthly, the man." First, then, Irving urged McLean "to grow in all knowledge and in all wisdom . . . but especially in the Holy Scriptures . . . This you must set yourself to do as a part of your bounden duty, perfecting yourself in the knowledge of the original tongues and applying yourself to the critical study of the Scriptures," which have a unique oneness.[24]

Irving then charged McLean, as a preacher or minister, to so thoroughly know and understand the church's ordinances so as to be able to conduct them "without the help of any service book." To properly understand the "sacraments," McLean should "study from the Scriptures, or any author older than a century; but at [his] peril from any later." He instructed McLean to use the biblical psalms wisely in worship, for "they are the essence of divine truth," and also to make the difficult task of public prayer his "especial care."[25]

Specifically with regard to preaching Irving said, "Take thy liberty . . . beat down the enemies of the Lord; wound and heal; break down and build up again. Be of no school; give heed to none of their rules or canons . . . be fettered by no times," as Irving never was, "accommodate no man's conveniency, spare no man's prejudice, yield to no man's inclinations . . . Preach the Gospel: not the Gospel of the last age, or of this age, but the everlasting Gospel; not Christ crucified merely, but Christ risen; not Christ risen merely, but Christ present in the Spirit, and Christ to be again present in person . . . Keep not thy people banqueting, but bring them out to do battle for the glory of God and of His church."[26]

Under the third heading, the pastoral, Irving said, "Be thou the pastor always; less than the pastor, never." He urged McLean to visit his people in the company of an elder, but also to be ready to receive his people when they sought his "counsel" and "prayers," and he told McLean, "Thou must be willing to give thy life for every one of them, to wash their feet, to minister to them in health and in sickness, in wealth and in poverty, in good and in bad report. For why? Because they are the Lord's."[27]

Fourthly, Irving urged McLean to follow in the traditions and teaching of the Scottish Church, "imbuing" himself "with the spirit of our reformers, and martyrs, and covenanters." With regard to relationships with other denominations, Irving said, "As a churchman thou owest brotherly love to

24. Irving, *CW*, 1:527–28.
25. Ibid., 1:530–31.
26. Ibid.
27. Ibid., 1:532–34.

the Church of England . . . but thou owest also rebuke and reproof for her backslidings in doctrine and discipline . . . To the Nonconformists also, who hold sound doctrine, thou owest brotherly love; and rebuke and reproof also thou owest them for their uncharitable spirit towards us . . . To the Papacy, and to the Socinian [who rejects the deity of Christ], thou owest no mercy. Unfold their vileness, cry against them with all thy might. Superstition on one hand, liberality on the other . . . thou must fight against with the two-edged sword of the faith."[28]

Yet all this would be wasted if McLean did not attend to the last point, the development of himself as a Christian man. Irving urged him to be hospitable, to "accumulate riches at [his] peril," and to "speak out against Mammon." Indeed, he should tell the rich "what they should do with their treasures [and to] reprove them and their accumulations sharply." No wonder many of the wealthy soon deserted Irving. "Oh, be thou a man far above this world living by faith in the world to come . . . Be thou of a bold countenance and a lion heart, of a single heart and a simple spirit . . . be faithful unto Christ and no other allegiance."

But "Who is sufficient for these things?" Irving asked. He knew as well as anyone that pastoral ministry was difficult and demanding. It could be suffocating or isolating, joyous or sad. It needed more than human strength. "Who is sufficient for these things? Thou art," he declared, "Christ strengthening thee."[29]

This remarkable address is powerful to read. One can only imagine how powerful it was to hear. It is kind, it is stern, it is intelligent, it is emotive, it is thought provoking, and it is, above all, challenging. To us, it appears in words that leap off the page. Hugh McLean must have been stirred to the very depths of his being by it. It is perhaps no coincidence that McLean was later expelled from the Presbyterian Church for taking the same view of the human nature of Christ as Irving would.[30]

THE IMPACT OF MARY IRVING

A second daughter called Mary was born to the Irvings in the spring of 1827, but she died that December. The birth and death of their daughter left Isabella in a poor physical state. Even her husband, in one of his more

---

28. Ibid., 1:534–36.
29. Ibid., 1:537–39.
30. Oliphant, *Life*, 2:121–22.

desperate moments, stated that he grieved over his "vexed life" and longed "to be delivered from it."[31]

It was probably the Sunday after Mary's death that he preached a remarkable sermon to a deeply moved congregation from the text, "I shall go to him, but he shall not return to me" (2 Sam 12:23), the words of David after the death of his infant son.[32] It is still a touching sermon to read today, when well removed from its original circumstances. The reader, even now, feels Irving's struggles.

He knew, of course, that others in his congregation had suffered similar blows, and this sermon was especially addressed to them to comfort and assist them as well as, no doubt, to minister to his own heart. "In the present life," he consoled, "the innocent infant may suffer with and for its parents," but "in the life that is to come it is regarded by God as standing in itself alone; and that the most unfortunate of infants in their birth and in their life may, after their death, pass at once into the most blessed of the saints of God . . . Yet . . . when it is God's will to take, He will take, even though the man after His own heart should lie low before Him in sackcloth and Ashes."[33]

Yet, he was still, as always, the theologian. He went on to argue that the death of infants demonstrated that death was not "the consequence of our personal sinfulness," as infants were "innocent of all actual transgression," but rather it was the "natural inheritance of all mankind."[34]

---

31. Ibid., 1:414.

32. Oliphant suggests that this sermon was preached in 1830 after the death of Samuel (Oliphant, *Life*, 2:147), but Grass argues cogently that it was after the death of Mary in 1827 (Grass, *Edward Irving*, 125–27).

33. Irving, "On the Death of Children," in Irving, *CW*, 4:367–68.

34. Ibid., 369–70.

11

The Albury Conferences

Oh Albury! most honoured of the King
And Potentate of heaven; whose presence here
We daily look for! In thy silent halls
His servants sought, and found such harmony
Of blessed expectation, as did fill
Their hearts with lively joy . . .
That the sweet odour of those hallowed hours
May never from our souls depart . . .

—EDWARD IRVING[1]

THE PROPHETIC SCHOOL

While Irving was translating Lacunza's book, two other related events took place with regard to the study of the Bible's teaching on the last days. In the summer of 1826, Irving, Way, and Frere formed the Society for the Investigation of Prophecy, and the members of that society met at different times that year to discuss prophetic issues. Henry Drummond and Irving then called a conference at Albury, Drummond's estate, just before the end of the year, at Advent, especially to discuss biblical prophecy and the Second

1. Ibid., "Preliminary Discourse," in Ben-Ezra, *Coming*, cxcii.

Advent. Drummond seems to have suggested the conference and its location, Irving its appropriate timing.[2] These Albury Conferences continued to be held at the end of each year until 1829.

These meetings were not mass events, but were each attended by twenty to twenty-five invited clergy and laity. They were think tanks rather than preaching extravaganzas—that is, "not a venue for the curious, but a workshop for the convinced."[3] All told, over forty men attended one or more of these conferences, and at least one woman, Lady Powerscourt, was a guest. These included nineteen Church of England clergymen, four ministers from the Church of Scotland, and eleven English laymen. Amongst them were Irving, Drummond, Robert Story, Way, Frere, and the eccentric Jewish convert Joseph Wolff. Hugh McNeile, Rector of Albury, chaired the meetings.[4] It can be correctly assumed from this that Irving had a considerable influence over numerous Anglican evangelicals.[5] In this chapter we will consider mainly the first two of these conferences, and in chapter 13 we will examine the third and fourth.

To set the scene we will use an unusual but wonderfully descriptive account of an Albury Conference (1828)[6] that appears in a letter from Irving to his three-year-old daughter Margaret. It says something unique about Albury and portrays the warmth of Irving's relationship with his children.

> My Maggy,
> Papa is living in a great house with a great many men who preach. The house is Mr. Drummond's and Lady Harriet Drummond's . . . This house where we live is all round with great trees, like grand-papa's, and the black crows build their nests, and always cry caw, caw, caw. There is a sweet, little river that runs murmuring along, making a gentle noise among the trees. And there is a large, large garden . . . We are all reading the Bible, which is God's word—the book we read at worship. God speaks to us in that book, and we tell one another what he tells to us. Every morning, about half-past six o'clock, a man goes round and awakens us all. Then, soon after, comes a maid, like Elizabeth, and puts on a fire in all our rooms, and then we get up . . .

2. Irving to Henry Drummond, September 4, 1826, in Irving, *DL*, 228.

3. Patterson, "Designing," 64.

4. Bennett, *Origins*, 218; Irving, "Preliminary Discourse," in Ben-Ezra, *Coming*, clxxxiii–clxxxix; Story, *Memoir*, 102.

5. See also Brown, "Victorian Anglican Evangelicalism," 675–704, especially 679–80.

6. Oliphant says that this was the second conference, but because the letter appears to have been written in 1828, it must have been the third (Oliphant, *Life*, 2:61).

Then we go down stairs into a great room and sit round a great table, and speak concerning God and Christ.[7]

Irving then drew a picture of the table with the names of the various delegates, indicating where each was sitting. He closed, "But it is time for dinner. Farewell, my dear Maggy. Mamma will tell all this to you, and you must tell it all to Miss McDonald and little brother. The Lord bless my Maggy! Your Papa, Edward Irving."[8]

Robert Story told a friend that the Albury Conference he attended consisted:

> of a great variety of talent and accomplishment, and, upon the whole, of singular unity of spirit and feeling. Its prominent character was at once devotional and rational. Freedom of judgment, earnestness of inquiry, willingness of persuasion, enthusiasm without rashness, zeal without intolerance, speculation without levity, prediction without bold presumption, unraveling without the destroying of mystery, examination without irreverence of the Divine decrees, are so many attributes expressive of the proceedings of those memorable days.[9]

Irving also gave a rough timetable of events at the first conference in his "Preliminary Discourse." According to this, they dealt with just one subject on each of the six days, except on one day when they combined two related topics. Each day was divided into three segments. The first was before breakfast at 8:00 a.m., in which they first sought "the Lord" for the graces "necessary and proper" for the day's labors, and then an appointed speaker briefly opened the day's subject. After breakfast they gathered again at eleven, and the Moderator asked each member to comment on the chosen subject. This session lasted four or five hours. They met once more after dinner at about 7:00 p.m. and discussed the day's subject in a more relaxed and informal way to try to sort out any difficulties that had arisen. They finally closed the day at about eleven by singing a hymn and praying.[10]

The prevailing hermeneutic at the conferences was to take the Bible literally, but allowing for "figures and metaphors" and seeing all through a premillennial lens. Allied with this was the use of biblical typology, which, ironically, at times forced them to interpret non-literally. In addition, they

7. Margaret Irving, December 1828, quoted in ibid., 2:62.

8. Ibid., 2:62.

9. Story, *Memoir*, 103–104.

10. Irving, "Preliminary Discourse," in Ben-Ezra, *Coming*, cxc–cxcii.

adopted the practice, probably inherited from Frere, of regarding each prophetic symbol as having only one meaning throughout the Bible.[11]

At the first Albury Conference, the topics discussed included "the times of the Gentiles," the state and prospects of the Jews, the "visions and numbers of Daniel and the Apocalypse," and the Second Advent. Irving claimed that they were generally in harmony on all these matters.[12] In fact, Drummond cited six points discussed at Albury that year on which there had been general agreement: first, this "present Christian dispensation [will] be terminated by judgments"; secondly, during those judgments "The Jews will be restored to their own land"; thirdly, these judgments would fall "principally, if not exclusively, upon Christendom"; fourthly, the Millennium will occur after these judgments; fifthly, Christ's return will be premillennial; and sixthly, "The 1260 *years* commenced in the reign of Justinian" (in the sixth century) and ended during the French Revolution, which means "that our blessed Lord will shortly appear."[13] So, in line with Irving at that time, Albury was premillennial and historicist and expected Christ to return soon—very soon. Attention was focused on Irving's edition of Lacunza's work in the conference of 1827.[14]

Irving stated that it was decided by the Albury Delegates "that nothing should go forth from the meeting with any stamp of authority, that the church might not take offence."[15] However, Drummond said that "a publication in the form of Dialogues was suggested" and he published a work, eventually printed in three volumes, called *Dialogues on Prophecy*, which gives a record of their deliberations.

But the accuracy of these volumes was doubted even by the author.[16] However, it does show correctly that the Albury delegates adopted historical and mythical nicknames under which they also sometimes wrote. Such names were commonly used by other writers of that time. However, as Columba Graham Flegg says, attempts "to identify these pseudonyms" has met with only "limited success."[17] It can be said with some certainty that Lewis Way was "Basilicus" and J. Hatley Frere was "Crito." Beyond that, it is very

---

11. Patterson has an extensive section on their hermeneutics; see Patterson, "Designing," 63–98.

12. Irving, "Preliminary Discourse," in Ben-Ezra, *Coming*, 1:clxxxix–cxc.

13. Drummond, *Dialogues*, 1:ii–iii, emphasis added.

14. Ladd, *Blessed*, 36–37.

15. Irving, "Preliminary Discourse," in Ben-Ezra, *Coming*, cxc.

16. Drummond, *Dialogues*, 1:iii; Bennett, *Origins*, 242 n.151.

17. Flegg, "*Gathered*," 38. I have also attempted to make these identifications, and my success has been very limited.

difficult to identify them. It has been claimed that Irving was "Aristo," but there has been a counter claim that he was "Anastasius."

The first "Conversation" recorded in volume one is portrayed as a discussion mainly between three delegates, "Philalethes" (possibly Lord Mandeville), "Anastasius," and "Aristo," with comments in the later stages by "Crito" (Frere), "Evander" (possibly John Bayford), "Theophilus," "Theodorus," "Philemon," "Josephus," "Polydorus," "Basilicus" (Way), and "Sophron." Yet it would seem highly unlikely that only three spoke during the first part of this debate. Indeed, according to this record, if Irving was Aristo, he did not speak until nearly a quarter of the way through, and it is frankly hard to believe that he would have remained silent that long. Perhaps this does suggest that he was Anastasius, who took more of a leading role.

Yet the whole presentation of the discussion sounds rather stage-managed, with, for example, Philalethes being portrayed as the doubter of the value of the study of prophecy who is convinced of its merit by Anastasius.[18] It is very unlikely that Philalethes would have been invited to the conference if he doubted the value of prophetic study, even if he did belong to the aristocracy. In addition, people who appear to have been present are referred to as though they were not. It is probably best to see these *Dialogues* as true in what was discussed and the ideas promoted, but as a very hazy record of the actual details of the discussions.

According to Drummond, the reception that the first edition of *Dialogues* received was very negative. He said that "all" the "Religious Magazines" called the teachings the book contained "novel," of "modern invention," and even heretical.[19] However, the word "all" has to be regarded as hyperbole considering that the Reverend Charles Hawtrey, the editor of *The Jewish Expositor* (the journal of the LSPCJ), attended Albury, though not necessarily in its first year. Hawtrey was an associate of Way and Drummond, and a premillennialist who would also have agreed with Albury's views on the Jews.[20]

It comes as no surprise then that Henry Drummond, in his preface to a later edition, argued that the "last" and "great Apostasy" prophesied in Scripture is "against the kingship of Christ" and that "the Evangelical party is raging as hotly [against it] as the most open infidels." Consequently, "The Kingship of Messiah seems now to be one chief doctrine to shew us who

18. Drummond, *Dialogues*, 1:1–44.

19. Ibid., 1:iv.

20. Stewart, "Millennial Maelstrom," in Gribben and Stunt, *Prisoners*, 138 n. 50, 146. Alexander Haldane, the editor of *The Record*, also attended at least one Albury Conference, though *The Record* did not begin publication until 1828 and Haldane was a strong critic of Irving's "embryo heresies" (Schlossberg, *Silent Revolution*, 76).

is on the Lord's side."[21] What Drummond and, indeed, Irving failed to see was that though many evangelicals opposed Albury's interpretation of the Bible's material on the last days, it did not mean that they were "against the kingship of Christ." They just understood it differently.

Even Irving's father-in-law found himself out of step with Albury's teaching on the end times. He told one of his daughters, "After giving the subject the most careful and impartial consideration I can, I am unable to see things as [Irving] and his friends do; nay, I am more and more convinced they are wrong." In addition, Irving's father-in-law strongly rejected the claim by at least some of the Albury delegates that their interpretations were taught them by the Holy Spirit.[22] And Robert Story, who attended at least one conference, said that he did not approve of the "exclusive way of preaching the advent" in which some of his associates engaged.[23]

THE NEW CHURCH

The foundation stone for Irving's new church had been laid at Regent's Square in the middle of 1824. The architect was William Tite (later Sir William) who also designed the Royal Exchange. The new building was not opened until Friday, May 11, 1827. It was Gothic in style, with twin towers at the front on either side of the main entrance, which originally led to a wide center aisle, and it could accommodate nearly two thousand people. It became known as the National Scotch Church or Regent Square Church.

Even before Irving had arrived in London there had been talk of building a major Scottish church in the capital to cater to Scots in exile. It was believed by some that there were about one hundred thousand Scots living in London at that time; Irving claimed 120,000, though the actual figure may have been much less. Either way, few of them attended a Presbyterian Church. Some attended Church of England churches, others non-conformist chapels, and many, perhaps most, went nowhere. Once Irving had landed and proven so popular, it was thought logical to build this special church to house his ministry.[24] And Irving was ever the Scot. He adored Scottish heritage. No amount of time in England would ever change that.

---

21. Drummond, *Dialogues*, 1:vi.

22. Quoted in Oliphant, *Life*, 2:62–63; John Martin to Elizabeth Martin, December 20, 1827, United Reformed Church Historical Society archive, Cambridge, UK, quoted in Grass, *Edward Irving*, 167 n. 85.

23. Story, *Memoir*, 104.

24. Drummond, *Edward Irving*, 102–105; Hair, *Regent*, 27–30, 185–86, appendix D; Oliphant, *Life*, 1:399–400, 402, 411; Grass, *Edward Irving*, 107–108, 135; Irving and

Dr. Chalmers officiated at the opening, and his account of the proceedings demonstrates one of the reasons why some people deserted Irving. Chalmers complained that the service lasted an hour and a half before it was his turn to rise to speak, with Irving's prayer taking forty minutes. Before the service Irving had told him that he would read a chapter from the Bible and, according to Chalmers, "He chose the very longest." It was, apparently, 1 Kgs 8 (not the longest, but certainly long). Chalmers knew his man when he said, "Irving certainly errs in the outrunning of sympathy." But Irving either did not understand the feelings of those in the pews or chose to ignore them.

On another occasion, according to Chalmers, Irving offered to read a chapter from the Bible for him, adding, "I can be short," having no doubt sensed the older man's concerns. But Chalmers was wary. "How long will it take you?" he asked. "Only an hour and forty minutes," responded Irving. This presumably was an exaggeration by Chalmers, but Irving simply did not know how to do things briefly. His short was another man's long. And his long taxed the patience of many of those who heard him as much as it taxed his own energy. The Reverend Gordon also reported that at around this time he heard Irving preach on the return of Christ in a sermon that lasted two-and-a-half hours. Not surprisingly, by the end of it "the people were dropping away."[25]

Upon the opening of the new church, the session issued a directive that was more significant than they knew at the time. The first part was taken from the *Directory for the Public Worship of God*, an official document dated 1645. It declared, "That all the people meet so timely for public worship that the whole congregation may be present at the beginning . . . and not depart till after the blessing." The elders added a statement urging their people to follow this instruction, that they might "maintain a just regard to the honour of the worship of God, and to the comfort and peace of their fellow-worshippers."[26] Yet later, there were many in the congregation who felt that certain events disrupted the worship of God and interfered with the comfort and peace of the congregation.

---

his Session to Thomas Chalmers, February 26, 1827, in Irving, *DL*, 235. London's population was about one-and-a-half million at that time, and it seems unlikely that over 7 percent of them would have been Scottish, even allowing for considerable migration from different parts of the British Isles, including Scotland (Inwood, *History of London*, 411–12).

25. Hanna, *Memoirs* (New York) 3:168, 171; Oliphant, *Life*, 1:403–404; Grass, *Edward Irving*, 109.

26. Hair, *Regent*, 42.

While many had left Irving by this time and an ever-increasing controversy raged around him, he was still attracting new people to his church. In one year in the late 1820s, nearly 180 new communicants were added at Regent Square.[27]

BACK TO SCOTLAND

In May 1828 Isabella, still unwell and pregnant again, went to visit her relatives in Scotland. Edward soon followed her. But his mission was not primarily to visit friends and old haunts, but rather to attend the Presbyterian Church's General Assembly and to promote the teachings of Albury in his native land. If one believes that the return of Christ is to occur within forty years, as Irving did by this time, it is easy to become obsessed by that idea and to desire to proclaim that message with great urgency to everyone.

He first joined his wife in Kirkcaldy and then preached in Annan and Dumfries before going on to Edinburgh. He was given a hero's welcome, particularly in his hometown, with nearby churches closing on Sunday so that their ministers and congregations could journey to Annan to hear him.

In Edinburgh he gave a series of twelve addresses on the subject of prophecy, initially at St. Andrew's Church. Even though each lecture began at 6:00 a.m., the church was always packed. The early hour was set to avoid clashing with the Assembly. Thomas Chalmers reported that Irving was drawing "prodigious crowds" and that one morning "We attempted to force our way into St. Andrew's Church; but it was all in vain."[28] Even at six in the morning one had to arrive early to gain admittance. When it became clear that St. Andrew's was too small, they moved to the West Church, which, with three galleries, was the largest in Edinburgh, but that too was uncomfortably filled each day.

This move, however, at least gave Chalmers a chance to hear Irving,[29] but he was not impressed. Chalmers complained to his sister "I scarcely understood a single word, nor do I comprehend the ground on which he goes in his violent allegorizations, chiefly of the Old Testament."[30] In his journal, Chalmers described Irving's address as "obscure" and "quite woeful. There is power and richness, and gleams of exquisite beauty, but withal, a mysticism and an extreme allegorization which I am sure must be pernicious to

27. Irving to Thomas Chalmers, n.d., quoted in Oliphant, *Life*, 2:118.

28. Oliphant, *Life*, 2:14–19.

29. Ibid., 23. See also Thomas Chalmers, journal entry, May 24, 1828, in Hanna, *Memoirs* (New York), 3:225.

30. Thomas Chalmers to his sister, June 18, 1828, in ibid., 3:225–26.

the general cause."[31] It is striking that Chalmers should twice charge Irving with allegorizing the Scriptures, for Irving would have insisted that he and his associates at Albury interpreted the Bible literally, not allegorically.

Thomas Carlyle was in town at this time, and he reported to his brother,

> We left Edward Irving [in Edinburgh], preaching like a Bo[a] nerges [on the return of Christ], with (as Henry Inglis very naively remarked) "the town quite divided about him, one party thinking that he was quite mad, another that he was an entire humbug." For my own share I would not be intolerant of any so worthy man; but I cannot help thinking that if Irving is on the road to truth, it is no straight one. We had a visit from him, and positively there does seem a touch of extreme exaltation in him: I do not think he will go altogether mad, yet what else he will do I cannot so well conjecture. Cant and Enthusiasm are strangely commingled in him.[32]

As Irving left Carlyle at the end of their brief meeting on this visit he said, "I must go, then—and suffer persecution, as my fathers have done."[33] Whether "persecution" was quite the right word might be argued, but there certainly was to be considerable opposition.

When the time for the Assembly arrived, Chalmers took one side on a particular issue, while Irving, who did not hold an official position at the Assembly, was still "wild upon the other side." In fact, Chalmers recorded that while he was addressing the meeting, Irving sat opposite him "as if his eye and looks, seen through the railing, were stationed there for my disquietude." They were two very different men. H. C. Whitley exaggerated only slightly when he said that "they had nothing in common."[34] In addition, according to Chalmers, at this time Irving "had a regular collision with a Dr. H., a violent sectarian, who denounced Irving as an enemy to the gospel of Jesus Christ."[35]

After the Assembly Irving journeyed to Glasgow, Carnwath, Rosneath, Row (also known as Ruh), and Bathgate, preaching in each place, usually on various aspects of the return of Christ. In Rosneath the church was too small to hold all those wishing to hear him, so Irving had to preach in a tent. Also in Rosneath, he met Alexander (Sandy) Scott (1805–1866), a ministerial probationer in the Church of Scotland who was at that time developing

31. Ibid., 3:225–26.
32. Thomas Carlyle to John A. Carlyle, June 10, 1828, CLO.
33. Carlyle, Reminiscences (Norton), 2:186.
34. Whitley, Blinded Eagle, 101.
35. Hanna, Memoirs (New York), 3:225.

the belief that the charismata of the New Testament church were still available. Irving said in a letter to his wife that he hoped God would deliver Scott from the "present deep waters" that covered him, caused, it would appear, by this teaching.[36]

In Row, Irving had an encounter with John McLeod Campbell (1800–1872), who was drifting from Westminster orthodoxy by teaching that Christ died for all.[37] However, in a letter to Isabella, Irving made it clear that Campbell's understanding was not that all would be saved, as in universalism, for it was still "the will of God to give eternal life by the Holy Ghost to whom it pleaseth Him." And Irving agreed with that "truth."[38]

Back in 1824 Irving had distinguished between favoritism and the grace that elects, the first being alien to God, the second being one of his most wonderful characteristics. No one can "attribute his religious condition," Irving declared:

> to favouritism. It is an act of grace but it is not an act of favouritism. An act of favouritism lies in exalting us at the expense of another, or over the head of another, who hath laboured as well for the prize. An act of grace lies in exalting us at all. An act of favouritism would cease if all were equally exalted. An act of grace would only be made the greater . . . An act of favouritism reflects upon others. An act of grace does not. An act of favouritism springs from weakness, and engenders vanity. An act of grace springs from goodness, and engenders gratitude.[39]

He, in fact, did not "object to the use of expressions that Scripture sanctions," such as "chosen of God, elect of God, people of God."[40]

In addition, in 1826 he had called Arminianism "false doctrine" and early in 1827 he had referred to "the Arminian heresy."[41] Even late in 1828 he could speak of "the commonness of the redemption and the personality of the election" being compatible doctrines. He went on "the former without

---

36. Irving to Isabella Irving, June 10, 1828, quoted in Oliphant, *Life*, 2:27. See also ibid., 2:23–29.

37. Dallimore, *Life*, 87–88 n. 597; Campbell, *Memorials*, 1:51–53; Strachan, *Pentecostal*, 15.

38. Irving to Isabella Irving, August 4, 1828, quoted in Oliphant, *Life*, 2:48. Thomas F. Torrance also argues that this was Campbell's view (Torrance, *Scottish Theology*, 287–88, 302).

39. Irving, "On Prayer," in Irving, *CW*, 3:54–55. For 1826, see ibid., *Babylon*, 2:184.

40. Ibid.

41. Ibid., *Babylon*, 2:346; ibid., "Preliminary Discourse," in Ben Ezra, *Coming*, viii.

the latter degenerates into universal salvation; the latter without the former degenerates into blind and absolute fate, partiality, or favouritism."[42]

An article in *The Quarterly Journal of Prophecy*, probably written by Horatius Bonar, pointed out a change in 1829. The article said that Irving's Calvinism was originally "high and uncompromising." Yet the writer detected a significant shift in a sermon preached in Scotland that year, in which Irving said that redemption preceded election. In other words, that God elected out of those already redeemed.[43] Yet even as late as 1830 Irving still believed that "our nature is all sinful" and that humanity was "altogether sinful without the power of" self-redemption,[44] so presumably he still held the doctrine of total depravity.

John McLeod Campbell, coincidentally, had considered the vacancy at the Caledonian Chapel some time before Irving became involved.[45] Irving told his wife that he was "much delighted" with both Campbell and Scott. When Irving returned to London, Campbell soon followed, and on three Sundays he preached in Irving's church, where he was well received.[46] Scott followed too and became Irving's assistant that same year.

How much Campbell influenced Irving might be debated, though they clearly had a lot of respect and time for one another. On one occasion Irving said to him, "Dear Campbell, may your bosom be a pillow for me to rest upon, and my arm a staff for you to lean upon." Campbell claimed that he was a major influence in Irving accepting universal atonement. For his part, Irving gladly acknowledged some of Campbell's input into his thinking.[47]

However, one area in which Campbell does not seem to have influenced Irving was with regard to Christ's death. Campbell had a very strong emphasis upon the cross of Christ, while Irving placed less stress upon it. Campbell once wrote, "Although I should live a thousand years of Christian usefulness, I would die looking to the Cross of Christ as I did at first—as simply as I would ask one to do who never looked at the Cross before . . . Look steadfastly at the Cross of Christ, and freely, and yield your heart to all the comfort of it and all the hope."[48]

---

42. Ibid., "Doctrine of the Incarnation," in Irving, *CW*, 5:181–82.

43. "Edward Irving," 234.

44. Irving to Marcus Dods, March 8, 1830, in Irving, *DL*, 267.

45. Campbell, *Memorials*, 1:8.

46. Oliphant, *Life*, 2:27, 34–35, quoting letters from Irving to his wife, June 10 and July 19, 1828.

47. Campbell, *Memorials*, 1:53–54. For a more detailed examination of Irving's view on the universality of the atonement, see Lee, "Christ's Sinful Flesh," 78–91. Lee argues that Irving's view was not exactly the same as Campbell's.

48. John McLeod Campbell to Neil Campbell, December 8, 1857, in Campbell,

Sandy Scott clearly influenced Irving. Irving called Scott "a most pre-cocious youth" who had "the finest and the strongest faculty for pure theol-ogy" that he had encountered, with "very great discernment in the truth."[49] Irving was already deeply considering the ministry of the Holy Spirit, so Scott's ideas about the charismata were fuel for the fire. In 1830, both Scott and Campbell were to be charged with heresy by the General Assembly.

To conclude the post-Assembly Scottish tour, it was back to Edinburgh and then on to the familiar territory of Kirkcaldy, where Irving's wife was soon to give birth and where one of her sisters was due to be married. What should have been a happy visit proved to be anything but. On the evening of Sunday, June 15, as Irving was on his way to the church to preach, he saw a man in an agitated state running to meet him. The messenger carried the terrible news that the gallery on the northern side of the church had col-lapsed under the weight of too many people, and panic had followed. Irving hurried to the scene and was confronted by chaos, with people battling their way down the stairs, pushing and falling. He then stationed himself at the foot of a staircase, hoping that his presence might bring calm and helping as many as he could to safety. The situation was clearly very serious, for already a growing number of injured people in varying degrees of distress were gathering on the grass outside the church.

Sandy Chalmers, the surgeon brother of Thomas, was in the church that evening with Thomas's wife and four of his children, who were on holi-day. Thomas's daughter, Eliza Chalmers, and Sandy's wife were actually in the gallery that fell, while other members of the family, including Thomas's wife, were seated below the opposite gallery, which everyone expected would also fall. Sandy Chalmers had to exit through a window. When he had made his escape, he quickly set to work attending the dozens of injured who were lying and sitting on the ground. It was later reported that no less than twenty-eight people were killed, most in the panic to reach the exits. All the members of the Chalmers family escaped injury, apart from a few bruises.

Irving was distraught. When he finally returned to his lodgings, he retreated into his room and wept. He spent the next few days visiting the bereaved and injured, offering what comfort he could. Sadly, in the way

Memorials, 1:304. See also Jinkins and Reid, "John McLeod Campbell," 135–49. My article titled "Was Edward Irving an Evangelical?" includes an examination of Irving's attitude to the cross; see my Edward Irving website, www.edwardirving.org.

49. Irving to Thomas Chalmers, December 1828, quoted in Oliphant, Life, 2:68; Irving to Rev. Martin, May 27, 1830, quoted in ibid., 2:126. David Brown, Scott's successor at Regent Square, had a much lower opinion of him (Brown, "Personal Remi-niscences," 219).

that logic twists after such events, some of the locals blamed him for the catastrophe.

Not surprisingly considering the chaos, different versions of the story emerged. Thomas Chalmers said that Irving was in the vestry at the time of the accident.[50] A third version appeared in a letter by an unnamed writer who does not seem to have been present. This was printed in a broadside (a one-sheet newspaper) that week stating that the service was nearing its end when the accident occurred.[51] However, Irving stated in a letter written later that evening that the accident "took place a few minutes before divine worship began. I was not in the Church, but on my way."[52] The tragedy in Kirkcaldy was sadly not unique. A similar catastrophe also occurred during the ministry of Charles Spurgeon in London in 1856.

Isabella gave birth to a son, Samuel, about ten days later, but what joy Irving experienced in that event was diluted by the terrible memories of the disaster. Two days after the tragedy, Irving conducted the wedding ceremony of his sister-in-law, Elizabeth, to William Hamilton. The Hamiltons were to live in London and became important members of Irving's church.

RETURN TO LONDON

Soon after the accident, Irving returned to London, but Isabella stayed in Scotland to recover her strength after the birth of Samuel. While they were apart, Edward sent frequent and lengthy letters to his wife. In one he wrote,

> To you, now lying on a bed of sickness and weakness, how sweet must be the thought that the Son of God himself bore your infirmities and carried your diseases and sorrows, and that He is able to succour you in your temptation; yea, that He is suffering with you, and will be a strength in you to overcome your suffering! Oh, my dear wife, how glad were I at this moment to stand beside your bed and speak comfort to your heart! But He, who is the head of all the members, heareth my prayer, and will minister grace unto you by His Spirit.[53]

It is striking that even in a letter of comfort to his wife, Irving's emerging theology rises to the surface. Christ did not just bear our sins, he also

---

50. Oliphant, *Life*, 2:29–31; Hanna, *Memoirs* (New York), 3:227–28; Wilks, *Edward Irving*, 189–90.

51. "Letter from Kirkaldy," June 16, 1828, National Library of Scotland, Word on the Street Digital Gallery, L.C.Fol.74(089).

52. Irving to an unknown recipient, June 15, 1828, in Irving, *DL*, 261.

53. Irving to Isabella Irving, July 15, 1828, quoted in Oliphant, *Life*, 2:37–38.

"carried [our] diseases." This understanding of such passages as Isa 53:4 and Matt 8:17 is common in today's Pentecostal and Charismatic circles, but it was to become prominent in Irving's thinking in the years ahead and would lead to much heart-searching.

In his own church, not all were comfortable with Irving's recent emphasis on the return of Christ, for he was once more preaching on the book of Revelation. He told Isabella, "The enemy seems stirring up the lukewarm and formalists to speak more and more against the blessed hope of our Lord's coming; but amongst us I find it findeth room and bringeth peace."[54] Whether the "lukewarm and formalists" were from his own church is not stated, but Irving did also mention an unpleasant encounter he had with one of his church members, who said, "I wish you were done with that subject altogether." We also notice here what was becoming a common Irving attitude: If you disagreed with his view, you were "lukewarm" or a "formalist." These people belonged to the "Religious World," a term Irving frequently used negatively for sections of the church he no longer believed were faithful or who failed to believe that the return of Christ was near. In his judgment, they would soon experience God's judgment.

Late that summer Irving began to feel unwell. As he expressed it, "there has been too great a sympathy between my head and my stomach, so much so as to cause slight headaches ever after eating . . . I doubt not that the root of the matter is study, which of late has been with me of a deeper, intenser, and clearer kind than at any former period of my life." In September, Isabella was just about ready to return home with the two children, so Irving decided to travel north to accompany her back to London. He resolved, at the suggestion of Drummond, that on the way he would stay a little while at Harrogate in Yorkshire, which was noted for its waters. It was hoped that they would help him recuperate. After a few days there he wrote to Isabella, saying, "I dare say this water would do me good, if I were to stay long enough. For it seems to enter into strong controversy with my complaint." But duty called, and he soon had to leave to travel north to Scotland to pick up Isabella and the children, then back to London.[55]

For some time after they returned to London they stayed with Irving's amanuensis, Miss McDonald. By this time Isabella had been away from the capital for over four months.

It was also at that time that Irving received a copy of "Dr. Hamilton's book against millenarianism," which was critical of Irving's views. Irving thought that it breathed "a virulent spirit." It accused him of having ideas

---

54. Ibid.

55. Irving to Isabella Irving, September 9 and 17, 1828, quoted in ibid., 2:53–55.

inconsistent with those of other millennialists. But Irving believed that he was "not called . . . to be consistent with any one but God's own Word." Yet it would seem that Hamilton believed that he was not being consistent even with that.

TO SCOTLAND AGAIN

At the end of 1828 Irving contacted Thomas Chalmers to ask him whether he thought any of the Scottish clergy would lend him their pulpits so that he could "preach a series of sermons on the Kingdom" if he were to journey north the following May.[56] Irving did, in fact, return to Scotland that May to speak on prophecy at another round of well-attended meetings. However, by this time, amidst rumors that he might be charged with heresy,[57] there was less support for Irving, and some of the Scottish clergy stayed away. Indeed, some refused to allow Irving to use their churches altogether, and he often had to preach in the open air or in tents. West Church, where he had preached several times the year before, was now closed to him, though he did have access to the more remotely situated Hope Park Chapel, the Kirk at Annan, and a few other places. Irving was determined to go ahead, even if he was in danger of being carried "bound hand and foot to prison," which was hardly likely. If Chalmers had done anything to enlist support for Irving amongst the Scottish clergy, it had at best only partly worked. But Chalmers was not sympathetic to this aspect of Irving's ministry, so he may not have responded positively to Irving's request in December.

Whatever official opposition there may have been, the crowds still went to hear him. One Sunday in the middle of May he was preparing to preach in a tent in Annan, but so many people came that he had to preach in a field. Irving estimated the crowd at nearly ten thousand. Nor was it a short sermon. According to Irving, he preached from noon until 5:30 p.m., "with an interval of only an hour." On other occasions he preached to ten thousand in Dumfries (thirteen thousand in some accounts) and to six or seven thousand in Holywood, and his "voice easily reached over them all." One woman claimed to have been sitting at her window "a quarter mile off" and was able to hear clearly what he said. Understandably, Irving believed that these "lectures [were] decidedly producing an impression upon the people" and that "the work of the Lord [was] prospering in [his] hand."[58]

56. Irving to Thomas Chalmers, December 1828, quoted in ibid., 2:68.

57. See the following chapter.

58. Dallimore, *Life*, 94–96; Murray, *Puritan*, 193; Oliphant, *Life*, 2:75–76, 78–79, 82–85. Estimates of crowd numbers vary, but one of the larger estimates was made by a

One Scot converted to a premillennial viewpoint at the meetings that year was Andrew Bonar (1810–1892), and also, it seems, his brother Horatius (1808–1889). On May 24, 1829, Andrew wrote in his diary: "Have been hearing Mr. Irving's lectures all the week, and am persuaded now that his views of the Coming of Christ are truth."[59] Horatius Bonar later wrote the preface to the second edition of Irving's *Last Days*, though he made it clear that he disagreed with Irving on certain points.[60] It was also probably Horatius who said that in the 1828 series of millennial addresses Irving was "more eloquent than logical."[61] The Bonars would go on to become two highly influential clergymen in the Free Church.

Yet Irving was less well received in Glasgow. As he emerged from a church there after one service, a restless crowd gathered around him and hurled abuse at him. "Ye're an awfu' man, Mr. Irving," one man shouted. "They say you preach a Roman Catholic baptism and a Mohammadan heeven." (The latter was presumably a reference to Irving's millennial views.) For a moment the situation looked dangerous, but Irving removed his hat, bowed to them, and said, "Fare ye well." He and his companion then moved forward, and the mob opened up "like a door on its hinges" to let them through.[62]

While Irving was in Scotland he gained a commission in Annan so that he could represent that Burgh as an elder at the General Assembly in Edinburgh. This was the only way he could hold an official position in the church's parliament, as his London church was outside the Scottish Church's boundaries. His primary aim in doing this seems to have been to champion the rights of Scots in exile. This rather unusual step was strongly opposed by some at the Assembly, though supported by others. Oliphant refers to the debate surrounding Irving's inclusion as "A warm discussion," though one must suspect that the temperature may have been some degrees higher than that. Irving was given opportunity to speak for himself, but, typical of him, his address was "too long to quote." In the end the debate went against him, and he was unable to remain in the Assembly as a delegate.[63]

In a letter reporting the incident he said,

> It gave me no pain to be cast out of the Assembly, except in as
> far as it wronged the burgh of Annan, and all the burghs in their

---

surveyor, which may lend it more authenticity.

59. Bonar and Bonar, *Andrew A. Bonar*, 5; Murray, *Puritan*, 195.
60. Horatius Bonar, quoted in Irving, *Last Days*, vii n.
61. "Edward Irving," 233.
62. Oliphant, *Life*, 2:86.
63. Ibid., 2:81–82.

rights . . . The attention and favour which I received was very marked, especially from the Commissioner and the Moderator; and unbounded was the wonder of men to find that I had not a rough tiger's skin, with tusks and horns and other savage instruments . . . Upon the whole, I am very well satisfied with this event in my life.[64]

However, Irving was still invited to attend the meetings, but he had to "sit in the body of the house."

In spite of this setback, Irving was given the honor of being one of two ministers who, as was the custom, went to visit the Commissioner (the sovereign's representative) to advise him when the Assembly was ready to receive him. The Commissioner also invited him to a dinner at which various dignitaries were present, including the author Walter Scott.[65] It would appear from this that Irving was excluded from an official position at the Assembly because of church polity rather than because of concerns about his theological orthodoxy.

Walter Scott's impression of Irving was not flattering, even though Scott "could hardly keep [his] eyes off him while [they] were at table." The author thought Irving's "dress, and the arrangement of his hair, indicated that much attention had been bestowed on his externals, and led [him] to suspect a degree of self-conceit, consistent both with genius and insanity." Scott also claimed that at the dinner Irving "boasted much of the tens of thousands that attended his ministry at the town of Annan, his native place." Scott thought that Irving must be the exception "to the rule that a prophet was not esteemed in his own country," but he said nothing during the meal.[66]

This Scottish visit was a mixed bag. He was accepted and rejected; he was praised and he was abused. And there would be much more trouble ahead, but not too much praise.

Yet some time after his return to London, Irving could say, "There is not a corner of this part of the island where the subject of Prophecy and the Second Advent have not in the Church firm and able supporters."[67] Albury's views on the return of Christ were spreading, and they would gain many supporters in the years to come.

64. Irving to Isabella Irving[?], May 26, 1829, quoted in Oliphant, *Life*, 2:82

65. Ibid.

66. Scott, "Journal of Sir Walter Scott: May 23, 1829."

67. Irving to Thomas Chalmers, n.d., quoted in Oliphant, *Life*, 2:118.

12

Heretic?

THE HUMANITY OF CHRIST

In 1828 and 1829 Irving published a three-volume collection of his sermons that included addresses on the Trinity and especially on the incarnation of Christ that he had begun to preach in 1825. Why had he preached on the Trinity and the Incarnation? Was it because they were traditional Christian beliefs and Irving wanted to show his orthodoxy? Certainly not! Everything we have seen of Irving so far clearly demonstrates that he did not toe the party line unless he sincerely believed that line was the correct one to toe. On a number of occasions he had gone contrary to the popular Christian beliefs and practices of his day, though he had not slipped into heresy.

Rather, Irving probably preached these sermons for two reasons. First, he truly believed in the doctrines they presented and, as a vital part of biblical truth, he held that they needed to be proclaimed. In fact, he regarded a good understanding of the Trinity "a first principle in all sound theology."[1] Secondly, he was very aware that in his age Unitarianism, which rejects the doctrines of the deity of Christ and the Trinity, was a considerable force. This belief system had ravaged the General Baptists in Britain late in the eighteenth century, and English Presbyterianism had also been badly affected by it.[2] Indeed, Irving's friend Coleridge had been a Unitarian, though by this time he had adopted Trinitarian beliefs.

1. Irving, *CW*, 4:252.
2. Nettles, *By His Grace*, 57, 73; Schlossberg, *Silent Revolution*, 26; Vidler, *Church*,

Irving's opposition to Unitarianism was clearly evident in one address he had earlier preached on John the Baptist, in which he called Unitarianism "a persecution of Christ in all His most essential characters" and accused it of robbing Christ "of His divinity" and "of His offices, leaving Him only the condition of a prophet." He continued, "if He had claimed no more than this, the Jews would never have quarrelled with Him. The Jews persecuted not the son of Mary, but the Son of God."[3]

These sermons, along with some other addresses from this period, deal mainly with the nature of Jesus Christ, the Son of God, and particularly with his humanity. And Irving's understanding of the human nature of Jesus Christ would prove highly controversial, though he always maintained that it was orthodox.

As it happens, these sermons were amongst Irving's most remarkable works. Irving regarded his addresses on the incarnation as containing "much more to God's glory . . . than in all [his] other writings put together." This no doubt was because, as he told Isabella, these themes "ravish my heart and fill me with most enlarged and exquisite delight."[4]

Oliphant thought that these orations were deeper even than Irving's usual addresses. It was as though he was saving his best for these expositions about the very nature of the Son of God. Oliphant also wondered "How any man could carry a large audience breathless through those close and lofty arguments, and lead them into the solemn courts of heaven to trace the eternal covenant there, preserving the mighty strain of intelligence and attention through hours of steadfast soaring into the ineffable mysteries." It was, she said, "a question I find it hard to solve."[5] That question still remains unsolved, for as one reads these addresses today, with all their overwhelming profundity, they sound like lectures to theological students. And even then, one would wonder if many of his listeners would grasp anything like all that he had said. But these addresses were preached to his congregation. In spite of their depth, or perhaps because of it, they are deeply moving and take one into the very presence of God.

When Irving was busy preparing one of these volumes for publication, he told Isabella, "It is a book for much good or evil, both to the Church and myself, I distinctly see. I intend to read it over with much diligence, and correct it with the greatest care."[6] It was, in fact, because of comments he

---

40, 142.

3. Irving, *CW*, 2:86–87.

4. Irving to Isabella Irving, September 9, 1828, quoted in Oliphant, *Life*, 2:54–55.

5. Ibid., 2:3.

6. Irving to Isabella Irving, August 18, 1828, quoted in ibid., 2:52.

made in some of these sermons that Irving was later branded a heretic. The theological aspect of this will not be dealt with here in great detail, for our concern is with the life of Irving rather than his theology. But this component in his theology, his Christology, and the controversy surrounding it played such a major part in his later years that some attention must be paid to it.

Irving was not just being theoretic in these addresses. Graham McFarlane says that Irving's interest in the nature of Christ was not just theological, but practical and pastoral. Christians in the pew know that they are sinners, but at their best, they desire to be holy. Yet they realize that they fall short. How can they live lives that honor God, as they want to do? Christ lived a holy life, so they should just follow His example.[7]

But the man Jesus Christ was different. Or was he?

Irving argued that in the incarnation the Word, Christ, not only took on human flesh but also took on *sinful* human flesh. That is, that Christ's flesh was the same as our flesh, our sinful human flesh, thus with the potential to sin. In other words, in his human nature Jesus was the same as us. This teaching is based in part on Rom 8:3, which says, "God sending his own Son in the likeness of sinful flesh, and for sin, condemned sin in the flesh" (AV). However, Irving also clearly taught that in spite of having "sinful flesh," Jesus never committed a sin. He was holy; he was sinless. But this was only possible through the power of the Holy Spirit in him, thus the third person of the Trinity comes crucially into the picture. As McFarlane puts it, in Irving's thought, "the Son of God himself was empowered by the Holy Spirit in order to fulfil the Father's will."[8] It is clear that Irving's theology of the Spirit was already well developed, and it evolved further in his final years.

From the pastoral perspective, Irving taught that "one great end and meaning of [Christ's] manifestation in sinful flesh, [is] to teach humanity how there resideth with the Spirit of God a power to fortify humanity, and make it victorious over all trials and temptations."[9] Thus his teaching was not just theoretic, but also practical, as McFarlane says.

Irving also taught, in line with traditional declarations and confessions, that Christ was truly God on earth, not *a* god or an emanation of the true God, but *the* God on earth as a human being. For example, in one sermon he said,

7. McFarlane, *Edward Irving*, 7–8.

8. Ibid., 11.

9. Irving, "John the Baptist," in ibid., *CW*, 2:98.

Although it is most true that the witness of the Spirit and of His servants the inspired apostles be to Jesus, yet it is also to the Father in Him. For what is the testimony to Jesus but that He is the Son of God who is come in the flesh? And what is a Son without a Father? In testifying to Christ's name, the Son, He doth also testify to God's name, the Father; not to the Father apart from Christ, but to the Father in connexion and union with the Son—as seen in the Son, as known by the knowledge of the Son, as manifest in the manifestation of the Son, preserving the distinctness of the person in the unity of the substance. And as no one can say that Jesus is the Son of God or the Christ but by the Spirit, I may say that it is in the Spirit we know both the Father and the Son, distinct from Himself in terms of personality, but as to substance one.[10]

To Irving, Jesus was "very God and very man in one indivisible Person,"[11] and this is strictly orthodox Trinitarian theology. In fact, as McFarlane says, "Irving's doctrine of God is thoroughly Trinitarian."[12]

To him, all this was not just a mere academic matter, for in Irving's understanding, the atonement depended upon it:

Doth the man become a serpent who graspeth the serpent in his gripe, and crusheth him? Do I become a devil, by wrestling with the devil and overcoming him? And doth Christ become sinful, by coming into flesh like this of mine, extirpating its sin, arresting its corruption, and attaining for it honour and glory for ever? Idle talk! They know not whether [whither?] they drive. They are making void the humanity of Christ, and destroying his mediation, as virtually as if they denied his Divinity. A mediator is not of one: how truly he is consubstantial with God, so truly is he consubstantial with me, or he cannot be mediator between me and God. The Days-man must be able to lay his hand upon us both.[13]

That is, to save us, Christ must be like us in our humanity, though without sin, and also be truly God.

10. Edward Irving, *God our Father*, quoted in McFarlane, *Edward Irving*, 18–19. See also ibid., 33.

11. Dorries, *Edward Irving's*, 79.

12. McFarlane, *Christ and the Spirit*, 176.

13. Irving, *Sermons*, 1:(140)cxliii. The unusual page numbering here is because the three volumes were printed with consecutive page numbers. When Irving added two extra sermons in volume 1, each additional page was numbered either (140) or (328) and distinguished by Roman numerals.

In these sermons, then, Irving plunged right in to search the complexities of the Trinity in his usual detailed way, while less adventurous souls might address these matters more superficially. Yet trouble was just around the corner, and disaster was not much farther off.

THE FIRST ACCUSATION

Enter the Reverend Henry Cole. Oliphant called him "An idle clergyman," while H. C. Whitley dubbed him an "obscure clerical busybody."[14] In fact, Cole seems to have been anything but idle, for he appears to have lived a very busy life. Nor was he particularly obscure. Cole was originally an Anglican parson, though at this time he was the minister at a Methodist Chapel in Islington, not far from where the Irvings lived. He was an ardent controversialist, writing mainly on theology and geology.[15]

Cole had heard that Irving had preached on the person of Christ at a meeting organized by the Gospel Tract Society, probably on July 10, 1827. What he was told disturbed him: that is, that Irving taught that Christ had a sinful human nature.

This was after Irving's original sermons on the person of Christ had been preached in his own church. These sermons had been proclaimed without any repercussions and were being prepared for publication in 1827–1828, at around the same time Cole entered the story. In other words, Irving had been teaching these ideas for some time, apparently without anyone finding fault with them.[16] Irving also presented similar ideas, though briefly and less clearly, in his "Preliminary Discourse" to Lacunza's book, which had been published early in 1827.[17]

On the evening of October 28, 1827, Cole, it appears, attended his own church and then went on to the Caledonian Chapel, where he heard the last twenty minutes of Irving's address. What he heard shocked him, and he wrote a letter to Irving that he published as a pamphlet before the year was out. In this letter Cole claimed that he heard Irving say, "'That sinful substance!' meaning the human body of the adorable Son of God." His letter continued by saying that Irving was:

---

14. Oliphant, *Life*, 2:5; Whitley, *Blinded Eagle*, 23.

15. Mortenson, "British Scriptural Geologists."

16. Irving, *Sermons*, 1:iii–iv, xiii; Dorries, *Edward Irving's*, 30–32, 66 n. 11; Oliphant, *Life*, 2:1–6, 9.

17. Irving, "Preliminary Discourse," in Ben Ezra, 1:cxxvi–vii, clxv–viii.

declaring "That the main part of His victory consisted in His overcoming the sin and corruption of His human nature." You stated, "He did *not* sin. But," you said, "there was that sinful substance against which he had to strive and with which he had to conflict during the whole of His life upon earth." What I felt at hearing such awful blasphemy against the person of the Son of God . . . I cannot describe.[18]

After the service Cole asked for an interview with Irving, which was soon arranged. Cole stated in the letter that he did this because he wanted to make sure that Irving had said what he had meant to say, and that there was no mistake or misunderstanding.

According to Cole's letter, at the interview he asked Irving if he had "asserted that the human body of Christ was sinful substance," to which Irving responded, "Yes, I did." Cole then asked, "But is that your real and considerate belief?" Irving answered, "Yes, it is, as far as I have considered the subject." At this point, said Cole, Irving pulled down a book of Presbyterian doctrine from the shelves in his vestry and pointed out a sentence that Cole remembered as "The flesh of Jesus Christ, which was by nature mortal and corruptible." Cole asked again whether this was Irving's own understanding of the body of Christ. Irving replied that it was.[19]

Then, according to Cole, Irving continued, "Christ did no sin; but his human nature was sinful and corrupt; and his strivings against these corruptions was the main part of his conflict. Or else what make you of all those passages in the Psalms, 'Mine iniquities have taken hold upon me that I am not able to look up: they are more in number than the hairs of my head.'" Irving also, it seems, gave some other examples that Cole did not quote. Cole responded, "But surely, Sir, by all those passages are represented the agonies of the blessed Saviour under the number and weight of all his people's sins imputed to and transferred upon him." To this Irving replied, "No, No! I admit imputation to its fullest extent, but that does not go far enough for me. Paul says, 'He hath made him to be sin for us, who knew no sin.'"[20]

Cole said that he then asked, "But, if, as you have already allowed, Christ did no sin, how can those passages in the Psalms refer to any sins, as being his own sins?" To this Irving answered, "Christ could always say with Paul, 'Yet, not I, but sin that dwelleth in me.'" Cole responded, "Do you mean that . . . Jesus Christ had that 'law of sin in his members' of which Paul

---

18. H. Cole, *Letter to the Rev. Edward Irving* (London: Eedes, 1827), 7–9, quoted in Strachan, *Pentecostal*, 26–27.

19. Ibid.

20. Ibid., 27–28.

speaks, when he says, 'I find another law in my members warring against the law of my mind, and bringing me into captivity to the law of sin in my members'?" Irving answered, "Not into captivity; but Christ experienced everything the same as Paul did, except the 'captivity.'"

Finally Cole asked, "Do you then, Sir, really believe that the body of the Son of God was a mortal, corrupt, and corruptible body, like that of all mankind? The same body as yours and mine?" Irving answered, "Yes, just so; certainly; that is what I believe."[21]

The book Irving used to support his arguments in this encounter was presumably the *Scots Confession of Faith* of 1560. In the twenty-first chapter, "Of the Sacraments," it says, "the eternal Godhood has given to the flesh of Christ Jesus, *which by nature was corruptible and mortal,* life and immortality."[22] The *Westminster Confession of Faith*, which in the seventeenth century replaced the *Scots Confession* in the Church of Scotland, was less clear on this matter, as shall be seen. Irving used the older confession because it was "greatly to be preferred" to the newer one. In fact, he read it to his congregation twice a year.[23]

Irving recalled this meeting with Cole in the prefaces to two of his books. Not surprisingly, he remembered that the time of the interview was "a moment of exhaustion."[24] Bearing in mind that he had just finished preaching and that a sermon from Irving was lengthy, involved, and very tiring to deliver, that is to be expected. His answers to Cole, therefore, *even if accurately recorded* by the latter, need to be viewed from that perspective, though Irving's more considered arguments on this doctrine do not vary much from what Cole reported.

Irving also said that he suggested that Cole return to discuss the matter the following Thursday. Cole, it would seem, made no attempt to do so. Nor did Cole give Irving a chance to examine the pamphlet before publication to check whether it was an accurate record of their conversation.[25]

21. Ibid., 28. See also Oliphant, *Life*, 2:6–8.

22. Presbyterian Church, "Scots Confession," emphasis added.

23. Irving, *Apology*, 9–10; Drummond, *Edward Irving*, 110. However, whether Irving knew it or not, the "Scots Confession" seems to have been hastily prepared, while much more time and attention had gone into the compilation of the *Westminster Confession* (Macleod, *Scottish Theology*, 14; Torrance, *Scottish Theology*, 125–30). However, this does not necessarily negate the value of the earlier confession.

24. Oliphant, *Life*, 2:8–10.

25. Preface to Irving, *Christ's Holiness in the Flesh* (Edinburgh: Lindsay, 1831), quoted in Oliphant, *Life*, 2:8.

IRVING'S VIEW OF CHRIST'S HUMANITY

What, then, did Irving say in his addresses about the human nature of Christ? In one he said that for Christ to deliver his people from sin, he must not only become man, but must submit "himself to the very condition of a sinner." In fact, he "must come into the very condition of that which he would redeem; become flesh, and take up into himself the very conditions of a human will, or human spirit; that is, become very man, and himself wrestle therein against flesh and blood—against principalities—against powers—against the rulers of the darkness of this world—against spiritual wickednesses in high places."[26]

While this does not specifically say that the flesh that Christ wore was sinful, it certainly fits with that idea and can be understood that way. Christ came "into the *very* condition[s]" of humanity in body and will. Indeed, it was necessary for him to "wrestle" against the powers of evil, implying that it was no easy path and that he experienced real temptation to sin, not just the appearance of such. Yet these words, being open to different understandings, would not in themselves shock the orthodox.

In other places Irving was clearer. In one sermon he said, as Cole had charged, that Christ, when compared with other humans, "was as sinful in his substance as they, tempted as they, liable to fall as they."[27]

Elsewhere he said that the Son of God joined

> himself unto the fallen creation and [took] up into his own eternal personality the human nature, after it had fallen . . . That Christ took our fallen nature is most manifest, because there was no other in existence to take . . . it was impossible to find in existence any human nature but human nature fallen, whereof Christ might partake with the brethren. I believe, therefore, in opposition to all . . . who say the contrary, that Christ took unto himself a true body and a reasonable soul; and that the flesh of Christ, like my flesh, was in its proper nature mortal and corruptible [a point later repeated] . . . he was of the seed of the woman after she fell, and not before she fell.

In fact, he took "the substance of the fallen Virgin Mary."[28] Here Irving was as clear as clear could be. Jesus Christ, the Son of God on earth, took on *sinful* human flesh because, quite simply, there was no other kind to take.

Irving also argued:

26. Irving, *Sermons*, 1:20.
27. Ibid., 1:(140)clii.
28. Ibid., 1:(140)ii–iii, (140)v.

Christ's flesh was as rebellious as ours, as fallen as ours. But what then? Is Christ's flesh the whole of his creature-being? No: it is his humanity inhabited by the Holy Ghost, which maketh up his creature-being. And, through the power of the Holy Ghost, acting powerfully and with effect to the resisting, to the staying, to the overcoming of the evil propensity of fallen man, it is, that the fallen manhood of Christ is made mighty, and holy, and good, and every way fit to express the will of the Divinity.[29]

In his lectures on the temptations of Christ, Irving argued that they were real temptations because of the flesh he had inherited. Jesus was genuinely "acted upon by temptation" and was liable "to err in all ways in which we are liable."[30] When faced with Satan's temptations, "the Saviour was not a stock or stone, that these visions and this offer of things should pass before Him without power or impression . . . It was of the very essence of His being to be touched by them, and moved with them, as another human being is."[31] Thus, it was only through the Holy Spirit that he was able to successfully resist the tempter.

In fact,

he took his humanity completely and wholly from the substance, from the sinful substance, of the fallen creatures he had come to redeem! He was passive to every sinful suggestion which the world through the flesh can hand up unto the will; he was liable to every sinful suggestion which Satan through the mind can hand up to the will; and with all such suggestions and temptations I believe him beyond all others to have been assailed, but further went they not. He gave them no inlet, he went not to seek them, he gave then no quarter, but with power Divine rejected and repulsed them all; and so, from his conception to his resurrection, his whole life was a series of active triumphings over sin in the flesh, Satan in the world, and spiritual wickednesses in high places.[32]

Indeed, Irving asked, "How could he be tempted like me, unless he were like me?" Yet while Christ's humanity could be so tempted, "his Godhead could not be tempted."[33] So Christ was tempted but was without sin.

---

29. Ibid., 1:(140)lxxv–lxxvi.

30. Irving, "The Temptation," Lecture III, in ibid., CW, 2:218.

31. Irving, "The Temptation," Lecture V, in ibid., CW, 2:242.

32. Ibid., Sermons, 1:vii.

33. Ibid., 1:(140)lxi.

He endured these great temptations "without once swerving from the path of blameless rectitude."[34] And all this to Irving was "orthodox doctrine."[35]

His opponents argued, Irving said, "that though [Christ's] body was changed in the generation, he was still our fellow in all temptations and sympathies." Irving responded that this could not be true, "for change is change; and if his body was changed in the conception it was not in its life as ours is." And if that was the case, this created "a chasm between him and us which no knowledge, not even imagination, can overleap."[36]

In May 1830, while the General Assembly was meeting, Irving published a booklet called *Opinions Circulating Concerning our Lord's Human Nature, Tried by the Westminster Confession of Faith*. As has been seen, Irving preferred the old *Scots Confession* to the *Westminster* standard, but because the later work was the current authority on Presbyterian doctrine he felt it necessary to focus attention on what it taught.

Irving argued that there were three usual ways of understanding Christ's human nature:

1. "That the nature of Christ was the nature of Adam as created and uninjured by the fall."

2. That Christ took his mother's nature, but it was "so wrought upon in the generation as to be purged from sin."

3. "That our Lord took the same nature, body and soul, as other men, and under the same disadvantages of every sort . . . his human will had lying against it, and upon it, exactly the same oppressions of devil, world, and flesh, which lay against Adam's will *after* he had fallen, and which lies upon every man's will unto this day. And yet, though 'tempted in all points like as we are,' and 'in the likeness of sinful flesh,'" He was kept from sinning by the power of the Holy Spirit.

The third, of course, was Irving's own view, still consistently held against all opposition.

He then tested these views against the *Westminster Confession* and concluded that it agreed with him. In chapter 8, clause 2, which deals with "Christ the Mediator," the *Westminster Confession* says that when the Son of God came to earth he took "upon him man's nature, with all the essential properties and common infirmities thereof, yet without sin." While it could be fairly argued that the word "all" refers only to "the essential properties" (not the "common infirmities") and that the sinful human nature could

---

34. Irving, "The Temptation," Lecture III, in ibid., *CW*, 2:219.
35. Ibid., "True Humanity," 422.
36. Ibid., *Orthodox*, vii–viii.

not be regarded as such, it still does say that Christ's nature was prone to "*common* [human] infirmities." This can be understood as referring to such infirmities as splinters in the hand of a carpenter, but it could also refer to having a sinful nature.[37] Thus, in Irving's mind at least, his view was in accord with Presbyterian orthodoxy.

If not in quite the same language quoted by Cole, the ideas expressed in Irving's writings are for the most part the same. However, this research has not uncovered that in his printed works Irving ever applied Ps 40:12 to Christ, as Cole claimed. That is, the verse "*Mine* iniquities have taken hold upon me, so that I am not able to look up: they are more in number than the hairs of my head." But if Irving did use that quotation in such a way, in what sense did he believe that the "iniquities" were Christ's? If, as Irving repeatedly asserted, Christ did not sin, this presumably could only refer to Christ taking our sins upon himself on the cross and thus making them his own.

Dallimore presents seven ideas that summarize Irving's teaching on the person of Christ, of which a précis follows:

1. Christ's flesh was the same as Adam's after the fall, not like Adam's before it.

2. Christ was subject to the same temptations and tendencies as we are.

3. There was nothing in his nature that gave him an advantage over us in fighting sin.

4. Yet Christ did not sin. This was because of the power of the Holy Spirit in him.

5. Therefore Christ is "the supreme Example" of how to live.

6. The Holy Spirit is "equally available" to each Christian.

7. That at the end of his life Jesus "was able to present to God a perfect human nature."

This summary, as it stands here, appears to be an accurate reflection of Irving's understanding of Christ's human nature.[38]

---

37. Edward Irving, *Opinions Circulating Concerning our Lord's Human Nature* (Edinburgh: Lindsay, 1830), quoted in Strachan, *Pentecostal*, 41–44, emphasis added; *Westminster Confession*, ch. 8:2.

38. Dallimore, *Irving*, 79–80. However, Dallimore continues in point seven that according to Edward Irving, Christ's work of reconciliation and atonement "was accomplished . . . not in His death, but in His life" (ibid.). While Irving did not place a strong emphasis upon Christ's death, what he did say about it seems to suggest that Dallimore is overstating his case. To Irving, we are saved by both Christ's incarnation, his perfect life, and his sacrificial death. See my "Was Edward Irving an Evangelical?" on my website, www.edwardirving.org.

The source of Christ's holiness—his sinlessness—is, in one respect, the crucial issue here. Irving's opponents were effectively arguing that he was sinless because of his distinctive human nature. Irving was stating that his sinlessness was not because of any uniqueness in his humanity, for his was the same as ours, but rather that it was through the power of the Spirit of God.

In Irving's *The Orthodox and Catholic Doctrine of Our Lord's Human Nature*, which according to David Brown, filled "all Scotland with alarm,"[39] he noted that those who opposed his view argued "for an identity of origin merely" while he and his supporters argued "for an identity of life also." Indeed, Irving continued, "They argue for an inherent holiness; we argue for a holiness maintained by the Person of the Son, through the operation of the Holy Ghost."[40]

To suddenly be accused of heresy came as a great shock to Irving. He later wrote, "I shall never forget the feeling which I had upon first hearing my name coupled with heresy. So much did it trouble me, that I once seriously meditated sending a paper to the *Christian Observer*, in order to contradict the man's false insinuations. But I thought it better to sit quiet and bear the reproach."[41] Not that his silence lasted long.

Irving believed and continued to believe that what he was proclaiming was orthodox, traditional Christian belief. In fact, to him, "To know and to understand how the Son of God took sinful flesh and yet was sinless, this is the alpha and omega, the beginning and the ending, of orthodox theology."[42]

Dorries argues that Irving had been preaching that same doctrine throughout his time in London. To demonstrate this, Dorries gives numerous examples of Irving's earlier sermons, in which Irving said such things as Christ was "in the likeness of fallen Adam," he took "a part of the fallen creature into union with Himself," he inhabited "sinful flesh," and "His manifestation in sinful flesh."[43] It is also possible that Irving taught this doctrine in his Glasgow ministry, though no record exists of those sermons. But now he stood accused of heresy for teaching it. And accusations of heresy are in danger of sticking whether they are true or not. Yet on this subject, even

39. Brown, "Personal Reminiscences," 264.
40. Irving, *Orthodox*, vii–viii.
41. Preface to Irving, *Christ's Holiness in the Flesh*, quoted in Oliphant, *Life*, 2:8.
42. Irving, "True Humanity," 422.
43. Dorries, *Edward Irving's*, 82–84.

today, the correct teaching is still debated. Some agree with Irving, some do not.[44]

THE DISPUTE RAGES

In Irving's time, the debate raged far and wide. It began with the publication of Cole's booklet at the end of 1827. The sermons themselves were not published until the close of 1828, being delayed some months so that Irving could add material to respond to Cole's accusations.[45] The responses were of three main types: those strongly opposed to the teaching, some even calling it heresy; those in favor; and those who did not seem to regard the issue as especially important, or at least not divisive.

In 1829, three separate reviews of Irving's new sermons appeared in *The Gospel Magazine and Theological Review* (*GM*), a journal with Anglican origins. In April, the reviewer cautiously stated that he could "not agree with [Irving's] assertion—for the Scripture declares, that [Christ] was *holy from the womb*." However, the reviewer did not seem to regard Irving's view as heresy and greeted Irving "with respect and affection." In June, the reviewer concentrated on Irving's comments on the Old Testament Law and predestination and, while critical in some respects, praised him for evincing "a holy enthusiasm in the cause of Divine truth." In August, the reviewer dealt with Irving's sermons on the Sower, plus a few other addresses not primarily related to the person of Christ. With regard to Irving's doctrine of Christ having sinful flesh, then, this reviewer[s] does not seem to have regarded it as a major issue. Certainly he did not give much space to it, and his opposition to it was very mild. He seemed more concerned about perceived Arminian tendencies in Irving's sermons and with his views on Christ's second coming.[46]

In April the following year, "Christiania," a Presbyterian, on behalf of "A little circle of friends," wrote to the *GM* expressing their distress at the way Irving's views were being condemned "by a part of the religious

---

44. Since the late nineteenth century, those against the view that Christ's flesh was fallen have included A. B. Bruce, Hugh MacKintosh, D. M. Baillie, Donald MacLeod, Martyn Lloyd-Jones, and Michael Harper. Those in favor have included Karl Barth, T. F. Torrance (a Moderator of the Church of Scotland), J. B. Torrance, W. Pannenburg, C. E. B. Cranfield, and David Dorries. See Martindale, "Edward Irving's," 9–12, 30–31, especially n. 42; Cranfield, *Epistle to the Romans*, 1:381–82; Lloyd-Jones, *Romans: 7:1–8:4*, 320–23; Harper, *Let My People*, 195, Dorries, *Edward Irving's*, 464–67.

45. Oliphant, *Life*, 2:10.

46. [Row?], Review of vol. 1 of *Sermons*, by Edward Irving, *GM*, April 1829, 181–83; ibid., *GM*, June 1829, 269–75; ibid., *GM*, August 1829, 368–74.

community." She also asked the editors for their opinion on the possible sinfulness of Christ's human nature and the mortality of his body.[47] The editors replied first of all that "the liberty taken by a set of *ruffianly* writers with Mr. Irving . . . is wicked and unpardonable." Yet they disagreed with Irving on the sinfulness of Christ's human nature, but they were still prepared to give him "the right hand of fellowship" because he held "up the lamb of God, as spotless, holy, harmless, undefiled, separate from sinners; who did no sin." They agreed with Irving that Christ's body was mortal, for after all he died. However, his resurrected body is immortal. Here the *GM* editors were being consistent with their earlier position: Irving was wrong about the sinful nature of Christ's body, but that did not make him a heretic.[48]

In July of that year the *GM* published a letter from "W." of Exeter in the southwest of England, who criticized some "monstrous assertions" that Irving had made in *The Morning Watch* on this same subject, including that "Christ had the same disposition and propensities as our sinful flesh." "W." argued that if Christ's flesh was mortal, then his death could not possibly be voluntary, which is what the Scriptures teach.[49] In this instance the editors replied very briefly, criticizing some of "W.'s" opinions but leaving Irving unscathed.

In 1829 James Haldane, a Baptist evangelist, said that he regarded as a contradiction Irving's stand that Christ had sinful flesh but was sinless. Haldane also argued, like "W.," that if Christ's flesh was mortal, then his death would be automatic, not voluntary as portrayed in the Bible.[50] Irving read Haldane's booklet, but thought that "there was no strength" in it.[51]

Also in 1829, Rev. R. H. Carne, an Anglican from Exeter, challenged Irving's doctrine in a pamphlet called *The Sinlessness, Immortality, and Incorruptibility of the Son of God*, which he appears to have sent to Irving.[52] Irving seems to have responded to this in *The Morning Watch* later that year, and he was supported by Dr. T. W. Chevalier, who had attended some of the Albury Conferences. In his response Irving complained of the "unsound . . . faith of many . . . in the true humanity of Christ," but did not mention Carne by name, though he did refer to Cole and Haldane.[53]

---

47. Christiania, "On the Sinfulness," 212.

48. [Row?], "Reply to the Above," 212–13.

49. W., "On Christ's Human Nature," 292–94.

50. James Haldane, *A Refutation of the Heretical Doctrine*, 16, 36, quoted in Martindale, "Edward Irving's," 14–15.

51. Irving to Isabella Irving, May 19, 1829, quoted in Oliphant, *Life*, 2:79.

52. W., "On Christ's Human Nature," 292.

53. Irving, "True Humanity," 421–22.

Chevalier enlisted the Athanasian Creed against Carne, which was particularly significant because the Athanasian Creed appears in the Anglican *Book of Common Prayer*, which Carne, as a clergyman of the Church of England, was supposed to believe and uphold. Indeed, this creed was expected to be recited on fourteen occasions in the Anglican Church year, including Christmas Day. It says that the Son of God was "Man, of the substance of his mother, born in the world," which Chevalier (and Irving) understood as meaning that as Christ's mother had sinful flesh, so did he.[54] But it is clear that not everybody interpreted it that way, including Carne. Carne responded by writing another pamphlet entitled, *The True Humanity of Christ*.[55]

John Nelson Darby of the Plymouth Brethren said in 1829 that he found some of Irving's output "deeply interesting" and "profitable," and regarded him as "a very holy man."[56] However, when he encountered Irving's understanding of the person of Christ, he called it "error," one of the "dreadful doctrines of Irvingism," "blasphemous," "wicked and evil," and a "ruinous doctrine."[57] Darby was noted for not pulling punches, though some of these remarks were made after Irving had died.

Early in 1830, *The Edinburgh Christian Instructor* published an anonymous but well-researched three-part series attacking Irving's views. This was written by Rev. Marcus Dods Sr., a fellow Presbyterian. He accused Irving and his supporters of misquoting the church fathers to support their case and of being ignorant and insolent.[58] This caused Irving to write to Dods challenging his views, even though he admitted that he had not read the articles but was rather going by hearsay. Irving said that he had heard that the articles were "very severe in their language and unkind in their spirit." Irving asked Dods to send him his views on the subject "in a brief form" that he might consider them, and then succinctly outlined his own position, though in softer terms than he sometimes used. (For example, Irving did not say on this occasion that Christ had sinful flesh.) Dods responded, but not entirely to Irving's satisfaction.[59]

54. Chevalier, "Defence," 446.

55. W., "On Christ's Human Nature," 292.

56. Darby, "Reflections upon the Prophetic Inquiry," in ibid., *Writings*, 2:19; Darby, "Our Separating Brethren," in ibid., 14:122.

57. Darby, "Sufferings of Christ," in ibid., 7:217, 226; Darby, "Mr. Newman's Remarks on Tongues," in ibid., 6:285; Darby, "Remarks on a Tract," in ibid., 15:2; Darby, "Brethren and their Reviewers," in ibid., 10:53.

58. Strachan, *Pentecostal*, 38–39.

59. Irving to Marcus Dods, March 8 and August 5, 1830, in Irving, *DL*, 266–68, 272–74; Oliphant, *Life*, 2:113–14; Grass, *Edward Irving*, 184–86. For further details, see

In 1833 Robert Meek, the curate of Yatton in Wiltshire, wrote two booklets against Irving's belief. In the first, the title described it as "Irving heresy." In the second, he called it "a doctrine of the most awful character and tendency" and an "obnoxious doctrine."[60] Meek also argued that if Christ had had "a fallen nature, an atonement for the sinfulness of his own nature would have been necessary."[61]

It is worth noting here that these criticisms came from a number of different denominations: Presbyterian, Anglican, and Baptist, plus in Cole's case, Anglican-Methodist.

Coleridge expressed a different concern about Irving's sermons on the Trinity. He had made extensive notes in his set of these books. In them he expressed his fear that Irving was slipping into "tritheism"—three Gods rather than one triune God—particularly with his emphasis on the Holy Spirit. In Coleridge's opinion, Irving presented "the Holy Ghost [as] clearly the superior person."[62] Others have argued that Irving's view divided the human from the divine in Christ, resulting in a form of Nestorianism.[63]

But there were also those who supported Irving. In fact, Meek complained that "certain brethren in the ministry . . . had embraced and zealously advocated this heresy," including some clergy in the Church of England.[64] H. T. Burne, another Anglican curate, who supported Irving in a pamphlet of his own, actually called Meek's view "false doctrine."[65]

Irving's old friend Thomas Carlyle, as well as Carlyle's mother, also supported him. Carlyle told a relative, "In my humble opinion, if the common interpretation of the Bible is to be followed, our friend is perfectly right, nay indubitably and palpably so: at all events, the gainsayers are utterly, hopelessly, and stone-blindly *wrong*. My Mother who is a better judge than I, declared it to be soundest doctrine, often preached in her hearing."[66]

Another Thomas Carlyle, a leading lawyer and later an Apostle in the CAC, also defended Irving. He wrote several books arguing in favor of

---

Irving to Samuel Martin, December 7, 1832, in Irving, *DL*, 326–28.

60. Meek, *True Nature*, 5, 8.

61. Meek, *The Sinless Humanity of Christ*, 12–13, quoted in Martindale, "Edward Irving's," 18.

62. Coleridge, *Collected Works*, 12, pt. 3:17, 41–43.

63. Grass, *Edward Irving*, 186–89.

64. Meek, *True Nature*, 5–6.

65. Ibid., 7. Burne's pamphlet was titled "The Scripture Doctrine of the Person and Humanity of our Divine Redeemer the Lord Jesus Christ."

66. Thomas Carlyle to John A. Carlyle, May 1, 1830, *CLO*, emphasis added. See also Carlyle, *Reminiscences* (Norton), 2:189–90.

Irving's doctrine in 1829 and 1830.[67] Irving also claimed that the Anglican Bishops of London and Gloucester held his view.[68]

It is important to note, as McFarlane says, that Irving's views "remained consistent throughout the debate," a point supported by Dorries.[69] While Irving may have flinched under the attacks of those who disagreed with him, he did not change his view. Perhaps surprisingly, in March 1830 Irving told Marcus Dods that before this issue blew up he "never knew that there were two opinions [on this doctrine] in any orthodox creed and true church."[70] Now he had discovered that there certainly was, and his view was in danger of being unacceptable to those in power.

It also needs to be noted, as Colin Gunton says, that Irving's "Christology and his understanding of the incarnation are essentially Trinitarian."[71] To Irving, Christ was human, truly human, but he was also the Son of God—indeed, truly God.

By this stage in his life Irving had succeeded in angering many of his evangelical brethren, including some in his own denomination, by the charges he had made against them in his *Orations*. He had angered leaders in the missionary movement by his controversial views on missionary support. He had taken what was then a minority premillennial view on the return of Christ. Now he had uttered heresy, or it was claimed that he had. In the minds of many, Irving was a maverick. It was time he was brought to task.

Wheels also began to move in Presbyterian circles that were eventually to crush Edward Irving and seal his fate. The charge was heresy no less, and that, in Presbyterian circles, was very serious. But Presbyterian wheels turn slowly. The official Presbyterian response to this and other matters will be considered in later chapters.

A century later, A. L. Drummond argued that Irving presented this issue "in such a one-sided, unguarded way as to give some people the impression that he believed Christ's body to be a mortal and corruptible body like that of all mankind, and his human nature to be identical with all human nature." To Drummond, Irving was just using "picturesque and popular

67. Dorries, *Edward Irving's*, 67 n. 33.

68. Irving to Chalmers, n.d., quoted in Oliphant, *Life*, 2:118.

69. McFarlane, *Edward Irving*, 7; Dorries, *Edward Irving's*, 73. Contrary to McFarlane and Dorries, Dallimore charged Irving with inconsistency on this issue, though the only quotations he gave come via Henry Cole (Dallimore, *Life*, 78–79). However, Dallimore claimed to have "more than once" spent hours examining Irving's teaching on this subject (ibid., 81).

70. Irving to Marcus Dods, March 8, 1830, in Irving, *DL*, 267.

71. Gunton, "Two Dogmas," 363–64.

phraseology," which was not meant to be taken literally.[72] In light of what Irving had clearly said, these are astonishing opinions to hold. As has been shown, Irving's presentation of these teachings was not truly "one-sided," nor was it "unguarded." Irving preached on both the divine and human natures of Christ and said what he had carefully thought out. What is more, that some people gained the impression that Irving taught that Christ's body was "mortal and corruptible" was simply because that is precisely what Irving had said. And it is clearly what he had meant to say.

If Irving's arguments seemed, as A. L. Drummond said, one-sided—that is, heavily weighted on the humanity of Christ—this was not because he chose to ignore Christ's divinity. It was rather because his view on Christ's humanity was so frequently attacked he had to repeatedly defend it. His opponents generally agreed with his view on Christ's deity, thus oft-repeated statements of that teaching were unnecessary. As Dorries remarks, "opposition forced" Irving "to write in defense" of his understanding of Christ's humanity, "Yet equally vital to his Christology was the doctrine of Christ's true divinity."[73]

Byung-Sun Lee hits the nail on the head in saying that Irving's idea of Christ having "sinful flesh . . . was not really understood by his contemporaries."[74] Certainly it was not by many of them. However, his use of the term "sinful flesh" in relation to Christ was always in danger of being misinterpreted. Irving probably realized that, for time and time again he stated that Christ was sinless. Irving clearly believed that Jesus Christ had never sinned.

Reading the criticism, one gets the impression that in this debate many of Irving's opponents believed he was saying that Christ had actually sinned or was at least subject to original sin. That would seem to be why some opposed him. Yet Irving clearly stated that Christ had never sinned, and just as clearly, if not as frequently, he said that Christ was not even subject to original sin.[75]

Irving's father-in-law "told him over and over, that his language, if not his meaning is heterodox." In his opinion, that language gave "abundant occasion for all that has been said and done against him." In addition, Rev. Martin said that he was not the only one close to Irving who has told him

---

72. Drummond, *Edward Irving*, 112, 159.

73. Dorries, *Edward Irving's*, 79.

74. Lee, "Christ's Sinful Flesh," 128.

75. See Irving, "Lord's Supper," in ibid., *CW*, 2:587; ibid., *Sermons*, 1:(140)lxii–lxiv; ibid., "True Humanity," 430–31.

so.[76] But Irving continued on, seemingly content to live in the danger he had raised.

As H. R. Mackintosh argued, this problem may also have been caused by Irving confusing "the idea of 'corrupt' with that of 'corruptible' (in the sense of liable to corruption or decay)."[77] There is no doubt that Irving frequently used the word "corruptible" in connection with Christ's flesh in his sermons and books. However, whether Irving used the even more controversial "corrupt" in such a context is unclear, but if he did so, it was very rarely.[78] Henry Cole certainly charged him with using "corrupt" in connection with Christ's flesh, though Cole may have misheard him.[79]

Within all this debate, it needs to be remembered that the *Scots Confession of Faith* says the Son "took the nature of humanity from the substance of a woman" and "the eternal Godhood has given to the flesh of Christ Jesus, *which by nature was corruptible and mortal,* life and immortality."[80] The main figure behind the production of that confession was the major Scottish Reformer John Knox.

In addition, in another place Knox spoke of Christ carrying "our flesh up to glory." In an exposition of Matthew's account of Christ's temptations, Knox also imagined Christ saying to Satan, "Lo, I am a man like to my brethren, having flesh and blood, and *all* properties of man's nature (sin . . . excepted)." Elsewhere Knox wrote, Jesus "proved [in the sense of tested or tried] our infirmities" and overcame them.[81] If not as clear as Irving, Knox sounds as though he was teaching the same doctrine.

In other words, Irving was in line with a major Presbyterian confession and, it seems, with John Knox, a Presbyterian of Presbyterians. Likewise, the *Westminster Confession* also seems to be open to this interpretation.

When we come to consider the view of John Calvin, of whom Irving had a high opinion and who is often regarded as the father of Presbyterian

76. John Martin to William Hamilton, June 1831, in Irving, *DL*, 281.

77. Mackintosh, *Person of Jesus Christ*, 207–208, quoted in Whitley, *Blinded Eagle*, 98–99.

78. He made some comments that might be interpreted that way, but it is probably not what he meant. See, for example, Irving, *Sermons*, 1:140 (xxxvii–xxxviii), 328.

79. H. Cole, *Letter to the Rev. Edward Irving*, 9, quoted in Strachan, *Pentecostal*, 28.

80. Presbyterian Church, "Scots Confession," chs. 6 and 21, emphasis added.

81. Knox, "A Godly Letter of Warning," in ibid., *Selected Writings*, 195; Knox, "An Exposition upon Matthew IV," in ibid., 300, emphasis added; Knox, "A Treatise on Prayer," in ibid., 88. However, Knox also implies that Christ was *kept from hunger* during the fast in the wilderness by "the invisible power of God" (presumably the Holy Spirit), which might suggest different flesh from us, though he also seems to hint that God could do this for others as well (Knox, "Matthew IV," in ibid., 305, 309).

doctrine,[82] the picture is not entirely clear. However, Calvin also seems to lean in Irving's direction. Commenting on the verse, Christ came "in the likeness of sinful flesh" (Rom 8:3), Calvin said, "Although the flesh of Christ was unpolluted by any stain, it had the appearance of being sinful, since it sustained the punishment due to our sins." In fact, "there appeared in Him a certain resemblance (*imago*) to our sinful nature."[83]

In the *Institutes of the Christian Religion*, Calvin referred to Jesus as "true God and true man" and said, "God's natural Son fashioned for himself a body from our body, flesh from our flesh, bones from our bones, that he might be one with us." In fact, his "flesh he received from us," and he "took our nature upon himself to impart to us what was his." In addition, Calvin argued that Christ had "a nature truly human" and "one bodily nature with us," being "comrade and partner in the same nature with us." Yet Christ is also "without fault and corruption" and "was exempted from common corruption!"[84] Whether Calvin meant the same thing as Irving in all this may be debatable. If he did, he certainly was not saying it as clearly.

While it can be regarded as certain that the *Scots Confession* was a major influence upon Irving's understanding of Christ's humanity, were there other sources from which he may have drawn these ideas? As we have seen, Carlyle's mother stated that what Irving taught was a view she had often heard preached, presumably in the secessationist church in Ecclefechan that the Carlyles attended. Irving also went to that church each Sunday for several years in his childhood. It is possible, even perhaps probable, that Irving heard that teaching from Rev. John Johnston, who was minister there when the Carlyles and Irving were in attendance.[85]

In addition, Patterson has said that Irving's "Christology appears more in keeping with that of Eastern Orthodoxy than the West," and Dorries has a large section in his *Incarnational Christology* noting the similarities between Irving's views and some of the early Eastern Church Fathers.[86]

82. Irving called Calvin "the most lion-hearted of churchmen" and believed that he "had given birth to valuable systems both of doctrine and polity" (Irving, *CW*, 3:350).

83. Calvin, *Epistles of Paul*, 159. See also Dorries, *Edward Irving's*, 236–47; Edmonson, *Calvin's Christology*, 183–96, 210; Martindale, "Edward Irving's," 26–27. These scholars argue that Calvin believed that "Christ assumed full humanity in its fallen state" (Martindale, "Edward Irving's," 26–27).

84. Calvin, *Institutes*, 1:464–67, 474–81 (Bk. 2, ch. xii, 1–3, and ch. xiii, 1–4).

85. Thomas Carlyle to John A. Carlyle, May 1, 1830, *CLO*; Campbell, "Carlyle," in Brown and Newlands, *Scottish Christianity*, 17. I have found nothing definite saying that Johnston did teach the same Christology as Irving, but Mrs. Carlyle sat under his ministry for many years, and her son said that she had often heard that doctrine taught, presumably by Johnston.

86. Patterson, "Designing," 16 n. 3; Dorries, *Edward Irving's*, 143–211. Gregory

However, a more likely direct influence is a bit closer to Irving in both time and geography: Richard Hooker, a sixteenth-century English Anglican. It is known that Irving had a copy of Hooker's *Laws of Ecclesiastical Polity*, greatly admired it, and drew some of his ideas from it. In March 1829 Irving published an article in *The Morning Watch* defending his Christology. It included a lengthy quotation from Hooker, part of which reads:

> If therefore it be demanded what the person of the Son of God hath attained by assuming manhood, surely the whole sum of all is this: to be, as we are, truly, really, and naturally man; by means whereof he is made capable of meaner offences than otherwise his person could have admitted . . .
>
> And as God hath in Christ unspeakably glorified the nobler, so likewise the meaner part of our nature, the very bodily substance of man . . . For in this respect his body, which by natural condition was corruptible, wanted the gift of everlasting immunity from death, passion, and dissolution, till God, which gave it to be slain for sin, had for righteousness sake restored it to life with certainty of endless continuance . . .
>
> For though it had a beginning from us, yet God hath given it vital efficacy, heaven hath endowed it with celestial power, that virtue it hath from above, in regard whereof all the angels of heaven adore it. Notwithstanding, a body still it continueth, a body consubstantial with our bodies, a body of the same, both nature and measure, which it had on earth.[87]

Hooker's teaching here is clearly very similar to Irving's.

The fact that Irving quoted Hooker in his defense strongly indicates that he noted these ideas when he was first reading Hooker. That he remembered them suggests that they influenced him. It is unlikely that Irving would have later gone to Hooker looking for support for his beliefs and just happened to come across this passage.

Yet whatever similarities exist between Irving's Christology and that of some other scholars, Gordon Strachan argues that in its fullness "Irving's

---

of Nazianzus (ca. 330–389), one of the eastern Cappadocian Fathers, famously said of Christ, "For that which he has not assumed he has not healed; but that which is united to his Godhead is also saved" ("Epistle 101," 7:440). Dorries argues that "the significance of the Cappadocian position was recaptured in the Christology of Edward Irving as few theologians had been able to achieve" (Dorries, *Edward Irving's*, 178). McFarlane also notes similarities between the Christologies of Irving and Theodore of Mopsuestia (ca. 350–428) in McFarlane, *Christ and the Spirit*, 190 n. 138.

87. Irving, "On the Human Nature," 80–82; Hooker, *Laws of Ecclesiastical Polity*, 299, 302–303. See also Lee, "Christ's Sinful Flesh," 114–15.

Christological position . . . appear[s] to be unique." Graham McFarlane agrees with him.[88]

THE POSSIBILITY OF A DOCTORATE

It seems that as far back as 1823, Sir John Sinclair, a Scottish politician, tried to have Irving awarded the degree of Doctor of Divinity. This move Irving rejected because he had not earned that degree. But there was "no honour upon earth" that he more desired, and when Thomas Chalmers was appointed to the Divinity Chair at Edinburgh University at the end of 1828, Irving wrote to him inquiring what he needed to do to work towards it.[89] This suggests that at that time Irving had little idea of the danger he was in. Indeed, one would expect Chalmers, because of his new position, to be involved in any future heresy trial. In 1830 Irving, perhaps becoming more aware of danger, wrote to Chalmers again on various issues but mainly on the nature of Christ's humanity and seems to have assumed that Chalmers would agree with and support him. Irving appears to have received no reply to that letter.[90]

88. Strachan, *Pentecostal,* 22; McFarlane, *Christ and the Spirit,* 179.

89. Oliphant, *Life,* 2:66–67.

90. Ibid., 2:117–19.

13

The Morning Watch

According to Irving, at the first Albury Conference on prophecy in late 1826 there had been general agreement amongst the members. However, this may not have been the case at the second conference, for when it came to selecting delegates for the 1828 Albury meetings, Drummond told Irving, "we must select with more caution, as some of the people last year have not been very faithful."[1] This comment probably meant that the unfaithful had expressed sentiments disagreeing with the views shared by Drummond and Irving either at the 1827 conference or afterwards.

By the time the 1829 conference was held, there was no shortage of differences amongst these interpreters of prophecy. One Albury delegate, Rev. William "Millennial" Marsh, who may have attended only in 1828, began his own annual conferences the next year, which suggests that he was not happy with the direction Albury was taking.[2] Lewis Way may have only attended the first conference, for later he became dissatisfied with the direction of Edward Irving's ministry.[3] Hugh McNeile, a leading figure at Albury, eventually split with Irving and Drummond over issues relating to the interpretation of biblical prophecy and Irving's beliefs about charismatic gifts.[4] In addition, in December 1829 Irving wrote an article that was highly critical of many sections of the church, particularly evangelicals,

1. Irving to Isabella Irving, August 4, 1828, in ibid., 2:49.

2. Carter, *Anglican Evangelicals*, 188; Irving to Isabella Irving, August 15, 1828, quoted in Oliphant, *Life*, 2:51.

3. Froom, *Prophetic Faith*, 3:425.

4. Grass, "Edward Irving," in Gribben and Stunt, *Prisoners*, 120–21; Patterson, "Designing," 214–15.

though no names were given.[5] It may have been this that caused Rev. Daniel Wilson and some others to leave the group after the 1829 conference,[6] and this was probably a factor in the ending of the Albury Conferences.

Soon after the 1828 conference Irving wrote to Thomas Chalmers advising him that:

> we . . . are more convinced than ever of the judgments which are about to be brought upon Christendom, and upon us most especially, if we should go into any league or confederacy with, or toleration of, the papal abomination . . . The second coming of the Lord is the 'point de vue,' the vantage ground, as one of my friends [probably Frere] is wont to word it, from which, and from which alone, the whole purpose of God can be contemplated and understood.[7]

To Irving, then, and presumably at least some of his associates, the return of Christ was the primary vantage ground from which God's purpose could be properly viewed. Yet, if that vision was skewed, then so was one's whole understanding of God's purpose.

Of the 1829 conference Irving admitted that there were "some diversities of opinion upon most subjects," though all the delegates appear to have been premillennial, yet they seemed to have viewed that era in slightly different ways. Irving told his wife that Lord Mandeville and the Reverend Dodsworth, both Anglicans, rated "the condition of men in the flesh" during the Millennium at a higher level than expected by Irving. In addition, Irving believed that people would still die during the Millennium, while Mandeville and Dodsworth did not.[8] But though there were variations of belief at Albury, they seemed agreed that Christ would return and then reign on earth for a thousand years. In fact, it has been claimed that it was "The Albury circle" that was "largely responsible for turning Britain to premillennialism."[9]

In successive days in 1829, the subjects under discussion were "Christ's office of judgment in the Millennium" introduced by Lord Mandeville; the Kingdom of God as seen in our Lord's parables, led by Dodsworth; "the Remnant of the Gentiles and their translation" (or rapture), led by Irving;

---

5. Irving, "Signs of the Times," 641–66. A second part of that article appeared in the next issue of *TMW* on pages 141–62.

6. Davenport, *Albury*, 26. For others disassociating themselves from Irving, see also Patterson, "Designing," 217, 223–24.

7. Irving to Thomas Chalmers, December 1828, quoted in Oliphant, *Life*, 2:67–68.

8. Irving to Isabella Irving, November 30, 1829, in ibid., 2:100–101.

9. Patterson, "Designing," 27.

the Apocalypse, led by the Reverend Whyte (or White); and "the Signs of the Times," opened by Drummond. Irving described Mandeville's presentation as being "truly sublime and soul-subduing." He also noticed that as his Lordship spoke, "everybody's pen stood still, as if they felt it a desecration to do anything but listen."[10]

This circle, with Irving at its center, was a major influence in the development of the form of last days thinking found in Dispensationalism. In the study entitled *The Origins of Left Behind Eschatology*, I searched through a substantial part of church history looking for eight elements essential to Dispensational (or Left Behind) end times thinking to discover their origins. These elements included futurism, a two-stage return of Christ prior to a millennial reign of Christ on earth, and a pretribulation rapture.[11] Six of these eight test criteria were taught by Irving and his associates.[12] Tim Grass has also discovered some comments by Irving that might be a seventh in embryo. These comments sound like a forerunner of Dispensationalism's sharp distinction between Israel and the church.

This is not to say, however, that Irving was the founder of Dispensationalism. That rather doubtful distinction goes to John Nelson Darby of the Brethren and C. I. Scofield.[13] But Irving was a key figure in the prophetic movement that gave it birth.[14]

One of the tools Irving used to develop and promote these ideas was *The Morning Watch; Or Quarterly Journal on Prophecy, and Theological Review*, which first appeared in March 1829. Irving was originally hesitant about producing such a publication because he did not like magazines,[15] presumably since they had not always been kind to him, but here was one he could control, so he eventually sanctioned it.

The catchcry of *The Morning Watch* was "Watchman, what of the night? Watchman, what of the night? The watchman said, 'The morning cometh and also the night: if ye will inquire, inquire ye: return, come'" (Isa 21:11–12). Patterson describes the publication's worldview as being "entirely shaped by Albury's *a priori* expectations regarding the Second Advent" and

10. Ibid.

11. See Bennett, *Origins*, 44–45.

12. See ibid., 212–35, especially 212 and 231.

13. See ibid., 247–97.

14. See Irving, "Interpretation of All," 788, as discussed in Grass, *Edward Irving*, 172. For a discussion on the relationship between Irving and Darby, see "Edward Irving and John Nelson Darby" on my Edward Irving website, www.edwardirving.org, which includes an examination of the passage mentioned by Grass.

15. Irving to Henry Drummond, December 1, 1828, in Irving, *DL*, 258.

the associated literal hermeneutic.[16] It was edited by John Tudor, though Irving still "pervade[d] the whole publication."[17] Irving and Tudor contributed most of that journal's material. During its four-year lifespan it was one of the most widely read publications of its type. Though its articles dealt with a range of Christian issues, its primary focus was biblical prophecy, and that from a very clear premillennial perspective.[18]

John Owen Tudor (1783–1861 or 1862) was an artist from Wales and a Church of England layman. He became associated with Irving and was later an Apostle in the CAC. Irving described him as "learned, modest, and devout,"[19] and in 1856 Tudor published a book entitled *On the Reconciliation of Geological Phenomena with Divine Revelation*.

The first article in the first issue of *The Morning Watch* was written by Tudor and was appropriately called "On the Study of Prophecy." It was followed by the first in a series entitled "Interpretations of All Those Passages of Prophecy Quoted in the New Testament," which was "Communicated" by Irving. Most of the articles it contained in its first year were on some aspect of interpreting the prophetic Scriptures. These included "On the Duty of Studying Unfulfilled Prophecy" by Tudor, "On the Apocalypse and the Millennium" also by Tudor, and "On the Gradual Unfolding of Prophecy" possibly by Irving or Tudor. But there were also articles on "The Texts and Versions of the Holy Scriptures" by Tudor, "On the Theology of the Periodical Journals of the Present Day" possibly by Irving, and two articles defending Irving's Christology—one by Irving and the other by Chevalier. It also included letters from a variety of correspondents as well as book reviews, including one review of Irving's *Last Days*.[20]

The second year's articles included the expected entries on matters concerning the last days, with issues as varied as "On the Seventh Vial of the Apocalypse," "The Parable of the Ten Virgins," and "Messiah's Reign on the Earth." It also contained responses to a number of criticisms. One article entitled "On Charges Brought against the *Morning Watch*" dealt with such concerns as its "Censure of the Religious World" and its "Bad Spirit." Another was a "Reply to Mr. J. A. Haldane" concerning the human nature of Christ.[21]

16. Patterson, "Designing," 104.
17. Oliphant, *Life*, 2:72.
18. Patterson, "Designing," 13, 17, 20, 60–61.
19. Irving to Isabella Irving, November 30, 1829, quoted in Oliphant, *Life*, 2:100.
20. See *TMW* 1 (1829).
21. See *TMW* 2 (1830).

In December 1829 and the following March, a two-part article by Irving, "Signs of the Times and the Characteristics of the Church," appeared in *The Morning Watch*. In this piece, Irving was again critical of the church, especially evangelicals. For example, commenting on the passage in Matt 23 in which Jesus declared various woes upon the "Scribes and the Pharisees," Irving called "the ministers and rulers and authorities in the church" the modern parallels of the Scribes and the Pharisees.[22] One of Irving's main criticisms of these church leaders was that they rejected Albury teaching about the last days. Indeed, "They have shut up four-fifths, yea, nine-tenths of the sacred volume. All the prophecies they have spiritualized away" and "They have scoffed at judgment." Indeed, Britain's "religious world . . . is a whited sepulcher . . . full of dead men's bones."[23]

He also argued that "the self-named Evangelicals" preached "justification by faith only," but did so in such a way that it became "truly the doctrine of works." In addition, he accused evangelicals of being more interested in "proselytizing unto a party"—that is, to their particular denomination—than in converting people to God and Christ.[24]

Irving further criticized those who believed that the "conversion of the whole world" was a realistic aim. To him now, as Coleridge had said, the world was to be judged, not converted. Indeed, the church in Britain would also be subject to that judgment. Amongst its many sins, "Protestant Britain" had allowed the rich to get richer at the expense of the poor. And, in a reminder of his missionary address, Irving poured scorn on those who believed that the "chief" means to pursue the fruitless aim of converting the world, indeed the "*only*" means, was "the pursuit of money." In fact, every valid institution and practice in the church seemed to be "held at nought, in comparison with the contributions of money, or of time or of talent" to service that end.[25]

Though much of what Irving said in this article is judgmental, exaggerated, and often unfair, there was at least one point on which he was right to focus, and he did it well, though in strong language. Irving began by quoting Jesus' words to the Scribes and the Pharisees, "Woe unto you . . . hypocrites! For ye make clean the outside of the cup and platter, but within they [? ye] are full of extortion and excess" (an Irving paraphrase of Luke 11:39). In Irving's opinion, the modern-day Scribes and Pharisees—church leaders, lay as well as cleric—had likewise taken great care to provide for

---

22. Irving, "Signs of the Times," 643.

23. Ibid., 142–43.

24. Ibid., 644–51.

25. Ibid., 655–56, 664–66.

their own needs, but they ceased "to give heed to [their] extortions and rapines, through [their] much heedfulness to these [their] systematic charities and appointments."

Indeed, more specifically, he accused them of charging "excessive and extortionate premiums and interests, the great gains, which you are daily, hourly practising, by calming your conscience with the decent and decorous domestic economy which you observe, and the regular fixed proportion of your income which you bestow upon charitable and religious uses." He also accused them of filling their coffers by "nefarious practices . . . false pretences" and applying "severe measures" to others in their daily business. Because of this, "Almost half" of Britain's "labouring population" was dependent on charity, "hardly able, at best, to obtain daily bread," and at times the "manufacturing population [was] brought into actual starvation." Yet at the same time, "the wealth of the superior order had increased."

In other words, Christians, leaders and others, were giving to the poor, but ignoring the fact that they were helping to create poverty by their business and domestic practices. Irving warned them that "God looks with an observant eye upon the secret machinations by which wealth is made, as he doth upon the outward and observable methods by which it is expended."[26]

Such accusations as these would win Irving no friends, and such strong language as "extortions and rapines" would make him many enemies. But Irving was by this time used to taking on the world, and when he believed that God was on his side, he was prepared to accept what came.

In fact, in this article Irving was well aware that he was using "penetrating and dividing words" which would "set [his] brethren" against him, but he felt compelled "to obey God rather than man." His accusations, in fact, were an extraordinary mixture of truth and misrepresentation. He claimed that what he said was "uttered in love,"[27] though sadly it did not always sound like it, and it was certain that many would not take it that way.

Irving's tackling of the wealth and poverty issue suggests that he had learned well from Thomas Chalmers. His comments on this matter were also in line with the philosophy of his old friend Thomas Carlyle, and this was almost certainly a subject that they had discussed. Carlyle wrote a book in 1843, during a period of economic crisis and unemployment, called *Past and Present*. In it Carlyle criticized "the Captains of Industry" for getting rich at the expense of the poor and British society generally for regarding the primary aim of human life as "making money," often at the expense of others. Carlyle stated that at that time, two million workers sat "in workhouses,

26. Ibid., 661–66.
27. Ibid., 653.

Poor-law Prisons, or have 'out-door' relief flung over the wall to them." Car-lyle warned that Britain was in danger of suffering a "Revolution and Reign of Terror" like that in France in the previous century if these abuses were not dealt with.[28] Though Carlyle's book was written nine years after Irving's death, the similarity of concern and thought is readily apparent.

In September 1830, an article appeared in *The Morning Watch* that seems to teach what is known as a pretribulation rapture. It was probably written by T. W. Chevalier,[29] who had been present at Albury. The concept the article presented is a little different from that in Dispensational (Left Behind) circles today, but it does seem to teach a rapture of living Christians to heaven before a tribulation, the judgment of God, on earth.[30]

The article also identified two stages in the return of Christ: the "epiphany" and the "parousia." In the first stage Christ would appear, but only in the sky and, in contrast to Left Behind, he is apparently to be seen by all on earth. The dead saints would then rise and ascend into heaven with living Christians. Then after "a certain period of time," which is not specified, Christ will actually return to earth with his saints.[31] This, then, presents a two-stage return and what seems to be a pretribulation rapture, but not a secret one as is common in Dispensational thinking. Irving had written something similar to this in March of that year,[32] and Chevalier was quite likely adapting his ideas. This demonstrates that the eschatology of Ir-ving's circle was moving in a Left Behind direction, with a two-stage return of Christ prior to the Millennium and, seemingly, a pretribulation rapture.

At the end of July 1829, Isabella gave birth to another boy named Gavin. He died the same day. He was buried on his father's birthday.[33] Of the five children born into their family up until this time, three—Edward,

---

28. Carlyle, *Past and Present*, 2–3, 271–73. General William Booth of The Salva-tion Army included extracts from Carlyle's *Past and Present* in an appendix to his *In Darkest England* at "the earnest request of a friend," probably journalist W. T. Stead, "who was struck by the coincidence of some ideas" in the two books (Booth, *In Darkest England*, xxv–xxix). However, Booth made it clear that he had not read Carlyle's book.

29. Only the initials T. W. C. are given in the article, and there were two men associated with Irving with those initials: Chevalier and Rev. T. W. Cole, an Anglican (Patterson, "Designing," 58). It is known that Chevalier wrote for *TMW*, but I have found no evidence that Cole did.

30. In the eighteenth century, Morgan Edwards, a Welsh-American Baptist, was the first to teach what is either a pretribulation rapture or a rapture that occurs in the middle of the tribulation (Bennett, *Origins*, 172–81). Chevalier's article is another early example of this teaching.

31. Chevalier, "On the Epiphany," 587–93.

32. Irving, "Signs of the Times," 156–58. See also Bennett, *Origins*, 224–25.

33. Grass, *Edward Irving*, 130.

Mary, and Gavin—had now died. That this was an era in which many children died in infancy made it no easier to bear. About a month after Gavin's death, Isabella's much-revered grandfather died as well.

In spite of the tragedy of Gavin's brief life, it was soon back to work for Irving. Even when the family holidayed in Brighton in September, he returned to London each Sunday to take the services.[34] Grass suggests that Irving threw himself into his work so vigorously as a means of "coping with loss,"[35] and that may be so, though in his London ministry Irving always bore a heavy workload. Isabella does not appear to have had a similar outlet. The woman's job in that era was in the home, and their home was full of loss and sadness. It was a difficult time for him, but it was worse for her.

The last of the Albury Conferences on the return of Christ was held that December. Another separate conference was held in the summer of 1830, mainly to discuss the charismata, the gifts of the Spirit.

As to *The Morning Watch*, it continued only until 1833. Early in May of that year, "The Lord" spoke to John Tudor at Irving's "breakfast-table," telling him that *The Morning Watch* should cease publication so that he could give more time to his duties as elder at their church. The magazine was then closed down.[36]

34. Oliphant, *Life*, 2:95–98.
35. Grass, *Edward Irving*, 131.
36. Irving to Henry Drummond, May 4, 1833, in Irving, *DL*, 360.

14

The Gifts of the Spirit

Perhaps few ministers in so short a period of time ever did more for the promulgation of the truths of Christianity than was accomplished by Mr. Irving.

—National Scotch Church trustees, August 10, 1832.[1]

IRVING'S CHANGING BELIEFS ABOUT THE MIRACULOUS

Irving's adoption of the charismata was not an instantaneous conversion, nor was it a smooth progression towards acceptance. His views progressed and developed, but not evenly. To examine this development adequately, we first need to go back to the mid-1820s.

It is possible, though unlikely, that as far back as 1823 Irving was considering charismatic issues. Thomas Carlyle reported in a letter to his future wife:

> Irving and I spoke about this project of his and my share in it; but we could come to no conclusion. He figured out purposes of unspeakable profit to me, which when strictly examined all melted into empty air. He seemed to think that if I set down in London streets some strange development of genius would take

1. Hair, *Regent*, 179, appendix C.

182

place in me, that by conversing with Coleridge and the opium eater [Thomas de Quincy] I should find out new channels for speculation, and soon learn *to speak in tongues.*[2]

One has to ask, what was meant by that last phrase, and was it actually said by Irving? Was it speaking in tongues in the Christian charismatic sense, or was it something else? That this was related to two writers who both used opium raises all sorts of additional questions. It may merely refer to Carlyle learning different languages to further his writing career. Yet even then the phrase, if it was indeed uttered by Irving (which must remain uncertain), might indicate the direction in which the preacher's mind was beginning to move. Yet it seems too early for this to be considered a stage in Irving's acceptance of the charismata, which the evidence suggests emerged in the second half of the 1820s.[3]

For example, in *Orations*, published in 1823, Irving had said, "But now the miracles of God have ceased, and Nature, secure and unmolested, is no longer called on for testimonies to her Creator's voice." In addition, with regard to the Scriptures, Irving said, "The vision is shut up, and the testimony is sealed, and the Word of the Lord is ended."[4] Addressing the London Missionary Society in 1824, Irving spoke of missionaries' "gifts of tongues and . . . interpretation of tongues" in a way that implied that the languages that they spoke were acquired by hard work rather than through miracle.[5] Even in the preface to the published form of that address the following year, he still argued that miracles had "ceased."[6] However, in the same place, he argued that the "five offices" in Ephesians: "'apostles, prophets, evangelists, pastors and teachers' are not offices for a time but all times."[7]

Then in *Babylon*, published early in 1826, he argued that "the latter Church" (presumably the post-apostolic church) was denied "a succession of prophets," for "the vision and the prophecy were sealed up." Instead, now the church's ministers did "not speak from immediate inspiration, or prophetic foresight." Yet, he continued, in this age, "every disciple" is being

---

2. Thomas Carlyle to Jane Baillie Welsh, October 22, 1823, *CLO*, emphasis added.

3. Sutherland, "Preaching," 11 n. 31 notes that the poet Tom Moore said that Coleridge claimed to have tried to "steady" Irving on "Daniel and the Revelations" and "the gift of tongues" in 1823. However, the date is incorrect. Moore's diary entry was dated November 9, 1833 (Moore, *Tom Moore's Diary*, 176–77).

4. Irving, *Oracles*, 1–2.

5. Ibid., *Missionaries*, 4.

6. Ibid., xxii–xxiii.

7. Ibid., xx–xxi.

"spiritually taught" by the Holy Spirit.[8] This was, perhaps, a hint that his view was changing.

On October 27, 1825, Irving told his wife that in his sermon preparation he found "a new style creeping upon" him, "whether for the better of for the worse" he did not know. It almost sounds as though he viewed the source of this style as something outside himself. Indeed, he went on, "I seek more and more earnestly to be a tongue unto the Holy Spirit."[9]

Nearly a month later he was probably more convinced that this new style was for the better. He wrote, "Oh, out of what a pit the Lord hath brought me! How I abhor my former self and all my former notions! I was an idolater of the understanding and its clear conceptions; of the spirit, the paralysed, dull, and benighted spirit, with its mysterious dawnings of infinite and everlasting truth, I was no better than a blasphemer."[10] The "spirit" referred to here appears to be his spirit rather than the Holy Spirit, but Irving seems to have had in mind much less dependence upon logic and reason in favor of a deeper communion with the Holy Spirit through his own spirit, which previously was "paralysed, dull, and benighted." Indeed, he almost sounds as though he was intending to dispense with human reason altogether. It is clear that there is a significant shift going on in Irving's thinking, and he did in later life place much less importance upon reason.

When hosting some people from his church at about the same time, he expounded "to them the doctrine of the Holy Spirit, and the withered trunk of form, ceremony and mere doctrine which remained when he was gone."[11]

One visitor he had early in November 1825 was Sarah Evans, "the wild girl." According to Irving, she had been "carried in her mind . . . at the beginning of a sermon" some time before. This seems to mean that on one occasion she cried out while Irving was preaching. Irving considered "that her temporary instability" that brought this about was "a somnambulism of the spirit," which, at this stage in Irving's thinking, probably meant an outburst while in a trance. The word "instability" suggests that Irving did not consider it to be a movement of the Spirit of God, which he might well have done a few years later.

Yet at this time, Irving still regarded her as "a spirit full of inspirations." He also thought that "her very words [we]re remarkable," and he found "a

---

8. Ibid., *Babylon*, 2:320–21.

9. Irving's journal, October 27, 1825, quoted in Oliphant, *Life*, 1:260.

10. Irving's journal, November 23, 1825, quoted in ibid., 1:351.

11. Irving's journal, November 25, 1825, quoted in ibid., 1:359.

strange abundance and fertility in her sayings" that astonished him.[12] This may be the first instance of charismatic gifts in Irving's church, though he did not seem to have seen it that way at the time, and the incident may not have had any direct connection with what was to happen later.

On the evening of that same day, a "very modest and backward" young Scot named Peter Samuel visited Irving. He was "one of the fruits" of Irving's ministry. Irving described him as having "such real utterance of the Spirit" and "such an uplifted and enlarged soul." On occasion, Peter Samuel even "seemed exalted into the third heavens, at times hardly knowing whether he was in the body or out of the body."[13] While one could read too much into incidents such as these, they do suggest that Irving was by this time moving in a charismatic direction.

An extraordinary event was drawn to Irving's attention near the end of November 1825. It concerned a Mrs. S., who was married to "a worthless husband." One night she had a vivid dream in which she clearly saw a church and saw and heard a minister preaching in it. She could describe the church and the preacher in detail, even down to the gown he was wearing. She also heard his text: "Blessed are ye poor, for yours is the kingdom of heaven." She discovered from a friend that the specific style of gown was only worn by the Scottish clergy, so she began to seek them out. At first she drew some blanks, but then turned up at the Caledonian Chapel. When Mrs. S. saw the building, she was sure that it was the church she had seen in her dream. She entered, saw Irving, and became just as certain that he was the preacher she had seen. That night he preached on "Blessed are ye poor."[14]

How accurate an account this is we cannot know, but the woman claimed it was true, and Irving saw no reason to doubt her. Yet this does not necessarily mean that by this time Irving had come to believe in the availability of all the charismata. Many non-Charismatics believe that God can direct his people through dreams, though they are often very cautious in the application of that belief. However, it does suggest that by this stage in his ministry Irving was very open to the supernatural.

In his "Preliminary Discourse" in Lacunza's book, completed at the end of 1826, he argued that "before the dreadful and terrible day of the Lord" Elijah would reappear, events he expected to occur within the next forty years. It would be the time of "the latter rain" during which "mighty and miraculous signs" would be seen.[15] Here Irving is more clearly moving

---

12. Irving's journal, November 2, 1825, quoted in ibid., 1:285.

13. Ibid., 1:287–88.

14. Irving's journal, November 21, 1825, quoted in ibid., 1:338–40.

15. Irving, "Preliminary Discourse," in Ben-Ezra, *Coming*, 1:v.

in a charismatic direction, with the reintroduction of the New Testament charismata being a sign that the end is not far away.

Indeed, he desired that all his people experience the same power of the Spirit that anointed Christ's ministry on earth.

> Now, if ye will receive these things which we have heard, and in your hearts believe them, ye must seek earnestly of the Father, that he would send forth his Spirit into your hearts, and anoint you with his power, as heretofore he anointed the man Jesus of Nazareth, that you also may go about doing good, and destroy the works of the devil. For though no one but the Son of God can discharge that ministry which brought life and immortality to those who were through the fear of death all their life time subject to bondage, yet every one who, like him, would condemn sin in the flesh, and obtain the victory over death and the grave, must walk in his footsteps, and in the same strength prevail over the enemy of souls and all his evil angels. But without the Holy Spirit ye can as little stir in this warfare, as without Christ ye could have known that such a warfare was to be undertaken, or such a victory to be achieved.[16]

In May 1827 Irving preached a sermon on baptism in which he said, "I cannot find by what writ of God any part of the spiritual gift was irrevocably removed from the church." He then went on to quote from the story of the conversion of Cornelius and his household, saying, "because that on the Gentiles also was poured out the gift of the Holy Ghost: for they heard them speak with tongues, and magnify God" (Acts 10:45–46), adding (in brackets in the published edition) "this being the visible sign of the invisible grace." Clearly, Irving's view on the charismata had changed. While in earlier published works he had argued that miracles had ceased, he had now come to believe that such spiritual gifts should still be expected. And tongues was "the visible sign" (really an audible sign) of the work of the inward working of God's Spirit.[17]

In this sermon he also argued against making a distinction between the ordinary gifts and the miraculous gifts. They were all gifts of the same Spirit, and none of them had been revoked. That these gifts did not now arise in the church was not because they were no longer available, but because the church was "under the judgment and wrath of God."[18]

---

16. Irving, "Preliminary Discourse," in ibid., 1:clxxxiv.

17. Irving, "Homilies on Baptism," in ibid., *CW*, 2:276–77.

18. Ibid.

The means to all these gifts, he declared, was through baptism. Baptism is the "solemn transaction of the Church, whereby she doth introduce believers, and the children of believers, into the inheritance of the Holy Ghost." But the gifts of the Spirit could only be "appropriated" through God-given faith, for which Christians needed to pray.[19] Apart from what all this says about the Spirit and spiritual gifts, this is also another example of Irving's firmly held belief that the sacraments were not just signs, but that they also endowed spiritual benefits. They were also seals of God's covenant with his people.

In August 1828 the Regent Square Church employed Sandy Scott as Irving's assistant. Carlyle described him as "a thin black-complexioned, vehement man; earnest, clear, and narrow as a tailor's listing."[20] Scott was appointed as Regent Square's "missionary to preach to the poor" of London.[21] His duties included preaching at Regent Square on Sunday afternoons and, on occasions when Irving was not available, ministering in the local schools and to the poor as well as accompanying elders on their visitation.[22]

Young Scott was to play a key role in the next major step in Irving's story. By this time Scott was convinced that the charismata, the supernatural gifts of the Spirit, were still available in the nineteenth century. Edward Irving also had come to that conclusion by 1827, as we have seen, though he was cautious in expressing it.

When Sandy Scott first arrived in London in August 1828, Irving confessed that he was "very little moved to seek myself or to stir up my people to seek these spiritual treasures." Irving also reported that when at this time he and Scott "went out and in together he used often to signify to me his conviction that the spiritual gifts ought still to be exercised in the Church; that we are at liberty, and indeed bound, to pray for them as being baptized into the assurance of 'the gift of the Holy Ghost,' as well as of repentance and remission of sins." Irving could think of no answer to contest this, and indeed, he regarded it as "altogether unanswerable." Thus Irving's pentecostal convictions were being strengthened by his young assistant, whose powers of argument, according to Irving, were second to none.[23]

Irving's understanding of the Spirit's work grew out of his eschatology, his Christology and understanding of the Trinity, and his sacramental

---

19. Irving, "Homilies on Baptism," in ibid., 2:279–80.

20. Thomas Carlyle to Jane Welsh Carlyle, August 22, 1831, *CLO*. A "listing" is a hem or border.

21. Irving, "Facts Connected," 4:756.

22. Hair, *Regent*, 49.

23. Irving, "Facts Connected," 4:756.

theology. As Elliott says, "Irving's Christology overflowed into his pneumatology." Elliott also argues, "By no later than 1831, Irving's views on the millennium, Christology and the charismata neatly dovetailed into a sophisticated, internally coherent and mutually reinforcing theological system through which he interpreted both the events of his own life and the world around him . . . if any one of these three areas came under doubt, it would have required of Irving nothing less than a wholesale re-evaluation of his theological position."[24] His doctrine of the Spirit, then, was essentially embedded in his Christological conviction that Jesus Christ did not sin because, though his flesh was just like ours, the Holy Spirit gave him the power to live a sinless life and to work miracles.

In his sermons on baptism published in 1828, Irving argued that "the baptised church was still held by God to be responsible for the full and perfect gift of the Holy Ghost, as the same had been received by our blessed Lord upon His ascension unto glory, and by Him shed down upon his church on the day of Pentecost, and by them exercised in all the ways recorded in the book of Acts and the epistles." In other words, the Holy Spirit still moved, or should move, in the church of Irving's day and in the lives of Christian people, complete with the supernatural gifts displayed in the first century, such as tongues and prophecy. The only reason that these gifts had disappeared, or at least seem to have done, was because of the church's "evil heart of unbelief," and 'the hiding of the light of the world' under 'the bushel' of human systems and ordinances." All this Irving claimed in 1832 to have believed for some years.[25]

However, it needs to be noted, as a number of writers point out, that for Irving belief in the charismata grew out of an intense study of Scripture. It was not an experience looking for a theology to support it.[26] As McFarlane says, in Irving's case it "was, if anything, a theology in search of experience, rather than an experience in need of theology."[27] Irving's beliefs about the Spirit, then, emerged first through his study of Scripture. The search for the experience to match those beliefs followed afterwards. In fact, he taught about the spiritual gifts in order "to prepare a people for receiving" them.[28]

24. Elliott, Edward Irving, 178, 182.

25. Irving, "Facts Connected," 4:754. Note that the varied capitalization of the Godhead is in the original.

26. Strachan, Pentecostal, 14–15, 18. See also ibid., 204 n.4, in which Strachan quotes Valentine Cunningham, "Texts and Their Stories—14," Redemption Tidings, October 1, 1970, 3. See also Roxborogh, "As at the Beginning," 2.

27. McFarlane, Edward Irving, 10.

28. Irving, "Facts Connected," 4:755.

In other words, the teaching, drawn from the conviction that this is what the Bible declared, came first; the manifestations came later.

Yet Tim Grass argues that this issue is not quite so one-sided,[29] and to a degree he is right. For while theological consideration appears to have led Irving to accept that these gifts were possible in his day, when they did emerge, this strengthened and extended his theological rationale to justify them. He appears to have been becoming sympathetic to the possible re-emergence of these gifts before he had heard of their apparent reappearance in Scotland, as will be discussed.

But in believing these things, Irving was setting out on a course for disaster. The *Westminster Confession* says that God revealed himself and declared his will "wholly" in the Scriptures, and that "those former ways of God's revealing his will unto his people [have] now ceased."[30] Thus Irving's emerging view was inevitably going to be seen as in conflict with the doctrinal standard of the Presbyterian Church.

THE GIFTS IN SCOTLAND

At the end of 1829, on a visit to Fernicarry (Gare Loch) in western Scotland, Sandy Scott encountered Mary Campbell, a young woman who had consumption and appeared close to death. However, she prayed "in faith" and was suddenly and miraculously healed.[31] It appears that in Scott's following conversations with this woman, he was unable "to convince her of the distinction between regeneration and baptism with the Holy Ghost" (a distinction that not all would accept). Scott urged her to read right through the Acts of the Apostles. This she did, plus John 14–16.

During this time of contemplation, Mary Campbell began to seriously consider missionary service. She believed that preparation in study and learning languages was not necessary because first, Christ would return soon and there was not time to complete the required study, and secondly, God had promised to "furnish his servants with every necessary qualification for their great work," including the ability to supernaturally speak foreign languages. (The expectation that the Spirit would give missionaries the ability to speak in foreign languages that they had not learned became

---

29. Grass, *Edward Irving*, 204.

30. *Westminster Confession*, 1:1.

31. Mary Campbell in A. Robertson, *A Vindication of the Religion of the Land*, quoted in Drummond, *Edward Irving*, 141.

surprisingly common towards the end of the nineteenth century, when the missionary movement was at its peak.)[32]

On a Sunday near the end of March 1830, in answer to prayer, Mary Campbell "began to utter sounds to them incomprehensible, and believed by her to be a tongue as of old might have been spoken on the day of Pentecost, or among the Christians at Corinth." She believed herself to be speaking in the language of the Pelew Islanders of the South Pacific, the group on which her missionary interest had been focused, a point that neither she nor anyone else in the Gare Loch locality could prove or disprove.[33]

Irving's secondhand report of this ran:

> one of her sisters, along with a female friend . . . had been spending the whole day in humiliation, and fasting, and prayer before God, with a special respect to the restoration of the gifts [of the Spirit]. They had come up in the evening to the sick-chamber of their sister . . . and along with one or two others of the household, they were engaged in prayer together. When in the midst of their devotion, the Holy Ghost came with mighty power upon the sick woman, as she lay in her weakness, and constrained her to speak at great length, and with superhuman strength, in an unknown tongue, to the astonishment of all who heard, and to her own great edification and enjoyment in God.

She also began to prophesy. This is a charismatic or pentecostal experience common enough in our own time, whatever one makes of it, but very rare in the early nineteenth century. As word about it got around, it attracted considerable attention.

Mary Campbell had had another sister called Isabella, who had recently died. Isabella had been noted for her saintliness and had frequently been visited by people from a wide area. Irving's old friend Robert Story had written a little book about her that had quickly sold over six thousand copies.[34] But the focus now turned upon Mary and to other people in the neighborhood who had also begun to demonstrate charismatic phenomena.

Among these were some members of a shipbuilding family named Macdonald, who had heard Sandy Scott preach about the Spirit. They lived across the Clyde in Port Glasgow. The daughter, Margaret, had become very ill, and the family feared that she would die. One day she experienced an ecstatic state in which she spoke "mingled praise, prayer and exhortation"

32. McGee, "Taking the Logic," 99–125.
33. Story, *Memoir*, 194–205, 210; Irving, "Facts Connected," 4:757–60.
34. Story, *Memoir*, 138.

for more than two hours. Amidst all this she prophesied, "There will be a mighty baptism of the Spirit this day."[35]

When her two brothers came home from work they found their sister in this state of spiritual ecstasy. In that condition she "addressed them at great length" and then prayed that her brother James would immediately "be endowed with the power of the Holy Ghost. Almost instantly, James calmly said, 'I have got it.' He walked to the window and stood silent for a minute or two." Those who saw him trembled, "there was such a change upon his whole countenance." He then moved to his sister's bedside and said, "Arise and stand upright."[36] This he repeated as he took her hand, and she rose from the bed apparently well. Then, as Oliphant reported, in a wonderful moment of "anti-climax," they all sat down and had dinner. But Margaret's health from that time was much improved, and she began to speak in tongues, as did other members of the household. She even engaged in writing in tongues, which she did at great speed.[37]

While Story was originally enthusiastic about these manifestations in western Scotland, he later strongly doubted that they were authentic. He told Irving that he found Mary Campbell's experiences a "stumbling-block" to any belief in the restoration of the charismata, and he knew her well. Indeed, he claimed that she later told him that she believed that she was wrong to call her "own impressions the voice of God."[38] Yet it does appear that there had been actual instances of healing through this work, and God was no doubt involved in that. They also came when the odds seemed heavily stacked against healing, and so they appeared miraculous to those close to the people involved. But whether any of these cures could be truly called miraculous is now unknowable. It also needs to be noted that both of the Macdonald brothers died of consumption in their mid-thirties.[39] That two leading figures in this spiritual movement died so young of disease suggests that if miraculous cures occurred in that community, they were not common.

Yet interest in the movement was widespread. The visitors came not only from Scotland, but soon from other parts of Britain as word about the manifestations traveled. Thomas Chalmers heard about it, showed much interest, and in typical fashion, reserved judgment on the veracity

---

35. Ibid., 205–206.

36. Ibid., 206–207. See also Oliphant, *Life*, 2:127–35.

37. Oliphant, *Life*, 2:132–35; [Empson?], "Pretended Miracles," 275.

38. Story, *Memoir*, 229–32.

39. Drummond, *Edward Irving*, 151.

of the occurrences.[40] McLeod Campbell, also in a state of uncertainty, told Chalmers, "Whether these things are what they seem to be and whether such things may—yea ought to be in the church are distinct questions."[41] John Nelson Darby of the Plymouth Brethren was one who visited the Macdonald home. Darby went, saw, heard, and left rather unimpressed.[42] Even Thomas Arnold of Rugby School took notice, but he was unsure whether the tongues were "real" or not.[43]

Thomas Erskine of Linlathen (1788–1870), a well-known lay theologian, also paid a visit to the region to investigate the gifts. His report was cautious but generally favorable: "It is certainly not a thing to be lightly or rashly believed," he said, "but neither is it a thing to be lightly or rashly rejected." He believed that the tongues were actual languages, though he could not identify them. Like others who heard these tongues, he described them as being "very loud." In the end, he decided "that it is of God."[44] However, according to Grass, he later changed his mind.[45]

Irving, inevitably, also heard about it. He told Chalmers that the accounts of the experiences of Mary Campbell and Margaret Macdonald "carry to me a spiritual conviction and a spiritual reproof which I cannot express." These events caused Irving to believe that now "The Church of Christ [was] recovering from a long sleep."[46]

In 1831 Mary Campbell married William Caird, a legal clerk, and stayed in London for a while with a member of Irving's congregation. Mary Caird would be referred to a number of times in the later accounts of the charismata at Regent Square.

It appears to have been on the last day of June in 1830 that Irving went to Albury for a three-day conference primarily on the gifts of the Spirit, leaving his family in the company of Isabella's mother. The conference must have been very difficult for him, for his little son Samuel was then seriously ill, which made discussion of these gifts very personal and also rather tricky. While there Irving wrote to his wife, telling her that while God had not given him "assured faith" for Samuel's recovery, God had given him "a

40. Hanna, *Memoirs* (New York), 3:254; Story, *Memoir*, 208–209; Oliphant, *Life*, 2:133–35.

41. McLeod Campbell to Thomas Chalmers, April 28, 1830, quoted in Roxborogh, "Charismatic Movement," 1.

42. Darby, "The Irrationalism of Infidelity," in ibid., *Writings*, 6:283–85.

43. Thomas Arnold to Rev. P. C. Blackstone, October 25, 1831, in Stanley, *Life and Correspondence*, 185.

44. Drummond, *Edward Irving*, 143; Erskine, quoted in Strachan, *Pentecostal*, 72.

45. Grass, *Edward Irving*, 212.

46. Oliphant, *Life*, 2:139; Irving to Mrs. Martin, July 1830, quoted in ibid., 2:148.

perfect resignedness to His will," which he believed was a "precious prepara-tion" for that healing. This does not mean that they were relying on spiritual healing alone, for doctors were summoned to Samuel's bedside. To Irving, sickness should be approached with both the "prayer of faith" and the "use of means."[47]

On the first night at this conference Irving was "afflicted" by some vi-sions and dreams, but he did not elaborate on their nature or any assumed significance. Irving gave few details about the deliberations at the confer-ence itself, though the first session was on the Jews and was "opened" by a Mr. W. Leach, a layman who had attended at least one of the millennial con-ferences.[48] They also discussed Alexander (Sandy) Scott's book, *Neglected Truths*, on the gifts of the Spirit.[49]

Significantly, this conference decided "That it is our duty to pray for the revival of the gifts manifested in the primitive Church; which are wis-dom, knowledge, faith, healing, miracles, prophecy, discerning of spirits, kinds of tongues, and interpretation of tongues; and that a responsibility lies on us to enquire into the state of those gifts said to be now present in the west of Scotland."[50] This was stated by the chairman, Hugh McNeile, but whether all the delegates were in agreement with that statement is unclear.

Irving returned to London mid-conference to take the services in his church, and, one would hope, so that he might see his son. Believing that Samuel would recover, he returned to Albury that Monday. Samuel died that same day. He was the fourth of the Irving children to do so. It is not sur-prising that Irving was criticized within the wider family for leaving Isabella and Samuel at this critical time.[51]

Irving told Henry Drummond in a letter that he was "stunned by the unexpected blow which it pleased the Father to give to what I had thought was my faith in him." Yet another such loss was enough to stun anyone, but Irving had now come to believe, if a little hesitantly, that God would answer the prayers of faithful Christians to heal the sick, so it was a double blow: a blow to his parental love and a blow to his faith. He felt that "God's word seemed to have failed" in this instance.[52] Some days later Irving, his wife,

---

47. Irving to Isabella Irving, July 1 and 2, 1830, quoted in ibid., 2:144–45.

48. Ibid.

49. Grass, "Edward Irving," in Gribben and Stunt, *Prisoners*, 109.

50. Miller, *History*, 1:45–46; Henry Drummond, *Narrative of the Circumstances*, 4, quoted in Grass, *Edward Irving*, 217.

51. Grass, *Edward Irving*, 217.

52. Irving to Henry Drummond, July 7, 1830, in Irving, *DL*, 268–70.

and Maggie, their lone remaining child, retreated to Albury for a chance to rest and mourn in peace.

In the letter to Drummond, Irving continued that while in the book of Acts miracles were commonly worked by the Apostles, we also:

> find that the gift of miracles was connected with certain persons in the Church who were not Apostles but distinct from them. This proves that this gift and the office for which it was the qualification were not limited to the persons of the Apostles nor to the Apostles' times, but belonged to the Church as much as pastors and teachers and governments do . . . If so, then see the conclusion which we come to, that though the prayers of the Church may be most faithful & fervent for healings and miracles and other works of the Holy Ghost which testify to the power of Christ and his presence in his Church, the answer is such cases cannot be obtained because there are no persons who are set apart to minister the gift which the Church has besought & which God waiteth to bestow . . . Think you not that if there was a person gifted of the H-Ghost with the power of miracles & whom I could send as the brethren sent to Peter, that my child might not now by his hand be raised up. For my part I dare not to doubt it, without doubting God and Christ.[53]

Here Irving is reasoning that faithful prayer alone is not enough. In New Testament times certain people were given the gift of healing by the Spirit, and such people needed to be identified in today's church to again fulfill that function. This was presumably a teaching discussed at the recent conference at Albury. In addition, as Elliott points out, "The prize Irving determined on here was nothing less than restoration of the charismata to the laity."[54] He did not suppose that the clergy were the only ones who could be so gifted by God, and in his mind, the Mary Campbell incident only confirmed that.

An article by Irving appeared in the September 1830 issue of *The Morning Watch*, called "The Church, with her Endowment of Holiness and Power." In it he argued that while "Perfect holiness is the inward law and condition of the church . . . Power in the Holy Ghost is her outward action."[55] However, as Gordon Strachan observed, the article said "little about the Church's endowment of holiness," but much more about its power.[56] This

---

53. Ibid. See also Elliott, *Edward Irving*, 172–73; Oliphant, *Life*, 2:141–43.

54. Elliott, *Edward Irving*, 173.

55. Irving, "Church, with Her Endowment," 633.

56. Strachan, *Pentecostal*, 76.

was presumably because of the controversial nature of the supernatural gifts, which thus demanded more explanation and defense.

One crucial question Irving asked in this paper was "how much of [Christ's] power is it his good pleasure to put forth upon this earth during this dispensation of his absence?" It was important enough for him to repeat it, though rephrased, on no less than two occasions.[57]

He answered it by first saying that on the Day of Pentecost the gift of the Holy Spirit was given, which "we are commanded to hold fast until he come." In other words, it was given then, but the same gift is still available today. He then expounded upon Mark 16:17–18, showing the "five particulars" of the Spirit's power still available to the church. They were: "casting out of devils," speaking "with new tongues," taking up "serpents" (which he argued showed that "animal creation" was once more subject to man as it had been before the fall, through what Christ had done), power over the effects of poisons "to him that believeth," and "power over diseases." And all this was "part and parcel of Christ's redemption."[58]

He then turned to chapter 12 of Paul's First Letter to the Corinthians. On that, Irving said that he regarded "the word of wisdom" and "the word of knowledge" (1 Cor 12:8) as the preaching and teaching offices in such churches as the Presbyterian,[59] not necessarily, in the strictest sense, miraculous gifts, but nonetheless Spirit-inspired. With regard to the gift of "faith" (v. 9), this was "not saving faith," but rather the type of faith that "one Christian may have . . . and another may not." That is, it is the kind of faith that, while distinguishable from the working of miracles, is "strong confidence in Christ's power." He understood "the gifts of healing" (v. 9), as noted above, as a gift(s) granted to specific persons in the church. This gift(s) "is part and parcel of the thing preached and by being so confirms it."

Irving continued explaining his understanding of the remaining gifts in this passage, but we will just look at two: prophecy and tongues. Prophecy is "not what is commonly understood by prophesying . . . the mere foretelling of future events, because it is unto men 'for edification and exhortation and comfort.'" This is most striking coming from Irving because in other places he understood *biblical* prophecy, particularly Daniel and Revelation, as very much the "foretelling of future events." Indeed, even here he admits that this is part of it, but one gets the impression that he believed it to be only a minor part. In this article, a prophet is rather, in line with the prophets in the Old Testament, "God's mouth to men." It is in fact, "the same

---

57. Irving, "Church, with Her Endowment," 631, 634.

58. Ibid., 632, 637–42.

59. Ibid., 645–46.

gift which was ministered by the Old Testament prophets—the faculty of shewing to all men their true estate in the sight of God . . . It is for building up and comforting the church, for converting sinners from the error of their ways, and warning the world of the evil to come."

But prophecies need to be tested. To show how this should be done, Irving brought in two other teachings that he had previously emphasized: the human nature of Christ and his millennial kingdom. Does the prophet believe that "Jesus Christ is come in the flesh" (1 John 4:1), and does he or she believe that "Jesus is Lord" (1 Cor 12:3), specifically Lord "of this earth"? If a prophet does not hold to these teachings (that is, in reality, Irving's understanding of them), then his or her prophecy cannot be genuine. This again shows how Irving's doctrines are not isolated units, but all integral parts of a complete theological system.[60]

Irving called tongues "the crowning act of all," for the Old Testament prophets did not have it, nor even did Christ.[61] He regarded the tongues of Acts 2 and the tongues of 1 Corinthians to be in principle the same insofar as he used the Corinthian passages to explain the nature of tongues in the second chapter of Acts. In Acts and Corinthians, the speaker did not understand what was said but was enabled to speak these words in and by the Spirit. It was the listeners in Acts and the interpreters in Corinth who understood what was said, not the speakers. These tongues are as important as prophecy, providing someone is available to interpret them (1 Cor 14:5)—and he did argue for interpretation, not translation. In addition, it was the church's duty to seek "this long-lost endowment," so that it could warn "the world . . . before the great and terrible day of the Lord."[62]

Towards the end of the article Irving further emphasized the interconnectedness of his doctrines when he said, "Christ came to do the Father's will *in our condition*, that we in the like case might be assured of power and ability through Him to do the same. He was the prototype of a perfect and holy man *under the conditions of the Fall*, that we, under those conditions, might know there was power and will in God that we all should be perfect and holy."[63] Just as the Spirit gave Christ, who had normal human nature, power to act and combat sin, the same Spirit is available to us today to do likewise.

Yet a question needs to be asked concerning that point. Did Irving really believe that Christians could be perfect in this life? If Christ had the

---

60. Ibid., 648–49, 651–55.

61. Ibid., 663.

62. Ibid., 657–61.

63. Ibid., 663, emphasis added.

same body as us, and the same Holy Spirit who aided him is also available to us, can we therefore also live without sin like him? Apart from the hint in the passage quoted above, no evidence of this has been found in Irving's writings. He does not appear to have drawn that conclusion from his Christology. Peter Elliott has a point when he says that if Irving had taught Christian perfection, his critics "would have pounced on it,"[64] and there does not appear to be any evidence of such criticism. Therefore, he presumably did not come to that conclusion.

In the foregoing article, Irving was clearly presenting the Spirit's power in mainly miraculous terms. Much of what he said there is echoed in modern Pentecostal and Charismatic circles, though there are differences—his understanding of words of wisdom and knowledge, for example.

Late in August 1830, John B. Cardale, a lawyer who knew a number of languages, led a delegation of six on Irving's behalf to visit the Macdonalds in western Scotland to ascertain the validity of their charismatic gifts. At this time Cardale belonged to an Anglican church under the ministry of the Reverend Baptist Noel, though he later joined forces with Irving.[65] Some of the delegates stayed for three weeks, some longer, visiting people and attending the gatherings. When they had all returned to London, a meeting was held at Regent Square so that they could report their findings. They stated that the tongues speakers claimed "that their organs of speech are made use of by the Spirit of God, and that they utter what is given them, and not an expression of their own conceptions or their own intention." Cardale said that his own observations confirmed that that was so.[66] In other words, their minds were not engaged in any significant sense in the process.

Cardale also wrote a letter reporting on this visit, which appeared in the December 1830 edition of *The Morning Watch*. He said that the tongue-speakers were sincere, devout, and godly, and that the tongues seemed genuine and appeared to be distinct, though different, languages. For example, he claimed that James Macdonald spoke two tongues that were "easily discernible from each other." And while James did not have a good singing voice, it being "harsh and unpleasing," when he sang in the Spirit his voice was "perfectly harmonious." In addition, when the different members of the family spoke in tongues or spoke "in the Spirit in their own language," it

64. Peter Elliott, e-mail message to author, March 14, 2013.

65. Drummond, *Edward Irving*, 153; Grass, "Edward Irving," in Gribben and Stunt, *Prisoners*, 112.

66. Drummond, *Edward Irving*, 152.

had "every appearance of being under supernatural direction." For example, their voices and manner were different from what they normally were.[67]

BACK TO REGENT SQUARE

In the middle of 1830, Sandy Scott left the Regent Square Church when he was called to the Scotch church at Woolwich in London. Irving was no doubt in one respect sad to see him go, but there had been a gap developing between these two men on church organization and other matters that must have made working together difficult. Nevertheless, Irving "praise[d] God for [Scott's new call] above all measure." It seemed to Irving that this appointment bordered on the miraculous, for Scott had "not a man . . . to speak for him."[68]

But Scott being accepted there was, as always, still in the hands of the local presbytery, which had first to approve his ordination. This was not an open-and-shut case. Just being associated with Irving brought suspicion upon Scott, plus it was known that some of his views were, shall we say, unusual. Rather strangely, Scott asked to deliver his trial sermons to the presbytery rather than to the church at large, a practice that, according to Irving, was permitted by "most presbyteries." Oliphant says that this was because of Scott's "delicate health," and he does appear to have been unwell at this time, though one wonders whether there was more to it than that. Whatever the reasons, the move certainly backfired, for Scott was subsequently accused by some sections of the religious press of trying to hide his controversial views. Yet addressing the presbytery was hardly hiding his opinions.[69]

David Brown, later known as a Bible commentator, followed Scott as Irving's assistant from the beginning of 1830 to, probably, the middle of 1832.[70] According to Irving, Brown's understanding of the nature of Christ's humanity was the same as his own. However, Brown's biographer later denied this, saying that he kept quiet on the subject, which might have given the impression of acceptance.[71] Brown also seems to have cautiously

---

67. Cardale, "Extraordinary Manifestations," 869–73.

68. Irving to Rev. Martin, n.d., quoted in Oliphant, *Life*, 2:110–11; Grass, *Edward Irving*, 213.

69. Oliphant, *Life*, 2:121–23, 126.

70. Brown, "Personal Reminiscences," 220; Dallimore, *Life*, 56. Drummond says that Brown remained with Irving until early 1833, but this seems contrary to what Brown says, and is also unlikely because that is at least seven months after Irving was forced to leave the Regent Square Church (Drummond, *Edward Irving*, 156).

71. Irving to Elizabeth Martin, October 13, 1830, quoted in Oliphant, *Life*, 2:151–52; Blaikie, *David Brown*, 42.

accepted the charismata, at least initially.[72] Yet on one occasion when Irving was away, Brown ordered a woman who was speaking in tongues "to be silent." He appears to have been a very hesitant supporter rather than an enthusiast.[73]

Interest in the gifts of the Spirit was stimulated in London in October 1830 when Eliza Fancourt, a clergyman's daughter, was apparently miraculously cured. It was claimed that Miss Fancourt had been healed of a curvature of the spine that had made her unable to walk or even stand. Inevitably, various people outside the movement argued that Miss Fancourt's health problems were caused by her excitable nature and that she did not really have a curvature of the spine at all. Thus, her cure was not anything out of the ordinary.

But an article in *The Morning Watch* the following March argued that Fancourt was not a particularly nervous or emotional person, so therefore that argument had no substance, and the writer then proceeded to give testimony to her condition prior to the healing. It quoted the opinion of a clergyman who had frequently visited Miss Fancourt during her "long confinement" and who spoke of her spirit of "patience and submission." In addition, the article referred to a letter in the *Christian Observer* that testified to her "sobriety of mind" and "the meekness and quietness of her spirit." *The Morning Watch* then gave the opinions and assumptions of various medical men confirming the very real nature of the young woman's spinal condition, though at least two of them rejected the idea that her cure was miraculous.

The article also quoted a letter from Miss Fancourt's father, which spoke of his daughter's "extraordinary restoration to health" and described her as a "restored cripple," the family of whom does not cease "to unite with her in the repetition of praise and thanksgiving, which ascribes to Jesus all the glory."[74] There would seem, then, that there was no doubt in Mr. Fancourt's mind that God was the cause of her healing.

Another article in the same edition of *The Morning Watch* stated, "So far from thinking the cure of Miss Fancourt extraordinary, *whether miraculous or not*, we believe that hundreds and thousands of similar cases have occurred in our own times, among the poor in spirit who are rich in faith" in answer to believing prayer.[75] Here Irving's people seem to be conceding that Fancourt's healing might not have been miraculous, though they may have

---

72. Oliphant, *Life*, 2:204.

73. Pilkington, *Unknown*, 8. See also ibid., 13, 19; Blaikie, *David Brown*, 42, 45; Drummond, *Edward Irving*, 157.

74. "Miracles, Signs, Powers," 150–60.

75. "On Miraculous Powers," 213, emphasis added.

done so because of frustration over the way the term was being bandied about. But even if it was not to be called "a miracle," they still regarded it to be of God in response to prayer, and as such, a remarkable, but not a rare, occurrence.

The *Edinburgh Review* of June 1831, while not rejecting the existence of the miraculous, claimed, "All the practitioners who attended Miss Fancourt, declare that the statement put forth by her friends may be received, every word of it, as true, yet accounted for by the operation of ordinary human causes. In defiance, however, of this unanimous opinion, persons are to be found who persist in crying, Miracle!"[76] Was it a miracle or a cure by "ordinary human causes"? Everybody would probably answer according to his or her own prejudices. However, it can be fairly argued that God is involved in all cures one way or another and that he does answer prayer, but that does not necessarily resolve this specific puzzle.

In the middle of 1831 Irving told a Dr. Orpen that "the raising up of the sick, and the restoring of those who have been long lame are now occurring more frequently amongst us." Indeed, he went on to state that some of the healings were as "wonderful" as those in the New Testament.[77] According to David Bebbington, Irving's church claimed forty-six miraculous healings in just one year, though this may have been a little later.[78] Irving and his associates, then, clearly believed that they were engaging in a Spirit-inspired healing ministry.

THE POWERSCOURT CONFERENCES

In the autumn of 1830 the Irvings went to Ireland and stayed with the Dowager Viscountess Powerscourt. It was hardly a rest, however, for Irving "preached thirteen times in eight days."[79] At one church in Dublin, which was "crowded to suffocation" a large window had been removed and benches placed outside so that the overflow congregation could hear the preacher. The congregation included "many highly respectable Roman Catholic gentlemen."[80]

Lady Powerscourt was a member of the Church of Ireland, though she was beginning to be influenced by some individuals soon to be known collectively as the Plymouth Brethren. Whether it was realized at that time or

76. [Empson?], "Pretended Miracles," 266.

77. Irving to Dr. C. E. H. Orpen, July 21, 1831, in Irving, *DL*, 282.

78. Bebbington, *Evangelicalism*, 91.

79. Isabella Irving to her sister, September 1830, quoted in Oliphant, *Life*, 2:150.

80. *Saunders's News-Letter*, September 18, 1830, quoted in ibid., 2:151.

not, the Albury Conferences had come to an end. It was now time to begin to plan their successors, the Powerscourt Conferences. These were eventually held at Powerscourt House in the years 1831 to 1833, with smaller, less significant conferences at another venue in the following few years. The three main conferences were larger affairs than those held at Albury, with about seventy in attendance at the first, mainly from the Irish Church and the emerging Brethren. The focus was once more the return of Christ and related issues.[81]

The leading figure in these conferences was, without question, John Nelson Darby, who, from this time or soon afterwards, belonged to the Brethren.[82] Irving is thought to have attended the first Powerscourt Conference in October 1831, though there is some doubt on this point. It is also probable that others from Regent Square went to that first Powerscourt gathering. In addition, it does seem that Irving and Darby had met the previous year. The relationship between Irving and Darby is not important in the story of Edward Irving, though it is very significant in the field of millennial studies. However, it will not be dealt with here.[83]

Though Irving intended on going to Edinburgh for the Presbyterian Church's Assembly in May 1831, affairs at home stopped him. This may have been a relief for everybody. But if absent in body, he was very much present in spirit. Irving led a prayer meeting in his church each morning at 6:30 during the week of the Assembly, specifically praying for its deliberations.[84] These morning prayer meetings became a regular feature of life at Regent Square and generally lasted about an hour-and-a-half; on occasions there were hundreds in attendance.[85]

In 1823 Irving had told William Hamilton, "I foresee infinite battles and contentions, not with the persons of men, but with their opinions. My rock of defence is my people. They are also my rock of refuge and consolation."[86] The "battles and contentions" were well under way. The question now became, would the "rock of defence . . . refuge and consolation" Irving found in his people remain a solid support?

---

81. Bennett, *Origins*, 270.

82. It is difficult to date precisely when the Brethren first came into being and when Darby left the Established Church to join them. See, for example, Stunt, *Awakening*, 287–95.

83. For more information on the relationship between Irving and Darby, see "Edward Irving and John Nelson Darby" on my Edward Irving website, www.edwardirving.org.

84. Oliphant, *Life*, 2:172–74.

85. Hair, *Regent*, 59; Pilkington, *Unknown*, 33.

86. Irving to William Hamilton, September 29, 1823, in Irving, *DL*, 187.

15

Dissent in London

Had he been prudent, he might have found some better way of deprecating the censures that threatened him; but he was not prudent.

—MARGARET OLIPHANT[1]

THE PRESBYTERY'S DECISION

It was clear to some at Regent Square, to members of the wider Presbyterian Church, and to observers from other churches that Irving could not go on unchecked. In fact, dissent was moving very close to home.

The period from 1830 to 1831 was a time of great change for the National Scotch Church. Regent Square's congregation was continually undergoing change as some departed because of Irving's extravagancies even as they drew new people to the church. As Oliphant observed, the newcomers, for the most part, were neither Scotch nor Presbyterian, which caused the very character of the church to change.[2]

On April 20, 1830, the London presbytery (made up of local ministers and some lay elders) met for the ordination examinations of Alexander Scott, who was at that time Irving's assistant. "In consequence of some doubts that existed concerning" Scott's Irving-like understanding of the humanity of

1. Oliphant, *Life*, 2:224.
2. Ibid., 2:231.

Christ, four ministers of that presbytery, including Irving, met with him again two days later. When the discussion with Scott had concluded, he left the meeting. But those who remained continued the debate, in which at least two of Irving's colleagues "freely stated their decided opposition" to Irving's views (and thus also to Scott's) and "pointed out several objectionable passages" in Irving's *The Orthodox and Catholic Doctrine of Our Lord's Human Nature.*[3]

A committee, which appears to have been the presbytery under another name and included Irving, was appointed to further consider the matter on May 20. From its deliberations this committee drew up a statement that read: "That the Son of God took human nature of ye substance of his mother, which (human nature) was wholly and perfectly sanctified by ye power of ye Holy Ghost, in the act of conception, and was upheld in the same state by the same power of the Holy Ghost, & underwent no process or progress of sanctification, as it needed none."[4]

Most members of this committee were against Irving's views and were delighted with this outcome. The presbytery recorded that this statement "struck at the root of Mr. Irving's peculiar sentiments" and the members hoped that "he would see the unscriptural character of his doctrine" and abandon it. Yet, according to the committee's report, Irving "fully acquiesced" to the statement.[5]

They, it seems, had won. But had they?

The next day, Irving wrote to Mr. MacDonald to tell him that the meeting had drawn up a statement that was agreed to "with one consent," which confirms that Irving had approved it. However, his wording of the statement in this letter, probably from memory, was a little different from the committee's record. He reported that it said, "That the human nature of our Lord was of the virgin's substance, perfectly and completely sanctified or purified in the generation of it by the work of the Holy Ghost, and underwent no process or progress of purification."[6]

A week after that meeting Irving wrote to his father-in-law, giving a third version of the statement. He told Mr. Martin that it said, "That the human nature of our Lord was of the virgin's substance, sanctified and purified by the work of the Holy Ghost in the generation, and sustained always in the

3. *Brief Statement,* 5.

4. *Minutes of the Scots Presbytery of London: April 28, 1823 to November 11, 1834,* vol. 2 of (United Reformed Church Historical Society, Cambridge) folios 189–93, quoted in Grass, *Edward Irving,* 184, 219–20.

5. *Brief Statement,* 6.

6. Irving to Mr. MacDonald, May 21, 1830, quoted in Oliphant, *Life,* 2:123.

same state by the same work of the Holy Ghost and underwent no process or progress of purification."[7]

These three accounts, though different, are not significantly so. The first, the meeting's record, must be regarded as the correct one, and the other two are either Irving working from memory or deliberately paraphrasing the original.

In the letter to his father-in-law Irving, like his opponents on the committee, seemed well pleased with this statement. Perhaps *he* had won after all.

But why is it that this statement was agreed to by both Irving and his opponents? The answer is that it was a compromise, blatantly ignoring the most divisive aspects of the subject. Those believing that Christ's humanity was like Adam's *before* the fall could have said "Amen!" to it, and so could those who held, like Irving, that Christ's humanity was like Adam *after* the fall. It seems astonishing that either side could have thought this statement settled the matter. It clearly did not. It avoided terms such as "sinful flesh" and "sinful substance," no doubt to please the majority of the committee, but it included nothing that Irving would have disagreed with. He quite probably made mental additions to the statement to bring it more fully in line with his beliefs, but the statement itself was neither a support nor a rejection of his position.

A few weeks later, a member of the presbytery warned Irving by letter that he intended to protest at their meeting on July 20, 1830, about some of Irving's views presented in his book on the incarnation. Irving argued that it would be unbiblical for the man to take his protest to "the Church" before they had met and had discussed the issues face-to-face.[8] The gentleman in question agreed, and since there was not time for them to meet one-on-one before the next meeting of the presbytery, he did not raise the matter then. However, another man did. Irving protested, and the presbytery agreed that the matter was not one for them to discuss until this second man had raised the matter with Irving personally.

Some weeks passed before anyone approached Irving about this, then the original protester did. When they met, Irving asked him to point out the parts of the book that he objected to. According to Irving, he "either would not or could not." Instead, the man said that he would put his objections in writing, but Irving claimed that he never did.[9]

---

7. Irving to Rev. Martin, May 27, 1830, in ibid., 2:126.

8. Irving had also argued for this principle in one of his homilies on baptism back in 1825 or 1826. See Irving, "Baptism," in ibid., *CW*, 2:402–403.

9. Oliphant, *Life*, 2:158–59.

Irving was away for the next meeting of the presbytery, and his main antagonist tried to raise the issue in his absence but was overruled. After this, it appears that two different members of the presbytery met with Irving privately to raise a couple of points in the book that they were uneasy about. However, according to Irving, this discussion passed without any difficulty or unpleasantness.

At the presbytery's meeting on October 19, which seems to have comprised four ministers, including Irving and three lay elders, the original protester brought before the meeting his concerns about Irving's book, *The The Orthodox and Catholic Doctrine of Our Lord's Human Nature*, reading "many passages to which he objected." His accusation seems to have been that Irving was teaching that Christ had actually sinned. Irving stood up to argue to the contrary and "moved that" his accuser "should be censured for setting at nought both the canon of the Lord and the order of the Presbytery." But to Irving's "astonishment and vexation" his associates, including the two men he had earlier met with privately, supported the protester.[10]

This was a major blow to Irving. Here he was being seriously challenged on his home ground. But this should have come as no surprise to him, for it seems that four of the six other members in this presbytery had already raised issues regarding his beliefs, and though he seems to have felt that two of those had been satisfied with his explanation at the prior private meeting, this was presumably not the case. But clearly Irving was shocked by this development. The only member of the presbytery who seems to have supported him in this latest meeting was William Hamilton, his brother-in-law, who was an elder from Regent Square.

For a second time at this meeting, Irving rose to his feet and told them that while he was prepared to submit to them "In everything that affected [his] conduct amongst them as a brother," he would not submit to them regarding his "standing as a preacher and ordained minister of the Church of Scotland as the minister of the National Scotch Church at Regent Square," because, in keeping with the "trust-deed," he had been "ordained by a Presbytery in Scotland."

According to Irving, the other members of the presbytery responded to this by arguing that he was "wholly and entirely at their tribunal." Irving rose to speak for a third time to respond to this, pleading his standing as a minister and a servant of the Scottish Church in London. But his colleagues did not respond favorably. Irving was clearly now in a quandary. In his later preface to *Christ's Holiness*, he said that he was faced with a choice between giving up "his standing as a minister of Christ to the judgment of these six

10. Ibid., 2:159–60; *Brief Statement*, 8.

men, or to dissolve [his] voluntary connection with them." He chose what he believed to be the lesser of these "two evils." He withdrew from the meeting and from the presbytery.[11]

In his absence, the presbytery appointed two committees. The first was to compare Irving's book on Christ's human nature with the Scriptures and "the Standards of the Church of Scotland." The second was to "receive Mr. Irving's reasons of protest." Both committees were to report back to the next meeting.

On October 25 Irving wrote the required response to the second committee, protesting about the presbytery's errors "with respect to discipline" in their conduct of this affair. The presbytery received the letter but was not impressed, and they laid the blame on Irving. The first committee reported later and found that Irving's book contained "errors subversive of the great doctrines of Christianity," condemning it.[12]

Thus far, Irving's exclusion had been his choice. However, at the meeting on December 14, 1830, the presbytery not only "condemned [his] writings," but also "excommunicated [him] from their body," announcing that he would not be readmitted until he recognized the "authority" of the presbytery and "openly renounced [his] errors." And this decision was "to be read from the pulpits."[13]

DECLARATION ON THE DIVINITY OF CHRIST

The day after his expulsion from the presbytery the Regent Square session met and, Irving said, "drew up, and subscribed with their hands, a solemn testimony to the truths taught by me and held by us," which was to be read from that pulpit the following Sunday. "We are as one man," he continued, "blessed be the Lord, and so is *all* my flock."[14]

The session's declaration read:

> We, the Minister, Missionary [David Brown], Elders, and Dea-
> cons of the National Scotch Church, Regent Square, feel it a duty
> we owe to ourselves, to the Congregation to which we belong, to
> the Church of Christ, and to all honest men, no longer to remain

11. Preface to Edward Irving, *Christ's Holiness in the Flesh*, quoted in Oliphant, *Life*, 2:158–60; Irving to Mr. MacDonald, mid-December 1830, quoted in ibid., 2:161; *Brief Statement*, 8.

12. *Brief Statement*, 9–12, 14–15.

13. Ibid., 14–16; Irving to Mr. MacDonald, mid-December 1830, quoted in Oliphant, *Life*, 2:161.

14. Ibid., emphasis added.

silent under the heavy charges that are brought against us . . . and therefore we Solemnly declare:

That we utterly detest and abhor any doctrine that would charge with Sin, original or actual, our Blessed Lord and Saviour Jesus Christ, whom we worship and adore as "the very and eternal God, of one substance and equal with the Father; who, when the fullness of time was come, did take upon Him man's nature, with all the essential properties and common infirmities thereof, yet without Sin; very God and very man, yet one Christ, the only Mediator between God and man;" who in the days of His flesh was "holy, harmless, undefiled, and full of grace and truth;" [*Westminster Confession*, ch. 8] "who through the Eternal Spirit offered Himself without spot to God" [Heb 9:14]; "The Lamb of God that taketh away the sin of the world" [John 1:29], "a Lamb without blemish and without spot" [1 Pet 1:19]; in which offering of Himself "He made a proper, real, and full satisfaction to His Father's justice in our behalf" [*Westminster Confession*, ch. 11]. And we further declare that all our peace of conscience, progress in Sanctification, and hope of Eternal blessedness, resteth upon the sinlessness of that Sacrifice, and the completeness of that atonement, which he hath made for us as our substitute.

And finally we do solemnly declare that these are the doctrines which are constantly taught in this Church, agreeably to the standards of the Church of Scotland, and the Word of God.[15]

This declaration was signed by Irving and Brown; elders Archibald Horn, David Blyth, William Hamilton, Duncan MacKenzie, and James Nisbet; and deacons Charles Vertue, Alex Gillespie, John Thomson, J. Henderson, Thomas Carswell, and David Ker. It was sent to each member of the London presbytery and was published in the major daily and weekly newspapers.[16]

One suspects that the wording of that declaration was mainly the work of Irving. It cleverly included extracts from the *Westminster Confession*, the Scottish Church's current standard, as well as biblical verses. The part about Christ having "common infirmities" with other human beings, as we saw before, may fit better with Christ's human nature being like Adam's *after* the fall, rather than *before* it, thus supporting Irving's position.

15. Oliphant, *Life*, 2:164; Hair, *Regent*, 55, 180, appendix C; Irving and the Elders of Regent Square to *The Times*, "Declaration on the Divinity of Christ," December 18, 1830, in Irving, *DL*, 276–77.

16. *Brief Statement*, 3.

However, here we may once more have an instance of Irving sensing unanimity where it did not exist. True, it appears that all the members of session were present at this meeting[17] and each one signed the document, but did some, perhaps, do so out of duty or with reluctance? Certainly it would soon become very clear that "all" his flock was not one with him.

The London presbytery met again on the first day of 1831 to discuss how to respond to the Regent Square declaration. Because Irving and his associates had gone public with their statement, the presbytery thought it necessary to do likewise and published their deliberations in *A Brief Statement* that ran to over thirty pages. This gave the presbytery's account of its dealings with Irving during this troublesome period.

As far back as the summer of 1828, Irving had warned his wife to prepare herself for their being cast "out of the synagogue."[18] Now with the London presbytery opposing him, this eventuality had moved a step closer, and when other ministers were dismissed from their positions by the General Assembly of 1831 for opinions Irving also held, it appeared inevitable.

---

17. William Dinwiddie's name is missing from the list, but he had died the previous January (Hair, *Regent*, 56).

18. Irving to Isabella Irving, July 25, 1828, quoted in Oliphant, *Life*, 2:45.

16

The Charismata at Regent Square

[Irving's] actual management of the manifestations was distinctly
muddle-headed.

—ANDREW LANDALE DRUMMOND[1]

THE TONGUES IN LONDON

An even more divisive issue was at hand. In September and December of
1830, Irving had two articles published in *The Morning Watch*: "The Church,
with Her Endowment of Holiness and Power" and "On the Gifts of the Holy
Ghost, Commonly called Supernatural," the latter being the first in a series
under that title.[2] Considering that little, if anything, had happened of a
charismatic nature so far at Regent Square, they were largely theoretic. But
they no doubt paved the way for what was to come.

On April 30, 1831, Emma Cardale, the wife of the leader of Regent
Square's delegation to Scotland, became the first person associated with
that church to speak in tongues. This was in a small private gathering, not
in a formal church service. She spoke what appeared to be three sentences
in an unknown tongue and then three in English, which were "The Lord

---

1. Drummond, *Edward Irving*, 272. Lee refers to Irving's "clumsy control" of
tongues, which "drove his church into chaos" (Lee, "Christ's Sinful Flesh," 205).

2. Irving, "Church, with Her Endowment," 630–68; ibid., "On the Gifts," 850–69.

will speak to His people. The Lord hasteneth His coming" and "The Lord cometh." Thus there was nothing particularly unusual in the message itself, just in the assumed nature of its delivery. It is also noteworthy that two of the sentences related to Christ's second coming, which demonstrated an Irving emphasis. Soon after this Mary Hall, the governess of the children of Spencer Perceval (a Member of Parliament and one of the Albury delegates), also spoke in tongues.[3] At last what had so long been prayed for had come about, or so it seemed.

In July Irving was delighted to be able to tell Robert Story, "two of my flock have received the gift of tongues and prophecy." However, speaking in tongues initially was kept to small gatherings in homes, by individuals in their private devotions, and in the church's prayer meetings. Irving did not at first allow it in the Sunday services.[4]

David Brown remembered that at around this time, a small number would go to Irving's home for breakfast after the morning prayer meetings. He recalled that on one such occasion, Emily, the daughter of Mr. and Mrs. Cardale, "began to breathe heavily and increasingly so, until at length she burst out into loud but abrupt short sentences in English, which after a few minutes ceased. The voice was certainly beyond her natural strength, and the subject-matter of it was the expected power of the Spirit not to be resisted by any who would hear." This was followed by "utterances" from Miss Hall and Edward Taplin, a teacher whom Brown found repellant.[5]

But why did Irving not allow it in the Sunday services? On the one hand, he sincerely believed that these happenings were God's answer to prayer and therefore should be permitted. But on the other, he still seems to have had a degree of uncertainty about them, and, no doubt, he felt that these practices also went against his experience of church and the traditions of the Church of Scotland, which he, up until now, had always sought to uphold. Before he was prepared to take that step, he set about testing these manifestations to see if they were genuine spiritual gifts.

As it happened, all the people that he heard prophesy in the early stages were folk he already knew. He felt that this was providential and important because he needed to be sure of the sincerity and character of those claiming these gifts and that they were not just putting on a show. He also paid careful attention to the content of the English-language prophecies to make sure that they were sound in doctrine. If they were not true to Scripture, then they could not be of God.

---

3. Drummond, *Edward Irving*, 153.

4. Irving to Robert Story, July 1831, quoted in Oliphant, *Life*, 2:186, 188.

5. Brown, "Personal Reminiscences," 268.

In Irving's words, the gifts were tested "first, by the walk and con-versation of the persons; secondly, by trying it according to the form of Scripture, seeing whether it had the sign of the tongue, and whether the prophesying was for edification, and exhortation, and comfort; thirdly, by the consciousness of the Spirit within myself, bringing conviction to my own heart; fourthly, by submitting it to *all* the people."[6] As far as Irving was concerned, these early prophecies passed each test, though not "*all* the people" accepted them.

Yet as the movement developed, some protested about Irving not al-lowing tongues in the church services. If these tongues and prophecies were truly from God, as the speakers and Irving believed, why should they not be heard in the church? This challenge troubled Irving's conscience for a number of weeks.

It appears to have been on Sunday, October 16, that he changed his mind. That morning he "went to the church, and after praying" he said to the congregation, "I cannot be a party in hindering that which I believe to be the voice of the Holy Ghost from being heard in the church. I feel that I have too long deferred." He then read two passages from the Bible, including 1 Cor 14:23, and continued, "I cannot longer forbid, but do, on the other hand, in the name of the Lord Jesus Christ . . . permit, at this meeting of the Church, that every one who has received the gift of the Holy Ghost, and is moved by the Holy Ghost, shall have liberty to speak." He then pointed to those that he had previously heard exhibit tongues and prophecy in private meetings. According to Irving's account, later during that service "It pleased the Lord . . . to sanctify it by His approval."[7]

Irving said that the first woman to speak in tongues in the church had felt a powerful impulse to do so and "fled out of the church into the vestry," perhaps from embarrassment or because she did not want to interrupt the meeting. This appears to have been Miss Hall, the governess. She found this impulse "quite irresistible" and gave "vent to that volume of majestic sound which passed through two closed doors, and filled the whole church."[8] The interpretation of her outburst, according to Irving, was "Why will ye flee from the voice of the Lord? The Lord is with ye; if ye flee now, where will

---

6. Oliphant, *Life*, 2:187–89; William Harding, *The Trial of the Rev. Edward Irving Before the London Presbytery*, 34, quoted in Grass, *Edward Irving*, 259, emphasis added.

7. Oliphant, *Life*, 2:194–95. Washington Wilks and the *Christian Advocate* of Oc-tober 31, 1831, also gave October 16 as the date, but George Pilkington said that it was October 9 (Wilks, *Edward Irving*, 205–206; Pilkington, *Unknown*, 5).

8. Irving, "Facts Connected," 4:760; Dallimore, *Life*, 114; "Disturbance at the National Scotch Church," *Country Times*, October 24, 1831, 339.

ye flee on the day of judgment?"[9] However, John Tudor claimed that she voiced criticism of tongues and prophecy being banned in the services. Yet Tudor also stated that not all her words were clearly heard.[10]

Another witness to this event was George Pilkington, who was soon to be recognized by Irving as a prophet, though he later regarded tongues and prophecy as a delusion. He also recalled the lady rushing down the aisle into the vestry and, it seems, another woman going down another aisle and right out of the building. This, he said, was followed by one or both of these women speaking loudly enough to be heard by the entire congregation of fifteen hundred to two thousand people.

It is impossible now to establish which of these accounts is the most accurate. They probably each hold some truth. Indeed, there is nothing actually contradictory in the three records. That one remembers that the woman said one thing and another something else could mean that she said both.

Not surprisingly though, these happenings resulted in "the utmost confusion" inside the church. Many stood up and craned their necks to try to see what was going on, and a babble of very ordinary English tongues arose from inside the building expressing that confusion. Irving, obviously, had to respond to this. He did with a brief explanation and a change of sermon topic. He preached from 1 Cor 14.[11]

That evening the church was even more crowded than usual, and there was an air of great excitement and expectancy. Irving began by explaining what had happened in the morning service, and he urged everybody to keep their seats and listen carefully if such a thing occurred again. It did.

George Pilkington said that as Irving concluded his sermon on 1 Cor 12 a "Brother . . . suddenly burst out" in a "crash of Tongue" and then said in English, "God is amongst us, and if you fly from him now, where will you fly in the day of judgment?" *The Times* of October 19, 1831, along with other papers, reported that at this service it was a "Mr. Taplin" who "commenced a violent harangue in the unknown tongue," which was followed by "several ladies [screaming] aloud," with some rushing to the doors and other members of the congregation standing on their seats to see what was going on. John Tudor also named Taplin as the speaker on this occasion, and his report of the words spoken is very similar to Pilkington's.

9. According to *The Morning Herald*, quoted in "The Rev. Edward Irving and the Unknown Tongue," *Baldwin's London Weekly Journal*, October 29, 1831, and in an article by the same name in the *Christian Advocate*, October 31, 1831, 3.

10. John Tudor to Robert Baxter, October 26, 1831, quoted in Grass, *Edward Irving*, 233. The original is held by the Banner of Truth Trust in Edinburgh.

11. Pilkington, *Unknown*, 10–11, 23–25.

This outburst resulted in even greater confusion than there had been in the morning. "One young lady" near Pilkington "screamed and fell in a fit upon her mother's lap." This caused further noise and bustle, and there were cries of "Order! Silence! Order!" Some in the congregation stood on their pews to see what was going on, while others walked out. But above the din, the "Brother's voice was still audible." *The Times* said that the whole occurrence "formed a scene which perhaps partook as much of the ridiculous as of the sublime."[12]

Irving later said that he regarded such tongue-speaking as the same as that which took place on the Day of Pentecost, though what happened in Acts 2 was in some respects unrepeatable. And the true speaker of these tongues "is not man [or woman], but the Holy Ghost." He believed that on the Day of Pentecost two different kinds of tongues were in operation, though he admitted that this could not be proven from Acts 2. Those tongues were an "unknown tongue" and normal, but Spirit-inspired, human language. This, Irving claimed, also commonly happened in the modern instances—an unintelligible tongue followed by a message in English.[13]

The Regent Square session met the following Friday. It seems to have been a very tense meeting, lasting four hours. One of the elders, James Nisbet, had previously expressed reservations about the gifts even before they had appeared in the Sunday services.[14] According to Nisbet, at the meeting Irving was "very decided in the expression of his views." The other members of session were either "doubtful" or "not convinced" about the validity of the manifestations and their place in the services.[15] Sadly, the minutes of session during Irving's ministry at Regent Square have been lost,[16] so we lack further details of this crucial meeting.

On the following Sunday morning, Irving began the service by explaining what had happened the previous week and then later preached upon Joel 2:28: "I will pour out my spirit upon all flesh." According to the *Morning Herald*, the only tongue to be heard as the service progressed was Irving's, except when a woman twice let out a "suppressed hysterical cry"

---

12. *The Times*, October 19, 1831 (originally published in *The World*), quoted in Oliphant, *Life*, 2:202–203. See also "Disturbance at the National Scotch Church," *Country Times*, October 24, 1831, 339; *Christian Advocate*, October 31, 1831, 3; Pilkington, *Unknown*, 11–12; John Tudor to Robert Baxter, October 26, 1831, quoted in Grass, *Edward Irving*, 233. Oliphant gives the month of *The Times* report as November, but it was October (Thomas Carlyle to Margaret A. Carlyle, October 20, 1831, n. 3, *CLO*).

13. Irving, "Facts Connected," 4:760–61. See ibid., 4:761 for the two tongues.

14. Irving to James Nisbet, September 7, 1831, in Irving, *DL*, 283–84.

15. James Nisbet's diary, quoted in Hair, *Regent*, 61.

16. Hair, *Regent*, 1.

during Irving's prayer.[17] It may have been that evening that Irving positioned his tongue-speakers at the front of the gallery so that they could be heard by the whole congregation. Miss Hall seems to have been the only one that obliged during the service, but Emily Cardale also did so at its conclusion. The English part of their prophecy was "Beware, beware it is a reality," oft repeated.[18]

According to Mrs. Hamilton, Irving's sister-in-law, at one Sunday evening service, probably early in November, the church was packed with "The galleries . . . fearfully full" and included some men out to make trouble. When Irving was approaching the end of his sermon, "another of the ladies" burst out in a tongue. While she did so, the congregation was mainly silent for a "few minutes," and even Irving presumably stopped speaking. Then "some fellows in the gallery" became restless and "began to hiss." Other people called out "Silence!" though whether to the woman or the "fellows" is unclear. Then still others began to cry out "one thing, and some another," which resulted in "a state of extreme commotion."[19]

Not surprisingly, as the large congregation became agitated, Mrs. Hamilton recalled the terrible tragedy of the gallery collapsing at the Kirkcaldy Kirk, as, no doubt, did Irving. An overcrowded church and "extreme commotion" spelled danger. Irving had sat down as the woman spoke, but he now rose to his feet and said, "Let us pray." He then led them in prayer "in an unfaltering voice" several times using the words, "Oh, Lord, still the tumult of the people." The tumult subsided. They sang. Irving next announced that there would be further opportunity in future morning services for people to "exercise their gifts," and he then dismissed the congregation, though some, perhaps for a variety of reasons, were very reluctant to leave. Mrs. Hamilton said that it all reminded her "of Paul at Ephesus."[20]

Ten days after the initial occurrence of tongues in the church Irving wrote to Rev. Martin, his father-in-law, in triumph, telling him:

> Thanks should be returned in all the churches for the work which the Lord has done and is doing amongst us. He has raised up the order of prophets amongst us, who, being filled with the Holy Ghost, do speak with tongues and prophesy. I have no doubt of this; and I believe that if the ministers of the Church

17. *The Morning Herald*, quoted in "The Rev. Edward Irving and the Unknown Tongue," *Baldwin's London Weekly Journal*, October 29, 1831.

18. *Christian Advocate*, November 28, 1831.

19. Undated letter from Mrs. Hamilton, quoted in Oliphant, *Life*, 2:201–2. Oliphant seems to have placed this incident out of sequence.

20. Ibid. Grass has another account of what appears to be the same incident in Grass, *Edward Irving*, 239.

will be faithful to preach the truth, as the Lord hath enabled me
to be, God will seal it in like manner with the baptism of the
Holy Ghost . . . I desire you to rejoice exceedingly, although it
may be the means, if God prevent not, of creating great confusion in the bosom of my dear flock . . . but the Lord's will be
done. I must forsake all for Him. I live by faith daily, for I daily
look for His appearing.[21]

Irving was already well aware that not all in his congregation accepted
that these manifestations were from God, and he suspected that trouble was
brewing.

Indeed, early in November he told Mr. MacDonald, "Most of the Session
dislike all this" and they were just a few amongst the "many adversaries."[22]
William Hamilton, Irving's brother-in-law and an elder at Regent Square,
retreated into the country to consider the issue and took time to write to
Rev. John Martin. In this letter he expressed his grave doubts about the
manifestations. Yet he acknowledged Irving's sincerity in the matter and
admitted that the people demonstrating these phenomena were "very holy
and exemplary persons." This probably meant that he did not believe that
they were faking it, but that did not remove the possibility that they were
deluded.[23] In fact, in what appears to have been a slightly later letter from
Hamilton to Martin, he actually called these manifestations "a delusion."[24]
In the end Hamilton opposed Irving on this, though reluctantly, and only
one member of the session, Duncan Mackenzie, supported Irving.[25] When
a Presbyterian minister does not have the support of his session, he is in
trouble.

There was also more opposition from within the family. Rev. Martin
wrote Irving a number of letters in which he criticized his son-in-law for
allowing these manifestations. These letters troubled Irving greatly. He responded by arguing that Martin was condemning him "without adequate
information" and even "without due tenderness and love."[26] While it was
true that Rev. Martin did not have firsthand experience of what was going
on at Regent Square, his main source of information concerning it seems to
have been William Hamilton, whom one would have expected to give a fair

21. Irving to Mr. Martin, October 26, 1831, in Oliphant, *Life*, 2:193.

22. Irving to Mr. MacDonald, November 7, 1831, quoted in ibid., 2:204–205.

23. William Hamilton to Mr. Martin, November 1831, quoted in ibid., 2:214.

24. William Hamilton to Mr. Martin, December 8, 1831, quoted in Hair, *Regent*,
64.

25. Oliphant, *Life*, 2:226–27. Mackenzie was later an apostle in the CAC (Hair,
Regent, 187, appendix E).

26. Irving to Rev. Martin, March 7, 1832, in Oliphant, *Life*, 2:252–53.

assessment of events even though he opposed them. Hamilton was certainly not anti-Irving, though he clearly found this whole issue very disturbing.

In one of the services on Sunday, November 20, Irving paused after reading the Scriptures (1 Cor 14 once more) and again after preaching specifically to allow for anyone so inspired to speak, whether in a tongue or in an English-language prophecy. Emily Cardale did so, apparently in English, "exhorting" the congregation to ask for "the waters of the Holy Spirit." Irving later wrote, "It was very solemn, and all was still attention." However, things did not remain still for long. Archibald Horn, a member of session, approached the pulpit carrying a Bible and asked Irving's "permission to read out of the Scriptures his reason for leaving the church and never entering it more." Irving refused to let him speak. Horn "went into the vestry, took his hat," and left. To Irving, this was "a fearful thing!"[27] Yet some would argue that here Irving allowed the wrong thing, but forbad the right. Eventually, Horn reconsidered his position and stayed at Regent Square, continuing as a trustee but resigning from the session.[28]

That same month, Irving met with the church's trustees and made it clear to them that he "could not . . . take any half measures." He pointed out that according to the trust deed, the conduct of the services at Regent Square was in the hands of the minister, so if he allowed tongues and prophecies in the services, then, in his opinion, that conduct was in keeping with the church's rules. No firm decision was made on whether the trust deed had been broken or not, and the matter was passed over to be considered the following week in a meeting at which Irving would not be present.[29]

Soon after this meeting with the trustees Irving wrote to them, advising them about proposed changes in the order of the Sunday services. He told them that he intended to pause after the Bible reading and after the sermon in each service to allow for someone to make an inspired utterance. But Irving knew that most of the trustees did not approve these practices.[30]

Two meetings of the session followed the deliberations by the trustees, in which attempts were made to persuade Irving to accept that permitting these manifestations in the Sunday services was contrary to the discipline of the Scottish Church and thus should not be allowed. But he was adamant

---

27. Irving to Mr. and Mrs. Hamilton, November 21, 1831, quoted in ibid., 2:216.

28. Hair, *Regent*, 62. It needs to be noted here that some men were both trustees and members of session.

29. Irving to Mr. and Mrs. Hamilton, November 21, 1831, in Oliphant, *Life*, 2:215–16.

30. Irving to the trustees of Regent Square Church, November 22, 1831, in Irving, *DL*, 287–89.

and would not give way.[31] To Irving, it was a case of obeying God or obeying man, and with those options, there was only one choice he could make.

The session, no doubt, would have agreed with obeying God rather than man but would have disagreed with Irving on who was commanding what. The explosion was bound to come. On November 25, Isabella told a friend, "Almost all the Elders and Deacons have left." Three days later, the *Christian Advocate* was more precise, reporting that eight of Regent Square's ten elders and deacons resigned in protest on the tongues issue.[32]

It is not surprising that these matters further separated Irving from Thomas and Jane Carlyle and, it would seem, from many of his early supporters. Carlyle frequently mentioned these events in his letters and in terms that did not hide his displeasure. But Carlyle is worth quoting on this because he gives the perspective of an outsider, and one who was usually sympathetic towards Irving.

In August 1831, Carlyle had told his wife:

> From all I can yet see Irving . . . is forgotten by the intellectual classes; but still flourishes as a green bay tree (or rather green cabbage tree) among the fanatical classes, whose ornament and beacon he is. Strangely enough is it all fashioned among these people: a certain everlasting *Truth*, even new Truth, reveals itself in them, but with a *Body* of mere froth, and soap-suds and other the like ephemeral impurities. Yet I love the man, and can trustfully take counsel of him. [33]

A week later Carlyle told Jane that he had spent some time with Irving

> in the *animali-parlanti* [talking-animals] region of the Supernatural. Understand, ladykin, that the "gift of tongues" is here also (chiefly among the women), and a positive belief that God is still working miracles in the Church—by hysterics . . . Irving hauled me off to Lincoln's Inn Fields to hear . . . (Mr. Scott); where I sat directly behind a Speaker with Tongues, who unhappily however did not perform, till after I was gone . . . The good Irving looked at me wistfully, for he knows I cannot take miracles in; yet he looks so piteously as if he implored me to believe. O dear O dear! was the Devil ever busier than now.[34]

31. Hair, *Regent*, 64.

32. Isabella Irving to Hon. J. J. Strutt, November 25, 1831, in Irving, *DL*, 290; *Christian Advocate*, November 28, 1831.

33. Thomas Carlyle to Jane Welsh Carlyle, August 15, 1831, *CLO*.

34. Thomas Carlyle to Jane Welsh Carlyle, August 22, 1831, *CLO*.

A couple of months later, just after the tongues were first heard in a Regent Square service, Carlyle told his mother that Irving's

> friends here are all much grieved about him. For many months, he has been puddling and muddling in the midst of certain insane jargoning of hysterical women, and crackbrained enthusiasts, who start up from time to time in public companies, and utter confused Stuff, mostly "Ohs" and "Ahs" and absurd interjections about "the Body of Jesus"; they also pretend to "work miracles," and have raised more than one weak bedrid woman, and cured people of "Nerves," or as they themselves say, "cast Devils out of them." All which poor Irving is pleased to consider as the "work of the Spirit"; and to *janner* [talk foolishly] about at great length, as making *his* Church the peculiarly blessed of Heaven, and equal to or greater than the primitive one at Corinth![35]

On one occasion at this time the Carlyles visited the Irvings at home and

> found the house all decked out for a "meeting" (that is, a bout at this same "speaking with tongues"); and as we talked a moment with Irving who had come down to us, there rose a shriek in the upper story of the house, and presently he exclaimed: "*There* is one prophecying [*sic*]; come and hear her!" we hesitated to go, but he forced us up into a back-room, and there we could hear the wretched creature raving like one possessed; *hoo*ing and *ha*-ing, and talking *as* sensibly as one would do with a pint of brandy in his stomach: till after some ten minutes she seemed to grow tired, and became silent. Nothing so shocking and altogether unspeakably deplorable was it ever my lot to hear. Poor Jane was on the verge of fainting; and did not recover the whole night . . . What the final issue for our most worthy but most misguided Friend may be, I dare not so much as guess.[36]

Then to his brother he wrote:

> Of poor Edward Irving I have seen little and wish I had heard nothing since you went away. Alas! the "gift of tongues" has now broken loud out (last Sunday) in his Church, the creature Campbell (or Caird or whatever she is) having started up in the forenoon; and (as the matter was encouraged by Irving) *four* others in the evening, when there ensued as I learn something like a

35. Thomas Carlyle to Margaret A. Carlyle, October 20, 1831, *CLO*.
36. Ibid.

perfect Bedlam scene, some groaning, some laughing, hooting, hooing, and several fainting. The Newspapers have got it, and call upon his people for the honour of Scotland to leave him, or muzzle him. The most general hypothesis is that he is a *quack;* the milder that he is getting cracked . . . My poor friend!"[37]

Jane Carlyle agreed with her husband, which was not by any means always the case. She told a cousin:

far worse Bedlam is poor Edward Irving's house where people are to be found at all hours *"speaking with tongues"* that is to say shrieking and howling in no tongue . . . it is truly distressing to see a man of such talents and such really good and pious dispositions as Mr. Irving given up to an infatuation so absurd . . . But a man more sincere in his professions does not exist.[38]

Two weeks later Carlyle told his mother,

Irving comes but little in our way; and one does not like to go and seek him in his own house, in a whole posse of enthusiasts, ranters and silly women. He was here once, taking tea, since that work of the "Tongues" began: I told him with great earnestness my deepseated unhesitating conviction that it was *no* special work of the Holy Spirit, or of any Spirit save of that black frightful unclean one that dwells in Bedlam. He persists mi[l] dly-obstinate in his Course; greatly strengthened therein by his wife, who is reckoned the beginner of it all.[39]

There is little doubt that Carlyle was mistaken to assume that Isabella was "the beginner of it all," though she appears to have encouraged Irving in it. As we have seen, the triggers seem to have been Mary Campbell, Sandy Scott, and especially Irving's own studies and reflections.

A month later Carlyle told a relative, "Irving does not come much here; only once since that gift-of-tongue work began, and we have not been even once with *him*. It was last week that he called. He looked hollow and haggard; thin, greywhiskered, almost an old man: yet he was composed and affectionate and patient: I could almost have wept over him, and did tell him my mind with all plainness."[40]

---

37. Thomas Carlyle to John A. Carlyle, October 21, 1831, *CLO*. Mary Campbell became Mary Caird.

38. Jane Welsh Carlyle to Helen Welsh, October 26, 1831, *CLO*.

39. Thomas Carlyle to Margaret A. Carlyle, November 10, 1831, *CLO*.

40. Thomas Carlyle to James Carlyle, December 13, 1831, *CLO*.

In these letters it is clear that the Carlyles had not become anti-Irving. They still loved and respected him. Their complaint was that in their opinion Irving was dabbling in nonsense, damaging his reputation, and wrecking whatever good he might do. It also seems that the stress of his work was prematurely aging him, leaving him "almost an old man" at thirty-nine.

Also in 1831 Carlyle published his translation of the great German hymn, "Ein Feste Burg." Part of the final verse runs, "Mit seinem Geist [Spirit] und Gaben [Gifts]." Carlyle translated this as "'Tis written by His finger," thus omitting any specific mention of the Spirit and gifts (whatever those gifts might be). It is easy to imagine that Carlyle's translation of that line was influenced by his rejection of Edward Irving's teaching on the Holy Spirit.

In his *Reminiscences*, Carlyle also recalled visiting the Irvings with Jane, probably early in 1832, when they also had visitors from their church. Isabella met with the church members in one room while Edward spoke to the Carlyles in another. Soon Carlyle heard a noise coming from the other room, which he described as "a shrieky hysterical 'Lal-lall-lall!' (little or nothing else but *l*'s and *a*'s continued for several minutes); to which Irving, with singular calmness, said only, 'There, hear you; there are the Tongues!'" The Carlyles left the Irvings' home that night "full of distress."[41]

Whether Carlyle's description of what he heard on that occasion was accurate we cannot know. As we have seen, he was strongly opposed to such manifestations, regarding them as nonsense, which presumably colored his record.

This now brings us to an examination of the nature of these tongues. What did they sound like? What were they? Oliphant said, "The character of the sound has perhaps received as many different descriptions as there are persons who have heard it. To some . . . it was imposing and awful, to others it was merely gibberish . . . to others an uneasy wonder, which it was a relief to find passing into English."[42] Robert Baxter, a one-time prophet himself, called such utterances "powerful and commanding" and "an intense and riveting power of expression."[43] But they always or nearly always seem to have been loud. That was a description of them made by a wide variety of listeners. Was it that loudness that made them impressive and sound supernatural?

Amongst the other descriptions, Thomas Erskine of Linlathen wrote a booklet called *Gifts of the Spirit*, in which he claimed that the tongues

41. Carlyle, *Reminiscences* (Norton), 2:205.

42. Oliphant, *Life*, 2:207. See also Cardale, "Extraordinary Manifestations," 870, 872–73.

43. Baxter, *Narrative*, 5, 9.

were "distinct" languages, "well inflected" and "well compacted," and were "composed of words of various lengths, with the natural variety, and yet possessing that commonness of character which marks them to be one distinct language." They were, he insisted, "not gibberish."[44]

George Pilkington, who knew several languages, began to attend the prayer meetings and he even uttered a prophecy, though in English. He described the tongues as being delivered "suddenly" and in "short sentences," with, at least from one male practitioner, "an astonishing and terrible crash" and "uttered in a tone of power and authority."

Fascinated by the tongues that he heard, Pilkington began to use his knowledge of languages by writing down some of these pronouncements and translating them. From this he deduced that the gifted people were speaking in intelligible languages, most commonly Latin and Spanish and mispronounced English. However, his attempts at deciphering the tongues were not approved, being regarded as unspiritual, even of "the Devil." Finally, Pilkington came to believe that these tongues were not due to "the influence of the Holy Spirit" and left the movement.[45] Yet the fact remains that, in Pilkington's opinion, at least some of these tongues sounded like genuine human languages, whatever their origin.

John Roxborogh refers to the comments in one newspaper of the time that reported that taking the outbursts down in shorthand proved very difficult, which suggests they were barely intelligible, and that a scribe claimed to have made "sad work of the orthography."[46]

One critic seemed to be employing a tongue of his own when he described the happenings at Regent Square as "the turbid visions of phrenzied enthusiasts, and the idle rhapsodies of delirious fanaticism," which "assume the privilege of celestial inspiration, and array themselves in the hallowed garb of prophecy."[47]

When one of Irving's prophets was asked, "how [do] you know when you speak by the Spirit of God?" he answered, "I can discern." The questioner, not unexpectedly, inquired, "How do you discern?" The man answered, "By its effect and its fruit." The prophet went on to say that he knew that his pronouncements were from the Spirit of God and were not the spirit of error because he was "filled with love to Christ and His church and [had] joy, and peace, and strength." This man also stated that he was unable to exercise

44. Erskine, quoted in Hanna, *Memoirs* (New York), 3:253.

45. Pilkington, *Unknown*, 5–6, 12, 15–16, 19–20, 23–24, 32, 36.

46. Roxborogh, "Charismatic Movement," 2.

47. Rev. A. C. L. D'Arblay, January 8, 1832, quoted in Drummond, *Edward Irving*, 179.

this gift at will. It was rather something that came from outside him. In addition, he confessed that when he spoke in a tongue he did not understand it, for he did not have "the gift of interpretation."[48]

Irving, who had witnessed these manifestations "hundreds of times," said that tongues (and he did use the word "tongues") had four purposes: "for revealing things hidden in the Word . . . for bringing to the knowledge of the Church things that are taking place beyond the reach of ordinary communication . . . for prophesying to the edification and comfort and exhortation of the Church, for the conviction and judgment, heart-searching and conversion, of the unbeliever," and finally, for the teaching of doctrine. That is, presumably, when the tongue is in the language of the listeners, or if in an unknown tongue, there is an interpreter present. Thus he appears to be including native language prophecy under the heading of "tongues." In Irving's thinking, it seems, they were different manifestations of the same gift.

Irving also described tongues as coming

> by the Holy Ghost . . . with a power and strength and fulness, and sometimes rapidity of voice, altogether different from that of the person's ordinary utterance in any mood; and I would say . . . quite supernatural. There is a power in the voice to thrill the heart and overawe the spirit after a manner which I have never felt. There is a march, and a majesty, and a sustained grandeur in the voice . . . which I have never heard even a resemblance to [except on rare occasions]. It is a mere abandonment of all truth to call it screaming or crying: it is the most majestic and divine utterance which I have ever heard . . . So far from being unmeaning gibberish, as the thoughtless and heedless sons of Belial have said, it is regularly formed, well pronounced, deeply felt discourse, which evidently wanteth only the ear of him whose native tongue it is to make it a very masterpiece of powerful speech. But as the Apostle declareth that it is not spoken to the ear of man, but to the ear of God . . . we ought to stand in awe, and endeavour to enter into spiritual communion with that member of Christ, who is the mouth of the whole Church unto God . . . it is the Spirit of Jesus carrying on a discourse with the invisible Father through one of our brethren.[49]

In this description Irving has four main points. When a person spoke in a tongue (or even prophesied) their voice was different from their normal voice. Secondly, he argued that these utterances sounded especially grand

48. Wilks, *Edward Irving*, 222–23, quoting the church's trustees and the London presbytery at Irving's trial.

49. Irving, "Facts Connected," 5:198–200.

and even divine, and thirdly, that they were, in fact, supernatural ("by the Holy Ghost"). Fourthly, that the speaker was merely the mouthpiece, as "it is the Spirit of Jesus" speaking to the Father through the human agent.

When Irving's two descriptions are placed together it is apparent that he believed tongues have a "known part," that is, a language known to the listeners, and an "unknown part." The latter confirmed that the former was truly "a message from God." In the instances Irving had witnessed, the known part was usually about 90 percent of what was spoken, the unknown only 10 percent.[50]

The people who spoke in tongues at Irving's church described it as an intense experience. According to Irving, one such person explained that when they prayed normally, they were well aware of matters other than their prayer, but when they prayed in tongues, "it was as if a deep covering of snow had fallen on all the country around, and I saw nothing but the object of my desire."[51]

Crucially, Irving regarded speaking in tongues as the sign of the baptism of the Holy Spirit, as is common in Pentecostal circles today. He also related it to the sacrament of baptism with water. In addition, he believed that it was also out of this language gift(s) that the other spiritual gifts would emerge.[52]

It is probably true to say that the secular press loved all this talk of tongues and regarded it as nonsense. Carlyle said, "The Newspaper accounts are sometimes overcharged," though, one supposes, at other times he considered the reports quite accurate.[53] Indeed, it is fair to say that sometimes Carlyle's own comments about these events were also "overcharged."

The Times was highly cynical about tongues. "The great body of Mr. Irving's adherents," it declared, "would probably have remained by him if, in his headlong course of enthusiasm, he could have found a resting-place." Indeed,

> They might pardon his nonsense about the time and circum-
> stances of the millennium. They might smile at unintelligible
> disquisitions about "heads," and "horns," and "trumpets," and
> "candlesticks," and "white and black horses," in Revelations.
> These things might offend the judgment, but did not affect the

50. Ibid, 5:203–204.

51. Ibid., 5:199–200.

52. Ibid., 5:204–205, 316–20. I have found Irving's earlier writings to be logical, powerful, and usually clear, even when I have disagreed with him. However, this three-part article in *Fraser's*, written near the end of his life, is, in my view, of a lesser order. At times it seems rather confused.

53. Thomas Carlyle to Margaret A. Carlyle, November 10, 1831, *CLO*.

nerves. But have we the same excuse for the recent exhibitions with which the metropolis has been scandalised? Are we to listen to the screaming of hysterical women, and the ravings of frantic men? Is bawling to be added to absurdity, and the disturber of a congregation to escape the police and the treadmill, because the person who occupies the pulpit vouches for his inspiration?[54]

The Age mischievously suggested that Irving was intending to change his calling and become a member of the Whig government. His aim was to introduce a new Reform Bill, "written by him in his unknown tongue." Irving's female prophets received special attention. *The Age* stated that having given "their *maiden* display of elocution" at Irving's chapel, they "are to be recommended as *Maids of Honour* to her Majesty."[55]

The Albion and the Star said that Irving's ventures into the miraculous were introduced merely to rekindle his fading popularity. Prominent within them was a "pretended prophetess . . . who claimed the gift of tongues." Indeed, the origins of this movement, the paper declared, were "half a dozen hypochondriacs in some remote corner of Scotland having discovered that they talk nonsense whenever they open their mouths, persuad[ing] themselves that the nonsense was inspiration, and that the gift of tongues was again come upon the earth. It would of course be idle, if not directly profane, to compare their brutish gabble to any work of miracle." But as a result of all this, the "crowds flock" to Irving's chapel "to listen to their fooleries."[56] *Baldwin's London Weekly Journal* called Irving's followers "deluded."[57]

In addition, books were also published attacking Irving's position. Amongst them was a book by William Kidd called *The Unknown Tongues! Or the Rev. Edward Irving Arraigned at the Bar of the Scriptures of Truth and Found "Guilty."* This appeared in at least four editions.[58]

Inevitably, *The Morning Watch* defended Irving. The December 1831 edition contained three articles on the charismata that supported Irving's position in different ways. The "Abuse of Spiritual Gifts," possibly written by the other Thomas Carlyle,[59] argued:

54. Quoted in Oliphant, *Life*, 2:210.

55. "A Ministerial Change!" *The Age*, November 20, 1831, 272.

56. *Albion and the Star*, November 1, 1831.

57. "The Rev. Edward Irving and the Unknown Tongue," *Baldwin's London Weekly Journal*, October 29, 1831.

58. *The Courier*, November 29, 1831, 1.

59. The article does not contain the writer's name, but Irving's long-term friend Thomas Carlyle said that an article on tongues in this issue of *TMW* was written by his namesake (Thomas Carlyle to Margaret A. Carlyle, February 18, 1832, CLO).

> When any one speaks in an extraordinary manner, and informs
> us that he is constrained to do so by a supernatural power acting
> upon, and within, him, the question is one simply of fact: if we
> love the person who makes the declaration, we do not doubt
> him, for confidence is the lowest ingredient in love: if we doubt
> him, it is a proof not to be gainsayed that we place no confidence
> in the truth of his assertions, that we entertain no love for him.
> [In addition, the people in question] are persons walking blame-
> lessly in all the ordinances of God and man . . . and making good
> and unquestionable confession of faith in Christ Jesus.[60]

In other words, if sincere and good Christian people claim that their
experiences are supernatural, we should believe them. Not to do so means
that we do not love them. This argument contains two obvious problems.
First, that sincere Christians might be mistaken about certain aspects of
their spiritual experience. Secondly, that one can love fellow Christians
without necessarily accepting everything that they claim.

The article continued, "there can be no healthy church without having
all the Spirit and all the gifts in it." That these gifts were so rare in their age
demonstrated "the low estate into which the church [had] fallen." In that age,
the church had abused the gifts by doubting their reality. In fact, "The first
point necessary to establish a true church on the apostolic model, is to have
a body of persons filled with spiritual gifts of speaking in unknown tongues,
prophesying, working miracles, raising the dead, curing the sick."[61]

It needs to be acknowledged that though Irving might be considered
rather easily persuaded in all this, he did at times reject some manifestations
that were claimed to be the work of the Holy Spirit. Tongues, in one form
or another, broke out in pockets in different parts of Britain. Some Irving
labeled demonic.

One such claim came out of Gloucester in the southwest of England,
where the seven-year-old twin children of Rev. E. C. Probyn "spoke in the
Spirit." Probyn, his wife, and one of the twins paid a visit to Regent Square.
While they were there, the twin who had been left back in Gloucester was
said to have given forth spiritual utterances at home. Later the other child
did too, and the two of them then ruled the family. Irving and his associates
were uneasy about the origin of these manifestations. Indeed, according to
Irving, when tested by the local church's curate, "The Spirit betrayed himself." He/it would not submit to the scriptural test of 1 John 4:1–3, forbad
marriage, "and played many more antics." He/it "disliked prayer, praise, and

---

60. "Abuse of Spiritual Gifts," 375–76.

61. Ibid., 378, 398.

reading the scriptures," yet "preached a wonderously sweet Gospel." Eventually the curate "expelled" the spirit.[62]

The question must now be asked: Did Edward Irving experience any of these spiritual gifts himself, or was his experience of them only secondhand? It has been stated that Irving "never claimed any charismatic or pentecostal experience for himself," and he "never spoke in a 'tongue,' or interpreted, or prophesied, or worked a miracle."[63] In fact, it appears that no one has yet uncovered any clear reference to such an event. In addition, Thomas Carlyle said that Irving never spoke in tongues,[64] which presumably was information that he received directly from Irving.

However, David Dorries argues that Irving was in fact "Spirit baptized and spoke in tongues," though he admits that "no documentation exists from Irving's own writings" to prove or disprove this claim. Dorries argues that Irving would not have been so enthusiastic about the gifts if he had not experienced them himself.[65] Yet it seems unlikely that Irving would have kept quiet about such experiences if he had in fact had them. Such an announcement would surely have strengthened the case in their favor and his position in his church. In addition, the reason that Irving was eventually downgraded in his church appears to have been because he had not received these gifts. It seems, therefore, much more than likely that Edward Irving did not personally experience such gifts.

If Irving did not speak in tongues, it says much for his integrity. Amidst all the displays of charismata going on around him (whether false, genuine, or mixed) he was obviously not prepared to pretend to have had an experience that had in fact passed him by. He must have wondered why he had been left out.

ROBERT BAXTER

One of the leading figures in this prophetic movement was Robert Baxter, a devout Anglican from Doncaster in the north of England. He was much concerned about the decline in the national church and was looking for its renewal. Baxter, a lawyer, became one of this new charismatic movement's

---

62. Irving to Rev. Probyn, November 10, 1831, in Irving, *DL*, 286–87; Irving to Mr. MacDonald, November 19, 1831, in Oliphant, *Life*, 2:211–12; "Abuse of Spiritual Gifts," 152–54; Stunt, "Trying the Spirits," 95–105.

63. McFarlane, *Edward Irving*, 10; Whitley, *Blinded Eagle*, 76. See also Elliott, *Edward Irving*, 192–93.

64. Carlyle, *Reminiscences* (Norton), 2:204.

65. David Dorries, "Edward Irving," in McGee, *Initial Evidence*, 53.

most significant prophets. He also contributed a few articles to *The Morning Watch*. Oliphant said that he spoke "with a force and fulness not yet attained by the other speakers."[66] In fact, he became "a prolific deliverer of prophecies."[67]

Baxter seems to have first met Edward Irving as early as 1823.[68] Baxter had heard about the Port Glasgow tongues movement from a relative, which seems to have stimulated his interest in the supernatural. During a business visit to London in the summer of 1831, he attended a Regent Square prayer meeting at which he heard Mr. Taplin speak in a tongue and heard Emily Cardale prophesy. This so greatly impressed him that he "was led to fall on [his] knees and cry in a loud voice, 'speak, Lord, for they servant heareth,'" which he "repeated many times." Baxter then went on to make a "prophecy," urging his listeners to proclaim "the near coming of the Lord Jesus." Thus, Baxter became further known to Irving, who invited him to read the Scriptures and pray at some later prayer meetings.[69]

Afterwards, Baxter returned to Doncaster, where he made no "spirit-inspired" pronouncements in public, but at times "the power" came down on him while he was engaged in private prayer. In addition, at the end of one communion service in his church, he felt "the power come upon [him] largely, though the impulse was not to utterance." Being "in the power" became Baxter's common way of describing his ecstatic experiences, over which he seems to have had little or no control.[70]

Some months later, in January 1832, Baxter returned to London and began once more to attend Irving's early morning prayer meetings. During his first visit on this trip, Irving noticed him and asked him to read the Scriptures, which he did. As he read, "the power came upon" him and he was "made to read in the power," his voice being "raised far beyond its natural pitch."

One evening Baxter, Irving, David Brown, Miss Hall, Mrs. Cardale, and perhaps one or two others met for dinner. After the meal a discussion ensued on the state of the church. Mrs. Cardale made what appears to have been considered a prophecy, and then "the power fell upon" Baxter, and he

---

66. Oliphant, *Life*, 2:233; Baxter, *Narrative*, 1, 4. See also Drummond, *Edward Irving*, 185–86.

67. Miller, *History*, 79.

68. Irving, "What Caused," 132.

69. Baxter, *Narrative*, 3–5, 147–48 (appendix A: letter dated December 29, 1831). More about Baxter's experiences can be found in ibid., 151–52, 155 (appendix B: letters dated October 14 and December 20, 1831); Oliphant, *Life*, 2:409–13; Drummond, *Edward Irving*, 186–88."

70. Baxter, *Narrative*, 8–10.

launched forth for two hours about "the Church and the Nation." At that time, Baxter believed himself to be "the passive instrument of the power that used" him.

Speaking about this occasion later, Baxter explained, "In the beginning of my utterances that evening, some observations were, in the power, addressed by me to the pastor, in a commanding tone; and the manner and course of utterance manifested in me, was so far differing from those which had been manifested in the members of his own flock, that he was much startled."[71]

So confident was Baxter of the power within him that on one occasion, he

> bid those present ask instruction upon any subject on which they sought to be taught of God; and, to several questions which were asked, answers were given by me in the power. One in particular was so answered with such reference to the circumstances of the case, of which, in myself, I was wholly ignorant, as to convince the person who asked it that the Spirit speaking in me knew those circumstances, and alluded to them in the answer.[72]

Robert Baxter said that he "never had any command over the power, and though [he] could refrain from speaking, yet [he] could not speak in power when [he] would, nor continue speaking when [he] had begun, unless the power continued with [him]."[73]

One might wonder why Irving was so startled by Baxter's pronouncement at the dinner party—after all, one would think that by this time he had seen and heard just about everything. But Irving, after initial doubts, sensed a new level in the Spirit's working. In a letter to Mr. MacDonald some days later, he said, "The Lord hath anointed Baxter of Doncaster *after another kind*, I think the apostolical; the prophetical being the ministration of the word, the apostolical being the ministration of the Spirit. He speaks from supernatural light . . . nevertheless the word is sealed in the utterance. It is more abiding than the prophetical, though sometimes for a snare he is locked up. It is authoritative, and always concludes with a benediction."[74] Indeed, in a later *Morning Watch* article, Irving *seems* to rate Baxter's pro-

---

71. Ibid., 13–14.

72. Ibid. In some cases, Baxter gave the initials of the people involved rather than full names, including "Mrs. J. C." and "Miss H.," who were presumably Mrs. Cardale and Miss Hall (ibid., 16). These meetings appear to have been gatherings of "gifted persons."

73. Ibid., 42.

74. Irving to Mr. MacDonald, January 24, 1832, quoted in Oliphant, *Life*, 2:234, emphasis added.

nouncements the equal of Scripture.[75] Mrs. Cardale also regarded Baxter as very special. She called him "a prophet, and more than a prophet."[76]

Why is it that Irving saw such a difference in Baxter's prophecies compared with the others? The answer is most probably that Baxter actually said something with a bit of depth. Up until this time, Irving's prophets such as Miss Hall, the Cardales (mother and daughter), and Mr. Taplin had been saying such things as: "Why will ye flee from the voice of the Lord? The Lord is with ye; if ye flee now, where will ye flee on the day of judgment?" and "The Lord will speak to His people. The Lord hasteneth His coming," as well as "The Lord cometh."[77] Irving's prophets had also been noted as saying, "God is amongst us, and if you fly from him now, where will you fly in the day of judgment?" as well as "Beware, beware it is a reality," which was repeated again and again,[78] and "When will ye repent? Why will ye not repent?" Also there was the spirit-inspired exhortation urging the congregation to ask for "the waters of the Holy Spirit."[79] Indeed, David Brown's opinion of these earlier prophecies was that they were rather "poor, and the same thing over again."[80]

In fact, all of these ideas could be easily gleaned from the Bible or ordinary human thought. Such pronouncements, no doubt, could have been heard in many churches and chapels up and down the country on any given Sunday without the preachers claiming direct inspiration from the Spirit of God. What Irving seems to have been looking for were prophecies that, while consistent with the teaching of Scripture, were more detailed and specific.

As Irving listened to these early prophecies, he must have wondered, "If God through His Spirit is speaking to us, why doesn't He say something more significant?" The utterances of these "gifted" people seemed rather mundane and normal, even if the delivery was believed to be supernatural.

But Robert Baxter was different. He made long, significant pronouncements that were clearly a cut above the rest. In fact, as shall be seen, he was

---

75. Irving, "What Caused," 130.

76. Baxter, *Narrative*, 73.

77. *Morning Herald* quoted in "The Rev. Edward Irving and the Unknown Tongue," *Baldwin's London Weekly Journal*, October 29, 1831, and an article by the same title in the *Christian Advocate*, October 31, 1831, 3; Drummond, *Edward Irving*, 153.

78. Pilkington, *Unknown*, 11; *Christian Advocate*, November 28, 1831.

79. "A Private Letter from a Visitor from Aberdeen," November 3, 1831, in *The Unknown Tongues of Rev. Edward Irving and Rev. Nicholas Armstrong Arraigned*, quoted in Drummond, *Edward Irving*, 167–68; Irving to Mr. and Mrs. Hamilton, November 21, 1831, quoted in Oliphant, *Life*, 2:216.

80. Brown, "Personal Reminiscences," 268.

to go on to make very specific, dated predictions, which Irving accepted as true.

Towards the end of January 1832 Irving wrote to Robert Story, telling him, "For the last six months, the Spirit hath been moving [Baxter] and uttering by him privately; but his mouth was not opened till Friday week" at the Regent Square prayer meeting, "when he was reading the Scripture and praying." Baxter continued to minister at Regent Square for more than a week, "speaking," according to Irving, "in the power and demonstration of the Spirit with great authority." Mrs. Cardale, when under "the power," also "declared that Jesus had touched [Baxter's] lips with a living coal" (Isa 6:6–7) and that he "should speak with authority as a prophet." However, when Irving arranged for Baxter to actually preach at an evening service at Regent Square, "the Spirit," through Mrs. Cardale's daughter, forbad it.[81]

Near the close of 1831, Baxter, after initial hesitation, had come to believe in a rapture of the faithful to heaven before a time of great trouble on earth, which he had learned from "Mr. Irving's writings." This belief was later reinforced by a revelation his wife had along the same lines.

On January 14, 1832, Baxter made a prophecy related to that rapture. He seems to have repeated it eight days later in a church that was probably Anglican. It was that in 1,260 days from the date of the prophecy, "the saints" would be translated from earth to heaven before a time of "destruction" on earth. These 1,260 days, also given as three-and-a-half years and forty-two months, are referred to in biblical passages such as Rev 11–13. The association of these periods is based on the belief that biblical years were 360 days' duration (a year being twelve months of thirty days each, totaling 360 days, then $360 \times 3\frac{1}{2} = 1{,}260$). Baxter appears to have originally stated this in a meeting at Irving's home.[82]

In other words, according to this prophecy, a key end times event, the rapture, would take place 1,260 days after January 14, 1832, so presumably on June 27, 1835. Baxter did not say before the end of the 1,260 days, but *at* the end of them, so he had effectively dated the rapture.

Irving seems initially to have accepted this as prophecy. But Irving did also qualify Baxter's prediction by saying, "This is not to date the Lord's

---

81. Irving to Robert Story, January 27, 1832, quoted in Oliphant, Life, 2:235–36; Baxter, Narrative, 73, 75–76.

82. Baxter, *Narrative*, 17–19; Irving to Robert Story, January 27, 1832, quoted in Oliphant, *Life*, 2:235. Baxter clearly gives the date of the original prediction, and Irving says in this letter that Baxter's visit to the other church was "last Sunday," hence January 22. See also Baxter, *Narrative*, 44, 46, 52, 56, 63.

coming, which is some time after His saints are with Him.”[83] In other words, Christ would return to Earth "some time after" the rapture.

Back in 1825 to 1826, in *Babylon and Infidelity Foredoomed of God*, Irving had argued that Christ would return *by* 1868, without giving a specific date.[84] Whether he still held to that precise belief is unclear, for there is an abundance of evidence that his eschatology was undergoing change at this time.[85] By 1832, then, while Irving and Baxter do not seem to have precisely dated Christ's actual return, Baxter had clearly dated the assumed preliminary rapture, and Irving had accepted that dating.

However, soon after Baxter's prediction, Emily Cardale appears to have made a prophecy in which she said that the day was not known, which presumably refers to this prophecy. This put Irving on the back foot. He confessed, "I am not equal to the work of commenting upon these words from the Lord. I am contented to walk in the darkness."[86]

Baxter also predicted that the British state and its churches would fall; indeed, they would be "destroyed," which was well in line with Irving's beliefs. In addition, he proclaimed that "pestilence would spread throughout the land, and that the sword would follow." And he seems to have expected all this in the same time frame, or perhaps only a little longer.[87]

This final prophecy may have had, in part at least, a very ordinary cause: existing disease. Cholera, originally observed in India, had arrived in Russia in 1823 and spread to Germany and the north of England in 1831, and it was much feared. By late October 1831, the prospect of cholera was "agitating the whole of Great Britain."[88] A little after this, in an utterance of "great power," Baxter referred to the cholera outbreak, which he expected to result in "carnage."[89]

The disease did not reach London until soon after these predictions. The epidemic subsided within a year, only to reemerge in 1848 to 1849, 1853 to 1854, and, for the last time in England, in 1866. Though it caused over thirty thousand deaths in 1832, it must be said that this "pestilence"

---

83. Irving to Robert Story, January 27, 1832, quoted in Oliphant, *Life*, 2:235.

84. Irving, *Babylon*, 1:173–75.

85. Bennett, *Origins*, 212–29. Indeed, in the January 27 letter to Story, Irving said, "These things I believe, some of them I understand, others I have not yet attained to," which also suggests that his eschatology was undergoing some change (Oliphant, *Life*, 2:236).

86. Irving to Robert Baxter, March 3, 1832, in Irving, *DL*, 295.

87. Baxter, *Narrative*, 54–63. See also Baxter, 31, 45; Irving to Robert Story, January 27, 1832, quoted in Oliphant, *Life*, 2:236.

88. A letter from ΣΦ in *Christian Advocate*, October 31, 1831.

89. Baxter, *Narrative*, 67. See also ibid., 70–71.

did not "overflow the land," insofar as it confined itself mainly to the poorer areas of some cities.[90] And no major conflict was fought in Britain during that century, so "the sword" also failed to arrive.

In another prophecy, Baxter announced that the "American Indians" were the lost tribes of Israel (a belief surprisingly common over the previous two centuries) and that they would return to Palestine before the three-and-a-half years of his rapture prophecy had expired.[91]

While it may seem superfluous to say that these predictions by Baxter were ultimately proven wrong, attention needs to be drawn to that fact because it is so significant. Baxter was one of the leading figures in this prophetic movement. Irving seems, after initial doubts, to have had implicit trust in his pronouncements, for Baxter was considered to be of the "apostolical" school. If Irving was wrong in his assessment of Baxter and his prophecies, where else was he wrong when assessing the validity of the assumed charismata surrounding him?

Baxter also later denied that his "Spirit-inspired" pronouncements were genuine. In fact, he did so even before the 1,260-day prophecy was proven wrong. In 1833 Baxter published his *Narrative of Facts* in which, while accepting that the charismata were still available, he called this particular movement a "snare" and "a false faith," and deemed its followers—including himself—"deceived" and "deluded."[92] Indeed, Baxter admitted that more than forty of his prophecies had been proven wrong and that while some of his attempts at healing and exorcism had appeared successful, others had clearly failed.[93] By 1833, he accepted that he had made the revelations "under a spiritual power," but that that power was not the Spirit of God.[94] He also called his prophecies a "delusion of Satan."[95]

It also is claimed that Miss Hall, who was the first to speak in tongues in a Sunday service at Regent Square, later confessed that she believed her outbursts were not genuine. In the spring of 1832, she was staying in the home of John Tizard. On March 26, Tizard told Baxter,

> It has pleased the Lord in His great faithfulness completely to discover the heart of poor Mary Hall . . . through a very powerful testimony from Mrs. Caird & Miss Emily Cardale that the whole work of utterance in her has been entirely of the flesh.

90. Inwood, *History of London*, 420; Luckin, "Final Catastrophe," 32–42.

91. Baxter, *Narrative*, 80–82.

92. Ibid., 1–2.

93. Dallimore, *Life*, 137; Baxter, *Narrative*, 118.

94. Baxter, *Narrative*, 65; Drummond, *Edward Irving*, 198.

95. Baxter, *Narrative*, 44.

By degrees her own conscience has been fully convicted of it, & she is suffering in the flesh much bitterness & grief from the consequences. I fear that all her knowledge of the Lord has gone no deeper than the intellect, for her heart appears now to be quite shut up from the Lord. The whole work in her she sees plainly to have been nothing else than strong excitements in the flesh . . . It is remarkable that the first utterance in public at the Morning Prayer Meeting in Mr. Irving's Church was by a Miss Dixon who it has since appeared has spoken only in the flesh, & the first utterance in the public Sunday Service was by poor Mary Hall, who now tells me that her own conscience shewed her at that very time that it was but the flesh. Even when Mr. Irving had all the gifted persons together, & by the command of the Spirit from Miss E. Cardale tried them all, the flesh was sufficient to enable Mary Hall to confess equally with them as she herself now acknowledges.[96]

How much value is this secondhand confession? Can it be regarded as truly representative of Mary Hall's beliefs? The wording of this letter suggests that Tizard, an otherwise unknown figure, had some reservations about the genuineness of the Regent Square manifestations, in spite of his acceptance of the "very powerful testimony" of Mary Caird and Emily Cardale. Therefore this missive has to be viewed through that lens.

Yet there would seem to be little doubt that by this time Mary Hall no longer believed that her pronouncements were genuine. However, it seems less likely that she doubted the genuineness of her prophecies at the time she made them, in spite of what Tizard says. She sounds as though she was a woman easily influenced by others. Though she was the first to prophesy in a Sunday service, she was not the first to do so at Regent Square meetings, so she had probably witnessed such outbursts. When in the company of other prophets, in front of a pastor who believed in such manifestations, she prophesied. When accused of speaking only in "the flesh" by two well-accepted prophets, she began to have doubts about her own utterances. After spending time with Tizard, who apparently had some reservations about these manifestations, she even confessed that she *never* believed her utterances were genuinely Spirit-inspired. She appears to have been a very confused lady. The question of whether any of her utterances were genuinely of the Spirit must now be regarded as impossible to answer. But if hers are accepted as genuine, this then casts doubt upon the prophecies of Mrs.

96. John Tizard to Robert Baxter, March 26, 1832, quoted in Grass, *Edward Irving*, 245. See also Miller, *History*, 75–76.

Caird and Miss Cardale, who said that they were false. That is, assuming that what Tizard says is true.

Once more then, we have to ask whether Irving was being gullible in all this. Robert Story, who had first approved the manifestations in western Scotland, later believed that they were not genuine, and it is clear that Story was a sober but sympathetic assessor of these phenomena and that he was close to them, so his view should not be lightly dismissed.[97] The charismatic experiences in the Regent Square Church were certainly influenced by the events in Scotland, but, even assuming Story was right, that does not necessarily mean that the Regent Square experiences were of the same kind.

However, Irving's friend and supporter Hugh McLean, after much consideration, believed the manifestations in London were not genuine. He gave thirty-two reasons why he rejected them as a genuine work of God. Amongst these reasons were "The failure of prophecy in a great variety of instances, erroneous interpretations of Scripture . . . contradictory utterances," and failed healings.[98]

While it is impossible at this time to make a fair assessment about the genuineness of all the phenomena at Regent Square, it must be noted that at least three of Irving's "prophets" later either retracted their prophecies or denied that they were genuine. That does not necessarily condemn the whole affair, but it certainly does cast doubt upon it.

Strikingly, Irving admitted to the failed prophecies in a letter to McLean, though as an honest man, he could hardly have failed to recognize them. But he blamed their failure on "the unbelief that is in us, preventing the fulfillment of His word." In fact, he went on, "we have caused His word to fail."[99] In other words, a prophecy is not certain to come true, for it can be hindered by unbelief.

Baxter claimed that when Irving was explaining to him the problem of unfulfilled prophecies, he said that a true prophet might "one moment, speak by the Spirit of God, and the next moment by an evil spirit."[100] The former would come to pass; the latter would not. If Irving did say that—and Baxter seemed very sure that he did—then it is unlikely it was an opinion he held for long, because so much else he said contradicts it. He may have merely adopted this view during this period of stress.

97. Robert Story to Edward Irving, late 1834, in Irving, *DL*, 412–13.

98. [Bonar ?], "Edward Irving," 238–40.

99. Irving to Rev. Hugh B. McLean, February 1, 1834, in Irving, *DL*, 384–85. See also [Bonar ?], "Edward Irving," 240–41. Irving linked "failed" biblical prophecies with the failed prophecies of his own people, and saw unbelief as the cause of both.

100. Baxter, *Narrative*, 119–20.

Indeed, Irving's mind at this time in his life was strongly biased in favor of such manifestations. While originally suspecting that the miraculous gifts would not again appear until the Millennium, he did come to believe that God had never retracted them, so that these gifts were available then and there. This was particularly so insofar as Irving also held that there would be an outpouring of such phenomena in the last days, which he believed were by then upon them. Therefore it was important to Irving that these manifestations be accepted as a genuine work of the Holy Spirit. They were an essential outworking of several components in his theology. They were very important not only for his pneumatology or even his doctrines of God, they were also vital for his eschatology and were also related to his understanding of the sacraments. In fact, Irving claimed that he established "the grounds of this doctrine . . . in [his] Lectures on the Apocalypse."[101] If the Holy Spirit was not moving in this way, then it meant that Edward Irving would have to conduct a crucial rethinking of a substantial part—perhaps virtually the whole—of his theology.[102]

That Irving was most favorably inclined towards believing that the gifts were genuine is supported by A. L. Drummond and Peter Elliott. Drummond explains that Irving "had strong prepossession in favour of the gifts," while Elliott puts it this way: "Irving was completely convinced that God's plan for the Church involved a pouring out of the Spirit on all believers, both men and women."[103] Therefore he would have been easier to convince that these phenomena were genuine than someone who approached them with an open mind.

It also needs to be noted that many of these gifts, if gifts they were, seem to have emerged when Irving was preaching or reading from passages that refer to them, such as 1 Cor 12 and 14, or soon afterwards. One might be more readily convinced that the gifts were genuine if they had emerged more often when other Scriptures were under consideration. Irving's reading of these passages and preaching upon them may have acted as prompts for people to respond as they did.

---

101. Irving to Rev. Martin, March 7, 1832, quoted in Oliphant, *Life*, 2:253. In one letter, Irving said that he had brought "forth from obscurity a whole system of precious truth," which included, most importantly, the "glad and glorious tidings of [Christ's] speedy coming" (Irving to the Trustees and Building Committee and to the Elders and Deacons of the National Scotch Church, March 17, 1832, in Irving, *DL*, 296).

102. Peter Elliott also argues this; see Elliott, *Edward Irving*, 182–83.

103. Drummond, *Edward Irving*, 155–56; see also ibid., 159; Elliott, *Edward Irving*, 190.

Yet it also needs to be recognized, as A. L. Drummond points out, that a number of the "gifted" were well educated, or at least reasonably so.[104] J. B. Cardale and Baxter were lawyers, Taplin a schoolteacher, Miss Hall a governess. Particularly in the cases of Cardale and Baxter, one would not have expected such men to be easily persuaded of these phenomena.

Pilkington, who was later critical of these manifestations, believed that the "gifted" people were intelligent, sincere, and even pious, so he did not feel that they were faking it. Rather he supposed that they were deluded. That is, they were sincere but mistaken.[105]

Hugh McNeile, who chaired the Albury Conferences and so was a close associate of Irving's, heard Taplin speak in tongues and described what he heard as "jargon" with a sprinkling of Latin words. McNeile, then, is the second person who claimed to have detected Latin in these pronouncements, and considering that Latin was a language that many of the people who attended Regent Square would have learned, perhaps some of the speakers were inadvertently regurgitating childhood memories.[106] It is also said that J. N. Darby detected similarities to Latin in the tongues he heard in Scotland,[107] though it is less likely that any of the speakers in that part of Scotland, not being as well educated, had ever learned that language. Robert Baxter also claimed to have spoken in Latin and French on one occasion while "in the power."[108]

David Brown remembered that "all that was uttered in English seemed to be so poor, and the same thing over again . . . the only thing that might seem to indicate 'a power not their own' as its source, was the unnatural—I could not say preternatural—strength of it."[109] Presumably by "strength" he meant the volume of these utterances and the force with which they came. As we have seen, numerous witnesses commented on their loudness and forcefulness. Likewise, Edward Miller also noted the repetitious aspect and the limited depth of some of the English pronouncements.[110]

Assessing these matters today, one has to admit that the whole pentecostal aspect of Regent Square *may* have been delusional, and parts of it (unfulfilled prophecies, for example) were definitely so. On the other hand,

104. Drummond, *Edward Irving*, 165.

105. Pilkington, *Unknown*, 12, 17, 34.

106. McNeile, cited in Miller, *History*, 1:72. See also Drummond, *Edward Irving*, 169–70.

107. Newman, *Phases*, 119.

108. Baxter, *Narrative*, 133.

109. Brown, "Personal Reminiscences," 268.

110. Miller, *History*, 1:72.

if the miraculous gifts of the Spirit are indeed still available today, then one cannot rule out that some of these manifestations came from a genuine movement of the Spirit of God.

Yet genuine or not, it sounds very presumptuous of Irving to accuse Robert Story of "grievously sinn[ing] in standing afar off from the work of the Lord, scanning it like a sceptic [sic] instead of proving it like a spiritual man!" for which Irving urged him to "repent."[111] After all, Story had originally sympathized with the outbreaks in Scotland, though he later doubted their validity. Story was not a skeptic, but one who had tested the spirits and believed that he had found them false.

In some of his comments on the charismata Irving also argued that one should set aside the intellect because it stood in the way of the Spirit's working. For example, in the letter to Robert Story quoted above, he urged Story to keep his "*conscience unfettered by [his] understanding.*"[112] On a later occasion he told John McLeod Campbell, "we [that is, Irving and his followers] are not a reasoning people."[113] Indeed, when a person was speaking in tongues or prophesying, it was God who was framing the words, not the human agent. Their spirits were active, but their mind was not. In fact, "it is the Spirit of Jesus carrying on a discourse with the invisible Father through one of our brethren." The words were not "accessible" to the speaker's "understanding."[114]

This is in stark contrast with some of Irving's earlier comments in which he considered the intellect to be of higher value. For example, just before he moved to London in 1822, Irving had told Jane Welsh, "my intellect long unused to expand itself, is now awakening again, and truth is revealing itself to my mind."[115] And there is abundant evidence of the power of Irving's intellect in his sermons preached at the Caledonian Chapel. At the beginning of his time in London he had also said that the Christian religion "doth not denounce the rational or intellectual man, but addeth thereto the spiritual man, and that the latter flourishes the more nobly under the fostering hand of the former."[116] Thus, the intellect and the spirit were partners, not opponents, and the intellect even fostered the spiritual.

111. Irving to Robert Story, January 27, 1832, quoted in Oliphant, *Life*, 2:236.

112. Irving to Robert Story, January 27, 1832, quoted in Drummond, *Edward Irving*, 150.

113. Irving to John McLeod Campbell, February 22, 1833, quoted in Oliphant, *Life*, 2:331.

114. Irving, "Facts Connected," 4:761, 5:199, 200.

115. Irving to Jane Baillie Welsh, February 9, 1822, in ibid., *DL*, 134.

116. Ibid., *Oracles*, 379.

Indeed, in Irving's early ministry, while he regarded Christianity as essentially a religion of the heart, that heart was fed, at least partly, through the intellect. To Irving, the "Doctrines" of the faith "should be like the mighty rivers which fertilize our island." They should "carry health and vitality to the whole soul and surface of Christian life."[117] But now the spirit, hopefully through the Holy Spirit, overruled the intellect.

Amidst all this charismata, Irving believed that he was fighting for "the faith once delivered to the saints."[118] To him, there was nothing novel in it all. It was essential Christianity. On Christmas Eve, 1831, Irving wrote to the Regent Square session pleading with them to accept these manifestations as being from God. He began:

> My Dear Brethren,
>   There is nothing I would not surrender to you, even to my life, except to hinder or retard in any way what I most clearly discern to be the work of God's Holy Spirit . . . I most solemnly warn you all, in the name of the most high God, for no earthly consideration whatever, to gainsay or impede the work of speaking in tongues and prophesying which God had begun amongst us.[119]

Irving was clearly on a collision course with most of the leaders of his church. The outcome looked black.

FOR KING AND CHURCH

Whatever question marks now hovered over Irving's ministry, he was still popular in some quarters. At about this time, he received a gift of nearly £100 from some friends in Edinburgh. This he thought best to spend on books that would be "profitable for the understanding of the Holy Scriptures,"[120] which, no doubt, would also engage his intellect.

In spite of all this difficulty, Irving also found time in 1829 and 1830 to raise a number of petitions on different issues. These tended to be presented with a prayer and a flourish. One was to Robert Peel, who was then Home Secretary, and concerned the Catholic Reform Bill of 1829. He and two of his elders went to Peel's office and, while waiting to be seen, Irving and his

---

117. Ibid., 41–42.

118. Letter from Irving, n.d., quoted in Oliphant, *Life*, 2:111.

119. Irving to the Regent Square session, December 24, 1831, quoted in ibid., 2:228.

120. Letter from Irving, quoted in ibid., 2:111.

companions knelt down as Irving prayed for success on their mission. When one of Peel's officials appeared to accept the petition, Irving rose to his feet and proceeded to lecture the poor man on the contents of the document.[121]

In 1830 Irving raised another petition urging the new King William IV to call a national fast. On December 21, this time accompanied by elders Hamilton, Nisbet, and McKenzie, Irving visited Lord Melbourne, the Home Secretary, to present the petition. As they waited to be received, the four men, as before, knelt down to pray. When finally ushered into his Lordship's presence, Irving was given leave to speak. This he did, reading the lengthy address that accompanied the petition in full, denouncing democracy, the selfishness of the rich, and the decline of doctrine in the church. It concluded by strongly urging the appointment of godly chaplains in the royal household, the observance of the Sabbath in court and in the nation generally, and the holding of a day of prayer and fasting to confess the country's failings.[122] Melbourne was not noted for rocking the boat, so, one suspects, while the petition was accepted, he either never presented it to the king or did not press him to take notice of it.

Even beyond all this, Irving was as busy as ever. According to Isabella, one day in October 1830 he was speaking from nine in the morning to nine at night, "what with expositions, dictating, and answering questions."[123] And this was not likely a rare occurrence. His sister Elizabeth reported that on one Sunday in 1831, Irving arrived home from the morning service at 2:00 p.m. After dining, he went to visit the sick. He had tea out and returned to the church "to talk with young communicants," then took the evening service "with great animation." After that, he "went to pray with a child." It was then on home and back to the church the next morning for the prayer meeting.[124] Some weeks he preached as many as seven times. In addition, Irving still believed that the way ahead looked bright for his church, which had good congregations and by this time hosted "more than two hundred" daily at the early morning prayer meetings.[125] Indeed, he could say in 1832, "The church has been enlarged; many souls have been converted by the voice of the Spirit . . . and altogether the work of the Lord has been proceeding."[126]

---

121. Wilks, *Edward Irving*, 197–98.

122. Oliphant, *Life*, 2:165; [Bonar ?], "Edward Irving," 235.

123. Letter from Isabella Irving, October 1830, quoted in Drummond, *Edward Irving*, 213–14.

124. Quoted in Oliphant, *Life*, 2:176–77.

125. Irving to Robert Story, January 27, 1832, quoted in ibid., 2:236.

126. Reported by William Hamilton [to Rev. Martin?], quoted in ibid., 2:245.

Amidst all this turmoil, on February 21, 1831, Isabella gave birth to a boy, Martin Howy Irving. Early in August the child was vaccinated by a surgeon named Richardson.[127] Unlike most of his siblings, Martin was robust; he became a powerful rower and lived until he was eighty, the only one of the Irving children to live past the age of fifty.

---

127. Irving to Mr. Richardson, August 8 1831, in Irving, *DL*, 283.

17

The London Trial

[I am] groaning under the reproach of ten thousand tongues in ten thousand ways.

—EDWARD IRVING[1]

STRESS AND STRAIN

In Irving's farewell discourse to the people of St. John's at Glasgow in 1822, he had urged them,

> put your trust in [God] continually. The strong man shall become as flax, and the mighty man as the clod of the valley; and friends shall be comfortless or fade from your sight; the strength of youth and the joy of life shall utterly fail, and the bonds of nature may dissolve, so that parents shall forget, and the mother cease to love the child whom she bore; but God, if ye trust in Him, shall be to you a shield and a buckler, and a strong tower and an everlasting portion. He shall feed you by the still waters, and anoint your head with oil, and make your cup to overflow.[2]

1. Irving to the Trustees and Building Committee to the Elders and Deacons of the National Scotch Church, March 17, 1832, in Irving, *DL*, 296.

2. Irving, *CW*, 3:347.

Now it was time for him to put that to the test.

The Presbyterian Assembly of 1831 had dismissed the Reverends John McLeod Campbell and Alexander Scott from the Church of Scotland ministry, and Hugh Mclean narrowly escaped the same fate, with his case being referred back to his presbytery, which eventually went against him. In Mclean's case, the problem was that he believed that the human nature of Christ was the same as Adam after the fall, as did Irving. Campbell's expulsion was primarily because he believed that the atonement was for everybody, not just the elect, as did Irving by this time. Scott was dismissed because he disagreed with the *Westminster Confession* on three points, including that Christ died only for the elect. This Assembly not only dismissed some members of the clergy who were close to Irving in both teaching and affection, it also condemned his book, *The Orthodox and Catholic Doctrine of Our Lord's Human Nature.*[3]

In addition, the Assembly issued a report that was directly aimed at him titled "Report upon Books and Pamphlets Containing Erroneous Opinions." This Irving had half-expected. The report urged any relevant presbytery to see whether Irving was the author of the works in question, and to take whatever action was possible and considered necessary.[4]

Irving found these actions by the Assembly deeply disturbing. The decisions relating to Campbell and Maclean he regarded as subverting "the whole truth the Father, Son and Holy Ghost, and being unanimous are . . . very fearful . . . very terrible [and] very horrible." In fact, the Assembly's opinions on the human nature of Christ contained "grievous absurdities and heresies."[5] The following year, in a letter to his father-in-law, Irving called the Church of Scotland "dead, and heretical, and all but apostate," and in need of "repentance and humiliation."[6] Very clear! Very bold! Very disturbing! It would seem that Edward Irving was fed up with being called a heretic and had decided to fight the battle of words with the same weapon.

Irving's father-in-law was also disturbed by the actions of the 1831 Assembly, but in a different way than Irving. He expressed that he was "grieved" at the Assembly's handling of the cases of Irving and McLean. He does not seem to have disagreed with the decisions so much as "the very

---

3. Irving, "Judgment upon the Deliberations," 84–85; Oliphant, *Life*, 2:177–79; Story, *Memoir*, 185–86, 391–92; Lee, "Christ's Sinful Flesh," 199–203.

4. Oliphant, *Life*, 2:178–79; Drummond, *Edward Irving*, 120; Lee, "Christ's Sinful Flesh," 203–204.

5. Irving, "Judgment upon the Deliberations," 86–87.

6. Irving to John Martin, March 7, 1832, quoted in Oliphant, *Life*, 2:253.

harsh and uncharitable spirit . . . exhibited by some of the speakers" on the matter. He thought that Irving deserved more consideration.[7]

Later that year, Irving published a book that examined the history of the Scottish Church and gave a detailed comparison of the old *Scots Confession* and the more recent *Westminster Confession*.[8] He came down firmly in favor of the older document, as he had always done. The *Scots Confession*, he argued, was closer to Christian truth, which effectively meant that it was more in line with his own beliefs. It has already been mentioned that Irving may have preferred the older confession because of its more Romantic bearing and because it was closer to his view on the humanity of Christ. It could also be argued that the earlier confession was stronger in its teaching on the Holy Spirit than the more recent one. Though the *Westminster Confession* makes numerous references to the Holy Spirit, it does not have a specific chapter on him; the *Scots Confession* does.[9]

Thomas Chalmers, in spite of his theological position and standing, remained silent on these matters at the Assembly.[10] In his journal, all he said with regard to the discussion about Irving was "General Assembly. Mr. Irving's case."[11] Chalmers, it appears, did have sympathy with some aspects of the teaching of Campbell and McLean, if not Irving, and he did not seem to have had the heart to speak against any of them.[12] A. L. Drummond suggests that Chalmers may have remained silent on the issue of Christ's human nature because he saw in Irving "a strain of fanaticism so potent" that it would inevitably destroy him, and it was thus pointless to try "shielding him temporarily."[13] But that doctrine was clearly not only held by Irving.

On the other hand, it has been claimed that Chalmers had a habit of avoiding "Assembly divisions."[14] If this was the case, then it may be that Chalmers' lack of comment was because he had little appetite for controversy and chose to avoid it. Back in 1820, Irving noted that Chalmers took a very cautious approach to the Scottish troubles of that time. Irving told

7. John Martin to William Hamilton, June 1831, in Irving *DL*, 280–81.

8. Irving, *Confessions*, xciii–civ.

9. Presbyterian Church, "Scots Confession," ch. 12. References to the Holy Spirit in the *Westminster Confession* can be found in ch. 1:5, 2:3, 7:3, 8:8, and 11:4 (Letham, *Westminster Assembly*, 72, 169–73).

10. Hanna, *Memoirs* (New York), 3:250–51; Oliphant, *Life*, 2:119–21; Torrance, *Scottish Theology*, 288–89.

11. Chalmers' Journal No. 7 (1827–34), 28 May 1831, quoted in Grass, *Edward Irving*, 226.

12. Torrance, *Scottish Theology*, 314–15.

13. Drummond, *Edward Irving*, 118.

14. Chambers, "Doctrinal Attitudes," 168.

Carlyle that Chalmers took "a safe course in all these difficulties" and that in politics he would "not side with" the Whigs, the Tories, or the radicals.[15] Four years later, Irving urged Chalmers to "Be on your guard against the fear of your fellow-men,"[16] which might indicate that he had observed such fear in the great man. It has also been suggested that Chalmers was held back from supporting Irving by his own conservatism, which rings true.[17]

All this suggests that Thomas Chalmers did not like taking sides or the personal conflict that was often involved. However, he was in the thick of the fight during the Disruption in 1843, which saw the emergence of the Free Church of Scotland. Then at least, he did take sides.

The last time Irving and Chalmers ever met appears to have been in October of 1830. Chalmers recorded in his diary, "Had a very interesting call from Mr. Irving between one and two, when I was in bed. He stopped two hours, wherein he gave his expositions; and I gave, at greater length and liberty than I had ever done before, my advices and my views. We parted from each other with great cordiality, after a prayer which he himself offered with great pathos and piety,"[18] and, one suspects, at great length. The following year, the two men had an exchange of letters that ended with Chalmers expressing his lost confidence in his one-time colleague.[19]

It is striking that when Irving's letters are examined, one cannot help but notice the differences between Irving's letters to Thomas Carlyle and those to Thomas Chalmers. He usually addressed Carlyle as "My Dear Carlyle." Most often he addressed Chalmers, "Dear Sir." The contents of the letters to Carlyle are generally warm, while those to Chalmers are businesslike. Irving and Carlyle were friends. Irving and Chalmers were never more than ministerial colleagues.

In July of 1831 Irving was bold enough to state in a letter to Robert Story that the ministers who had passed censure on Campbell, Mclean, and himself at the Assembly had cast out not just a number of ministers, but also "the truth of God" and that "by denying that Christ came in the flesh," were in fact "Antichrist" and "enemies of Christ and His truth."[20] The ministers of the Assembly, if they had been advised of those charges, would no doubt have responded that they were not "denying that Christ came in the flesh," but were only rejecting Irving's understanding of it. As to being Antichrist

15. Irving to Thomas Carlyle, April 15, 1820, in Irving, *DL*, 84.

16. Irving to Thomas Chalmers, September 21, 1824, in ibid., 202.

17. Drummond and Bulloch, *Scottish Church*, 206.

18. Quoted in Oliphant, *Life*, 2:140.

19. Grass, *Edward Irving*, 227–28.

20. Irving to Robert Story, July 1831, quoted in Oliphant, *Life*, 2:185–86.

and "enemies of Christ," some might well have wondered in their more heated moments whether those charges could have been better applied to Irving himself.

It seems to have been in the late winter or early spring of 1832 that Irving preached to his congregation on healing from 1 Cor 12:9. Irving believed at this time that disease only afflicted Christians if they had sinned or if God had allowed it as a test of faith, as with Job. Indeed, to him, "Sickness is sin apparent in the body." He also said, "*every* instance of sickness in the Church ought to be confessed as a judicial visitation for sin and treated accordingly,"[21] and any such disease in the Christian could normally be cured through faith.

The next day, Irving was taken ill with what he later believed to have been cholera. There had been a terrible outbreak of the disease in Britain that year. According to his own account, which appeared in *The Morning Watch* in June, on that day he "arose in perfect health, at the usual hour," and went to meet with his flock for the early morning prayer meeting. He continued,

> During the prayer-meeting I began to feel pain, but was able to go through the service. A number of friends accompanied me home to breakfast. On reaching home, I became very chill, and had a very severe pain in my stomach and bowels, and my bowels were much relaxed . . . After sitting awhile, I felt a little relieved, and entered the room where my friends were, and sat down by the fire, unable to taste anything. The hour's pain I had endured, and the other trial of my constitution, had even then had such an effect on my frame that my appearance shocked my friends. I . . . endeavoured to lift up my heart to my God, having a presentiment that I was called upon to show forth the faith which I had on the preceding evening been led to exhort my people to have in the heavenly Father.

He was able to lead family worship, but he was "so enfeebled" that he could not kneel or stand, so he had to sit to pray. After that Irving went to his room, confessed his sins, and cast himself on God for the strength to preach later that morning and again in the evening. By this time he was "very sick," with a "wringing or gnawing pain through [his] whole body." He asked to be left alone until it was time to prepare to leave for the morning service. The diarrhea continued, and he also began to vomit.[22]

---

21. Irving, "Holiness and Power," in ibid., *CW*, 5:464; Irving to Henry Drummond, April 26, 1833, in Irving, *DL*, 355, emphasis added.

22. Irving, "Visions—Miraculous Cures—Cholera," letter to the editors in *TMW*

At the prescribed time, a very worried Isabella went to attend to him and prepared some "arrowroot and brandy" for him, but he was unable to take it. She later said that his eyes were "sunken," his cheeks "pallid," and his whole appearance was "ghastly." In spite of another bowel movement and more vomiting, he managed to walk to the church located about four hundred yards away accompanied by his wife and a friend, but "With slow and difficult steps."

He refused to allow anyone to take his place conducting the service, though David Brown was present. Upon mounting the pulpit, he began to read a chapter from the Bible, "expecting the power of spiritual exposition" he normally experienced, but to his "astonishment," nothing came to his mind. He continued reading, but his voice began to fade, his breathing became difficult and his eyes hazy, which impeded his reading. He also became dizzy, and in a desperate attempt to stay upright he held on to the sides of the pulpit.[23]

Irving was convinced that it was his "unbelief" that was the cause of these ailments, and he feared that he would fall before the people and thus shame his Savior. Silently he prayed, "Surely Thou, O Jesus, art stronger in my spirit, than Satan is in my flesh!" Instantly, "a cold sweat . . . broke out all over [his] body, and stood in large drops" upon his forehead and hands. But he "seemed to be strengthened," and he began to read more clearly, though he was still unable "to add one word of exposition." At the end of the reading, the congregation sang "a few stanzas of a Psalm."

He then read from John 3, intending to preach on the final verse. At this stage in his life and with his understanding of the Holy Spirit's ministry, he often did not prepare his sermons but instead spoke as the Spirit moved.[24] While this strategy may have normally worked well for him, on this occasion it did not. As he proceeded with the Bible reading, Irving found himself "utterly incapable of originating anything." Eventually, "Slowly and with great weakness the words dropped from" him, but he remained unable to bring them together "into regular discourse." Thus, presumably, what he said was a number of disconnected thoughts. But he gave himself "to the Spirit, and went forward."

Suddenly, "the Holy Ghost, in one of the prophets, burst in upon [his] discourse, speaking with tongues and prophesying." This brought Irving

---

(June 1832) 5:427.

23. Ibid., 5:428–29.

24. Irving gives the impression here that he had completely given up sermon preparation. However, Margaret Oliphant said that she knew of a woman who was still acting as his amanuensis in the preparation of at least some of his sermons at this time (Oliphant, *Life*, 2:313).

"rest and refreshing," and though "dead . . . in respect of body and of mind," he was able to recommence his address "with fresh strength," being "alive in respect of the Spirit." Dead or alive, or dead and alive, he continued to speak for "about an hour, with more unction . . . than [he] had ever preached before."

After arriving home, he ate "little or nothing," but he was able to preach again later that day "with more power" than he could remember experiencing before. The next day he arose with "renewed strength" and continued in reasonable health.[25]

Whether this sickness was cholera or not might be debated. The major symptom of cholera is diarrhea, of which Irving clearly had a bad case. Other symptoms include vomiting, which he also experienced, and great thirst, which he did not mention. Another cholera symptom is muscle cramps, which could be the cause of the "very severe pain" that he spoke of. But whether it was cholera or not, clearly Irving was very unwell, but this was not surprising considering the strain he had been under for so long.

In the days ahead his health improved, but reports by a number of people state that he never looked well in these later years. For example, six months later Mrs. Montagu told Jane Carlyle that "he looked dreadfully pale, and was much emaciated."[26] A couple of months later Jane herself described him as "gray, toilworn, haggard."[27] He was worn out, exhausted by his own great efforts and stressed by continual opposition. If Irving had experienced a healing of whatever had laid him low, it seems to have been at best a temporary and partial one.

THE TRUSTEES TAKE ACTION

But the opposition Irving faced was to continue. When the National Scotch Church at Regent Square had originally been planned in 1823, it had been proposed that it would retain its "connection with the Church of Scotland, and that the doctrines, forms of worship and mode of discipline of" the Scottish Church "shall be taught, observed and practised therein."[28] This had been enshrined in the Regent Square's trust deed and so remained

25. Irving, "Visions—Miraculous Cures—Cholera," letter to the editors in *TMW* (June 1832) 5:429. Another account mentions the presence of David Brown; see Grass, *Edward Irving*, 262–63.

26. Anna Montagu to Jane Carlyle, January 2, 1833, *CLO*; Thomas Carlyle to Margaret A. Carlyle, January 27, 1833, *CLO*.

27. Jane Carlyle quoted in Thomas Carlyle to John A. Carlyle, March 29, 1833, *CLO*.

28. *The New Times*, July 29, 1823, 1.

unchanged. What had changed were some of Irving's beliefs and his conduct of the church's worship. The new ways he had allowed were seen by
many as in conflict with Presbyterian teachings and practices.

Early in 1832 the Regent Square trustees enlisted the aid of Sir Edward
Sugden, a prominent lawyer and politician, to consider whether Irving was
right in saying that he was solely responsible for the way the church services were run. Sir Edward perused the trust deed and advised that Irving
was wrong, concluding that the presbytery would be in its rights to dismiss
Irving.

In the middle of February the trustees approached Irving to give him a
copy of that report. This meeting appears to have been quite amiable, though
tensions must have boiled beneath the surface. Irving told the trustees that
he would consider the matter and get back to them.[29]

At about the same time, Thomas Carlyle told his brother,

> I saw Irving yesternight [February 15], for the *fourth* time since
> you left us. He is still goodnatured and patient; but enveloped
> in the vain sound of the "Tongues": I am glad to think that he
> will not go utterly *mad* (not madder than a Don Quixote was);
> but his intellect seems quietly settling into a superstitious *caput
> mortuum;* he has no longer any opinion to deliver worth listen-
> ing to on any secular matter. The Chancellor *can* eject him, thus:
> It is provided by the original Deed of his Chapel that the wor-
> ship there shall be that of the Established Church of Scotland:
> his Managers, I know, have already consulted Sugden; whether
> and how *soon* they may drive the question to extremities, is not
> to be guessed. Indeed, the whole matter is getting stale here, and
> is little heeded. I pity poor Irving, and cannot prophecy of him:
> his "Morning Watch" he gave me yesternight is simply the howl-
> ing of a Bedlam.[30]

Two days later Carlyle told his mother:

> Meeting Irving the other day on the street, he appointed me
> to come and take tea with him. The "inspired-tongue" work, I
> think, is getting a little dulled; at least I heard or saw nothing
> of it going on, that night; only Irving still full of its importance,
> and his Wife (a melancholic half-hollow sort of person, not
> wholly to my mind) still fuller . . . He put into my hands, as "the
> deepest view he had ever seen" a Paper (in his Prophetic Maga-
> zine "the Morning Watch") written by a namesake of mine [the

29. Oliphant, *Life,* 2:245, 248. Sugden had been the nation's Solicitor-General.
30. Thomas Carlyle to John A. Carlyle, February 16, 1832, *CLO.*

lawyer Thomas Carlyle (1803–1855)] in Edinburgh, or rather *not* by him, "for it was given him" by the spirit! This deepest view I glanced into, and found to be simply the insanest Babble, without top bottom or centre, that ever was emitted even from Bedlam itself. Poor Irving! It is still said they are taking steps to cast him out of his Church: what next he is to bring out upon the world I cannot prophecy. A good truehearted man he will continue; the truer, the more he suffers from the world: but he has once for all surrounded himself with Delirium, and with the Delirious; and so stands quite exiled from all general usefulness.[31]

The Sunday after Irving had received Sugden's report, before he had responded to the trustees, he made an announcement from the pulpit that showed that he would take no backward step and that he was well aware of what his fate would be. He told his people that he had "something of great importance" to say to them and continued:

> I do not know whether I may ever look this congregation again in the face in this place, and whether the doors of the church will not be shut against me during this week. If it be so, it will be simply because I have refused to allow the voice of the Spirit of God to be silenced in this church . . . No one has found any fault with me at all except in the matter of my God [echoes of Dan 6:5] . . . The church has been enlarged; many souls have been converted by the voice of the Spirit; the church has fallen off in nothing; and altogether the work of the Lord has been proceeding. But because I am firm in my honour of God and reverence for his ordinances, we are come to this. Now I must provide for my flock. What are you to do? You must not come here. Here the Spirit of God has been cast out, and none can prosper who come here to worship. Go not to any church where they look shyly on the work of the Spirit. We must "not forsake the assembling of ourselves together" . . . If we should be cast out for the truth, let us rejoice; yea, let us exceedingly rejoice.[32]

He also proposed that if, or more likely when, the church's doors would be shut against him that the people meet temporarily in what today would be called house churches, and he promised to help them as best he could.

Irving was, perhaps, being less than honest when he also said in this address, "Let no one be troubled for me: I am not troubled."[33] The great

31. Thomas Carlyle to Margaret A. Carlyle, February 18, 1832, *CLO*.

32. William Hamilton to the Martins, n.d., quoted in Oliphant, *Life*, 2:244–46. Part of Irving's address is contained in this letter.

33. Ibid.

work he had established was being split apart before him. If he was not troubled, then it was indeed a miracle.

The next day he penned a reply to the trustees, which read:

> My Dear Brethren,
>
> I have read over the opinion of Sir Edward Sugden . . . and I have taken a full week to consider of it. The principle on which I have acted is to preserve the integrity of my ministerial character unimpaired, and to fulfil my office according to the word of God. If the trust-deed do fetter me therein, I knew it not when the trust-deed was drawn, and am sure that it never was intended in the drawing of it . . . But if it be so that you, the trustees, must act to prevent me and my flock from assembling to worship God, according to the word of God, in the house committed into your trust, we will look unto our God for preservation and safe keeping. Farewell! May the Lord have you in His holy keeping.[34]

At the end of February 1832, then, Edward Irving knew that he would no longer be able to minister in the church that he had established and made famous. Soon he would no longer be its minister. It was sad, oh, so very sad. And there was probably no one sadder than Edward Irving.

On March 17 Irving wrote a lengthy letter to the Regent Square trustees and session. In it he warned,

> I do you solemnly to wit, men and Brethren, before Almighty God, the Heart-searcher, that whosoever lifteth a finger against the work which is proceeding in the Church of Christ under my pastoral care, is rising up against the Holy Ghost; and I warn him even with tears to beware and stand back, for he will assuredly bring upon himself the wrath and indignation of the God of Heaven and Earth if he dare to go forward.[35]

Irving went on to state that he had undertaken "Many months of most painstaking and searching observation" to test these gifts and had received "the most varied proofs of every kind" to confirm that they were genuine. To speak or move against them was "to blaspheme the Holy Ghost [and] to act against the Holy Ghost."

He also asked them "if the trust-deed could have been intended to prevent the spiritual gifts from ever being exercised within the building . . . ?"

---

34. Irving to the Regent Square trustees, February 28, 1832, quoted in ibid., 2:247–48.

35. Irving to the Regent Square trustees and London presbytery, March 17, 1832, in Irving, *DL*, 296–99.

The simple answer to that was no. But until Irving had begun to think along those lines it is highly unlikely that any of his church leaders had considered that kind of gifting, so they had not then thought about the issue. There was nothing in the trust deed to permit the gifts, nor to specifically disallow them. The real question was: Did the trust deed forbid lay people shouting out from the pews during the church services? Doing so was certainly contrary to normal Church of Scotland practice, and that church's practice was enshrined in the Regent Square trust deed, as noted above.

In addition, Irving also went on to warn the Regent Square trustees and session that if they "cast forth" the Holy Spirit from their church, which he believed they were doing, that church "will never prosper or come to any good until it hath been cleansed from this abomination by sore and sorrowful repentance." If they did not repent, "disappointment and defeat will rest upon it for ever." Indeed, this act "will bring down judgment upon all who take part in it." The letter was signed, "Your faithful & loving Pastor and Friend, Edwd Irving."[36]

Through all this, Irving never seems to have doubted that he was right in his beliefs about these manifestations. Peter Elliott puts this down to his Romantic inclinations. The charismata were in line with the "heroic and visionary," and thus in keeping with Romantic ideals. In addition, in Elliott's terms, when attacked Irving always "defaulted to the standard Romantic hermeneutic of opposition." That is, the authorities always opposed the new and the different. The charismata were in one sense new and were certainly different, so those in charge opposed them. Such "Opposition was more a confirmation that you were doing something right than possible evidence that you were doing something wrong," for as Elliott also suggests, "Irving seemed to equate sincerity of motive with authenticity of vision." He and his followers were sincere, and therefore what emerged from their ministry must be genuine.[37] Few, if any, doubt Irving's sincerity, but his sincerity did not guarantee the truth of his beliefs or the genuine giftedness of his followers.

Though Irving's days at the Regent Square Church were clearly numbered, he was still officially its minister. On March 17, 1832, Regent Square's trustees approached the London presbytery to have him dismissed. They made five charges against him:

> 1. [That he] suffered and permitted, and still allows, the public
>   services of the church in the worship of God, on the Sabbath

36. Ibid.

37. Elliott, *Edward Irving*, 188.

and other days, to be interrupted by persons not being either ministers or licentiates of the Church of Scotland.

2. [That he] suffered and permitted, and still allows, the public services of the said church in the worship of God, to be interrupted by persons not being either members or seatholders of the said church.

3. [That he] suffered and permitted, and also publicly encourages, females to speak in the same church, and to interrupt and disturb the public worship of God in the church on Sabbath and other days.

4. [That he] suffered and permitted, and also publicly encourages, other individuals, members of the said church, to interrupt and disturb the public worship of God in the church on Sabbath and other days.

5. [That he], for the purpose of encouraging and exciting the said interruptions, has appointed times when a suspension of the usual worship in the said church takes place, for said persons to exercise the supposed gifts with which they profess to be endowed.[38]

Whether these interruptions were strictly interruptions might be argued, for Irving had deliberately set aside a time in the services so that the regular worship would not be interrupted. It is also striking that these charges do not argue biblically, though certain Scriptures undoubtedly dwelt beneath the surface. Strictly speaking, to argue from the Scriptures was not the task of the trustees, who were the legal overseers of the church's affairs rather than its theological guardians. To argue scripturally and theologically was more the role of the presbytery. The real issue to the trustees here was who had the right to make theological pronouncements in the services in the Presbyterian church under their watch? Presbyterian discipline dictated that only properly and officially trained men (and only men) were allowed to do so. The National Scotch Church at Regent Square was officially committed to that view.

THE TRIAL

These charges were to be brought by the Regent Square trustees to a special meeting of the London presbytery on April 26, 1832, a meeting at which Irving was to be present. On the morning of that day Irving breakfasted

38. Oliphant, *Life*, 2:261.

with some who had remained loyal to him, including David Brown (whose loyalty was being put to a stern test and would not last much longer) and the Cardales. That morning one of the "gifted" spoke a brief message of encouragement.

Soon afterwards a visitor arrived with a message that was strikingly discouraging. It was Robert Baxter, upon whose detailed prophecies Irving had staked so much. He was met by Irving and Cardale. Baxter shocked them by telling them that he felt certain that the pronouncements he had made were the outpourings of "a lying spirit," not "the Spirit of the Lord." He had come to believe that some of Irving's doctrines were "erroneous," and because these teachings were endorsed by the words of various prophets, including himself, this meant that their prophecies must also be false.

Irving had, in fact, been aware for more than a month that Baxter had begun to reject some of his teachings.[39] But this was hardly what Irving wanted to hear the morning before a meeting in which he would have to defend the authenticity of the manifestations and the legitimacy of his actions in allowing them. It was yet another body blow to him.

Yet this disappointment does not seem to have dented his belief in the genuineness of the tongues and prophecies. He and Cardale returned to the others, and Irving led them in a prayer:

> Have mercy, Lord, on thy dear servant, who has come up to tell us that he has been deceived, that his word has never been from above, but from beneath, and that it is all a lie. Have mercy on him, Lord; the enemy has prevailed against him, and hither he has come in this time of trouble and rebuke and blasphemy, to break the power of the testimony we have to bear this day to this work of Thine. But let Thy work and power appear unto Thy poor servant.[40]

Once more, Irving does not seem to have considered that he, Edward Irving, might be wrong. Earlier he had said that he had received "the most varied proofs" to confirm the genuineness of these gifts. Yet on this occasion he seems to have been ignoring some striking evidence that at least some of these gifts were not genuine. In Baxter's opinion, on this issue Irving was "utterly deluded."[41]

39. Baxter's *Narrative*, 117–18; Oliphant, *Life*, 2:263–64; Hair, *Regent*, 66–67; Irving to Robert Baxter, March 21, 1832, in Irving, *DL*, 300–303. See also Robert Baxter to "Mrs. P.," April 30, 1832, quoted in [Bonar ?], "Edward Irving," 236.

40. Brown, "Personal Reminiscences," 272.

41. Robert Baxter to "Mrs. P.," April 30, 1832, quoted in [Bonar?], "Edward Irving," 236.

After Baxter's defection, Irving still continued to believe in his prophecies. But Irving believed that now, as a person, Baxter was "a vessel marred upon the wheel of the Potter," who fought "sore against the gracious purpose of his Maker." Indeed, in Irving's opinion he had made "a shipwreck . . . of heavenly treasure," for which Irving urged him to repent.[42]

The official meeting that day of the presbytery and the trustees was held at the London Wall church and was effectively Irving's trial. A number of Irving's supporters were also present. It was continued the next day, April 27, and was reconvened on May 2.[43] Put simply, the issue was: Had he allowed practices in his church contrary to the discipline and teaching of the Church of Scotland?

The meeting began with a prayer. Suddenly Taplin, the schoolteacher, burst forth in "a tongue" and followed it with a prophecy in English. This must have shocked Irving's accusers, but it at least gave a demonstration of what they were considering. It also, one suspects, further distanced the antagonists on this gloom-ridden day.

Mr. J. H. Mann laid the charges against Irving on behalf of the trustees, and Mr. Cardale, who was a solicitor, acted in his defense. The prosecution called three of Irving's followers to give evidence, including Taplin, but strangely, they called no one else. Those three no doubt would rather have been defending the preacher, but in these circumstances almost anything they could say would go against him. The first of these witnesses was Duncan Mackenzie, the only elder who had totally supported Irving in the tongues issue.

After Mann had begun with what Oliphant called some "loose and confused interrogations," Irving was allowed to question the witness. Irving drew out of Mackenzie that when the "gifted" people were so inspired, it was not strictly they who were speaking, but rather the Holy Spirit. Irving then asked him if he believed that the prophesying "agree[d] with the things written in the Scripture or not?" According to Oliphant, "immediately a tumult of opposition arose." This was halted when the Moderator, James Brown, pointed out that the issue under consideration was not whether these manifestations agreed with Scripture, but whether they were allowable according to Presbyterian Church order. A heated discussion broke out, with Irving opposing that view and each member of the court individually supporting it. It was thus confirmed, contrary to Irving, that the issue the court had to

---

42. Irving, "What Caused," 130, 138, 140.
43. Hair, *Regent*, 176–77, appendix B.

decide was whether these practices agreed with the denomination's standards and the trust deed of the Regent Square Church.[44]

Technically, of course, the court's ruling was correct. That was the charge originally brought against Irving, and it had to be dealt with. In addition, at his ordination Edward Irving must have agreed to abide by the *Westminster Confession*, the church's doctrinal standard. That was normal practice. But now his views and practices seemed to contradict that confession. So it could be fairly argued that he was going against his ordination vows. But it is a sad day when, at a Christian meeting, one cannot use the Scriptures to support one's position. Indeed, the *Westminster Confession* stated, "all controversies of religion are to be determined [by] the Holy Spirit speaking in the scripture." And while the *Westminster Confession* also allowed "synods and councils ministerially to determine controversies of faith," it recognized that at times those bodies have erred.[45] (The trial of John McLeod Campbell in 1831 had also included a Scriptures versus *Westminster Confession* debate.)[46] But such controversies could never be settled by the opinion of one man.

The next witness was Mr. Taplin. He testified that he had spoken once, but only once, during a church service "at the close of Mr. Irving's sermon" one Sunday in October 1831. The Moderator then asked Taplin whether he had spoken at that particular time "by a previous arrangement with Mr. Irving," thereby suggesting collusion. This Taplin emphatically denied. While Irving had later set aside particular times for these manifestations, Taplin pointed out that he had not yet done so at that stage, and when Irving eventually did so, Taplin said that he had disagreed with it.

The Moderator then asked Taplin whether he had previously heard teaching about the gifts prior to his speaking out in the church service. The witness answered,

> I heard Mr. Irving, I believe, first teach that he saw no reason why the gifts of the Spirit should have been withdrawn from the Church; and I was led by that, and hearing of their revival in Scotland, to read the Scriptures for myself on the subject; and I found in the last chapter of Mark, the Lord had promised "that signs should follow them that believe;" and I thought, "What is

---

44. Oliphant, *Life*, 2:263–67.

45. *Westminster Confession*, ch. 1:10, 31:3, 4. Biblically-based creeds and confessions are necessary and useful, but there is always the danger that in areas under debate a confession will take priority over the Scriptures.

46. Lee, "Christ's Sinful Flesh," 75–76; Torrance, *Scottish Theology*, 288.

a Church, or the authority of a Church, if it set aside the plain
promise of Scripture?"[47]

Thus, he was arguing that though Irving triggered the idea in his mind,
his conclusions emerged from his own reading and consideration of the
matter. But Taplin was clearly aware of the possibility of tongues and in
favor of them before he had publicly engaged in them.

Later Mann asked Taplin, "Were the exhibition of tongues in the
Church, by you and others, similar to the exhibition you made this morning?" Taplin objected to the word "exhibition" and refused to answer the
question. Mann substituted the word "display," but Taplin again protested
and refused to answer. Mann tried again; once more the witness would not
answer. Finally Mann found an acceptable wording: "Were the manifestations in the Church, by you and others, similar to that we heard this morning?" Taplin replied, "Our gifts differ in some respects, though they are
similar in kind. We each speak a different tongue." Mann then asked Taplin
whether he understood what he had said in his outburst that morning; the
teacher responded, "I understood the English." The interrogation of Taplin
continued, though not all the questions seemed relevant to the matter at
hand.[48]

Next Mr. Ker, Irving's only remaining supportive deacon, was called
to the stand. Mr. MacLean, a member of the presbytery, asked him whether
doctrinal matters such as those related to the second coming of Christ had
been confirmed by the gifted people. At this point Irving's solicitor objected
that such questions were "irrelevant" to the case, but Irving asked that the
question be retained and answered, for he desired "no concealment or re-
serve in respect to [his] doctrine."

Irving's stand made it possible for the trial to consider other quite different matters than tongues. Inevitably, it seems, the next question to Ker
was "Have you heard . . . That Christ's humanity was fallen and corrupt
humanity?" He answered, "I have heard it declared that His flesh was fallen."
This Maclean paraphrased to "He has heard it declared that our Lord's flesh
was fallen and *corrupt*." Immediately Irving rose to his feet to ask, "He has
not said any such word, Sir, as 'corrupt'; why will you make additions of
your own to the evidence?" Ker added his voice to the protest. The mood
was becoming very tense.

After a host of other questions, the Moderator asked Ker, "Is there anything which you wish to add in exoneration of your minister?" Ker seized
the opportunity: "I would only say, that I believe nothing could be so painful

47. Oliphant, *Life*, 2:267–68.
48. Ibid., 2:269.

to Mr. Irving as that any one should interrupt the public services of the Church, except those persons through whom the Holy Ghost speaks." Ker's well-intentioned statement had left a gaping hole through which Irving's accusers soon rushed. Who was to be the judge of whether or not the Holy Spirit was speaking? Could anyone really know such a thing? How could one judge?

Once more someone asked a question about Irving's understanding of the humanity of Christ, but this time in a more legitimate context. Had the manifestations "commended" Irving's Christology, the questioner asked. "Yes!" came the reply. This ended the case for the accusers and the first day of the trial.[49]

Yet not quite! Edward Irving had the last word. Just before he left the building, Irving is said to have thrown a sheet of paper onto the table. Written on it was his protest about not being allowed to refer to the Scriptures in his examination of the witnesses.[50]

Oliphant was scathing in her criticism of the day's deliberations: "Had the reverend judges confined themselves to the real evidence which the complaint demanded, their sitting need not have lasted above an hour or two."[51] She had a point. Time was certainly wasted with irrelevant questions. Yet the issues at stake were more complex and momentous than Oliphant seems to have realized, and when Irving was involved, few things lasted just "an hour or two." In this case his accusers wanted their time, and so did he.

Robert Baxter called on Irving again that evening. One suspects that Irving was not pleased. After a hard day at his trial, he hardly needed one of his friends telling him that he was wrong, but that is precisely what Baxter did. The next morning Baxter once more visited Irving, hoping "to convince him of his error of doctrine, and our delusions concerning the work of the Spirit, but he was so shut up, he could not see either."[52] No doubt, Baxter's motives were good, but his persistent denial of what Irving still held to be true must have hurt the preacher deeply. Yet Irving's faith in the authenticity of these charismatic phenomena does not seem to have wavered.

On the trial's second day, the presbytery gave Irving opportunity to defend himself. His address was lengthy and, inevitably, was interrupted a number of times "by hot discussions and calls to order."[53]

49. Oliphant, *Life*, 2:270–72, emphasis added.

50. Irving to the London Presbytery, April 26, 1832, in Irving, *DL*, 303.

51. Oliphant, *Life*, 2:272.

52. Baxter, *Narrative*, 119.

53. Oliphant, *Life*, 2:282.

He began, "[It is] for the name of Jesus, the Baptizer with the Holy Ghost, that I now stand here before all this people, and am called in question this day." This sounds like a muffled echo of Paul's words before the Sanhedrin (Acts 23:6), and that was probably what Irving intended. In fact, his phrase "am called in question" is the precise wording of part of that verse in the Authorized Version. He, the modern Paul, was being called to defend his God-given mission before the modern Sanhedrin. Indeed, he must have felt his position to be also like Paul before Agrippa, and he was not going to be disobedient to what he considered a "vision from heaven" (Acts 26:19).

He continued,

> First, as I am to justify the thing which I have done, it is needful to show the grounds on which I did it; and to show the grounds on which I did it, it is needful to show the thing in the Word of God, which I believe God has given us. Next, it is needful that I show you that the thing which we have received is the very thing contained in the Word of God, and held out to the hope and expectation of the Church of God; yea, of every baptized man. Thirdly, that I show you how I have ordered it as minister of the church; and show also that the way in which I have ordered it is according to the Word of God, and in nothing contradictory to the standards of the Church of Scotland. Fourthly, to speak a little concerning the use of the gifts: and, finally, to show how we stand as parties, and how the case stands before this court.[54]

Clearly, it was going to be a long day.

When he came to refer to the complaints against him of violating the trust deed and the Church of Scotland's constitution, Irving once more assumed the mantle of Paul. "That unto this day," he declared, "not only have I done nothing contrary to the word of God; but, 'Men and brethren, I have done nothing against the people or the customs of our fathers'" (Acts 28:17). Yet, he went on to say, his responsibility was ultimately to Christ, for "He is the Head of every man."

On the previous day, the Moderator had declared that with regard to development in doctrine—in this case tongues and this specific type of prophecy—that it first had to be taken to the General Assembly through the local presbytery for approval. Irving had no chance to answer this at the time, but it must have festered in his mind overnight. Now he had opportunity to respond to it. He did so in his best military mood:

> And if any person or court, or the Pope of Rome, or any court
> in Christendom, come between a man, or a minister, and his

54. Ibid., 2:275–76.

Master, and say, "Before obeying Jesus, you must consult us," be
they called by what name they please, they are Antichrist. I say
no Protestant Church hath ever done so. I deny this doctrine
that was held forth yesterday, that it is needful for a minister to
go to the General Assembly before he does his duty. I deny the
doctrine that he can be required to go up to the General Assembly for authority to enable him to do that which he discerneth
to be his duty.[55]

By this time the Moderator must have been sitting on the edge of his
seat. "Let these words be taken down," he ordered.

"Aye, take them down," responded Irving. "Take them down!" And in
case there was any doubt about what he had just said, he repeated it.[56]

He went on:

It is the command of your ordination vow that you serve Jesus.
You are ministers of Jesus, and not ministers of any Assembly.
You are ministers of the Word of God, and not the ministers of
the standards of any Church. I abominate the doctrine. It is an
Antichrist—it is the very essence of Antichrist. It is Popery in
all its horrors . . . When were the statutes of the Church made
the mete and measure of preaching? The liberty of preaching, or
prophesying, is the basis of all liberty; when was it ever bound up
within six-and-twenty, or nine-and-thirty, articles? Never, never
since the world began; and never, never shall it be endured.[57]

In spite of all his troubles, Edward Irving had clearly not lost his fire.
But he was fighting a losing battle, and he must have known it.

He then proceeded to defend his ventures into allowing the charismata, saying that his practice was not contrary to the methods of the ancient
church or even that of "the early Reformation Church." Nor was it contrary
to the standards of the Church of Scotland. But even if it had been contrary
to Presbyterian Church discipline, he argued, he still would have allowed it
because it was consistent with Scripture.

Irving then argued once more that the pronouncements made by the
"gifted" people were not their own words, but rather the words of the Holy

55. Ibid., 2:276.

56. Ibid., 2:277–78.

57. Wilks, *Edward Irving*, 225–226. There are slight variations in wording between Oliphant and Wilks, which probably means that one of them paraphrased the original record, or perhaps both of them did. Wilks is used where he records something significant not found in Oliphant.

Spirit. This belief he pressed on "the conscience of the Presbytery," presumably even knowing that its members would not accept it.

He continued that he could present "not less than five hundred persons" to support the three court-appointed witnesses who had testified that the manifestations were genuine.[58] Again, this may be a deliberate echo of the Apostle Paul, who told the Corinthians that the risen Jesus had been seen by "above five hundred brethren at once" (1 Cor 15:6). But Irving seems to have failed to see the limitations of his argument. For five hundred to say that they believed these pronouncements were genuine did not mean that they were so. If a parallel was indeed intended between his five hundred and Paul's, it needs to be said that Paul's band were bearing witness to something physical that they could see and touch—something concrete—while Irving's supporters were speaking of something that they believed to be true. It was an opinion rather than a testimony. If a thousand truly Christian witnesses said they believed the gifts were not genuine, did that, on the strength of superior numbers, mean that they must be false?

He continued, "It would be a burdensome thing, not to this Presbytery alone, but to this city, if you should shut the only church within it in which the voice of the Holy Ghost is heard—if you should shut the only church in Britain in which the voice of the Holy Ghost is heard."[59] Here Irving is engaging in Romantic fantasy rather than truth, with his heroic church standing alone against the forces of evil. Whether the manifestations at Regent Square were genuine was then under debate and still is, but whatever the truth of that, he did know that a few other churches in London and other parts of Britain also claimed to be experiencing similar manifestations at the time. His church was not alone in this.

In closing, Irving criticized the members of the presbytery for sitting in judgment on something that they had not personally witnessed and had not "attempted to prove." He urged them to attend some of the meetings at Regent Square to judge for themselves. Yet some of the presbytery almost certainly had witnessed them, though undoubtedly in Irving's opinion, they had done so with closed minds.

When Irving had finished, Mr. Mann, on behalf of the trustees, responded by criticizing Irving's "unseemly and untimely denunciations, with which he . . . had attempted to stem the torrent of justice."[60] How much the court had to do with justice might be argued, but Irving was clearly battling

---

58. Oliphant, *Life*, 2:278–80.

59. Harding, *The Trial of the Rev. Edward Irving Before the London Presbytery*, 49, quoted in Grass, *Edward Irving*, 259.

60. Oliphant, *Life*, 2:281–82.

against a torrent of opposition that would eventually flush him from his church.

The third day of the trial was to be held the following Wednesday, which would be the final, decisive day. But had the decision already been made? Irving preached one last sermon at the Regent Square Church on Thursday evening before the trustees locked the doors against him. The next morning, he and his loyal followers defiantly held a service in front of the church's doors.[61]

In addition, in the interval between the second and third day of the trial, some members of the Regent Square Church drew up a petition supporting Irving. It stated that the majority at the church was on Irving's side, and it also advised that the presbytery needed to act with caution.[62]

On the final day of the trial Irving continued the struggle, asking,

> Was it a small matter for me, when planted a minister of the church of Christ, and secured in the possession of that house during my life . . . to surrender the post in which God, and the Church, and the covenants of men, had planted me, to the discontents of a few men, to the opinions of any number of men, whom I believed in my heart to be grieving both God and His Church, by their rash and indiscriminate, their hasty, hardy, and unfounded judgments? . . . I ask if it was a small matter that should move me to consent to go forth from the habitation and home of our souls, and wander, we know not whither, over this wide and wicked city, *where there is no church that will call us sister, or welcome us to an hour's shelter under their roof.*[63]

Irving also focused on what he considered the real issue in this debate: Were the tongues and prophecy the work of the Holy Spirit or not? After all, he argued, Presbyterian tradition could not be used to try the case because "the canons of the Church of Scotland are entirely silent" on the subject. The real issue, then, was: Were these phenomena genuine or not? If these manifestations were the work of God's Spirit, Irving argued, surely none would dare deny them. And in Irving's opinion, "the evidence upon the table is *unanimous* to this point, that it is the voice of the Holy Ghost."[64]

The evidence given during the trial may indeed have been unanimous in that the three witnesses called, plus Irving, were all believers in the gifts.

61. Grass, *Edward Irving*, 260–61.

62. Harding, *The Trial of the Rev. Edward Irving Before the London Presbytery*, 89, quoted in ibid., 259–60.

63. Wilks, *Edward Irving*, 233–34.

64. Oliphant, *Life*, 2:283–84, emphasis added.

Documentary evidence had also been tabled, but the precise content is unknown. But, as Irving well knew, Robert Baxter had recently declared his prophecies a delusion, and, it would seem, Miss Hall had also denied the authenticity of hers. Thus the overall evidence could not possibly be considered unanimous in favor of authenticity. Not for the first time, Irving seems to have been blocking out voices and evidence that disagreed with his views.[65]

Yet in the course of his defense, he did mention his "dear friend" Baxter. Irving argued that Baxter had "been taken in this very snare of endeavouring to interpret by means of a mind remarkably formal in its natural structure the spiritual utterances which he was made to give forth."[66] Thus, to Irving, the prophecies were genuine—only Baxter's unspiritual understanding of them was in error.

As he proceeded, Irving also pointed out that since tongues had come to his church two hundred people had been accepted as members in six months, some converted "from the depths of immorality and vice." It was as if he was asking, "If this is so, how could such a ministry be wrong?" (Indeed, he claimed that at the very least a thousand, probably many more, had been converted during his entire London ministry.)[67]

At one stage the trustees stated that they would accept the use of tongues in the prayer meetings, but not in the Sunday services.[68] Not surprisingly, Irving would not make that compromise. He had already painfully worked through that issue and would not now backtrack.

He also charged his accusers with hypocrisy in that they were arguing that he did not keep the *Westminster Confession* while they barely took notice of it themselves. "I believe," he argued, "that no book in the English language hath been more out of mind of preachers in the pulpit or in the closet than the Westminster Confession of Faith—whereof, till it become a convenient weapon for dashing out the brains of faithful ministers, far more than half of the clergy were ignorant despisers or hearty haters. Oh, the hypocrisy, the seven fold hypocrisy, of this generation of Churchmen!"[69]

This stunning accusation, while no doubt an exaggeration, had some truth in it. At least some of the moderates appear to have rejected key parts of the *Westminster Confession* but preferred not to say so directly, and even

65. By this time, Irving knew of Mary Hall's apparent retraction as well as Baxter's, and Oliphant quotes a letter from the presbytery dated May 2, 1832, which states that the "documentary evidence" was given (Oliphant, *Life*, 2:289–90, 297).

66. Ibid., 2:285.

67. Ibid., 2:288.

68. Drummond, *Edward Irving*, 212.

69. Wilks, *Edward Irving*, 238.

some of the church's evangelicals did not hold to all of it.[70] Irving closed by claiming that he had "offended neither against the ordinances of God or the covenants of man."[71] However, the presbytery was not to see it that way.

In spite of Irving's urging, at no time did his accusers consider the most important matters in this controversy. That is, were the manifestations genuine or not and were they in keeping with the Scriptures?[72] Irving dealt with this question. The witnesses dealt with it. But the presbytery studiously ignored it. The presbyters would have argued, no doubt, that this was not what the trial was about, which was technically true. Yet there was no shortage of irrelevant questions asked on the first day, which suggests a double standard. But when it came to the question of authenticity—which, it is true, was very hard to prove or disprove—their minds seem to have been made up against it before the trial began.

It is also noticeable that in this trial the dispute about Irving's Christology lurked in the background. The case was clearly about Irving allowing the charismatic manifestations, but his Christology, which was seen by many as an earlier departure from sound doctrine, was always going to rear its head again in such controversial circumstances. There is no point in beating a man with one stick if you can just as easily beat him with two.

The court's decision was deferred to that evening. At the evening session the five ministerial members of the presbytery, one by one, delivered their verdict against Irving. "While deploring the painful necessity," tragically but inevitably, they unanimously decided that "the Rev. Edward Irving has rendered himself unfit to remain the minister of the National Scotch Church," and they advised the trustees that he "ought to be removed" from that position. The next day, J. H. Mann sent Irving a letter advising him of the court's decision that he could no longer serve as that church's minister.[73]

Edward Irving had been sacked.

The press applauded the decision to remove Irving. The Times stated, "The blasphemous absurdities which have for some months past been enacted in the Caledonian Church, Regent Square, are now, we trust, brought to an effectual conclusion." This paper also accused Irving of "partnership with knaves and imposters."[74] The Record, an Anglican paper whose editor regarded the tongues as a delusion and had fought an ongoing verbal battle

70. Drummond and Bulloch, Scottish Church, 56–57, 104–113.

71. Oliphant, Life, 2:289.

72. Ibid., 2:283–84.

73. Hair, Regent, 67, 176–78, appendix B; Oliphant, Life, 2:290, 298; Wilks, Edward Irving, 242–43.

74. The Times, quoted in Oliphant, Life, 2:298–99. The editor was apparently unaware of the church's name change.

with Irving's people, not only noted Irving's fate, but also seemed to rejoice in "Baxter's recantation" and David Brown's decision to leave Irving.[75] (It would appear that Brown left Irving because of unease about both the charismatic issue and Irving's Christological views.)[76]

Oliphant, in her much later work, took a very different stand. She called the presbytery's decision "perfectly illogical and indefensible" and made by "reckless Presbyters." She was most unimpressed by how the presbytery and the trustees handled the case.[77]

The June 1832 issue of *The Morning Watch* published an article on the sacking called "The Ark of God in the Temple of Dagon." It began, "Mr. Irving and his church have been ejected from Babylon." The writer considered Irving's deposing so significant that he declared, "it will mark an era of far greater importance than the ejection of Luther from the Papacy." In fact, Edward Irving "seems designed to take" an "important part . . . in fulfilling the purpose of God." Those remarkable statements only make sense if one recognizes that Irving and his associates believed that the worldwide church was in serious decline—to them it was "Babylon"—and that the charismata marked the start of a new age. Indeed, these things were all part of the lead-up to the appearance of the Antichrist and the eventual return of Christ himself. In preparation for these things, "God will now clear a way for the reception of all His gifts, to gather and constitute an Apostolic church."[78]

IN EXILE

The deposing of Irving gave rise to many uncertainties. Who would go with him? Where would they meet? What kind of church would they establish? And who would stay at Regent Square? Who would pastor that church?

Only a minority of the congregation remained loyal to the National Scotch Church. As William Hamilton put it, in the closing months of the year that church was "thinly attended."[79] This presented the church's leaders with a number of problems, not least of which were financial, for they still had a large debt to repay. However, the church did grow again to

75. *Record*, quoted in Oliphant, *Life*, 2:298–99. The article "Mr. Irving's Church and the Record Newspaper" contains some quotations from the *Record*, in which the manifestations are called "delusive and visionary" and "awful delusions" ("Mr. Irving's Church," 181, 186).

76. See, for example, Brown, "Personal Reminiscences," 201, 273; Grass, *Edward Irving*, 250–51.

77. Oliphant, *Life*, 2:299.

78. "Ark of God," 441–42.

79. William Hamilton to Samuel Martin, December 1832, in Irving, *DL*, 329.

become a significant Scottish Christian witness in London for many years ahead. Nevertheless, its glory days were past. Irving was replaced on a temporary basis by Rev. James Marshall of Edinburgh and later by Rev. Peter MacMorland of Paisley. A number of other preachers also filled the vacancy on occasions, some of whom were on trial for the position of minister. It was probably in February of 1835 that Regent Square called Rev. MacMorland to be its minister, and he was inducted in April of that year.[80]

Irving and the leaders who had remained loyal to him first hired a hall in north London's Gray's Inn Road for their services the Sunday following the dismissal. This building was also used by Robert Owen, a social reformer and, in the opinion of *The Morning Watch*, "an infidel." It was reported that nearly eight hundred congregants were present on the first Sunday. If all those people had usually attended the Regent Square church, it must have left some gaping holes there, though Irving's service did not begin until 2:00 p.m.[81]

In the next few weeks Irving also began to preach in a variety of outdoor locations, including Britannia Fields near the Regent Square Church. He had, as discussed above, previously preached in the open air on his Scottish trips.[82] It was estimated that between two or four thousand attended one of these outdoor services at Britannia Fields, which some rechristened "The Field of the Tongues." On this occasion he preached for an hour and forty-five minutes and is said to have declared that the destruction of the world would soon come to pass. Wicked London, which had been so blessed by God's favor, "would be the first example" of God's judgments.[83]

Other members of his flock also took their turn in this outdoors preaching. Before May was halfway through, John Sayers Orr, one of Irving's supporters, was taken to court because he had preached in the open air, and he was just one of "thirty or forty" of Irving's associates then engaging in evangelism in the fields.[84] However, according to Oliphant, this practice

80. Hair, *Regent*, 69–70, 73–74. Hair says that it was in February and April 1834 that MacMorland was called and inducted, but William Hamilton makes it clear that they were still searching for a minister in January 1835 (William Hamilton to John Martin, January 30, 1835, in Irving, *DL*, 435). This letter was clearly written soon after Irving's death, so if the date is wrong, it is not by much.

81. "Ark of God," 444–45.

82. Drummond, *Edward Irving*, 211; Oliphant, *Life*, 2:301. Back in 1824 Irving had stated that he believed outdoor preaching was valid, though he did not expect it to be "so useful as worship within doors" (Irving, "On Prayer," in Irving, *CW*, 3:31).

83. *The Newcastle Courant*, April 7, 1832, quoted in Grass, *Edward Irving*, 256–57.

84. *The Examiner*, quoted in Thomas Carlyle to John A. Carlyle, May 22, 1832, n. 18, *CLO*; Isabella and Edward Irving to Rev. and Mrs. Martin, August 1832, quoted in Oliphant, *Life*, 2:318.

did not continue after 1832, which seems to have been because Irving believed that he had sent them out without being "ordained" through the Holy Spirit.[85] Yet this outdoor preaching does seem to have been triggered by a prophecy from Robert Baxter, who had been so ordained.[86]

While Irving was preaching during one of the outdoor services, there was a disturbance in one section of the large crowd assembled to hear him. It centered around a lost infant looking for its mother. Irving, seeing the problem, interrupted his sermon and called out, "Give me the child!" The child was brought to him, and he cradled it in his arms as he carried on preaching, using the infant as an illustration for his sermon.[87]

These events were belatedly noted by Thomas Carlyle. In July Carlyle observed, "Edward Irving is out of his Chapel, and seems to be preaching often in the fields. He has rented Owen's huge ugly Bazaar (they say) in Grey's [sic] Inn Road, at 7 guineas a week, and lectures there every morning: Owen the Atheist, and Irving the Gift-of Tongueist time about [by turns]: it is a mad world."[88]

The Times also thought it odd. Irving and Owen presented "perhaps, the strangest conjunction that ever design or accident produced. The former will give his 'new readings' of the Apocalypse, with occasional interludes on 'the tongues'; and the other his 'new view of society,' with a little fiddling and a sixpenny hop, 'for the benefit of the working class.'"[89] Not that Irving and Owen had joined forces; their beliefs were far too different for that. They were just sharing the same building. Yet, as W. H. Oliver points out, while Owen was not a Christian, he used Christian millennial language and ideas in his quest for the ideal society,[90] so there was a little overlapping between them.

All this inevitably placed a great strain upon relationships with Irving's wider family. His father-in-law, Rev. Martin, as we have seen, strongly disagreed with Irving's views on the charismata. Irving's brother-in-law, William Hamilton, also disagreed with him, and he was an elder at Regent Square. These disagreements were in a practical sense quite significant, for Irving and his followers were moving into uncharted and controversial

85. Irving to his church, October 1834, quoted in Oliphant, *Life*, 2:369; Wilks, *Edward Irving*, 281–82.

86. Baxter, *Narrative*, 37–38. Though Baxter had recanted, Irving and his people still regarded his prophecies as genuine.

87. Oliphant, *Life*, 2: 303–305.

88. Thomas Carlyle to John A. Carlyle, July 2, 1832, *CLO*.

89. *The Times*, May 5, 1832, quoted in ibid., n. 10.

90. Oliver, *Prophets*, 175–91.

territory and antagonizing many in the process—both those close to them and those who viewed it all from afar.

In August the Irvings wrote a letter to Rev. and Mrs. Martin seeking some measure of reconciliation. Isabella began the letter, and Edward finished it. As part of this process Isabella invited her parents to come to London and stay with them. Edward acknowledged that staying with them would expose the Martins to the charismata, as "the voice of the Good Shepherd . . . is more spoke under our roof" than anywhere else, which could cause problems for the in-laws. He suggested that if they did not feel comfortable with that, they could stay with the Hamiltons. However, it seems that the Martins did not take up the invitation to visit either home at that time.[91]

If all this was not enough trouble, there were also disputes amongst the prophets. A Regent Square woman named Jane Simpson claimed to have prophetic gifts. She was the wife of James Gilliland Simpson, whom Irving had approached about being an elder back in 1824.[92] But the Cardales and Mary (Campbell) Caird denied that Mrs. Simpson had any such gifts, and in the case of the Cardales, this appears to have been done with some hostility. Irving tested Mrs. Simpson's gift in May 1832 and also rejected her claim, at least in part because of the testimony of his long-established prophets. It became rather messy, with claims and counter-claims concerning spiritual authenticity coming from the various parties.[93]

Not happy with Irving's decision, Jane decided to head for western Scotland and meet with the gifted there, presumably hoping to have her gift recognized. She and her husband left London on July 22 bound for Port Glasgow. While they were there Margaret Macdonald, not knowing about this incident, said in the Spirit that there were divisions at Irving's church. But this may have been little more than an uninspired guess. However, Jane Simpson was suitably moved to confirm the prophecy by reading an account of her problems with Irving and his prophets. James Macdonald then prayed that Irving would be humbled, and further prophecies were uttered saying, "bring him *down*, down, down to the *dust*, to the dust."[94]

91. Isabella and Edward Irving, August 1832, quoted in Oliphant, *Life*, 2:317–18.

92. Irving to James Gilliand Simpson, June 2, 1824, in Irving, *DL*, 197.

93. Grass, *Edward Irving*, 265. Details of the dispute can be found in Jane Simpson to Edward Irving, May 8 [?] and 31, June 16 and 27, 1832, in Irving, *DL*, 304–310, 312–16; J. G. Simpson to Edward Irving, June 16, 19, and 27, 1832, in ibid., 311, 313–314, 317.

94. "A Brief Account of Mr. and Mrs. Simpson's visit to Portglasgow [*sic*] in 1832" Acc. 12489/11, National Library of Scotland, Edinburgh, quoted in Grass, *Edward Irving*, 266.

In the late summer or early fall the Simpsons officially resigned from Irving's church, but he refused to accept their resignations. Instead Irving attempted to get them to succumb to his authority, but failed. Finally, on December 6, Irving wrote Jane Simpson a rather unpleasant letter, telling her that she had "grievously offended against the Lord Jesus Christ . . . resisted the Holy Ghost," and rebelled against the authority of Irving and his church. He then advised her that she and her husband were no longer communicant members of his church, though he said that he would keep the door open for their return if they were repentant.[95] The Simpsons eventually joined a church in Scotland.

A NEW HOME

In the weeks after Irving's dismissal, he and his officers first considered building a new church, but they believed that the Holy Spirit forbad them to do so at that time. So instead they looked for a suitable place to hire. Their search eventually led them to Newman Street, near Oxford Street, where there was a large hall that had previously been the gallery of Benjamin West, an Anglo-American artist. On his first visit there, some time elapsed before the caretaker appeared in answer to Irving's knock. The man apologized for the delay and explained that this delay was because his child was very ill in an upper room. Irving, moved as ever by the plight of others, offered to pray for the youngster. The caretaker led Irving up the stairs and into the room where the child lay. The preacher fell to his knees and prayed fervently for healing. By the time Irving visited again, the sick child had recovered.

After an examination of the property and negotiations with the owner, the decision was made to hire it. In the following weeks, alterations were made so that the building would be suitable both for accommodating the Irving family and for the public worship of Irving's exiles. The Irvings moved in early in the fall of 1832, and their group soon began to hold services there.[96]

This move must have been especially difficult for Isabella, for she was nearing the end of another pregnancy at the time. Mid-September she gave birth to a boy, Ebenezer,[97] who sadly died on April 21 the following year. Thus the distressing sequence of Irving fatalities continued.

---

95. Irving to Jane Simpson, December 6, 1832, ibid., 325–26.

96. Oliphant, *Life*, 2:308, 316–17.

97. Oliphant, *Life*, 2:318; Irving to Henry Drummond, September 14, 1832, in Irving, *DL*, 320.

At the beginning of 1833, Anna Montagu went to see the Irvings in their new home and visited the new "chapel." She described the hall as being "beautifully fitted up," with "a place beyond, for visitors, pious Clergymen, Travellers &c containing six Bed rooms and a sitting room and the Front House is a very Handsome one." But all this came at a cost. Montagu continued, "He has *taken upon himself* a rent of 400£ a year & Taxes in proportion—while he is popular this may do—but with this rent they must collect 1000£ at the Chapel to enable him to live at all—I know not where all this will end."[98] Mrs. Montagu was not alone in that concern. But in this respect it was as well that the wealthy Henry Drummond was still with them.

Before entering their new building, Irving proposed some changes in the services that may have been adopted in the closing weeks at Gray's Inn Road. He had been concerned for a while that the "multitude of strangers and gazers" attending the services were just spectators attracted by the publicity who were only waiting for the next thrill. The worship of God was far from their minds. So Irving's plan was that his loyal people would meet an hour before the usual time for confession and appropriate teaching. Afterwards, outsiders would be granted admittance and Irving would make a specific presentation of the gospel. He was also considering holding the Lord's Supper weekly.[99] It seems that a variation of this dividing of the services was tried but did not work, so it was soon abandoned.

It is clear, though, that at this stage Irving was still in charge. However, whether Irving knew it or not, he was beginning to lose his standing even amongst his own people.

The first service in the new premises was held on Friday, October 19, 1832, at which Ebenezer Irving was baptized. The service also included a number of outbursts from Emily Cardale, Mary Caird, Mr. Taplin, and especially Henry Drummond, who was by then very much in his element.[100]

At the Wednesday evening service five days later, Irving preached from 1 Sam 1 on the events surrounding the birth of the prophet Samuel. The subject was reconciliation to God. During his sermon, Irving described the church as "conceiving, but not having brought forth." Suddenly, a voice rose up from the congregation: "Oh, but she shall be fruitful. Oh! Oh! Oh! She shall replenish the earth! Oh! Oh! She shall replenish the earth and subdue it—and subdue it." Another voice cried out, "Oh, you do grieve the Spirit— you do grieve the Spirit! Oh, the body of Jesus is to be sorrowful in spirit!

---

98. Letter from Anna Montagu to Jane Carlyle, January 2, 1833, *CLO*. See also Thomas Carlyle to Margaret A. Carlyle, January 27, 1833, *CLO*.

99. Oliphant, *Life*, 2:321–22.

100. Grass, *Edward Irving*, 269–70.

You are to cry to your Father—to cry, to cry in the bitterness of your souls! Oh, it is a mourning, a mourning, a mourning before the Lord—a sighing and crying unto the Lord because of the desolations of Zion—because of the desolations of Zion—because of the desolations of Zion!"[101]

Irving must have been put on the back foot by these interruptions. For the most part, earlier prophecies had been given at certain times in the services designated by Irving himself. By contrast, these outbursts were in the middle of his sermon.

Irving recommenced his address, but then Henry Drummond spoke forth: "Ah, shut Him not out—shut not out your Saviour! Ah, you are proud of your dignity! Ah, truly your power is fearful! Ah, you have a power of resisting your God—you have a power of resisting your salvation! Ah, you are not straitened in your Father; you are straitened in yourselves! Oh, receive Him now! The day is almost closed. Ah, enter now! Delay not! Delay not! Delay not! Ah, wherefore stand you back?"

Yet Irving took this in his stride and responded to the interruptions: "Shut not the Lord out," he cried, "the Spirit of the Lord speaking in his servants." At once another servant called out, "Oh, I have set before thee—oh, I have set before thee an open door; O, let no man shut it—oh, let no man shut it!"

Irving took up his sermon again and this time was able to speak for longer, but then a woman cried,

> Ah! Will ye despise—Ah! Will ye despise the blood of Jesus? Will ye pass by the cross, the cross of Jesus? Oh! Oh! Oh! Will you crucify the Lord of glory? Will ye put Him to an open shame? He died, He died, He died for you—He died for you! Believe ye, believe ye the Lamb of God! Oh, He was slain, He was slain, and He hath redeemed you—He hath redeemed you—He hath redeemed you—He hath redeemed you with His blood! Oh the blood, the blood, the blood that speaketh better things than the blood of Abel—which crieth mercy to you now—mercy to you now! Despise not His love—Despise not His love—Despise not His love!
>
> Oh grieve Him not! Oh, grieve not your Father! Rest in his love! Oh, rejoice in your Father's love! Oh, rejoice in the love of Jesus, in the love of Jesus, oh, for it passeth knowledge! Oh, the length, oh, the breadth, oh, the height, oh, the depth of the love of Jesus! Oh, it passeth knowledge! Oh, rejoice in the love of Jesus! Oh, sinner! For what, for what, what, oh sinner, what can separate, separate, separate from the love of Jesus? Oh, nothing,

---

101. Oliphant, *Life*, 2:323–26.

nothing! Oh, none can pluck you out of His hands! Oh, none shall be able to pluck you out of your Father's hand![102]

Irving concluded his sermon and made an announcement, then Drummond reentered the fray. "Ah, be ye warned!" he declared.

> Be ye warned! Ye have been warned. The Lord hath prepared for you a table, but it is a table in the presence of your enemies. Ah, look you well to it! The city shall be builded—Ah! every jot, every piece of the edifice. Be faithful each under his load—each under his load; but see that ye build with one hand, and with a weapon in the other. Look to it—Look to it! Ye have been warned. Ah! Sanballat, Sanballat, Sanballat; the Horonite, the Moabite, the Ammonite! Ah! Confederate, confederate, confederate with the Horonite! Ah! Look ye to it, look ye to it![103]

Here seems to be a good place to make a further assessment of the charismata as associated with Edward Irving. Earlier, we noted that three of Irving's prophets later retracted their prophecies, and some of their prophecies—Baxter's timed prediction of the rapture, for example—were shown to be false. A common criticism that these pronouncements were often very repetitious was also noted.

With regard to these prophecies at Newman Street, it needs to be noted that the speakers used a little King James English (e.g., "hath," "ye," and "crieth"), which, along with the relative absence of "thees" and "thous," suggests that their target is not one person but rather a group, groups, or members of a group. So they were presumably not directly aimed at Irving. While allusions to the Scriptures appear frequently, the multiple repetitions are most unlike the Bible's prophecies. Certainly the Bible's prophets did use repetition at times (e.g., Isa 5:18–22; 6:3, or in the New Testament, Rev 2:7, 11, 17, 29; 3:6, 13, 22), but not so frequently or so unimaginatively—or, shall we say, so repeatedly. These prophecies, if they were indeed prophecies, were very, very different from those in the Bible. Likewise, the multiplicity of "Ohs!" and "Ahs!" sound more theatrical than prophetic. In addition, it is very hard to accept that these disordered statements are exclusively the outpouring of the Spirit of God, who is a God of order.

The "she" in the first outburst (about replenishing the earth) appears to be the church, so the idea presumably would then be that the church would be "fruitful" and "replenish the earth." But the church that the

102. Ibid.

103. Ibid. In this account, Oliphant *seems* to suggest that all these interruptions took place during one sermon, but the wording is not completely clear and she may be referring to two sermons.

speaker presumably referred to was Irving's church, later to be known as the Catholic Apostolic Church (CAC), not the wider church made up of numerous denominations that the CAC, following Irving's lead, initially rejected as "Babylon." The "body of Jesus" in the second instance is most likely also in reference to the church, though presumably the wider church, as it "grieve[s] the Spirit." The longest of these efforts is very repetitious, contains a number of scriptural quotations, and everything in it might often be heard in normal sermons.

With regard to Drummond's second interruption, Sanballat, a Horonite (possibly a branch of the Moabites), was a leader of those who opposed the rebuilding of the walls of Jerusalem after the exile. He was supported by Tobiah, an Ammonite (Neh 2:10, 19; 4:1–3; 6:1). With that background in mind, the idea would seem to be that the CAC were building a new church (Jerusalem), and Drummond was warning his people against their critics, the Sanballats and Tobiahs of the modern age, who were intent on knocking it down. Whether many of those who heard this pronouncement would have understood it that way, however, must be regarded as doubtful.

Was, then, the Holy Spirit speaking through Irving's people? To be frank, the pronouncements quoted above generally sound as though they have no direct divine source. They are, for example, very different from the Spirit-inspired Scriptures. Also, some of them sound as if they were spoken by people who, unused to public speaking, were struggling for words and so fell back on repeating what they knew best. In other words, they sound like words produced by their minds, not by the Spirit of God, as was claimed. While it is true these messages are generally consistent with Scripture and even quote Scripture, they are often muddled, unhelpfully repetitious, and vague. This does not necessarily mean that all of the CAC's claimed charismata were false, but it does shed great doubt upon the authenticity of this aspect of the movement.

Margaret Oliphant also asked the question that must be in the minds of many who have read this account. While there is nothing in these statements "to which the orthodox believer could object," why interrupt the sermon to make pronouncements that "convey so little"? This is particularly so, as Oliphant points out, in that sermons from Irving were far more "profound and instructive" than the limited utterances here recorded. Fortunately, it appears, not all of Irving's sermons at Newman Street were as badly interrupted as this one.[104]

In February 1833 Irving wrote to John McLeod Campbell, sounding quite content and in a mood of confidence in his chosen path, though sad

104. Ibid., 2:326.

and perhaps a little surprised that Campbell and Sandy Scott had not sought to join the CAC.[105] Yet, though they may have had points of agreement with Irving, there were also areas where they disagreed.

Amidst all these dramatic events, two things remained the same for Edward Irving. First, he never seemed to lose confidence in the rightness of his path. His letters of that time show that he believed that God would use his church to bring great blessing to London, Britain, and indeed, "the whole world."[106] Second, he was still a minister of the Church of Scotland. And the London presbytery was powerless to dethrone him because he had been ordained at Annan in Scotland.

105. Irving to John McLeod Campbell, February 22, 1833, quoted in ibid., 2:329–32.

106. Ibid., 2:318–19.

18

The Scottish Trial

They had met to find him guilty, and so they did.

—H. C. WHITLEY[1]

In March 1832 an Assembly committee was set up to investigate Irving. Arising out of its findings, by May Principal MacFarlane of Glasgow had instructed the presbytery of Annan to take action against Irving. It did so first by sending Irving a letter in August asking him whether he was the author of three books, namely *The Orthodox and Catholic Doctrine of Our Lord's Human Nature*, as well as *The Day of Pentecost; or, the Baptism with the Holy Ghost*, and *A Judgment, as to What Course the Ministers and the People of the Church of Scotland Should Take in Consequence of the Decisions of the Last General Assembly*. Thus, Irving's views on Christ's humanity, his encouragement of spiritual manifestations, and his attack on the church's Assembly were all in question.

Irving responded to that request in a letter dated October 13 admitting authorship. His letter was fiery, even raving. In it he told the presbytery that he regarded that Assembly as "one of the most *wicked of all Gods enemies.*" It was "that wicked Assembly," and he "grieved" that the members of the presbytery "should yield obedience to the desires of that *synagogue*

1. Whitley, *Blinded Eagle*, 33.

of Satan." Likewise, the Scottish Church was "*Babylon.*" Yet the letter was signed "Your humble & faithful servant in the Lord."[2]

Arising from this, Irving was called to appear before the Annan Presbytery the following year. According to Oliphant, the members of this presbytery were "obscure," with the exception of Dr. Henry Duncan. Duncan, like a number of other Church of Scotland ministers, dabbled in many areas. He was a preacher, author, newspaper editor, geologist, and also the founder of the first savings bank.[3] He seems to have written a pamphlet on Socinianism when he was still quite young, which should mean that he was well versed in Christological controversies.

Irving arrived in Annan on the morning of March 13, 1833, the day of the trial, and was met by a small gathering that included one of his brothers-in-law, David Ker, an ardent supporter from his church, and David Dow, a tongue-speaking minister of the church in Scotland. By the time Irving had made his way to the parish church at midday, a large crowd had gathered to catch a glimpse of him. There were so many—two thousand by one count—that they could not all press into the building.

The trial began with Irving confirming that he was the author of the books denounced by the Assembly committee. He objected, however, to the wording of the case against him, which gave the impression that he had taught that Christ was sinful. Irving was asked to leave the church for a few minutes while the presbytery debated the issue. The presbyters made a slight change to it, and Irving was brought back in.

The Moderator then asked, "Did you teach the fallen state and sinfulness of Christ's nature?" Irving answered the question on his own terms: "I have said and taught Christ was fashioned as a man, that he took our sinful nature upon him, but that, by the grace of God, he was upheld and yielded not to the motions of that sinful nature." This he called "a glorious doctrine," which he intended to "maintain . . . even unto death."[4]

As the members of the presbytery gave their opinions on the issue one by one, Irving sat with his head in his hands, frequently emitting a deep sigh. At one stage there was such an outburst of sympathy for Irving from the assembled people that the Moderator threatened to continue proceedings in a private room.

When Irving made his defense, he spoke for two hours, his great voice trembling with emotion. He first defended himself against what he correctly

2. Grass, *Edward Irving*, 271–72; Irving to the Presbytery of Annan, October 13, 1832, in Irving, *DL*, 324–25.

3. Oliphant, *Life*, 2:341; "Henry Duncan."

4. Wilks, *Edward Irving*, 244–45.

argued were false accusations. For example, he declared, "As to my maintaining that Christ is other than most holy, I do protest that it is not true." In case that was misheard, he repeated, "It is not true! Before the living God I do declare it is false." Indeed, he had never taught that Christ was unholy. He also denied that he taught doctrines that were "inconsistent with the unity of God," as some accused him of doing.[5]

He then presented what he did teach:

> He took your flesh and made it holy, thereby to make you holy; and therefore He will make everyone holy who believes in Him. He came into your battle and trampled underfoot Satan, the world, the flesh, yea, all enemies of living men, and He saith to every one 'Be ye holy, for I am holy.' Do you say that that man was unacquainted with grief—that He was unacquainted with the warrings of the flesh? . . . Is this your gratitude to the Captain of your salvation?[6]

At one stage, Dr. Duncan interrupted him and accused Irving of preaching to the crowd rather than defending himself before his accusers. This, no doubt, was a case of once a preacher, always a preacher. Irving protested that he must be allowed to say what he wanted in his own defense. The Moderator supported Duncan, stating that Irving sounded like he was addressing his congregation in London. At this, Irving protested that he knew very well where he was and why he was there.

He continued,

> Ye ministers, elders, and presbytery! This is no question of scholastic theology. I speak for the sanctification of men. I wish my flock to be holy; and, unless the Lord Jesus has contended with sin, as they are commanded to do, how can they be holy when they follow Him? . . . Can a soldier who is sick, wounded, or dead, be expected to follow a leader who is filled with the omnipotence of God? Nay! But if his captain be sick, wounded, and dead, too, may he not ask the soldier to do the like? Now Jesus was sick for us, contended with sinful flesh for us, and hence it is that He can call on us to follow Him in our contending with sin, our sicknesses and deaths. Yea, and He does call on us . . . Ah, was He not holy? Did He not gain for us a victory? Holy in His mother's womb; holy in His childhood; holy in His advancing years Holy in his nativity; Holy in His resurrection, and not

---

5. Oliphant, *Life*, 2:344.
6. Ibid., 2:345.

more holy in one than in another? And He calls upon you to be holy.[7]

Irving appears to have once more slipped into sermon mode. But clearly Irving was arguing that Jesus was sinless; he was holy from the womb to the resurrection, and was thus without sin.

Then Irving focused upon how much all this battle had cost him: "Ye know not what I have suffered—ye know not what it is to be severed from a flock you love, to be banished from your house, to be driven from a place of worship in which ye have been honoured, as God's servants, by the tokens of His approbation. Yet, though thus scorned and trampled on, truth is prevailing."[8]

He closed by most clearly addressing the "Ministers and Elders of the Presbytery of Annan," whom he defiantly told:

> I stand at your bar by no constraint of man. You could not—no person on earth could—have brought me hither. I am a free man on a free soil, and living beyond your bounds; neither General Assembly or Pope has a right to meddle with me. Yea, I know ye have sinned against the Head of the Church in stretching thus beyond your measure, and this sin ye must repent of. Ye have sinned against the Lord in my person . . . and, if ye repent not, your consciences will tell you hereafter that you have been guilty in this matter . . . Ye offend Him, for in the least of his little ones he may be offended. But I forgive it, and will pray for you . . . Do what you like. I ask not judgment of you; my judgment is with my God, and as to the General Assembly, the spirit of judgment is departed from it. Oh! Ye know not how near ye are to the brink of destruction.[9]

Irving's words were powerful, but he knew that his fate was sealed, at least as far as being a minister in the Church of Scotland was concerned. Yet, this climactic moment makes Elliott ask, "Was the Church of Scotland deposing Irving or was Irving rejecting the Church of Scotland?" He correctly answers, "It appears that both took place."[10]

Outside the church, the sun was sinking. Inside the church, one of Christianity's brightest lights was about to be removed from its candlestick.

The members of presbytery then pronounced sentence: "Guilty!" The Moderator gave Irving opportunity to object to his being deposed as a

7. Ibid., 2:346.

8. Ibid. See also ibid., 2:350–51.

9. Oliphant, *Life*, 2:346–47; Wilks, *Edward Irving*, 248–49.

10. Elliott, *Edward Irving*, 191.

minister in the Church of Scotland. This he did by warning his accusers of God's judgment.

Nicholas Sloan, a member of the presbytery, then rose to pray, but even that was not to pass without incident. David Dow, one of Irving's supporters, cried out, "Arise, depart! Arise, depart! Flee ye out of her! Flee ye out of her! Ye cannot pray! How can ye pray? How can ye pray to Christ, whom ye deny? Ye cannot pray. Depart! Depart! Flee! Flee!"

For a moment, the members of the presbytery were flummoxed by the interruption. Dow stood and began to move towards the exit. Irving also rose and shouted, "Stand forth! Stand forth! What! Will ye not obey the voice of the Holy Ghost? As many as will obey the voice of the Holy Ghost let them depart." At that, Irving, along with Dow, strode down the aisle followed by their supporters and left the church.

The delayed prayer was then offered. The court's final decision was due to be given next, but Irving was no longer there to hear it. Three times a member of the court called Irving to return, but he was either out of earshot or had no intention of subjecting himself to what he knew was coming. In his absence, it was announced that Edward Irving was deposed from his position as a minister of the Church of Scotland. He had been officially deposed for heresy concerning the human nature of Christ.

Irving was now out of the church—not just physically out of his old home church at Annan and his new church at Regent Square, but also right out of the Church of Scotland.

At eleven the next day, Irving preached in a nearby field to about two thousand people. This was the start of a brief but exhausting preaching tour of that part of Scotland. Crowds continued to gather to hear him in the fields and streets.[11] Jamie Carlyle, brother of Thomas, heard him preach at this time in Ecclefechan to an "assemblage . . . large and earnest." Irving stood on a table or chair anchored to a large tree. The weather was "grim, with windy snow-showers flying." Irving's hair and clothing were violently tossed by the biting winds, but his "eloquent voice [was] well audible under the groaning of the boughs and piping of the winds."[12] If Irving had been dethroned from the Church of Scotland, he had not been dethroned from the hearts of the people.

Thomas Carlyle was more cynical:

> poor Edward Irving . . . He came to Annan to be deposed; made a heroico-distracted Speech there, Dow finishing off with a Holy-Ghost shriek or two; wher[e]upon Irving calling on them to

11. Oliphant, *Life*, 2:347–49, 352–53; Wilks, *Edward Irving*, 249–52.

12. Carlyle, *Reminiscences* (Norton), 2:209–10.

"hear that" indignantly withdrew. He says in a Letter printed in the Newspapers that he "did purpose to tarry in those parts certain days, and publish in the towns of the coast the great name of the Lord"; which purpose it appears he did accomplish; "publishing" everywhere a variety of things. He was at Ecclefechan Jean writes us: gray, toilworn, haggard, with "an immense cravat the size of a sowing-sheet covering all his breast": the country people are full of zeal for him; but everywhere else his very name is an offence to decent society.[13]

But what was the real reason that Edward Irving had been deposed? Officially, it was because of heresy concerning the humanity of Christ. Originally the presbytery had cited three of his books covering different issues against him, including one about the charismata. But at the trial the presbytery seems to have concentrated on his Christological teaching. However, it is most likely that the heresy issue was one of several reasons he was dismissed, and it was probably not the major one. It is commonly believed that it was more because of irregular church order and discipline relating to tongues and prophecy.

For example, less than thirty years after Irving's death R. H. Story said that it was the "manifestations" that occurred at Regent Square that "were the efficient cause" of Irving's expulsion from the church.[14] In more recent times Martin Sutherland has stated, "It is clear that his deposition in 1833 had much to do with issues beyond heresy. Indeed it is arguable that his Christology may have suffered from indifference more than from condemnation" if it had not coincided with the tongues phenomenon in his church.[15] And in Patterson's opinion, "Had tongues not occurred at Regent Square it is doubtful Irving would ever have been put on trial, at least in London."[16]

He was probably sacked for a complex mixture of reasons. Irving had angered many people during his London ministry. In *Orations* he had strongly criticized "evangelicals." In *Missionaries* he had, some thought, criticized missionary societies and had also proposed a unrealistic method of financial support. His criticism of the churches in *Babylon* was over the top. His millennial views, while gaining some support, were still not generally favored. His ventures into the charismata troubled many. In addition, his negative comments about the Scottish Church were increasingly losing

13. Thomas Carlyle to John A. Carlyle, March 29, 1833, *CLO*.
14. Story, *Memoir*, 226.
15. Sutherland, "Preaching," 4.
16. Patterson, "Designing," 203–204.

him the support of those who had once been sympathetic towards him. The *Christian Observer* hit the nail on the head when it described Irving as "the Ishmael of the Christian world, his hand being against every man."[17] Yet Edward Irving had been popular, very popular. Perhaps that was his greatest heresy.

However, it needs to be noted that not all of the Church of Scotland's clergy approved of the presbytery's action. A. L. Drummond says that six members of the General Assembly opposed it, "including Principal Mac-Farlane of Glasgow." But Thomas Chalmers said nothing.[18]

An intriguing additional feature in all this is that when he was giving his defense, Irving appeared to be advocating a congregational form of government. That is, an ecclesiology in which the control is vested in the local church, not in a presbytery or in synod or in the edicts of a pope. He told the court, "I stand at your bar by no constraint of man. You could not—no person on earth could—have brought me hither. I am a free man on a free soil, and living beyond your bounds; *neither General Assembly or Pope has a right to meddle with me.*"[19]

Indeed, two years earlier Irving had advocated a congregational form of government even more clearly in his *Confessions of Faith and the Books of Discipline of the Church of Scotland.* There he maintained:

> that a church with its minister, one or more, its doctor, one or more, its elders and its deacons, is complete within itself for all purposes whatsoever, either of self-preservation or of propagation: and that the Presbytery, mentioned in Scripture, and in our Books of Discipline, consisted of the eldership of such a church, and I do feel in this respect perfect liberty, acting as the head of the eldership of a church, to do all the acts to which a bishop in the Church of England or a Presbytery in the Church of Scotland feel themselves to be competent. Moreover, I feel assured that it is the duty of every church so to act.[20]

However, Irving was now to return to London and experience a form of church government quite different from the Presbyterian or the congregational, one in which he would have the power of neither a bishop nor a presbytery.

17. *COB* (1829) 510–11, quoted in Schlossberg, *Silent Revolution*, 76.

18. Drummond, *Edward Irving*, 221.

19. Oliphant, *Life*, 2:347, emphasis added.

20. Irving, *Confessions*, cxxii–cxxiii.

19

Irving and the Catholic Apostolic Church

With resignation [he] accepted a nominal position in the sect established in
Newman Street.

—Andrew Landale Drummond[1]

IRVINGISM?

It is not intended here to paint a complete picture of the Catholic Apostolic
Church (CAC). We will examine it as far as it connects with the life of Edward Irving. Its later history, for the most part, does not concern us.

The CAC and its members were frequently called "Irvingites" and
their teaching "Irvingism," and this continued long after Irving had died.
Robert Baxter's second publication in 1836 (after Irving's death) was called
Irvingism, in Its Rise, Progress and Present State. J. N. Darby of the Plymouth
Brethren called the CAC "Irvingites," as did a writer he was criticizing.[2]
Catherine Mumford (later Booth), while staying with a friend in 1854, paid
a visit to an "Irvanite" chapel in Burnham, Essex, where she heard one of the

1. Drummond, *Edward Irving,* 272.

2. Darby, "On the Presence and Action of the Holy Ghost in the Church," in
ibid., *Writings,* 3:235, 247, 265.

CAC angels. She was not impressed.[3] Even A. L. Drummond seems to refer to "Irvingites" in his biography of Irving in 1937.[4] Yet, Irving appears to have objected to the movement being named after him, a wish Dorries says was respected by its members.[5]

But the question needs to be asked: Was Irving the founder of the CAC? The answer is complex and at least two-sided. First, it must be said that without Edward Irving, the CAC would almost certainly never have existed. H. C. Whitley puts it this way: "You can no more explain the Franciscan Order without Francis and his followers than you can explain the Catholic Apostolic Church without Irving and his friends."[6]

Irving was the leader of the church out of which the CAC emerged and the one who had attracted thousands to that church. He was also the primary teacher of some of the doctrines that made it distinctive. He believed in modern-day apostles, and they had apostles. He taught that the charismata were as available in their age as in the first century, and the members of the CAC believed that these gifts were evident in their church. In fact, tongues were still being heard in CAC services into the twentieth century.[7] Irving regarded the mainstream churches as "Babylon," and the CAC did likewise, though the CAC view on this changed later. The CAC clearly taught and practiced a number of Irving distinguishing ideas. Indeed, according to Whitley, Irving's writings continued to be "tested and studied" by CAC leaders after his death.[8]

Yet, on the other side, Irving died two years after the breakaway movement began, so his direct influence was short-lived. In addition, as shall be seen, Irving was downgraded very early in the CAC's history, and thus his influence lessened. It would seem to be true that even before Irving died, other leaders in the movement had more influence over it than he did. It was they who plotted the CAC's course and determined its beliefs. The CAC became what they believed it should be, not necessarily what Irving had advocated. Indeed, Tim Grass argues, "Ultimately, the development of the Catholic Apostolic Church owed at least as much to [Henry] Drummond

---

3. Catherine Booth, letter CM 92, September 8 or 9, 1854, in Booth and Booth, *Letters*, 229–30. Irving had died when Catherine was only five, so she probably knew little about him, hence the odd spelling.

4. Drummond, *Edward Irving*, 181.

5. Irving to his church, October 25, 1834, in Irving, *DL*, 408; Dorries, *Edward Irving's*, 62–63.

6. Whitley, *Blinded Eagle*, 72.

7. Ibid., 75; Elliott, "Nineteenth-century Australian Charismata," 31–33.

8. Whitley, *Blinded Eagle*, 81.

as it did to Irving."[9] Columba Graham Flegg is more specific. He puts it this way: "the eventual liturgical and ecclesiological developments" in the movement "went far beyond anything Irving could have envisaged." He regards Cardale and Drummond as being their architects.[10]

But when did they adopt the name of Catholic Apostolic Church? According to A. L. Drummond, the name was originally used by a man answering a census question. The census-taker asked which church the man belonged to and he replied, "the Catholic and Apostolic Church, worshiping in Newman Street." Flegg also accepts this explanation.[11] However, this seems to be impossible. The true origins of the name would seem to be more formal and more official.

The only British census in the nineteenth century that asked religious questions was the one taken in 1851, and the name is known to have been in use before then. CAC records show that it was towards the end of 1847 that the CAC apostles declared that the correct name for the Newman Street congregation was to be "The One, Holy, Catholic and Apostolic Church, London, The Central Church." Then in 1849, Cardale ordered that the name "Catholic Apostolic Church," without the definite article, be attached to all their English churches.[12]

This name presumably grew out of the Newman Street leaders frequently referring to their church informally as a Catholic Church, in the sense of it being universal, and as an Apostolic Church, in that they had apostles. The informal usage gradually became formal, and thus the new name was coined.

NEWMAN STREET

The new church at Newman Street was opened in October 1832. The structure of the Newman Street building was different from other churches and reflected CAC theology. While it had galleries and an arrangement of pews like many other churches, there was no pulpit. Instead there was a large platform. At the front of this platform in the early days were seven seats, the middle of which was for the angel, while the other six were for the elders, who included John Tudor, editor of *The Morning Watch*.

Just below the platform were another seven chairs belonging to "the prophets." In the early period, the middle of these was occupied by Mr.

9. Grass, *Edward Irving*, 104.

10. Flegg, *Gathered*, 63.

11. Drummond, *Edward Irving*, 234; Flegg, *Gathered*, 74–75.

12. Grass, "Albury," 6–7, 14 n. 23; Henke, "Catholic Apostolic Church," 3.

Taplin. Lower down still were another seven chairs occupied by the dea-cons. The services were led by the angel; the angel and the elders expounded the word, and the prophets spoke as the Spirit moved them.[13] In the most elevated position, at least in later days, was the altar, showing how highly they regarded the Eucharist.[14]

The term "angel" refers to the pastor, and in the case of Newman Street, that role was occupied by Edward Irving, though there were other churches being established in various towns, each with its own angel. This title comes from Rev 2 and 3, in which the seven letters to the churches are in fact addressed to the angel of each church, rather than directly to each church. Some biblical scholars regard the angels mentioned in those chapters as supernatural beings—angels as we normally think of them—while others believe them to be ordinary church leaders, pastors, or preachers (the Greek term *angelos* originally meant "messenger"). Irving, and later the CAC, ad-opted this latter view. Irving seems to have held to this understanding of angel at least as far back as November 1831.[15]

As the church developed, there were also twelve apostles, the senior figures in the church. Even as early as 1824 and 1825, Irving had stated in his missionary address and book that he regarded the apostolic office as still current,[16] though his understanding then seems to have been that missionaries were modern-day apostles, which is a different interpretation than what would later emerged. In the CAC, the apostles were the same in number as those in the New Testament and assumed a similar authority.

An article in the June 1832 edition of *The Morning Watch* explained the importance of this new brand of apostles. It reported, "the apostle of the New Testament answers to the prophet of the old, as *the living expositor* of the word of God. *This office is constantly needed.*" It continued, "The apostle must stand in the place of Christ, if he will be his minister: he must teach as one having authority . . . he must say, 'These are the laws of the Lord Jesus Christ, and by his authority committed unto me, I command you to obey them.'" In fact, he is "the representative of Christ in the church, the visible Head of the visible body."[17]

The twelve apostles were J. B. Cardale (the "Pillar of Apostles"), Henry Drummond, H. King-Church, S. Perceval, N. Armstrong, F. V. Woodhouse,

13. Baxter, *Irvingism*, quoted in Oliphant, *Life*, 2:322–23.

14. Flegg, *Gathered*, 265.

15. Irving to Mr. MacDonald, November 7, 1831, quoted in Drummond, *Edward Irving*, 158. See also Irving, *Confessions*, cxxii.

16. Ibid., *Missionaries*, xx–xxi.

17. "Prophets and Apostles," 333–34, emphasis added.

H. Dalton, J. O. Tudor, the other Thomas Carlyle, F. Sitwell, W. Dow, and D. Mackenzie. Eight of these had previously belonged to the Church of England and three to the Scottish Church. Three were clergymen, three were solicitors, and two had been members of Parliament.[18] The first was appointed in November 1832, when Henry Drummond, in a prophecy, declared that Cardale was to be an apostle. In September of the following year, Drummond was appointed an apostle.[19]

How did these offices relate to each other? In February 1833 Irving told Alan Ker, brother of the ever-loyal David Ker, that "the apostle is over the angel," that is, over Irving and other such pastors, but, on the other hand, "The angel of the Church is over the apostle." The way it worked—or should work, according to Irving—was that as the Apostle John addressed Revelation to the angels of the different churches such that Irving, as an angel, received his "instructions" from an apostle such as Cardale. Yet, it was Irving the angel's job to make sure that all, including the apostles, "bow" to those instructions.[20] Irving believed that it was not his role to deliver "Spiritual utterance," but it was his job to see that such utterances were "obeyed" by everybody. He told Apostle Drummond, "As a man you are under me, as a spiritual Minister bringing the word of God I am under you."[21]

In addition, as has been seen, there were prophets. Before Robert Baxter's recantation, he had been the most highly regarded of all of Irving's prophets. Once, while in "the power," he had prophesied that the church's traditional practice of ordination should cease and that the church's spiritual offices should instead be bestowed upon the "gifted" or those appointed by the Spirit through the "gifted." Even after Baxter had left the movement, this prophecy still held sway.[22]

This made it very difficult for Edward Irving. He had been ordained by the Church of Scotland, which was now hardly relevant, but because he does not appear to have personally received any of the charismata, he was not regarded as amongst the spiritually gifted. This meant that others in his church had now been elevated above him.

As we have seen, after Irving was sacked from the Church of Scotland he toured some of his old haunts preaching the gospel. When he returned to

18. Flegg, *Gathered*, 44, 65–66, 71; Kolde, "Catholic Apostolic Church," 458.

19. Irving to Henry Drummond, September 26, 1833, in Irving, *DL*, 368; Flegg, *Gathered*, 58–59, 64–65; Stunt, *Awakening*, 268.

20. Irving to Alan Ker, April 30, 1833, quoted in Oliphant, *Life*, 2:334. See also Irving to D. Dow, April 1833, in Irving, *DL*, 341–43.

21. Irving to Drummond, April 2 and 7, 1834, in Irving, *DL*, 391, 393.

22. Baxter, *Narrative*, 28; Oliphant, *Life*, 2:319–20.

London, he discovered that this prolonged stay had not pleased the leaders of the CAC.[23]

It seems to have been on March 31, soon after his return to London, that he was preparing to accept a recently baptized infant into the new church during a service. Suddenly, he was stopped by Apostle Cardale. Cardale stated that because Irving's ordination by the Church of Scotland had been rescinded and since he had not yet been re-ordained by his new church, he should not be allowed to perform such an act. And that re-ordination could only come through a specific and identifiable word from the Spirit. Irving took that message as a word from God's Spirit and did not go ahead with the procedure. If initially surprised by Cardale's interruption, he does not seem to have been distressed by his pronouncement. After reflection, he appears to have agreed with it. Irving's new ordination followed on April 5.[24]

Yet a similar incident occurred when Irving was about to baptize a child that August. A prophet, "by a word," stopped him from conducting the ceremony. However, the issue on this occasion does not appear to have been Irving's right to baptize, but some perceived "unholy thing" in the church. Nevertheless, it still remains that Irving was told not to conduct the ceremony by someone else.[25]

In addition, in a letter Isabella told her mother that "Edward was truly grieved" that he was not able to go and see her on a visit to Scotland early in 1834. "But," she continued, "truly his time is not his own, neither is he his own master."[26] Who was his master? Was it Christ, or was it the apostles and prophets of the CAC? Soon after this visit, Apostles Cardale and Drummond rescinded some appointments that Irving had made while they were away.[27]

Who, then, was in charge? Who governed whom, and in what ways? The problem was that though they all argued that the structures they were introducing originated in New Testament times, in some respects they were new, and how the various offices should relate to each other was far from clear. Confusion and disagreement on this matter continued for some time.

---

23. Ibid., 2:358.

24. Irving to D. Dow, April 1833, in Irving, *DL*, 337–40; Grass, *Edward Irving*, 276–77; Oliphant, *Life*, 2:354 (see note with comments by Cardale), 355–56. Oliphant says that this was an actual baptism, but Irving's letter to Dow, written soon after the event, indicates that the baptism had been carried out earlier in the child's home.

25. Irving to Henry Drummond, August 7, 1833, in Irving, *DL*, 364.

26. Isabella Irving to Mrs. Martin, early 1834, quoted in Drummond, *Edward Irving*, 232.

27. Oliphant, *Life*, 2:373.

At its best, the debate seemed like godly men seeking God's will, but at times it sounded like little more than a power struggle.

Irving wrote to Henry Drummond and others on a number of occasions stating his views on the various offices.[28] In 1834 he told Drummond, "I do well know that it pertaineth to an Angel [such as Irving] fully accomplished of the Holy Ghost for his office to minister and *to rule* and to discern in a fourfold measure, Apostolical, Prophetical, Evangelical & Pastoral, whereby he is enabled consciously to apprehend and with discernment *to obey every thing spoken by the Lord through this fourfold headship in the house.*"[29] It was complicated, and not everybody agreed on specifics.

But one thing was clear: Edward Irving was no longer in charge of his church.

As has been noted, Irving did not speak in tongues and he did not prophesy in the charismatic sense. This obviously put him at a disadvantage in a charismatic church. Suddenly, though perhaps not so suddenly, Edward Irving, the greatest preacher of his age, a profound theologian, a godly man, and a caring pastor, had been severely downgraded. By 1832 and perhaps even before, Baxter (while still loyal), the Cardales, and others were regarded as "spiritual" ministers. But a minister who had only been ordained "by laying on of hands," like Irving, was only a "fleshly" minister,[30] and a "fleshly" minister could not expect to lead a "spiritual" church. A "spiritual" prophet, then, was above a "fleshly" angel, like Irving.

Thus Edward Irving was dethroned by his own congregation—not, in the end, by an official church body, but by a group of prophets, a spiritual elite of doubtful distinction. Edward Irving had become a victim of his own teaching.

In fact, Irving himself clearly elevated this "spiritual" class above men such as himself. He said,

> tongues and prophesying . . . are the constant demonstrations of
> God dwelling in a man, and teaching him all spiritual things by
> the Holy Ghost, without help of any third thing or third party,
> *to the great undervaluing and entire disannulling of the powers of
> natural reason and speech as a fountain-head of divine instruc-
> tion*: therefore they must ever be fatal to the pride of intellect,
> to the prudence and wisdom of the world, to the scheming,

28. See, for example, two long and rather confusing letters from Irving showing his understanding of how he believed these positions should relate to each other: Irving to D. Dow, April 1833, in ibid., *DL*, 337–47; Irving to D. Dow, April 25, 1833, in ibid., 348–54. See also Irving to Henry Drummond, May 4, 1833, in ibid., 358–60.

29. Irving to Drummond, April 7, 1834, in ibid., 394, emphasis added.

30. Baxter, *Narrative*, 43, 77–78.

counselling, and wise dealing of the natural man; to all mere philosophers, theologians [including, presumably, Edward Irving], poets, sages, and wits of every name; yea, makes war upon them, brings them to nought, and utterly defeats their pretensions.[31]

To Irving, the Spirit-inspired prophet was well ahead of the reason-based preacher, like himself. He did not seem to allow for the valid belief that reasoned-out sermons could and should also be inspired by the Spirit of God. So Edward Irving had played a major part, perhaps *the* major part, in his own demotion.

As Columba Graham Flegg says, "For the remainder of his life, Irving was required to accept apostolic rule and to be guided by the words of the prophets."[32] Eventually—and it was a small mercy—on April 5 he was ordained by Apostle Cardale as the London church's angel on the instruction of one of the prophets. But even in this office he had to be taught his duties by lesser men.[33] However, even after ordination, how much authority Irving still held in his church seems to have remained both unclear and changing.[34]

In his trial before the London Presbytery, Irving had optimistically argued, "No authority comes between the angel of the church and Christ. See you in the seven epistles of Christ to the angels, if it tells them to go up to any synod of general assembly? . . . It is not sound doctrine which teacheth that the Presbytery or General Assembly, or any men, or bishops, or popes, interveneth or interposeth between the minister of a church and Christ."[35] He no longer had a presbytery or General Assembly to deal with, but something had arisen to take their place—the CAC offices of apostle, elder and prophet—and they did come between the angel (or minister) and Christ.

However, David Dorries argues that this view of the relationship between Irving and the CAC leadership is shrouded by "A cloud of misunderstanding" and "does not bear even remote correspondence with the facts." Rather, according to Dorries, Irving himself admitted that he had earlier "assumed a place of stature" in the church "reserved only for Christ." This suggests that Irving elevated, or tried to elevate, himself above other CAC

---

31. Edward Irving, "On the Gifts," in ibid., *CW*, 5:558, emphasis added.

32. Flegg, *Gathered*, 60.

33. Oliphant, *Life*, 2:356, 363–64; Drummond, *Edward Irving*, 221.

34. Flegg, *Gathered*, 60–61.

35. Irving, *The Trial of Edward Irving before the London Presbytery*, 41, quoted in Elliott, *Edward Irving*, 191.

leaders. As evidence for his position, Dorries quotes part of a letter Irving wrote to his church shortly before his death, which says,

> Understand, dearly beloved, that such a fullness of the Spirit as our God proposeth to give to His Church in London can only stand under the headship, government, and administration of the Lord Jesus. No Apostle, Prophet, Evangelist, nor Pastor, no Angel of any church, no man, nor creature, hath more than a measure of the Spirit, nor can occupy nor administer more than a measure or proportion of the Spirit. To Jesus alone pertaineth the fullness, and to the Church over which He ruleth . . . But we were beguiled to think that the full measure of the Tabernacle of the Lord would be given to that church over which I preside as Angel; which was no less than the exalting of the Angel of the Church into the place of Christ. I tremble when I think of the awfully perilous place into which I was thrust. [Now, the figure by which the eldership is known in Scripture is the calf;] and this exaltation of the Angel of the Church to sit head over the fullness of the Spirit, was truly the making of the calf to worship it, instead of worshipping Him who sitteth between the cherubim . . . In the same light I see the naming of Evangelists by me, which pertains not to any one but the Second Adam . . . [And of this also I do repent and call upon the whole flock to repent along with me. In the same light] also do I see the sending forth of the Evangelists unordained, which was the slighting of Jesus, the Apostle in His Apostles, to whom it appertaineth to send forth. In all these things I grievously sinned against the Lord, and you with me . . .
>
> He had mercy upon us, and began to take the veil from off our eyes by the hand of His Apostles, to whom He gave timeous discernment of these things, with utterance of that which they discerned; but I confess for myself that I was very slow, yes, and reluctant to turn back from my evil way.[36]

The main problem here seems to have concerned the role that the Newman Street Church would have in relation to the other CAC churches that were springing up. Would Newman Street be preeminent? Irving seems to have assumed that it would, and he does not appear to have been the only one in the CAC leadership that came to this conclusion. The second issue was his "naming" and sending out evangelists. In this Irving was also not

---

36. Dorries, *Edward Irving's*, 59–62; Irving to his church, October 1834, in Irving, *DL*, 428–31. The sections in square brackets are in the full text of the original letter, but not in the quotation made by Dorries. They are included here for further clarification.

alone, for he was acting on "a word" from the prophet Robert Baxter,[37] who at the time was still highly regarded and his ministry accepted as being of the Spirit.

So is it right to say, then, that Irving "*assumed* a place of stature" in his church, which was rightfully Christ's, as Dorries says? First, it needs to be noted that Irving spoke of being "thrust" into what he considered "a perilous place," in a way that sounds as though others did the thrusting, not him. He is also clearly confessing the sins of his church, not just his own: "we were beguiled" and "you [sinned] with me." Therefore Dorries may be going too far.[38] Yet Irving did begin the letter, in a passage Dorries does not quote, "It well becometh me, who was the *chief instrument* of bringing in that sin for which the hand of the Lord hath long laid heavy upon us, to do my utmost part to remove the same."[39] So Irving was well aware of his playing a leading role in that "sin."

Dorries also argues that Irving bore no bitterness about the way the leadership of the CAC was structured and that he continued to have good relationships with the other leaders.[40] In Dorries' opinion, Irving "was as committed to the introduction of an apostolic church order as were any of his leaders."[41] Certainly it was consistent with what Irving taught, so he could hardly have objected to it. That Irving supported his apostles is evident in his letters to Henry Drummond, one of the apostles, though he did at times challenge him.[42]

Two months before he died, Irving still believed that the CAC was "a complete and perfect pattern of what [Christ's] church should be, endowed with a fullness of the Holy Ghost," though not without sin. And his final letters to that church breathe an air of deep pastoral concern. Indeed, he regarded himself as still their "faithful and loving Pastor," the "shepherd of the flock." Death could not snap his "bond of love" with them.[43] Even near the end, he told Cardale that he loved his flock and was "thankful to them" and that he knew they loved him.[44]

---

37. Baxter, *Narrative*, 37–38.

38. Elliott argues along similar lines (Elliott, *Edward Irving*, 55).

39. Irving to his church, October 1834, in Irving, *DL*, 428, emphasis added.

40. Dorries, *Edward Irving's*, 62–64.

41. Ibid., 60.

42. See, for example, Irving to Henry Drummond, September 26, October 3 and 21, 1833, June 28, July 10 and 26, 1834, in Irving, *DL*, 368–70, 373, 400–404.

43. Wilks, *Edward Irving*, 280–86; Irving to his church, October 25, 1834, in Irving, *DL*, 407–409.

44. Irving to Mr. Cardale, November 5, 1834, in ibid., 409.

While Irving may have had no bitterness about his downgraded position, he must have felt a sense of loss and even some confusion. In May 1833 Irving had said, "I am oftimes sore troubled, and much cast down and broken in spirit."[45] Elliott sums up the situation well when he explains, "The final months of Irving's life demonstrate alternate periods of acceptance and chafing against this new order."[46] One gets the impression that in this new situation, Irving was acting at times as he had done at the Caledonian and Regent Square Churches as the minister and primary leader of the church, before realizing or being told that such actions did not fit into the new leadership structure. This is evident, for example, when Irving, prepared to receive an infant into the church, was told he was not qualified to do so. He was no longer *the* leader. This change must have taken some getting used to both emotionally and practically. As Dorries says, Irving had to make "a painful adjustment,"[47] and it must have been very painful indeed.

In addition, some of the leaders, such as Drummond and Cardale, do not seem to have been easy to get along with, and considering that they were both apostles, this must have presented problems. Irving's relationship with the CAC leaders, then, was probably not as good as Dorries suggests, at least in some cases.

The CAC envisioned that their movement would have seven churches in London, as in chapters two and three of the book of Revelation, and others as directed by the Spirit. They opened up a number of churches in Irving's time, including four more in London. Two of these were led by Rev. Nicholas Armstrong, an Irishman as tall as Irving, and Rev. H. J. Owen, both previously of the Anglican Church and believers in the charismata. Owen had also been a delegate at the Albury Conferences. Another of the CAC's London churches was led by a Congregational clergyman named Miller. These men were, in CAC terminology, "angels."

The CAC also opened a church in Edinburgh under the leadership of William Tait, a minister from the Scottish Church, as well as another in Albury and about twenty more in other parts of England, Scotland, Wales, and Ireland.[48] H. C. Whitley, who came from a CAC family, claimed that clergy from "the Baptists, Anglicans, Congregationalists and Roman Catholics" joined the movement. Whitley called the church at Newman Street

---

45. Irving to Henry Drummond, May 1, 1833, in ibid., 357.

46. Elliott, *Edward Irving*, 200.

47. Dorries, *Edward Irving's*, 60.

48. Oliphant, *Life*, 2:305, 361, 370; Drummond, *Edward Irving*, 167, 231; Grass has a list of early CAC churches in Britain (Grass, *Edward Irving*, 284 n. 42).

the CAC's "Jerusalem," while Albury was its "Rome," its "spiritual centre."[49] According to Grass, Albury became "the chief seat" of the movement's apostles.[50]

The CAC changed in a number of ways after Irving's death, though perhaps in some directions that could be traced back to him. For example, the CAC became very liturgical in its worship, demonstrating the influence of Old Testament, Roman Catholic, and Orthodox ritual. It also adopted the doctrine of the real presence of Christ with regard to the elements in the communion service. By 1851 the movement had at least thirty-two churches, including a number overseas, and over four thousand members. It became especially strong in Germany.[51]

In the Albury tradition, they continued to expect Christ to return soon. C. F. Andrews, Christian missionary to India and friend of Gandhi, was brought up in a CAC family. Andrews was not born until 1871, but he claimed that "Every chapter in the Book of Revelation was explained" by his parents "as certain to come to pass in our own days," and "The Second Coming of our Lord was daily expected."[52] The CAC expected Christ to return while at least one of its original apostles was still alive. The last one, F. V. Woodhouse, died on February 3, 1901. However, the movement continued on. The CAC today has no churches in Britain, but still has a few in Germany and the Netherlands.[53] In addition, a movement known as the New Apostolic Church that broke away from the CAC in the 1860s is still a thriving body.[54]

MORE DEATH IN THE FAMILY

As if Irving was not experiencing enough trouble, at the end of March 1833 his sons Martin and Ebenezer were both ill, the latter dangerously so. On one occasion, perhaps more, Edward and Isabella spent most of the night nursing the boys. Martin recovered. Ebenezer did not. He died on April 23.[55] It may be easy for us to shrug off the deaths of infants in the nine-

49. Whitley, *Blinded Eagle*, 77–78.

50. Grass, "Albury," 5.

51. Henke, "Catholic Apostolic Church." Grass says that there were fifty-six in 1851 (Grass, "Albury," 7–8).

52. Kerr and Mulder, *Famous Conversions*, 173–75.

53. Drummond, *Edward Irving*, 234; Flegg, *Gathered*, 90; Grass, "Albury," 8–9.

54. Henke, "Catholic Apostolic Church," 9–10; Irving, *Edward Irving's*, xvii–xix. For the New Apostolic Church, see http://www.nak.org.

55. Oliphant, *Life*, 2:358; Irving to Henry Drummond, March 27, 1833, in Irving,

teenth century with a "That was always happening in those days," but each death was heartbreaking for the parents, and Edward and Isabella Irving had already experienced much of this kind of tragedy. Irving wrote to his father-in-law telling him: "The Lord in His severity and His goodness, hath been pleased to chastise us for our sin and the sins of the flock by removing from us our darling Ebenezer."[56] In Irving's charismatic theology, illness was always, or nearly always, the direct result of someone's sin, be it the sin of the afflicted individual or a parent, or the collective sin of a group.

DL, 337; Irving to D. Dow, April 25, 1833, in ibid., 354.

56. Irving to Rev. Martin, April 23, 1833, quoted in Oliphant, *Life*, 2:359.

20

The Decline and Death of Edward Irving

His sun rose to noon, and at noon disastrously went down, carrying with it a
world of hopes.

—Margaret Oliphant[1]

Irving made a brief visit to Edinburgh in January and February of 1834 with
Taplin and William Tait to visit the CAC church there. The church was being
troubled by "an evil spirit," and it was Irving's task to deal with it. This visit
was very different from his earlier Scottish preaching tours. This time, he
seems to have ministered to a few rather than to many. It would appear that
this Scottish outpost "recovered" and was "strengthened, and comforted" by
Irving's visit. Quite what happened to the evil spirit is unclear.[2]

Some of Irving's old supporters went to hear him on this visit. They
were saddened by what they saw. The service was held in a poorly lit chapel, and the congregation was small. "An 'apostle' . . . was in the pulpit and
Mr. Irving occupied the desk under him." In that dim light, "Irving looked
twenty years older; his black hair had become grey; his cheeks thin and sunk

---

1. Oliphant, *Life*, 1:76.
2. Ibid., 2:370–73; Drummond, *Edward Irving*, 232.

. . . Even his voice was not what it had been. He looked dispirited and wan and feeble; a man whose heart had already begun to break."[3]

When Irving returned to London, Apostles Cardale and Drummond went to Scotland to ordain the angel of their Scottish church. While they were away, Taplin, the "Pillar of Prophets,"[4] spoke a prophecy instructing the appointment of some of the CAC members to certain positions in the church. Irving accepted the prophecy and appointed them. When Cardale and Drummond heard about it, they were not pleased. They declared the prophecy to be a delusion, advised Irving and Taplin that they had acted without proper authority, and canceled the appointments.

Irving seems to have remonstrated with Drummond about this, but later he, in his own words "a poor rebellious worm," apologized in writing and asked for Drummond's forgiveness. But this all had left Irving in "great darkness" and rather confused. Even in May he still could say, "Ofttimes in looking back I think I have been hardly dealt with," yet he confessed that he was aware of a "great disorder" in his own spirit. Taplin was also unhappy with the action taken and left the CAC for a while.[5]

In May Irving bumped into Thomas Carlyle while the latter was on a trip to London. This had been their first meeting for some time. Carlyle wrote that as he was out walking that day, "a large figure starts from a seat and clutches my hand: it is Edward Irving! Good Edward, poor Edward, he looks ill, very ill; a pale yet flushed complexion, eyes with a dim glazy trouble in them: I was heartily affected. He is to be in Bayswater (after tomorrow) for some months, by the Doctor [Darling's] peremptory order: I could not see him last night in Newman Street, but only his unutterable Pagoda. To think that he should *die* of that cursed rubbis[h] is very painful [to] me."[6]

Of this same meeting Carlyle told his wife, "Edward Irving! . . . The poor friend looks like death rather than life; pale and yet flushed, a flaccid, boiled appearance; and one short peal of his old Annandale laugh went thro' me with the wofullest [sic] tone."[7] Later Carlyle recorded that Irving "had suddenly become an old man." His hair was gray, his face "hollow, wrinkly collapsed," and his body, while "still perfectly erect, seemed to have lost all its elasticity and strength . . . He was very kind and loving . . . He admitted

---

3. [Bonar?], "Edward Irving," 238. The writer gets a little confused with the CAC's apostles and angels, but "apostle" it should be.

4. Flegg, *Gathered*, 44.

5. Oliphant, *Life*, 2:373; Irving to Henry Drummond, February 24 and May 1, 1834, in Irving, *DL*, 385–86, 397.

6. Thomas Carlyle to John A. Carlyle, May 18, 1834, *CLO*.

7. Thomas Carlyle to Jane Welsh Carlyle, May 17, 1834, *CLO*.

his weak health, but treated it as temporary . . . His tone was not despondent; but it was low, pensive, full of silent sorrow."[8]

It appears to have been in June or July that Irving crossed paths with Thomas Carlyle again, not once, but twice. "I saw our worthy Edward twice, a good while ago" Carlyle told a friend, and continued:

> They seem to have a kind of synagogue in Newman Street, and are a "self-contained house" in many senses . . . If Irving live, he will, as I still keep prophecying, kick it to the Devil (who is mostly the father of it), and, in new shape be himself again one day . . . I often think I might do something for him, were we in free intercourse; but the "four-and-twenty elders" will it not, and must have their way.[9]

Carlyle, according to his *Reminiscences*, had earlier determined that he would tell Irving exactly what he thought about the direction of his ministry. This encounter may have been one of the occasions on which he did this. Carlyle stated his views clearly, warning Irving that he was on a course "full of danger to him" and arguing against what he considered to be the preacher's blind acceptance of a chapter in Paul's First Letter to the Corinthians. Jane said "hardly anything," but what she did say was in agreement with her husband.

During Carlyle's "twenty minutes" of earnest talk, Irving, "head down, his face indicating great pain," said nothing. When Carlyle had finished, Irving responded in a mild, "low tone" with his "face full of kindness and composed distress," briefly defending his position. What he actually said Carlyle did not record. Probably neither man expected to convince the other, and each remained unconvinced.[10]

In the first seven months of the year Irving was faced with a string of significant family events and crises, some of which were very difficult to deal with. In March the eighth and last of the Irving children was born. The infant was named Isabella, and she lived to maturity.[11] Then in June little Margaret went missing "in the ocean of London." Quite what happened is unknown, but the girl's disappearance inevitably caused considerable distress until she was eventually found.

In July Isabella appears to have had a gynecological problem, the details of which are unclear, but it was serious enough to force Irving to

8. Carlyle, *Reminiscences* (Norton), 2:211–12.

9. Thomas Carlyle to William Graham, August 5, 1834, *CLO*, 2007.

10. Carlyle, *Reminiscences* (Norton), 2:205–207.

11. Grass, *Edward Irving*, 308; Isabella Irving to Henry Drummond, October 19, 1834, in Irving, *DL*, 405–406.

cancel a trip to Albury.[12] Later that same month Isabella was struck down with what was assumed to be cholera. This cast Irving "down to the greatest depths." The elders of the church were summoned to her bedside, as, apparently, was Dr. Darling. The elders prayed, the doctor seems to have ministered some relief, and she recovered.[13]

In June Irving had told Drummond, "My health is quite restored and my strength growing apace."[14] However, this seems to have been wishful thinking, for Edward Irving was still very ill. In fact, soon after this, Irving's father-in-law said that he "Grows weaker and weaker and no Doctor can find the least disease in him. So weak . . . he could not lift his little baby to his neck!"[15]

It is important to note here that though Irving believed passionately in divine healing, he also accepted the ministrations of doctors. Indeed, when his wife recovered from the just-mentioned illness, he referred to Dr. Darling as "a blessed instrument" in God's hand and said that he could "see the hand of the Lord in the means."[16] Back in 1831 he even had had one of his children vaccinated.[17]

On August 14, Irving and Carlyle met again when the latter was admitted to "Newman Street, after *four* prior ineffectual attempts." Carlyle indicates that these earlier visits had been thwarted by CAC officials. But on this occasion, he said, "with an insuppressible indignation mixed with my pity: after some shying, I was admitted!" He recorded:

> Poor Irving! he lay there on a sofa, begged my pardon for not rising; his Wife, who also did not and probably could not well rise, sat at his feet, and watched all the time I was there, miserable haggard [she was still recovering], like a watchful Hysperides [*sic*] dragon. I was civil to her, but could not be more: I never in my time was concerned in another such despicability as I was forced to suspect her of. Irving once lovingly ordered her away; but she lovingly excused herself, and sat still. He complains of biliousness, of a pain at his right short-rib; has a short thick cough which comes on at the smallest irritation. Poor fellow! I brought a short gleam of old Scottish laughter into his face into his voice, and that too set him coughing. He said it was the Lord's will; looked weak, dispirited, partly embarrassed.

12. Irving to Drummond, July 10, 1834, in ibid., 401.

13. Irving to Rev. Martin, July 1834, in ibid., 402–403; Oliphant, *Life*, 2:374–75.

14. Irving to Henry Drummond, June 6, 1834, in Irving, *DL*, 400.

15. Carlyle, *Reminiscences* (Norton), 2:215.

16. Irving to Rev. Martin, July 1834, in Irving, *DL*, 403.

17. Irving to Mr. Richardson, August 8, 1831, in ibid., 283.

He continues toiling daily, tho' the Doctor (Darling) says, rest only can cure him. Is it not mournful, hyper-tragical? There are moments when I determine on sweeping in upon all Tongue-work and Martindoms and accursed choking Cobwebberies, and snatching away my old best Friend, to save him from Death and the Grave! It seems too likely he will die there."[18]

A couple of weeks later they met again. "We had Irving down," wrote Carlyle. Carlyle described him at around this time as "a touching, rather sad sight, yet with kind remembrances clinging to it: he is *white* in beard and whiskers, looks very weak, coughs, and seemed disposed to do what I pressingly wished and insisted on: go and rest himself in the country."[19]

So Irving went to the country—the country of Scotland. The reasons for this northern trip are debated, but they appear to have had little to do with the rest Carlyle had advised. Some argue that Irving was sent there by the CAC leadership, others say that it was in obedience to a prophecy made some years before that he would carry out further significant ministry in Scotland, while it is also claimed that Irving merely wanted to go because Scotland "was his native air." While it seems that not all the CAC's leadership agreed to this venture, it is clear that its main purpose was to do CAC work and that his ministry included a number of places well south of his homeland. It is also very unlikely that Irving would have made this trip without apostolic approval.[20] But whatever the reason, Irving headed north and was never to see London again.

He left London at the beginning of September and journeyed via Birmingham. Isabella spent at least part of the time while he was traveling at Brighton on the southern coast, which was a popular place of escape for Londoners in the nineteenth century. Irving next stayed at Blymhill in Staffordshire, moved on to Bridgnorth in Shropshire, and then returned to Blymhill. On this second visit to Blymhill he received news that his son, Martin, was unwell. This caused Irving much anxiety, and he wrote to Isabella to make sure that the elders visited the boy to pray for him. Mercifully, the boy quickly recovered.

While at Blymhill on the second visit, Irving also wrote to William Hamilton, his brother-in-law, asking him to look after his business dealings with his publishers, which sounds as though he knew he might not have much longer to live. Why did he choose Hamilton, who was now in some

18. Thomas Carlyle to John A. Carlyle, August 15, 1834, *CLO*.

19. Thomas Carlyle to Alexander Carlyle, August 28, 1834, *CLO*.

20. Oliphant, *Life*, 2:375–76; Drummond, *Edward Irving*, 223–24; Grass, *Edward Irving*, 289–91.

respects estranged from him? Why did he not choose one of "the deacons and under-deacons" of his present church, whom he judged as "worthy of all confidence"? It seems to have been because Hamilton had always assisted him in these business matters, and it was more convenient to continue with him. Though they had parted on religious matters, Hamilton remained a close relative, and there was no animosity between them. And perhaps Irving had *more* confidence in Hamilton than in his present deacons?[21]

Next it was back to Shropshire, this time to Ironbridge and Shrewsbury, then on to Herefordshire and into Wales. Irving usually seems to have traveled on horseback, journeying sometimes twenty-five miles a day or more.

His comings and goings in the Midlands and Wales seem to have been because the CAC was hoping to establish a church or churches in that region. He met with numerous clergymen and conducted a number of services, mainly, it seems, in homes. This certainly indicates that his trip was more than just a personal visit to Scotland.

Irving's letters at this time also show that he still had a great love of the natural world. He frequently mentioned the wonderful sights he saw, from the rivers in the valleys to the highest mountains. Indeed, the way to Hereford "seemed a very wilderness of beauty and fruitfulness," and his "eye was never satisfied with beholding it." Likewise, "the valley of Usk . . . hath a beauty of its own, so soft, with such a feathery wood scattered over it, gracing with modesty, but not hiding, the well-cultivated sides of the mountains, whose tops are resigned to nature's wilderness." One day's journey was "among the well-sunned, well-aired mountains, where every breeze seemed to breathe health upon" him.

In fact, his letters in September also state repeatedly that he believed that his health was improving. For example, on September 26 he told his wife that his health was "better," for he had a good appetite and his pulse had now gone "under 100." This was certainly an improvement, for at times it was as high as 120. A day later Irving reported that he was "hardly conscious of an invalid's feelings." A few days later, he was strong enough to descend "320 feet below the level of the road" into a ravine and then climb out again. On another occasion he walked "eight miles" through the countryside. It must have brought back many memories of his early days.[22]

21. Oliphant, *Life*, 2:378–81. For an example of Hamilton handling Irving's business affairs back in 1829, see Grass, *Edward Irving*, 114.

22. Oliphant, *Life*, 2:381–91; Drummond, *Edward Irving*, 225.

"THE DYING APOSTLE, WHO WAS NOT AN APOSTLE"[23]

As the October days flicked past, it became a little colder and rain set in. It was probably on October 9 that Irving got rather wet while viewing the Menai Bridge, which had been completed only eight years before. He was feverish that night and into the next day, to which was added a headache. However, he was still able to ride. Two mornings later he felt much better, but by the end of that day his headache had returned "with sickness." He became worse, experiencing "the most severe bilious fever." On the night of October 11 to the morning of October 12 he slept for over four hours, then lay awake listening, he said, to the clock chime, "parched with thirst and inward heat, and yet chilly, my head full of pain, my heart of fainting, but my faith steadfast." Just as morning was breaking, he "threw off flannels and stockings" and stood in a "footpan" of cold water and poured more cold water over his shoulders. "All at once [he] was a changed man" (not surprisingly) and he managed to gain some more sleep.

In the morning he was brought breakfast in bed and thought of staying there the whole day, but that would have been "yielding to the disease," so he arose and walked for half an hour. But for the next day or two he suffered a bad fever and slept little.

In his letters to Isabella at this time, Irving often said how much he missed her and frequently expressed his desire for her to join him. Though one gets the impression that she also was still not well, Isabella traveled north and joined him in Liverpool. She found him "looking much worse" than when he had left home.[24] Whether this decline had set in because of the recent bout of fever or whether it had come on gradually throughout his travels we will never know. Irving believed that disease could be defeated with faith, and one wonders whether his comments in his letters about getting better were little more than a denial of the seriousness of his condition.

Towards the end of October, Irving wrote two letters to his church. In one of these he did acknowledge his ill health, telling his people, "I am greatly weakened and wasted, and have little strength for anything save to pray unto the Lord. Yet am I nowise cast down in spirit, desiring only the glory of the Lord in whatever way He shall be pleased to reveal it."[25]

In the other letter he expressed his belief that his people were "called, and chosen, and set apart to a great work, which the Lord seeketh to

---

23. Oliphant, *Life*, 2:399.

24. Ibid., 2:393–97.

25. Irving to his church, October 25, 1834, in Irving, *DL*, 407.

accomplish in us, and by us." And he said that he believed that this work would extend throughout the world.[26]

It was next on to Glasgow. Cold Scotland was not the best place for Irving to be as winter approached, and his declining health meant that he would not fulfill his mission. The weather became stormy, and Irving's health grew worse. He adapted his habits and diet. Every morning he was "sponged with vinegar and rubbed with a course towel." He also ate "only the most nourishing meats with bread [and drank] one or two glasses" of the finest Madeira or "a tumbler of excellent ale." He also rode for about two hours every day.

Irving took up a few opportunities to preach, but his efforts were puny compared with former times. He also met McLeod Campbell again, but the meeting does not seem to have been a happy one. They had a number of theological disagreements.[27]

One friend recorded, "He is sinking under a deep consumption. His gigantic frame bears all the marks of age and weakness; his tremendous voice is now often faltering, and when occasionally he breaks forth with his former feeling, one sees his bodily powers are exhausted."[28] As the fever continued Irving spent more time in bed, but as his strength ebbed, his faith remained firm. Even in this most weakened condition Irving seemed to believe that God would raise him from his bed of sickness. Someone even prophesied that he would recover. Doctors attended him. His mother and a sister visited him, as did some of Isabella's relatives. As late as November 21 he could describe himself as being "in pretty good health,"[29] though, judging by all other accounts, this assertion was far from true.

F. V. Woodhouse, a future CAC apostle, also visited him. Woodhouse described Irving at that time as "the Pride of Scotland moral intellectual and personal brought to naught by the hand of the Lord," so weak that he was only able to move slowly, with "a little child [Woodhouse] leading him."[30]

As December dawned it seemed clear to nearly everybody that Irving did not have much longer to live. However, Irving himself, Isabella, and a few of Irving's most faithful followers still expected him to recover. But on December 4 Isabella's faith was put to a severe test. Irving's body was clearly still declining, and his mind began to wander. He was now a shadow of the man whose powerful preaching had stirred so many. At one stage he

---

26. Irving to his church, October 1834, in ibid., 430.
27. Irving to Henry Drummond, November 11, 1834, in ibid., 410–11.
28. Mrs. Stewart Ker, quoted in Drummond, *Edward Irving*, 225.
29. Irving to John Martin, November 21, 1834, in Irving, *DL*, 416–17.
30. F. V. Woodhouse to Henry Drummond, November 20, 1834, in ibid., 415.

seemed to be uttering something in an unknown tongue, an experience he had never had, but Dr. Martin recognized the sounds as the twenty-third Psalm in Hebrew. Perhaps the reciting of this Psalm, with its "walk through the valley of the shadow of death," indicated that Irving was at last aware that his death was drawing close.

On Sunday, December 7, 1834, it was clear that there was no hope of recovery. As evening approached, Irving's mind rambled further and his speech became largely unintelligible. He prayed, "Lord pardon all," and his last coherent words were "If I die, I die unto the Lord. Amen!" Was this his acceptance of the inevitable? Either way, in the first hour of the next morning, Edward Irving went to be with his Lord.[31]

He had died at the age of forty-two. But what an amazing forty-two years they had been, four decades packed with a ceaseless round of useful activity and achievement matched by very few who have lived twice as long. His death so young was a sad end to his sad, yet tumultuous life.

Indeed, the story of Edward Irving is a strange one. Its strangeness continued even after his death. The Scottish Church had rejected him, but his funeral service was held in a crowded Glasgow Cathedral on December 12, and he was buried in its crypt, an honor open to only the most worthy of Scottish saints.[32] He was rejected, but still honored! Yet two of the pallbearers were future apostles in the CAC: F. V. Woodhouse and Frank Sitwell, the latter being a brother-in-law of the Archbishop of Canterbury.[33]

The Reverend John Cumming of the Crown Court Church at Covent Garden led a memorial service in London two days later. He said in his address that Irving had the great gift of being "able to arrest the attention, and gain the hearts, and mould the doings of his audience."[34] And so he had.

It is said that some of Irving's followers expected him to rise from the dead and waited around his tomb. Whether this claim was true or not, no miracle was forthcoming. After the funeral, F. V. Woodhouse accompanied Isabella back to London.[35]

Thomas Carlyle mourned the death of his dear friend. In a letter to David Hope he said, "Poor Irving's death I had anticipated like yourself; especially since I saw him last in autumn. Nevertheless, the news of it shocked

---

31. John Martin to William Hamilton, December 7, 1834, in ibid., 420–22; Samuel Martin to Henry Drummond, December 8, 1834, in ibid., 423; Oliphant, *Life*, 2:397–405; [Bonar?], "Edward Irving," 242.

32. Oliphant, *Life*, 2:404–405.

33. F. Sitwell to Henry Drummond, December 24, 1834, in Irving, *DL*, 433–34.

34. Quoted in Drummond, *Edward Irving*, 276. See also Grass, *Edward Irving*, 298.

35. Drummond, *Edward Irving*, 227–28.

me, as only a few such occurrences now can. Poor fellow! . . . This mad City (for it is mad as Bedlam, nine-tenths of it) killed him; he might have lived prosperous and strong in Scotland, but there was in him a quality which the influences here took fatal hold of; and now—Alas! alas!"[36]

Many tributes to Irving soon followed. One in *Fraser's Magazine* of January 1835, usually attributed to Carlyle, paid him the ultimate compliment in saying, "The first great feature in Edward Irving's character was godliness" and next to it was his "purity and simplicity." This tribute continued, "Oft times has he fasted, whilst the food prepared for himself was sent to his poor brethren," and "He was never heard to speak an unkind word of any of his numerous opponents, far less of any of his friends."[37]

Chalmers, quoting Burns, called him "one of the nobles of nature." In fact, Chalmers went on, "His talents were so commanding, that you could not but admire him, and he was so open and generous it was impossible not to love him."[38] Dr. James Hamilton, one of Irving's successors at Regent Square, said, "It was not his fault, but the world's that life is not the thing of wonder, and nobility, and delight, which his creative eye beheld it . . . With all his love of human love, he had no fear of man . . . In the pulpit, as bold as the Baptist, he was in private a very Barnabas—a son of consolation."[39]

The Reverend George Leon Walker remembered, "If there has been in modern times a man with the old apostolic fire and fervor for the salvation of men and the glory of the Savior, Irving was that man." It was probably Dr. Hanna who recalled, "There was a kind of sublime humility in his egotism . . . and while he believed in himself, in his powers, his missions, his convictions . . . he was yet quite willing to become a nothing, if only the world would just believe with him."[40] It seems to have been Robert Story who said that Irving "stood up and spoke to his generation, and . . . to the heads and leaders of his generation—to the sages and peers and senators who thronged around him—out of the fullness of an intense conviction."[41]

In addition, his brother-in-law William Hamilton said, "For years he was my bosom friend, and my most intimate and constant companion. The affection we cherished for each other was strong and sincere . . . I loved him sincerely, both as my friend, and former Pastor, from whose faithful and

---

36. Thomas Carlyle to David Hope, December 19, 1834, *CLO*.

37. Carlyle, "Death of Edward Irving," 3, 100.

38. Thomas Chalmers, quoted in "Obituary: Rev. Edward Irving," *Gentleman's Magazine* 3 (1835) 665.

39. James Hamilton, quoted in Root, *Edward Irving*, 130–31.

40. George Leon Walker, quoted in ibid., 134; William Hanna, quoted in ibid., 143. Dr. Hanna's words originally appeared in vol. 39 of the *North British Review*.

41. [Robert Story?], *Macmillan's Magazine*, quoted in Root, *Edward Irving*, 147.

powerful ministration I chiefly derived whatever knowledge I have attained to . . . in divine things."[42]

When the saintly Robert Murray M'Cheyne (at that time still a student) heard of Irving's death, he wrote in his journal that he looked back on Irving "with awe, as on the saints and martyrs of old. A holy man, in spite of all his delusions and errors. He is now with his God and Saviour, whom he wronged so much, yet, I am persuaded, loved so sincerely."[43]

It is an oddity of western society that it is considered bad form to speak ill of the dead unless they are long dead, but one can more or less say what you like about the living. Yet there is no reason to suppose that any of these tributes were insincere. Rather, it took Irving's death to make some proclaim his greatness.

As to the press, the *Scottish Guardian* and *Bell's New Weekly Messenger* both announced Irving's death "with the sincerest regret," with the *Scottish Guardian* adding that "Irving, with all his faults, was a good man." *Baldwin's London Weekly Journal* referred to him as "an amiable man" of "thorough honesty," but of "grievously misdirected piety."[44]

Yet Carlyle indicated that even in his death, some still found call to despise Irving. "It is a very mournful thing," he wrote, "for me to find how *universally*, except among his own sect, the noble Edward is regarded here, even by tolerant, reasonable men, as little better than an empty quack! Such is the nature of popularity: today in the clouds; to-morrow down in the gutter, and even there not low enough."[45]

However, it does need to be admitted that in his later years Irving himself had become increasingly intolerant towards those who disagreed with him. His good nature thus became badly tarnished. He even seemed to save his most vicious barbs for other Christian leaders who failed to see things his way. By contrast, Carlyle generally seemed to escape such criticism. Perhaps this was because Irving did not expect too much from Carlyle other than friendship, but he expected other Christians to understand things from the right perspective—that is, his perspective—and few did. In those later years, there was to Irving only one way of understanding any

---

42. William Hamilton to John Martin, January 30, 1835, in Irving, *DL*, 434.

43. Bonar, *Memoir and Remains*, 27; Bonar, *Life*, 35. Strangely, these two records of M'Cheyne's journal each have him writing about Irving's death on November 9, 1834, a month before it happened. While it is possible that M'Cheyne had heard a rumor about Irving's death before it occurred, it is more likely that the November entries should be dated December.

44. *Scottish Guardian*, December 9, 1834; *Bell's New Weekly Messenger*, December 14, 1834, 600; *Baldwin's London Weekly Journal*, December 13, 1834.

45. Thomas Carlyle to David Hope, December 24, 1834, *CLO*.

subject, and that was the Irving way. If you saw it differently, then you were rejecting the testimony of Scripture and disobeying God. This was another sad aspect of Irving's sad life, and it gave his enemies, even his friends, just cause to speak against him.

Edward Irving was a great man who took on the world even when he did not need to do so. And in the end, he lost.

21

A Brief Assessment of Irving as a Theologian

Was Edward Irving a good and consistent theologian? There is not and has never been agreement about that.

Strachan states, "The centre of [Irving's] ministry was the systematic, doctrinal exposition of the Word of God," and "He was a systematic, expository and doctrinal preacher."[1] Dorries says that Irving's "doctrinal system" had an "internal coherence,"[2] while Patterson calls Irving "an intelligent theologian."[3] Gunton states that Irving's Christological arguments "range over every aspect of the case and . . . reveal the breadth of his systematic theology."[4]

Yet Dallimore argues against the claim "that Irving was a precise theologian and that his ministry was one of careful exposition of the Scriptures." Instead, "One may read through Irving's entire *Works* without finding anything that can truly be termed expository preaching. He takes a text, but uses it merely as a peg on which to hang his own numerous ideas."[5] In addition, A. L. Drummond stated that "it is hopeless to look for consistency in Irving."[6]

---

1. Strachan, *Pentecostal*, 18, 58.
2. Dorries, *Edward Irving's*, 139.
3. Patterson, "Designing," 150.
4. Gunton, "Two Dogmas," 365.
5. Dallimore, *Life*, 59.
6. Drummond, *Edward Irving*, 135.

We will deal first with the matter of consistency on specific theological issues, for this is easily resolved. While one may find some evidence of that type of inconsistency in his writings, it is rare. The supposed inconsistency is usually caused by development in his theological thinking. That is, some of Irving's later theology certainly differed from that of his early days (which is not in itself a bad thing) and in some cases quite dramatically. But one can usually trace the process.

For example, there was distinct, traceable development in Irving's eschatology. One instance of this is that Irving originally believed that the world would be gradually made better, more Christian. He later came to believe instead that the world would be dramatically judged and destroyed because of its sin. He originally believed in one divine judgment, but later in more than one. He also developed a historicist understanding of the book of Revelation, though he later swung to a futurist view. Yet there is evidence that Irving tried to blend historicism and futurism (perhaps there was an inconsistency there). Though these examples do demonstrate changes in his eschatology, he was not usually being inconsistent.[7] His views may have changed, but they generally remained in their new form, sometimes with further development.

It is also clear that his pneumatology altered over the years. Early on, Irving did not believe that miracles were available today. Later he believed that they were, but once he came to that belief, he clung most tenaciously to it. He did not chop and change.

However, his understanding of Christ's human nature was rock solid. From 1825 and probably earlier, he believed that Christ's flesh was as in Adam after the fall,[8] and this view did not change in spite of the strongest opposition. When one examines his sermons, lectures, and letters on this teaching, his views are the model of consistency.

But what can be said generally about his theology? Was Edward Irving a profound and significant Christian theologian? It is not proposed to examine his theology fully here, for this book is essentially a biography, and there have been many other studies on Irving's theology in recent years that can be consulted.[9] Rather, it is proposed here to note the depth of

---

7. Bennett, *Origins*, 212–31.

8. This is discussed in greater depth in Dorries, *Edward Irving's*, 73–105, 109–39. Grass argues that Irving's early sermons on Christ's temptations (1823) are consistent with Christ's humanity being as in man after the fall, though they do not specifically teach it (Grass, *Edward Irving*, 175).

9. Two recent detailed theological studies are Elliott, *Edward Irving* (as well as his 2010 PhD dissertation of the same title), and Lee, "Christ's Sinful Flesh." Each of these researchers sees an overall consistency in Irving's theology.

his theology and how it all blended together. Whether one agrees with it or disagrees with it, can Irving's theology be regarded as significant, with each teaching consistent with the others?

It first needs to be said that Irving's work on the person of Christ was outstanding. These sermons and lectures are thorough, thought-provoking, and challenging. On this subject he was forced to give of his very best because of the controversy that continually surrounded him. In fact, some of his sermons on Christ's humanity are beautiful, moving, and instructive. They contain great depth, but at the same time rise to great heights. They seem to take one into the very presence of Christ, and that is preaching—that is theology—at its very best. One may disagree with him, but his arguments are strong, biblical, and well-rounded. Indeed, the fact that they are still so frequently debated nearly two hundred years after they were delivered demonstrates how very significant they are.

As to whether his Christology was heretical or not, Patterson correctly warns that "in the end, even today, the 'heresy' of Irving is often misunderstood, misstated, or uncritically assumed."[10] The charge of heresy at times seems to have been made by people who believed that Irving taught that Jesus Christ committed sin or at least was subject to original sin. But while a hasty reading of some sections of his writings might give those impressions, Irving went to great lengths to state that Christ was holy and sinless. Irving definitely and frequently taught that Jesus was without sin. In addition, if Irving's view was heretical, he has some good company. John Knox seems to have held Irving's view, for Irving frequently used the language of the *Scottish Confession* (mainly the work of Knox) to state his Christological doctrine. Also, at least one later Moderator of the Church of Scotland, T. F. Torrance, agreed with Irving's "heretical" view.

As a theologian of the Holy Spirit, Irving has to be seen as a major forerunner of the modern Pentecostal and Charismatic movements. There have, perhaps, been few Pentecostal theologians who have presented as thorough a biblical and theological rationale of the Holy Spirit's ongoing ministry through the miraculous as did Irving. Peter Elliott says that Irving's "works contain a more capable and reflective theology of the Holy Spirit than any that was written during the first fifty years of the twentieth century Pentecostal movement."[11] How much the modern movement rests on Irving's shoulders, if it does at all, will be examined in the appendix.

When one examines Irving's overall theology, it must be said that he had formed a remarkable interlocking and generally consistent scheme.

10. Patterson, "Designing," 203.
11. Elliott, *Edward Irving*, 208.

After leaving Irving's movement, Robert Baxter made a criticism of Irving that is strikingly thought-provoking and seems to have been both true and untrue. He said that with Irving, "one line of truth swells over its parallel line, and converging lines cut where they should only meet."[12] Yet one cannot neatly separate the different Christian doctrines into isolated units. They not only meet each other, they do swell over and converge with one another. And for anyone delving into biblical truth, they should do so. This is something that Irving understood very well, and here he was in principle correct.

For example, his Christology and his understanding of the sacraments influenced and blended with his pneumatology, as has been seen. In whatever ways they were right or wrong, they were beautifully consistent with each other. His eschatology influenced probably every component of his theology.

Indeed, in 1828 Irving told Chalmers, "The second coming of the Lord is the '*point de vue*,' the vantage ground . . . from which, and from which alone, the whole purpose of God can be contemplated and understood."[13] In connecting this approach with his belief formed in the mid-1820s that Christ would return by the 1860s, major problems were bound to arise. To predict Christ's return, even approximately, when the Scriptures forbid it and when so many before him had been proven wrong, was very foolish. Irving should have known better.

David Brown, his one-time associate, described Irving has having "a rich and surging imagination, never under sufficient control." Brown thought that stemming from such an imagination, Irving's eschatology "laid him open to influences fitted seriously to warp his judgment."[14] Brown was right. They did warp it.

Martin Sutherland says that Irving's "expectation of Spirit-driven revolutions was both his strength and his Achilles' heel."[15] While there can be little doubt that it was his teaching about the Holy Spirit and the current availability of the charismata that finally brought him down, this teaching emerged from at least one key component in Irving's eschatology. He believed, first, that Christ would return very soon, probably in his lifetime. He also came to believe that before that return, the charismata would reappear. Therefore those spiritual gifts simply had to be discovered—and soon.

12. Baxter, *Narrative*, 129–30.

13. Irving to Thomas Chalmers, late December, 1828, quoted in Oliphant, *Life*, 2:67–68.

14. Brown, "Personal Reminiscences," 258.

15. Sutherland, "Preaching," 19.

Whitley is correct in saying that it was Irving's "apocalyptic preoccupation which led him most astray."[16] So it was that Irving, not always known for sound discernment, appears to have seen those gifts where they may not have existed. And it destroyed him.

It is also one of the mysteries of Irving's life that he, a man of such great intelligence and biblical and theological knowledge, could have had his theology so strongly influenced by people who possessed less intelligence, a much poorer understanding, and may have been less close to God than he. While that might show humility, it also often displayed considerable gullibility.

It is easy to pick holes in Irving's theology. He has, after all, been proven wrong in some respects. But overall, he proclaimed a living theology that warms the heart and strikes the mind with living echoes of biblical truth. He was an important and consistent theologian, in spite of his errors.

16. Whitley, *Blinded Eagle*, 45.

Appendix

Edward Irving
and the Pentecostal Movement

Strachan noted that "the beliefs and experiences of the various branches of the contemporary Pentecostal Churches are so similar to Irving and his followers that one might suspect that they had been handed down by word of mouth or rediscovered by some Deuteronomy of the Spirit."[1] Mark Patterson states, "Contemporary Pentecostalism, despite a separation of time and differences in theological detail, nevertheless reflects significant similarities to that which was practiced at Regent Square and interpreted in *The Morning Watch*."[2]

In addition, many in the modern Pentecostal movement are well aware of the Irving phenomenon and see him as a forerunner of that movement. For example, *The New International Dictionary of Pentecostal and Charismatic Movements*, published in 2003, contains numerous references to Irving, including an article on him that, together with its bibliography, runs to a page-and-a-half. It also includes an article on the CAC. The author of the Irving article, David Bundy, argues that "the Irving phenomenon became an interpretive grid by which pentecostal theologians came to understand and evaluate their own experience."[3] Indeed, according to Bundy, Edward Irving is one of the writers most commonly quoted in "several early European pentecostal periodicals."[4] Larry Christenson, a Lutheran Charismatic,

---

1. Strachan, *Pentecostal*, 19.
2. Patterson, "Designing," 21.
3. Bundy, "Irving, Edward," 803–4.
4. Bundy, "European Pietist Roots," 612.

called Irving "a forerunner . . . of the entire Pentecostal phenomenon of the twentieth century."[5]

Yet Strachan argued that, in spite of its many similarities, the modern Pentecostal movement has no direct connection with Irving's venture into the charismata. Christenson also wrote against the idea that the CAC, and by implication Irving, influenced modern Pentecostalism. Those who share similar views include Vinson Synan, David Dorries, and Sheridan Gilley.[6]

But is that true? It would seem the question still needs to be asked: Did Irving, directly or indirectly, influence the early stages of the modern Pentecostal movement? This is the question we will consider in this appendix. In addition, we will briefly examine to what degree today's Pentecostals regard him as a fellow traveler.

First, we need to establish what we mean by the term "modern Pentecostal movement." Claims about the reappearance of prophecy and other charismata associated with Pentecostals have been made in different places, by different movements, and throughout much of church history. Take, for example, the Montanists of Asia Minor in the late second and early third centuries, whose main prophets were Montanus, Priscilla, and Maximilla. In the late thirteenth and early fourteenth centuries, the Order of Apostles, which displayed some of these gifts, arose in Italy under the leadership of Gerard Segarelli and particularly Fra Dolcino. Francis Xavier, the Catholic Missionary of the sixteenth century, is said to have spoken in tongues. There were also the French Prophets of the eighteenth century, a movement that arose in France but soon became active in a number of other European countries, including Britain. In addition, there were the Shakers, who originated in England in the late eighteenth century before moving to America. Christians in various holiness churches in America in the late nineteenth century also claimed to have had charismatic experiences such as speaking in tongues. These are only a few of the many reappearances of prophecy and other charismata, though some were outside the mainstream.

But the modern Pentecostal movement is usually regarded as having commenced at the very beginning of the twentieth century. In October of 1900, Charles Fox Parham (1873–1929), as a product of the holiness movement, opened the Bethel Bible College in Topeka, Kansas. He has been called "the founding father" of modern Pentecostalism, though some reject that title.[7]

5. Christenson, "Pentecostalism's Forgotten Forerunner," 20.

6. Strachan, *Pentecostal*, 19–20; Christenson, "Pentecostalism's Forgotten Forerunner," 36 n. 6; Dorries, "Edward Irving and the 'Standing Sign,'" in McGee, *Initial Evidence*, 41; Gilley, "Edward Irving: Prophet," 103.

7. James R. Goff, "Initial Tongues in the Theology of Charles Fox Parham," in

Parham believed that a worldwide revival would soon occur that would herald the return of Christ. Within that revival, and essential to it, many Christians would be given the ability to proclaim the gospel in human languages that they had not learned (*xenolalia* or *xenoglossia*), as in Acts 2. In two of these points—Christ's forthcoming return and speaking in tongues—Parham's views were much like Irving's, although Irving did not believe in a last days worldwide revival.

Parham shared these teachings at his short-term school. On January 1, 1901, one of his students, Agnes Ozman, was filled with the Spirit and spoke in tongues. Parham, like Irving, came to believe that these tongues were, in fact, the "initial evidence" or "initial sign" of the baptism of the Spirit. It is this initial evidence idea that makes that occurrence so significant, and this event is commonly believed to be the start of today's Pentecostal movement.[8] (Though in the Pentecostal movement these tongues were originally thought of as unlearned human languages [*xenolalia*], it later became more common to regard such outbursts as just unknown languages [*glossolalia*].)[9]

The date January 1, 1901, on which Ms. Ozman spoke in tongues, is a very neat and convenient date to regard as the beginning of the Pentecostal movement, though when looking for the these origins, we find that the real truth may not be quite so tidy. However, for our purposes it will suffice to regard modern Pentecostalism as beginning on that first day of the twentieth century.

A group of churches emerged out of Parham's college that became known as Apostolic Faith, but it never became a major denomination. However, others began to adopt Parham's ideas. In December 1905 Parham opened another school in Houston. At this school, William J. Seymour, an African-American evangelist, came under Parham's teaching.

Seymour absorbed Parham's doctrine before moving to Los Angeles as a pastor in February 1906. It was not long before Seymour was locked out of his church for his teaching on tongues, at which point he began holding meetings in homes. Soon he and some of his supporters began to speak in tongues. This stirred interest, and Seymour had to hire a meeting place in Azusa Street to accommodate the larger numbers. This church began to

McGee, *Initial Evidence*, 57; Synan, *Holiness-Pentecostal*, 89 n. 13.

8. Parham, *Voice*, 20, 26, 28; Goff, "Parham, Charles," 955–56; Goff, *Fields*, 69–71. For Irving's view on tongues, see Irving, "Homilies on Baptism," in *CW*, 2:276–77; Irving, "Facts Connected," 5:204–5, 316–20. Dorries points out that Irving preferred to refer to it as the initial "sign" or "gift" rather than the initial "evidence," but the idea is the same. See McGee, *Initial Evidence*, 48–50.

9. Goff, *Fields*, 72; McGee, "Initial Evidence," 786–91; McGee, "Taking the Logic," 120–21; Parham, *Voice*, 28.

grow fairly quickly, and its influence soon spread to churches and denominations in other cities and even spawned new churches. Eventually, its message also spread overseas. Though the Azusa Street Mission never became
a major center and closed in the 1920s, its influence has been extensive and
long-lasting.[10] Today the Azusa Street Mission is remembered with affection
and awe by Pentecostals around the world.

The contemporary Pentecostal/Charismatic movement is massive,
with a claimed five hundred million adherents, and it extends around the
world, having gained an especially strong following in poorer countries.[11]
It is also quite diverse and includes numerous denominations. Not all accept tongues as the initial evidence, though many do. The largest of the
Pentecostal denominations is the Assemblies of God, which began in 1914
and today has about sixty million adherents worldwide. Others include the
International Church of the Four Square Gospel, with nearly eight million
adherents; the Church of God (Cleveland, Tennessee), with about six million adherents; and the Church of God in Christ, with over five million
adherents.

There may be three links between Irving and modern Pentecostalism:
John Alexander Dowie, Charles Parham, and A. B. Simpson.[12] Certainly
all three of these men, who each influenced Pentecostalism, were aware of
Irving's charismatic experiences.

While not a Pentecostal, A. B. Simpson (1843–1919), a Canadian-born
American holiness teacher, believed in a number of Pentecostal teachings
and influenced many in the Pentecostal movement. He believed in tongues,
but he was very concerned about their misuse and rejected the initial evidence idea. He was the founder of the Christian and Missionary Alliance
(CMA), a linking of two existing missions that though not Pentecostal, has
through most of its history counted some Pentecostals among its ranks.[13]

As far back as 1892, the CMA convention discussed the validity of
supernatural speaking in tongues for overseas missionaries. Emerging from
that debate, the convention urged its people to "avoid the dangers of Irvingism." Six years later, Simpson advised his readers not to "unduly exaggerate the gift of tongues" and once more warned his people against Irving's
ideas.[14] It is clear from this that Simpson and the CMA were well aware

10. Robeck, "Azusa Street Revival," 344–49.

11. Synan, *Century*, 388.

12. Anderson, *Spreading Fires*, 38; Vreeland, "Edward Irving."

13. See "Use of Terms" at the beginning of this book for the distinction between
Pentecostal and Charismatic. See also Nienkirchen, "Christian and Missionary," 523–
25; Nienkirchen, "Simpson," 1069–70.

14. Simpson, "Connection between Supernatural Gifts," *Christian Alliance and*

of Irving and his ventures into the charismata, and may have passed that awareness on to some early Pentecostals.

J. A. Dowie (1847–1907), born in Scotland, was pre-Pentecostal but does seem to have been a bridge between Irving and the modern Pentecostal movement. Barry Chant calls him "a major contributor to the early development of Pentecostalism," while William Faupel says that "many" Pentecostal churches around the world "trace their origins" to Dowie.[15]

Soon after Dowie's birth, his father was converted through the ministry of Rev. Henry Wight, a barrister turned preacher. Wight appears to have been influenced by Irving.[16] If this is correct, the young Dowie would probably have had an early awareness of his Scottish predecessor. In addition, the boy was also later brought to Christ through Wight's ministry.[17]

His family was, however, attached to a Congregational church. The Dowie family moved to Adelaide in South Australia in 1860, but Dowie returned to Scotland to study seven years later. There he learned from Congregationalists and Presbyterians (though he was not always impressed by what he was taught), and he also met Andrew and Horatius Bonar. Thus, he had some association with those who had heard Irving.

Dowie then rejoined his family in Australia and was ordained as a Congregational minister in May 1872. But six years later he left the Congregationalists to become an independent evangelist and faith healer, going on to exercise an influential ministry first in Australia and then from 1888 onwards in America. He founded and ruled a city north of Chicago called Zion City, which included his multi-seat Shiloh Tabernacle. For a number of years he also published a newsletter called *Leaves of Healing*, which was distributed to thousands in America, Canada, Australia, New Zealand, and other countries.[18]

Dowie's career developed in three main stages. First, in the early and mid-1870s he was an ordinary, though enthusiastic, Congregational minister in Australia. Second, from the late 1870s he was an independent healing evangelist, and leading from that, from the late 1880s Dowie was the President of the Divine Healing Association in Australia and America. Third, in

(Foreign) Missionary Weekly (1892) 226, quoted in McGee, "Shortcut," 3; Simpson, "The Worship and Fellowship," *Christian Alliance and (Foreign) Missionary Weekly* (1898) 126, quoted in McGee, "Shortcut," 4.

15. Chant, *Australian Career*, 2; Faupel, "Theological Influences," 227.

16. Dowie, *Leaves* 2:30 (1896) 466; Vreeland, "Edward Irving."

17. Dowie, *Leaves* 1:48 (1895) 760; 5:48 (1899) 935.

18. Blumhofer, "Dowie," 586–87; Chant, *Australian Career*, 2–7; Dowie, *Leaves* 1:4 (1894) 60; 1:18 (1894) 280; 1:31 (1895) 490; 2:30 (1896) 467; 3:17 (1897) 257–61; 5:25 (1899) 471; 6:16 (1900) 481–83; Gardiner, "Apostle."

1896 he founded a new church, and at the turn of the century he became "Elijah the Restorer," eventually with a base in Zion City. For a brief while in 1881 he was even a leading figure in the early stages of The Salvation Army in Australia.[19]

When one compares Dowie's letters of 1872, written when he was a Congregational minister, against his writings in *Leaves of Healing* and other later works, the contrast is stunning. The earlier letters cover ordinary personal issues and everyday ministerial problems and are generally low-key. *Leaves of Healing*, by contrast, is high-powered and obsessed by divine healing, and at times gives the impression that everything else is subordinate to divine healing.[20] While this contrast can be partly blamed on the different media (personal letters as distinct from a dedicated journal), they still seem to be propelled by a different dynamic and display markedly different thinking.

What caused this change in Dowie's thinking and approach? The main cause seems to have occurred after Dowie moved from South Australia to a church in Sydney in 1876. Soon after his arrival there, many of his congregation fell sick with fever, and some died. Dowie began to reason why this should have happened, and he became convinced that sickness was of the devil and that God desired its cure. He then specifically prayed for the healing of a sick girl, and she made a remarkable recovery. He next prayed for her brother and sister, who were also sick. They too were cured. Their recovery made such a deep impression upon Dowie that his primary focus gradually changed to divine healing.[21]

But were these changes also influenced in any way by Edward Irving? As suggested above, Dowie probably had an awareness of Irving from his childhood. In addition, his time studying in Scotland may also have exposed him to the CAC and to Irving's teachings. In fact, Mark Hutchinson points out that Dowie's period of study in Scotland was when "the CAC was growing in influence there."[22] But what might be considered Dowie's charis-

19. Dowie seems to have dubbed himself the Australian Salvation Army's "General-in-Command" (Hentzschel, "Hidden Turmoil," 17–18). One can only wonder what General William Booth thought of that.

20. Lewis, *Times*, 7–12; Dowie, *Leaves* 1:1 (1894) 1–7; 2:1 (1895) 1–2, 8–14; 3:2 (1896) 18–22. These are just a few of the many such sections in *Leaves*, but the front page of almost any issue will give a good idea. Faupel states that divine healing was "so close to the heart of his thinking that he could hardly speak of any subject without at least an allusion to this doctrine" ("Theological Influences," 233).

21. Gardiner, "Apostle." Note that Dowie never used the phrase "faith healing," for faith does not heal. It is rather the channel for healing. For Dowie's comments on the term "faith healing," see Dowie, *Leaves*, 1st ser., 1 (1890) 136.

22. Hutchinson, "Edward Irving's Antipodean Shadow," n. 56.

matic conversion seems to have occurred later and to have been triggered by other events. However, Hutchinson also notes that Dowie's major churches in Melbourne and Sydney were established near CAC churches. Association with CAC leaders may, therefore, have been a factor in his adoption of a belief in divine healing.

William Faupel claims, "Dowie never acknowledged receiving anything from anybody,"[23] and the research conducted here confirms that conclusion. Therefore, evidence of any Irving influence on him is inevitably limited. However, it can be established that Dowie was very aware of Irving and his charismatic leanings and had a high regard for him. Apart from apparent early contact with Irving's associates, Irving is mentioned occasionally in Dowie's *Leaves of Healing*. In 1895 Dowie published an article by James Douglas of the London Missionary Society that ironically made a favorable mention of Irving's understanding of prudence. The following year, in a tribute to his father, Dowie referred to "Edward Irving's wonderful ministry, which so thrilled Scotland."[24]

In 1898 Dowie published in two parts his address on tongues and their interpretation. In the second part, Dowie referred to Irving and to what he called "the Holy Catholic Apostolic Church." Dowie went on to say that it was "false prophets" in that church who "deceived" him, "broke his heart [and] closed his mouth." Dowie added that he thought that Irving "might have been the man who would have brought back the Gifts of Healings, and the various Gifts that have been lost to the church, as no other man could have done in his time."[25] This rather ambiguous comment presumably meant that Dowie believed Irving would have brought back these gifts to the worldwide church if he had had opportunity to do so. Dowie clearly must have been aware of the charismatic nature of Irving's ministry by no later than 1898.

Then in a 1904 issue of *Leaves of Healing*, Dowie paid a tribute to Edward Irving by calling him his "predecessor" and stating that "a greater and mightier man of God never stood upon this earth." Dowie added that he had "*often* wished that [Irving] could have lived out the beautiful life that he began," which indicates that Dowie had frequently thought about Irving and

23. Faupel, *Everlasting Gospel*, 133 n. 60. See also Faupel, "Theological Influences," 241.

24. James Douglas, in Dowie, *Leaves* 2:9 (1895) 135; Dowie, *Leaves* 2:30 (1896) 466.

25. Dowie, *Leaves* 4:24 (1898) 468–69.

his unique ministry.[26] Later that year one of Dowie's associates noted that Irving had "attempted the restoration of the Apostleship."[27]

The following year Dowie again called Irving "a mighty man of God" and said that Irving's work failed "because his brethren were jealous of him." In fact, Dowie believed that Irving had "Apostolic power . . . but he allowed himself to be overcome by poor, foolish people, who said they were prophets."[28]

All this suggests that Dowie had absorbed a biography or two about Irving and probably some of Irving's own writings, though he was clearly placing his own interpretation on events, for Irving never claimed to possess "Apostolic power." It is unclear, however, exactly when Dowie's reading about Irving took place. It could have been when studying in Scotland (during the late 1860s to early 1870s), or after possible contact with CAC people in Australia (in the 1870s), or maybe even later.

In 1895 Dowie decided to establish a church that he intended to name the Christian Catholic Apostolic Church. It was founded a year later, but initially without the word "Apostolic" in the title. However, he later reverted to the original title, with "in Zion" added. While he argued that his church's name was drawn from words used in the New Testament and in early church documents, particularly the Apostles' Creed, it does also suggest an awareness of Irving and the Catholic Apostolic Church. As we have seen, Dowie appears to have known of the CAC from quite early in life, and he mentioned it specifically in a list of denominations in America that appeared in an 1895 edition of *Leaves of Healing*. His original coining of the full name for his church appeared in *Leaves* very soon after that.[29]

In addition, towards the end of his life he dressed in priestly robes, like those worn by Old Testament priests; in fact, it was argued that they "were designed by God Himself."[30] CAC leaders also wore vestments, though theirs seem to have been based more on New Testament ideas and imagery than those of the Old Testament. However, CAC influence on Dowie concerning the issue of clerical dress still seems likely.

In addition, when Dowie sent out his people two by two on visitation, the phrase with which he instructed them to greet each homeowner

26. Ibid., 15:14 (1904) 433, emphasis added.

27. Elder W. H. Cossum, quoted in Dowie, *Leaves* 15:21 (1904) 743.

28. Dowie, *Leaves* 16:20 (1905) 643; 16:12 (1905) 379.

29. Dowie, *Leaves* 1:27 (1895) 427; 1:28 (1895) 443; 1:30 (1895) 478–79; 1:31 (1895) 490; 1:34 (1895) 531; 2:14 (1896) 221; 2:17 (1896) 259–60, 265, 267; 2:18 (1896) 274–75, 279; 16:12 (1905) 379.

30. "God Gave Design of the Robes," *The Zion Banner*, September 20, 1904, 414.

was "Peace be unto this house," just like Irving did when he went visiting.[31] Irving's influence here is possible, though far from certain.

Dowie held a number of later pentecostal beliefs. As we have seen, His main emphasis was on what he called "divine healing." That was his strong emphasis. But this was all part of his belief in the restoration of the nine gifts of the Spirit in 1 Cor 12:4–11, which included prophecy and tongues. He also believed in leadership by twelve apostles.[32] In fact, towards the end of his life Dowie believed himself to be Elijah the prophet and an apostle, and there were in his movement other prophets and apostles.[33] But he did not teach that the gift of tongues is the initial evidence.[34] In fact, the gift of tongues seems to have been a late arrival in his charismatic ministry. It had not been heard by April 1897, though he believed that it would come.[35] The gift of healing was the key gift to him, not, as with Irving, the gift of tongues.[36]

In September 1898 Dowie claimed to have "in a measure" the first seven of those nine gifts, but not tongues and not the interpretation of tongues. He said that he did experience tongues on one occasion, but it did not stay with him. In his thinking at that time, this lack disqualified him from being an apostle, for he believed an apostle must have all nine gifts.[37] However, he did later become an apostle.

Dowie's attitude to apostleship may have been influenced by Irving. However, it was also clearly influenced by the Mormons, who have apostles. He had taken a great interest in the Mormons, and though he regarded much of their teaching as false, he admired their organizational structure.[38]

Though Dowie's personality often irritated both friends and enemies (he was, for example, rather dogmatic), his preaching and writing ministry

31. Lindsay, *Dowie*, 116.

32. Blumhofer, "Dowie," 586–87; Dowie, *Leaves* 1:10 (1894) 147; 2:47 (1896) 746; 3:6 (1896) 91; Gardiner, "Apostle"; Lindsay, *Dowie*. For CAC vestments, see Flegg, *Gathered*, 265–67.

33. Lewis, *Times*, 17–19; Dowie, *Leaves* 9:7 (1901) 196; 10:3 (1901) 87.

34. Vreeland, "Edward Irving."

35. Dowie, *Leaves* 3:24 (1897) 378. In fact, though he mentioned tongues fairly frequently, he did not emphasize it. See, for example, *Leaves* 1:27 (1895) 424; 1:28 (1895) 443; 1:48 (1895) 761; 2:4 (1896) 61; 2:14 (1896) 218; 2:15 (1896) 229–30; 2:17 (1896) 265; 2:18 (1896), 278; 2:19 (1896) 300; 3:29 (1897) 454; 3:45 (1897) 713. This was probably because he was well into his charismatic ministry before it was manifested in his church.

36. Ibid., 3:49 (1897) 774–75.

37. Ibid., 4:47 (1898) 926.

38. Ibid., 6:11 (1900) 324. Faupel also notes the influence of the Mormons on Dowie ("Theological Influences," 243–44, 250–53).

did influence a large number of people, including many in the emerging Pentecostal movement. For example, as James R. Goff notes, "Dowie's ministry undoubtedly influenced Charles Parham."[39] In September 1906 Parham visited Zion City, where Dowie's hold over his people was waning, and many of them attached themselves to Parham and his work.[40]

In fact, the following people were involved in Dowie's churches: F. F. Bosworth, J. Roswell Flower, Frederick Graves, John G. Lake (who later moved to South Africa), Charles E. Robinson (an author and editor), and Daniel Opperman. Flower and Opperman also became early workers in the Assemblies of God. Other early Pentecostals who came under Dowie's influence were Aimee Semple McPherson, Geritt and Whilhelmine Polman (founders of Pentecostal work in the Netherlands), Daniel Bryant (an early Pentecostal in South Africa), John Adams and Henry Roberts (early New Zealand Pentecostals), and Polly Wigglesworth.[41] In fact, Edith Blumhofer argues that over one hundred of Dowie's followers later occupied leadership roles in the Assemblies of God.[42] This does not necessarily mean that all or any of these people had read Irving's books or were even aware of him, but it can at least be said that they were influenced by a leader who seems to have been influenced by Irving, and that influence was widespread.

In addition, Dowie was frequently quoted in a number of "early European pentecostal periodicals."[43] Some of those same periodicals that quoted Dowie also quoted Irving.

William Faupel says that in his "judgment, Dowie links the Irvingite movement to Pentecostalism." Faupel also observes, "Dowie represents a direct historical link for Pentecostalism to the Irvingite movement."[44]

In fact, it is clear from all this that Dowie had a major influence upon the early Pentecostal movement. But there is some uncertainty about how much influence Irving had on Dowie and in what ways. We know that Dowie was exposed to Irving's life and teachings, but when that exposure took place and to what degree is unclear. However, Faupel lists eight ways in

39. Goff, *Fields*, 50. See also Synan, *Holiness-Pentecostal*, 90.

40. Goff, "Initial Tongues," 68, 73; Cecil M Robeck Jr., "William Seymour," in McGee, *Initial Evidence*, 79–80; Synan, *Holiness-Pentecostal*, 101.

41. *NIDPCM*, 26, 184, 187, 227–28, 308, 439, 642, 680, 828, 946–47, 1026; Gardiner, "Apostle," 21. Lyman Stewart, one of the two financiers behind *The Fundamentals*, was treasurer of the Los Angeles "branch" of Dowie's work in 1890, according to Dowie, *Leaves*, 1st ser., 1:5 (1890) 114.

42. Edith L. Blumhofer, "A Pentecostal Branch Grows in Dowie's Zion," *Assemblies of God Heritage* 6 (1986) 3–5, quoted in Faupel, "Theological Influences," 247 n. 65.

43. Bundy, "European Pietist," 612. See also Faupel, *Everlasting Gospel*, 133 n. 60.

44. Faupel, *Everlasting Gospel*, 133 n. 60, 135.

which Dowie's church echoed the CAC. These included: the two churches had similar names; each of the two movements believed themselves to be forerunners of the return of Christ; the two churches each believed that they were to be witnesses to the nations, warning them of the coming judgment of God; they also each believed in the restoration of the fourfold office (Apostles, Prophets, Evangelists, and Teachers) and in the restoration of the nine gifts of the Spirit. To this can be added that Irving and Dowie both had some reverence for the non-canonical Book of Enoch[45] and that Dowie, like the CAC leaders, wore vestments.

Yet there were differences, though these were mainly in emphasis. Dowie placed a much stronger emphasis on healing than did Irving, while Irving's emphasis on tongues was much stronger than Dowie's, considering that Dowie did not believe that tongues were the initial evidence. One striking difference between the two in the area of the charismata is that Irving accepted the ministrations of doctors and nurses in addition to spiritual healing to cure the sick, but Dowie vigorously rejected non-spiritual methods. When all this is considered, there does appear to be a link, via Dowie, between Edward Irving and early Pentecostalism. But it is unclear how strong that link might be.

Now we come to Charles Parham. We have already noted his role in the launching of the modern Pentecostal movement, but it also needs to be recognized that he continues to be regarded as a major figure in the early years of the development of Pentecostalism and as a great influence upon the movement. Apart from founding his own denomination, he was a significant influence upon the Assemblies of God, the largest Pentecostal church. In fact, H. V. Synan explains, "It was Parham who . . . formulated the 'initial evidence' teaching that is central to the theology of most of the classical pentecostal churches of the world," while G. B. McGee says that the initial evidence idea "became the hallmark of classical Pentecostal theology."[46] Parham is also mentioned more frequently in *NIDPCM* than any other individual. Parham's importance is clear. So what did he know of Irving, how did that impact him, and did his knowledge of Irving influence others?

While Charles Parham *may* not have known of Edward Irving prior to his founding of the Topeka Bible College, he certainly knew about Irving very soon afterwards. On January 22, 1901, a mere twenty-one days after Agnes Ozman spoke in tongues, Parham mentioned Irving in a sermon that appeared in a book first published in 1902. Parham said, "We have found . . .

45. Faupel, "Theological Influences," 242–44. See n. 56 for Enoch.
46. Synan, "Classical Pentecostalism," 553; McGee, "Initial Evidence," 786.

that the Irvingites, a sect that arose under the teachings of Irving, a Scotchman, during the last century, received not only the eight recorded gifts of
1 Cor 12, but also the speaking in other tongues, which the Holy Ghost
reserved as the evidence of his oncoming."[47] This does not necessarily mean
that Parham gleaned his belief in tongues as the initial evidence or any other
teachings from Irving's writings, but he clearly knew about Irving's view
soon after the Agnes Ozman incident, and it is quite likely that he knew of it
even before then. Therefore it is possible that Irving influenced him in that
direction. Parham was also influenced by Dowie, who could have been the
source of his information about Irving.[48]

Another person to consider is Carrie Judd Montgomery (1858–1946).
She was not originally a member of a Pentecostal church, having belonged
instead to the Christian and Missionary Alliance and then The Salvation
Army. However, she later joined the Assemblies of God and became a charter member of the General Council of that denomination.[49] She produced
a monthly journal called *Triumphs of Faith*. In the April 1884 issue, she re-
published an article by Edward Irving that had originally appeared in the
June 1832 edition of *TMW*, which told of an occasion when he was very ill,
but God had given him the strength to preach powerfully.[50]

All this indicates that one leading figure in the early Pentecostal movement, Parham, knew of Irving and may have been directly influenced by
him. It is also clear that Irving had some indirect influence on the early
movement through Simpson and Dowie, especially the latter. This certainly
does not mean that Irving's teaching gave birth to the Pentecostal movement. Rather, that movement seems to have emerged from other sources
such as the holiness churches, for example, and the direct study of Scripture.
Nevertheless, there does appear to have been some Irving influence on Pentecostalism during its early years, though how much is debatable.

One of today's Charismatic churches that can clearly trace its origins
back to Edward Irving is the New Apostolic Church (NAC). The NAC is not
strictly a Pentecostal church in the sense of the term used here (see "Use of
Terms" at the beginning of this book), but the NAC strongly emphasizes the
ministry of the Holy Spirit and also recognizes contemporary prophecy and

47. Parham, *Voice*, 29. For the date of the sermon, see 25. I have only seen the 1910
edition of this book, but this reference appears also to have been in the 1902 edition; see
Vreeland, "Edward Irving," n. 46, and Dorries, "New Apostolic Church," 929.

48. Goff, *Fields*, 50–51.

49. Warner, "Montgomery, Carrie Judd," 904–6.

50. Edward Irving, *TMW* 5 (1832) 425–29, quoted in Montgomery, "Edward Irving's Experience," *Triumphs of Faith* 4:4 (1884) 76–79. Other references to Irving appeared in *Triumphs of Faith* 27:6 (1907) 129; 27:11 (1907) 244–45.

tongues, though the latter does not seem to be stressed. Its website makes it clear that it traces its history directly back to Edward Irving and the CAC.[51]

The NAC originated in 1863, when a group broke away from the CAC because of a dispute over the appointment of additional apostles. The new body, unlike its parent, continued to appoint apostles. Today the NAC is a movement with churches in dozens of countries around the world and over ten million members, having seen significant gains between 1980 and 2000. Its "Creed" shares a number of similar emphases with Irving, though also some differences. Like Irving, the NAC places a strong emphasis upon the significance of the return of Christ.[52] However, the NAC does not appear to be a major influence in the Pentecostal world, as such.

There is no doubt at all that many of today's Pentecostals have a high regard for Edward Irving and see him as a fellow traveler. For example, the *NIDPCM* speaks favorably of Irving in a number of articles, while David Dorries and Derek Vreeland utter barely a criticism of him, while loudly praising him.[53] As David Hilborn says, "Irving is now widely credited by Pentecostal theologians with having provided a crucial precedent for their own tradition."[54]

According to G. B. McGee, "More than any other figure" in the nineteenth century, Irving "became identified with belief in the availability of the gifts of the Holy Spirit." McGee argues, "To Irving, speaking in tongues signified the 'standing sign' of the church's inheritance won through the redemptive work of Jesus Christ." In the early twentieth century, "Pentecostals found" in Irving "a recent precedent for their own experiences of tongues, but they seemed [generally] unaware of Irving's belief in its evidential value."[55]

In the Pentecostal/Charismatic publications referring to Irving that have been examined in research for this appendix, criticism of him is noticeable in its almost total absence, though in some cases this may be because the reference is very brief. Yet a number of Pentecostal/Charismatic books written in the last thirty years or so examined in the course of this study do not mention him, even when they might have been expected to do so. This may be because these writers were not aware of him, or it may be

---

51. New Apostolic Church International, "History of Our Church"; New Apostolic Church International, "Creed"; New Apostolic Church International, "Holy Spirit and Its Diverse Ways."

52. Ibid.

53. Dorries, *Edward Irving's Incarnational Christology*, 23–142; Dorries, "Edward Irving and the 'Standing Sign,'" 41–56; Vreeland, "Edward Irving," 1–7.

54. Hilborn, "Charismatic Renewal."

55. McGee, "Initial Evidence," 784–85.

because the charge of heresy that still hangs over Irving makes some reticent to quote him.

Peter Elliott argues that Irving's "works contain a more capable and reflective theology of the Holy Spirit than any that was written during the first fifty years of the twentieth century Pentecostal movement."[56] Whatever may be said about Edward Irving, he was certainly a man ahead of his times.

---

56. Elliott, *Edward Irving*, 208.

Bibliography

"Abuse of Spiritual Gifts." *TMW* 4 (1831) 375–402.

Allen, Hubert. *Roland Allen: Pioneer, Priest and Prophet.* Grand Rapids: Eerdmans, 1995.

Allen, Roland. *Missionary Methods: St. Paul's or Ours? A Study of the Church in the Four Provinces.* 2nd ed. London: World Dominion, 1927.

Anderson, Allan. *Spreading Fires: The Missionary Nature of Early Pentecostalism.* Maryknoll: Orbis, 2007.

Annan Academy. "Our History." *AnnanAcademy.org.* 2014. http://annanacademy.org. uk/wp/. "Annan Academy History," Online: www.annanacademy.org.uk/School_ info/School%20info.htm#ANNAN ACADEMY HISTORY.

"The Ark of God in the Temple of Dagon." *TMW* 5 (1832) 441–46.

Basilicus [Lewis Way]. "Thoughts on the Scriptural Expectations of the Church." *Jewish Expositor and Friend of Israel* 6 (1821) 102–12.

Baxter, Robert. *A Narrative of Facts Characterizing the Supernatural Manifestations in Members of Mr. Irving's Congregation, and Other Individuals in England and Scotland, and Formerly in the Writer Himself.* London: Nisbet, 1833.

Beales, Derek Edward Dawson. *From Castlereagh to Gladstone: 1815–1885.* Sphere Library 15156. London: Sphere, 1971.

Bebbington, David W. *The Dominance of Evangelicalism: The Age of Spurgeon and Moody.* History of Evangelicalism 3. Leicester, UK: InterVarsity, 2005.

———. *Evangelicalism in Modern Britain: A History from the 1730s to the 1980s.* London: Unwin Hyman, 1989.

Ben-Ezra, Juan Josafat [Manuel Lacunza.]. *The Coming of Messiah in Majesty and Glory.* 2 vols. Translated by Edward Irving. London: Seeley, 1827.

Bennett, David Malcolm. *The Origins of Left Behind Eschatology.* Longwood, FL: Xulon, 2010.

Berkhof, Louis. *The History of Christian Doctrines.* Edinburgh: Banner of Truth Trust, 1972.

———. *Systematic Theology.* London: Banner of Truth Trust, 1941.

Blackburn, Simon. *The Oxford Dictionary of Philosophy.* 2nd rev. ed. Oxford: Oxford University Press, 2005.

Blaikie, William Garden. *David Brown: A Memoir.* London: Hodder & Stoughton, 1898.

Blake, Robert. *The Conservative Party from Peel to Thatcher: Based on the Ford Lectures Delivered before the University of Oxford in the Hilary Term of 1968.* London: Fontana, 1985.

Bloch, Ruth H. *Visionary Republic: Millennial Themes in American Thought: 1756–1800.* Cambridge: Cambridge University Press, 1985.

Blumhofer, Edith L. "Dowie, John Alexander." In *NIDPCM*, edited by Stanley M. Burgess and Eduard M. Van der Maas, 586–87. Rev. ed. Grand Rapids: Zondervan, 2003.

Bohr, P. Richard. "The Legacy of Timothy Richard." *The International Bulletin of Missionary Research* 24 (2000) 75–80.

Bonar, Andrew A. *The Life of Robert Murray M'Cheyne.* 1844. Reprint, London: Banner of Truth Trust, 1960.

———. *Memoir and Remains of the Rev. Robert Murray M'Cheyne: Minister of St. Peter's Church, Dundee.* 1844. Reprint, Edinburgh: Oliphant, 1892.

Bonar, Andrew A., and Marjory Bonar. *Andrew A. Bonar: Diary and Life.* 1893. Reprint, Edinburgh: Banner of Truth Trust, 1960.

[Bonar, Horatius?]. "Edward Irving." *The Quarterly Journal of Prophecy* 14 (1862) 224–47.

Booth, William. *In Darkest England, and the Way Out.* London: Salvation Army, 1890.

Booth, William, and Catherine Booth. *The Letters of William and Catherine Booth.* Edited by David Malcolm Bennett. Brisbane, Australia: Camp Hill, 2003.

Brief Statement of the Proceedings of the London Presbytery, in Communion with the Established Church of Scotland, in the Case of the Rev. Edward Irving, and of a Book Written by Him and Entitled "The Orthodox and Catholic Doctrine of Our Lord's Human Nature." London: Steuart, 1831.

Brown, David. "Personal Reminiscences of Edward Irving." *The Expositor* 6 (1887) 216–28, 257–73.

Brown, Ralph. "Victorian Anglican Evangelicalism: The Radical Legacy of Edward Irving." *Journal of Ecclesiastical History* 58 (2007) 675–704.

Brown, Stewart J., and George M. Newlands, eds. *Scottish Christianity and the Modern World: In Honour of A. C. Cheyne.* Edinburgh: T. & T. Clark, 2000.

Browne, George. *The History of the British and Foreign Bible Society: From Its Institution in 1804, to the Close of Its Jubilee in 1854.* 2 vols. London: Bagster, 1859.

Bruce-Lockhart, Jamie. *A Sailor in the Sahara: The Life and Travels in Africa of Hugh Clapperton.* London: Tauris, 2007.

Bundy, D. D. "European Pietist Roots of Pentecostalism." In *NIDPCM*, edited by Stanley M. Burgess and Eduard M. Van der Maas, 610–13. Rev. ed. Grand Rapids: Zondervan, 2003.

———. "Irving, Edward." In *NIDPCM*, edited by Stanley M. Burgess and Eduard M. Van der Maas, 803–4. Rev. ed. Grand Rapids: Zondervan, 2003.

Calvin, John. *The Epistles of Paul the Apostle to the Romans and to the Thessalonians.* Vol. 8 of *Calvin's Commentaries.* Edited by David W. Torrance and Thomas F. Torrance, translated by Ross Mackenzie. Edinburgh: Oliver & Boyd, 1961.

———. *Institutes of the Christian Religion.* 2 vols. Edited by John T. McNeill and translated by Ford Lewis Battles. Library of Christian Classics 20–21. Philadelphia: Westminster, 1960.

Campbell, John McLeod. *Memorials of John McLeod Campbell: Being Selections from His Correspondence.* 2 vols. Edited by Donald Campbell. London: Macmillan, 1877.

Cardale, J. B. "On the Extraordinary Manifestations in Port Glasgow." *TMW* 2 (1830) 869–73.

Carlyle, Thomas. *A Carlyle Reader: Selections from the Writings of Thomas Carlyle.* Edited by G. B. Tennyson. Cambridge: Cambridge University Press, 1984.

————. "The Death of Edward Irving." *Fraser's Magazine* 61 (1835) 99–103.

————. *Past and Present; Chartism.* New ed., complete in one volume. New York: Putnam, 1848.

————. *Reminiscences.* 2 vols. Edited by Charles Eliot Norton. Elibron Classics. 1887. Reprint, Chestnut Hill, MA: Adamant Media, 2004.

————. *Reminiscences.* 2 vols. Edited by J. A. Froude. 1881. Reprint, Cambridge: Cambridge University Press, 2012.

Carlyle, Thomas, and Jane Carlyle. *The Carlyle Letters Online (CLO).* Edited by Brent E. Kinser. Duke University Press, September 14, 2007. http:carlyleletters. dukejournals.org.

Carter, Grayson. *Anglican Evangelicals: Protestant Secessions from the Via Media, c. 1800–1850.* Oxford: Oxford University Press, 2001.

Cauchi, Tony. "John Alexander Dowie." *Smith Wigglesworth Revival Library.* www. smithwigglesworth.com/pensketches/dowiej.htm.

Chambers, D. "Doctrinal Attitudes in the Church of Scotland in the Pre-Disruption Era: The Age of John McLeod Campbell and Edward Irving." *Journal of Religious History* 8 (1974) 159–82.

Chant, Barry. *The Australian Career of John Alexander Dowie.* CSAC Working Papers, Series 1:10. North Ryde, Australia: Macquarie University Centre for the Study of Australian Christianity, 1993.

Chevalier, T. W. "Defence of the Athanasian Creed." *TMW* 1 (1829) 446–68.

————. "On the Epiphany of our Lord Jesus." *TMW* 2 (1830) 587–93.

Christenson, Larry. "Pentecostalism's Forgotten Forerunner." In *Aspects of Pentecostal-Charismatic Origins,* edited by Vinson Synan, 15–37. Plainfield, NY: Logos, 1975.

Christiania. "On the Sinfulness of Christ's Human Nature, and the Immortality of the Soul." Letter to the editors in *GM* 5 (July 1830) 212.

Clej, Alma. "Coleridge, Samuel Taylor." In *Encyclopedia of Literature and Politics: Censorship, Revolution, and Writing,* edited by M. Keith Booker, 162. 3 vols. Westport, CT: Greenwood, 2005.

Coleridge, Samuel Taylor. *Aids to Reflection.* Edited by Henry Nelson Coleridge. 4th ed. London: Pickering, 1839.

————. *The Collected Letters of Samuel Taylor Coleridge.* 6 vols. Edited by Earl Leslie Griggs. Oxford: Clarendon, 1971.

————. *The Collected Works of Samuel Taylor Coleridge: Marginalia.* Vol. 12, pt.3. Edited by H. J. Jackson and George Whalley. Princeton: Princeton University Press, 2001.

————. *On the Constitution of the Church and State According to the Idea of Each: With Aids toward a Right Judgement on the Late Catholic Bill.* Library of English Literature 12572. London: Hurst, Chance, & Co., 1830.

————. *1819–1826: Text.* Vol. 4, pt. 1 of *The Notebooks of Samuel Taylor Coleridge.* 5 vols. Edited by Kathleen Coburn and Merton Christensen. Princeton: Princeton University Press, 1973.

————. *1819–1826: Notes.* Vol. 4, pt. 2 of *The Notebooks of Samuel Taylor Coleridge.* 5 vols. Edited by Kathleen Coburn and Merton Christensen. Bollingen Series 50. Princeton: Princeton University Press, 1973.

Coolahan, John. *Irish Education: Its History and Structure.* Dublin: Institute of Public Administration, 1981.

Cranfield, C. E. B. *A Critical and Exegetical Commentary on the Epistle to the Romans.* 2 vols. International Critical Commentary 32. Edinburgh: T. & T. Clark, 1990.

Cuthbertson, W. "Young Men's Christian Association Lecture on Edward Irving." *The Sydney Morning Herald*, September 11, 1860, 8. http://nla.gov.au/nla.news-article13045695.

Dallimore, Arnold A. *The Life of Edward Irving: Forerunner of the Charismatic Movement.* Edinburgh: Banner of Truth Trust, 1983.

Darby, John Nelson. *Writings of J. N. Darby.* Jackson, NJ: Present Truth, 2005. CD-ROM.

Davenport, Rowland A. *Albury Apostles: The Story of the Body Known as the Catholic Apostolic Church.* London: Free Society, 1973.

Dayton, Donald W. *Theological Roots of Pentecostalism.* Studies in Evangelicalism 5. Metuchen, NJ: Scarecrow, 1987.

Dorries, David W. *Edward Irving's Incarnational Christology.* Fairfax, VA: Xulon, 2002.

———. "New Apostolic Church." In *NIDPCM*, edited by Stanley M. Burgess and Eduard M. Van der Maas, 929–30. Rev. ed. Grand Rapids: Zondervan, 2003.

Dowie, John Alexander. *Leaves of Healing (1894–1906).* In *Healing Evangelists, 1881–1957.* Springfield, MO: Flower Pentecostal Heritage Center, 2006. CD-ROM.

Drabble, Margaret, ed. "Coleridge, Samuel Taylor." In *OCEL*, 214–15. Rev. 5th ed. Oxford: Oxford University Press, 1995.

———. "Wordsworth, Dorothy." In *OCEL*, 1094–95. Rev. 5th ed. Oxford: Oxford University Press, 1995.

———. "Wordsworth, William." In *OCEL*, 1095–96. Rev. 5th ed. Oxford: Oxford University Press, 1995.

Drummond, A. L. *Edward Irving and His Circle.* 1937. Reprint, Eugene, OR: Wipf & Stock, 2009.

Drummond, A. L., and James Bulloch. *The Scottish Church: 1688–1843.* Edinburgh: Saint Andrew, 1973.

Drummond, Henry. *Dialogues on Prophecy.* Vol. 1. London: Nisbet, 1828.

Edmonson, Stephen. *Calvin's Christology.* Cambridge: Cambridge University Press, 2004.

Elliott, E. B. *Horae Apocalypticae; or A Commentary on the Apocalypse.* 4 vols. 5th ed. London: Seeley, 1862.

Elliott, Peter. "Edward Irving: Romantic Theology in Crisis." PhD diss., Murdoch University, 2010.

———. *Edward Irving: Romantic Theology in Crisis.* Studies in Christian History and Thought Series. Milton Keynes, UK: Paternoster, 2013.

———. "Nineteenth-century Australian Charismata: Edward Irving's Legacy." *Pneuma* 34 (2012) 26–36.

Faupel, D. William. *The Everlasting Gospel: The Significance of Eschatology in the Development of Pentecostal Thought.* Journal of Pentecostal Theology Supplement Series 10. Sheffield: Sheffield Academic Press, 1996.

———. "Theological Influences on the Teachings and Practices of John Alexander Dowie." *Pneuma* 29 (2007) 226–53.

Flegg, Columba Graham. *"Gathered under Apostles": A Study of the Catholic Apostolic Church.* Oxford: Clarendon, 1992.

Froom, Le Roy Edwin. *The Prophetic Faith of Our Fathers: The Historical Development of Prophetic Interpretation*. 4 vols. Washington, DC: Review & Herald, 1946, 1948, 1950, 1954.

Gardiner, Gordon P. "The Apostle of Divine Healing: The Story of John Alexander Dowie." *Leaves of Healing: The Life, Ministry, and Message of John Alexander Dowie*. Edited by David K. Eames. Last modified March 2007. http:sites.google. com/site/leavesofhealing/leavesofhealingthelifegardiner.

Gilfillan, George. *A Third Gallery of Portraits*. New York: Sheldon, Lamport, & Blakeman, 1855.

Gilley, Sheridan. "Edward Irving: Prophet of the Millennium." In *Revival and Religion Since 1700: Essays for John Walsh*, edited by J. Garnett, and Colin Matthew. London: Hambledon, 1993.

Gilpin, William. *The Life of Bernard Gilpin*. Glasgow: Chalmers & Collins, 1824.

Goff, James R. *Fields White Unto Harvest: Charles F. Parham and the Missionary Origins of Pentecostalism*. Fayetteville: University of Arkansas, 1988.

———. "Parham, Charles Fox." In *NIDPCM*, edited by Stanley M. Burgess and Eduard M. Van der Maas, 955–57. Rev. ed. Grand Rapids: Zondervan, 2003.

Grass, Tim. "Albury and the Catholic Apostolic Church." Presentation to the Albury Historical Society, March 21, 2007. Last modified April 29, 2010. http://www. apostolischekritiek.nl/albury_and_the_catholic_apostoli.htm.

———. *Edward Irving: The Lord's Watchman*. Studies in Christian History and Thought Series. Milton Keynes, UK: Paternoster, 2011.

Gregory of Nazianzus. "Epistle 101." In *Cyril of Jerusalem, Gregory Nazienzen*, vol. 7 of *Nicene and Post-Nicene Fathers*, Second Series, edited by Phillip Schaff and Henry Wace, 440. Peabody: Hendrickson, 1994.

Gribben, Crawford, and Timothy C. F. Stunt. *Prisoners of Hope: Aspects of Evangelical Millennialism in Britain and Ireland, 1800–1880*. Studies in Evangelical History and Thought. Bletchley, UK: Paternoster, 2004.

Gumerlock, Francis X. *The Day and the Hour*. Powder Springs, GA: American Vision, 2000.

Gunton, Colin. "Two Dogmas Revisited: Edward Irving's Christology." *Scottish Journal of Theology* 41 (1988) 359–76.

Hair, John. *Regent Square: Eighty Years of a London Congregation*. 1899. Reprint, Memphis, TN: General Books, 2009.

Halliday, James. "The 1820 Rising: The Radical War." Stirling, Scotland: Scots Independent, 1993. www.electricscotland.com/history/1820/index.htm.

Hanna, William. *Memoirs of the Life and Writings of Thomas Chalmers*. 4 vols. Edinburgh: Sutherland, 1850.

———. *Memoirs of the Life and Writings of Thomas Chalmers*. 4 vols. New York: Harper, 1851.

Harper, Michael. *Let My People Grow: Ministry and Leadership in the Church*. London: Hodder & Stoughton, 1977.

Hazlitt, William. *The Spirit of the Age; or, Contemporary Portraits*. 2nd ed. London: Colburn, 1825.

Henke, Manfred. "The Catholic Apostolic Church and Its Gordon Square Cathedral: Bloomsbury, the 'Irvingites,' and the Catholic Apostolic Church." *University College London Bloomsbury Project*. Last modified April 14, 2011. www.ucl.ac.uk/ bloomsbury-project/articles/articles/CAC-Gordon_Square.pdf.

"Henry Duncan." *Savings Banks Museum.* Last modified 2002. http://www. savingsbanksmuseum.co.uk/henry_duncan.html.

Hentzschel, Garth R. "Hidden Turmoil of Army's Early Days." *Pipeline* (2013) 16–18.

Hibbert, Christopher. *Africa Explored: Europeans in the Dark Continent.* Harmondsworth, UK: Penguin, 1984.

Hilborn, David. "Charismatic Renewal in Britain: Roots, Influences, and Later Developments." *Evangelical Alliance.* August 3, 2006. http://www.eauk.org/church/ resources/theological-articles/upload/Charismatic-renewal-in-Britain.pdf.

Hitchcock, Thomas. *Unhappy Loves of Men of Genius.* New York: Harper, 1891.

Hooker, Richard. *On the Laws of Ecclesiastical Polity.* Vol. 2 of *The Works of Richard Hooker: With an Account of His Life and Death.* Edited by John Keble. 3 vols. Oxford: Oxford University Press, 1836.

Hutchinson, Mark. "Edward Irving's Antipodean Shadow." *Webjournals.* http:// webjournals.ac.edu.au/journals/aps/issue-10/edward-irvings-antipodean- shadow/.

Ice, Thomas D. "Alleged Irvingite Influence on Darby and the Rapture." *Pre-Trib Research Center,* Article Archives, Paper 126. May 2009. http://www.pre-trib.org/ data/pdf/Ice-AllegedIrvingiteInfl.pdf.

Inwood, Stephen. *A History of London.* London: Macmillan, 1998.

Irving, Edward. *An Apology for the Ancient Fulness and Purity of the Doctrine of the Kirk of Scotland.* London: Nisbet, 1828.

———. *Babylon and Infidelity Foredoomed of God: A Discourse on the Prophecies of Daniel and the Apocalypse, Which Relate to These Latter Times.* 2 vols. 1826. Reprint, Eugene, OR: Wipf & Stock, 2004.

———. "The Church, with Her Endowment of Holiness and Power." *TMW* 2 (1830) 630–68.

———. *The Collected Writings of Edward Irving.* 5 vols. Edited by Gavin Carlyle. London: Strahan, 1864–1865.

———. *The Confessions of Faith and the Books of Discipline of the Church of Scotland, of Date Anterior to the Westminster Confession.* London: Baldwin & Cradock, 1831.

———. *The Day of Pentecost; or, the Baptism with the Holy Ghost.* London: Baldwin & Craddock, 1831.

———. *The Diary and Letters of Edward Irving.* Edited by Barbara Waddington. Eugene, OR: Pickwick, 2012.

———. *Edward Irving's Holy Spirit Writings.* Edited by David Dorries. North Charleston, SC: Create Space, 2011.

———. "Facts Connected with Recent Manifestations of Spiritual Gifts." *Fraser's Magazine* 4 (1832) 754–61.

———. "Facts Connected with Recent Manifestations of Spiritual Gifts." *Fraser's Magazine* 5 (1832) 198–205, 316–20.

———. *For Missionaries after the Apostolical School: A Series of Orations.* London: Hamilton, Adams, & Co, 1825.

———. *For the Oracles of God: Four Orations. For Judgment to Come: An Argument, in Nine Parts.* 2nd ed. London: Hamilton, 1823.

———. "Interpretation of All the Old Testament Prophecies Quoted in the New." *TMW* 2 (1830) 777–804.

———. "A Judgment upon the Deliberations of the Last General Assembly." *TMW* 5 (1832) 84–115.

———. *The Last Days: A Discourse on the Evil Character of Our Times.* 2nd ed. London: Nisbet, 1850.

———. "On the Gifts of the Holy Ghost, Commonly Called Supernatural." *TMW* 2 (1830) 850–69.

———. "On the Human Nature of Christ." *TMW* 1 (1829) 75–99.

———. "On the True Humanity of Christ." *TMW* 1 (1829) 421–45.

———. *The Orthodox and Catholic Doctrine of Our Lord's Human Nature Set Forth in Four Parts.* London: Baldwin & Cradock, 1830.

———. *Sermons, Lectures, and Occasional Discourses.* 3 vols. London: Seeley & Burnside, 1828.

———. "Signs of the Times and the Characteristics of the Church." *TMW* 1 (1829) 641–66.

———. "Signs of the Times and the Characteristics of the Church." *TMW* 2 (1830) 141–62.

———. "What Caused Mr. Baxter's Fall?" *TMW* 7 (1833) 129–40.

"Irving's *Missionary Orations.*" Review of *For Missionaries after the Apostolical School: A Series of Orations,* by Edward Irving, and "Expostulatory Letter to the Rev. Edward Irving," by William Orme. *Eclectic Review* n.s. 24 (1825) 343–54.

"Irving the Rhapsodist and His Gold Repeater." *The Examiner,* May 14, 1826, 314.

Ishmael, Odeen. "The Demerara Slave Uprising." In *The Guyana Story: From Earliest Times to Independence,* 144–50. Blomingtoon, IN: Xlibris, 2013. Last modified May 10, 2014. www.guyana.org/features/guyanastory/chapter43.html.

Jinkins, Michael, and Stephen Breck Reid. "John McLeod Campbell on Christ's Cry of Dereliction: A Case Study in Trinitarian Hermeneutics." *Evangelical Quarterly* 70 (1998) 135–49.

Jurieu, Pierre. *The Accomplishment of the Scripture Prophecies; or, The Approaching Deliverance of the Church.* 2 vols. London: s.n., 1687.

Keay, John, and Julia Keay, eds. *Collins Encyclopaedia of Scotland.* Glasgow: HarperCollins, 1994.

Kerr, Hugh T., and John M. Mulder, eds. *Famous Conversions: The Christian Experience.* Grand Rapids: Eerdmans, 1983.

Knox, John. *Selected Writings of John Knox.* Edited by Kevin Reed. Dallas: Presbyterian Heritage, 1995.

Knox, John, et al. "The Scottish Confession of Faith (1560)." Edited by Kevin Reed. Dallas: Presbyterian Heritage, 1995. *Still Waters Revival Books.* www.swrb.com/newslett/actualNLs/ScotConf.htm#CH03.

Kolde, T. "Catholic Apostolic Church." In *Basilica–Chambers,* vol. 2 of *The New Schaff-Herzog Encyclopedia of Religious Knowledge,* edited by Samuel Macauley Jackson et al., 457–59. Grand Rapids: Baker, 1952. Christian Classics Ethereal Library at Calvin College. Last modified May 10, 2004. www.ccel.org/s/schaff/encyc/encyc02/htm/iv.vi.cxcix.htm.

Krapohl, Robert Henry. "A Search for Purity: The Controversial Life of J. N. Darby." PhD diss., Baylor University, 1998.

Ladd, George Eldon. *The Blessed Hope.* Grand Rapids: Eerdmans, 1956.

Lang, G. H. *Anthony Norris Groves: Saint and Pioneer.* London: Paternoster, 1949.

Lee, Byung-Sun. "'Christ's Sinful Flesh,' Edward Irving's Christological Theology within the Context of his Life and Times." PhD diss., University of Edinburgh, 2011.

Letham, Robert. *The Westminster Assembly: Reading Its Theology in Historical Context.* Westminster Assembly and the Reformed Faith. Phillipsburg, NJ: P. & R., 2009.

"Letter from Kirkaldy." June 16, 1828. National Library of Scotland, Word on the Street Digital Gallery, L.C.Fol.74(089). http://digital.nls.uk/broadsides/broadside.cfm/id/15361.

Lewis, Donald M. *Lighten Their Darkness: The Evangelical Mission to Working-Class London, 1828–1860.* Carlisle, UK: Paternoster, 2001.

Lewis, John A. *The Times of the Restoration of All Things.* Zion City, IL: Lewis, 1917.

Lindsay, Gordon. *John Alexander Dowie: A Life Story of Trials, Tragedies, and Triumphs.* Dallas: Christ for the Nations, 1980.

Lloyd-Jones, David Martyn. *Romans: An Exposition of Chapters 7:1–8:4; the Law, Its Functions and Limits.* Edinburgh: Banner of Truth Trust, 1973.

Luckin, W. "The Final Catastrophe—Cholera in London, 1866." *Medical History* 21 (1977) 32–42.

Mackenzie, Robert. *John Brown of Haddington.* 1918. Reprint, London: Banner of Truth Trust, 1964.

Macleod, John. *Scottish Theology in Relation to Church History Since the Reformation.* Greenville, SC: Reformed Academic, 1995.

Madden, Mrs. Hamilton. *Memoir of the Late Right Rev. Robert Daly.* London: Nisbet, 1875.

Martindale, Trevor W. "Edward Irving's Incarnational Christology." PhD diss., University of Aberdeen, 2009. *Pneuma Foundation.* www.pneumafoundation.org/resources/articles/TMartindale-EdwardIrvingIncarnationalChristology.pdf.

Mather, Increase. *A Dissertation, wherein the Strange Doctrine Lately Published in a Sermon, the Tendency of which is to Encourage Unsanctified Persons (while Such) to Approach the Holy Table of the Lord, Is Examined and Confuted.* Boston: Green, 1708.

McFarlane, Graham W. P. *Christ and the Spirit: The Doctrine of the Incarnation According to Edward Irving.* Carlisle, UK: Paternoster, 1996.

———, ed. *Edward Irving: The Trinitarian Face of God.* The Devotional Library. Edinburgh: Saint Andrew, 1996.

McGee, Gary B. "Initial Evidence." In *NIDPCM*, edited by Stanley M. Burgess and Eduard M. Van der Maas, 784–91. Rev. ed. Grand Rapids: Zondervan, 2003.

———, ed. *Initial Evidence: Historical and Biblical Perspectives on the Pentecostal Doctrine of Spirit Baptism.* Peabody, MA: Hendrickson, 1991.

———. "Shortcut to Language Preparation? Radical Evangelicals, Missions, and the Gift of Tongues." *International Bulletin of Missionary Research* 25 (2001) 118–20, 122–23. http://www.agts.edu/faculty/faculty_publications/articles/shorcut_mcgee.pdf.

———. "Taking the Logic 'A Little Further': Late Nineteenth-Century References to the Gift of Tongues in Mission-Related Literature and Their Influence on Early Pentecostalism." *Asian Journal of Pentecostal Studies* 9 (2006) 99–125.

McKenzie, Fred A. *Booth-Tucker: Sadhu and Saint.* London: Hodder & Stoughton, 1930.

Meek, R. *The True Nature of Our Lord's Humanity and Atonement.* London: Hatchard, 1833.

Miller, Edward. *The History and Doctrines of Irvingism, or of the So-called Catholic and Apostolic Church.* 2 vols. London: Kegan Paul, 1878.

Miller, James. *The Lamp of Lothian; or, The History of Haddington.* Haddington, Scotland: Allan, 1844.

"Miracles, Signs, Powers." *TMW* 3 (1831) 138–60.

Montague, Bruce R. "Family Research and History: Basil Montagu, 1770–1851." *The Montague Millennium.* Last modified February 22, 2006 http://www.montaguemillennium.com/familyresearch/h_1851_basil.htm.

Montgomery, Carrie Judd. "Edward Irving's Experience of Faith Healing." *Triumphs of Faith*, 4:4 (1884) 76–79. In *Healing Evangelists, 1881–1957.* Springfield, MO: Flower Pentecostal Heritage Center, 2006. CD-ROM.

Moore, Thomas. *Tom Moore's Diary, 1818–1884: A Selection.* Edited by J. B. Priestley. Cambridge: Cambridge University Press, 1925.

Morley, John. *The Life of William Ewart Gladstone.* 3 vols. London: Macmillan, 1903.

Mortenson, Terry. "British Scriptural Geologists in the First Half of the Nineteenth Century: Part 5, Henry Cole (1792?–1858)." *Journal of Creation* 13 (1999) 92–99. http://creation.com/british-scriptural-geologists-in-the-first-half-of-the-nineteenth-century-part-5.

"Mr. Irving's Church and the Record Newspaper." *TMW* 5 (1832) 179–202.

Murray, Iain Hamish. *The Puritan Hope: A Study in Revival and the Interpretation of Prophecy.* Edinburgh: Banner of Truth Trust, 1975.

Nettles, Thomas J. *By His Grace and for His Glory: A Historical, Theological, and Practical Study of the Doctrines of Grace in Baptist Life.* Grand Rapids: Baker, 1986.

New Apostolic Church International. "Creed." *Nak.org.* Last modified November 6, 2011. www.nak.org/faith-and-church/creed.

———. "History of Our Church." *Nak.org.* Last modified April 2, 2013. www.nak.org/about-the-nac/history-of-our-church.

———. "The Holy Spirit and Its Diverse Ways of Activity." Remarks on the Doctrinal Statement of January 24, 2006, Zurich, Switzerland. *Nak.org.* Last modified October 19, 2006. www.nak.org/fileadmin/download/pdf/HlGeistundWirkungsweisen_100107_engl.pdf.

Newble, Alan. "Thomas Chalmers: Biography." *Thomas Chalmers Sermons and Writings.* Last modified February 7, 2001. www.newble.co.uk/chalmers/biography.html.

———. "Thomas Chalmers: Poverty and the Poor Law." *Thomas Chalmers Sermons and Writings.* Last modified February 7, 2001. www.newble.co.uk/chalmers/poverty.html.

———. "Thomas Chalmers: Quotes About Chalmers." *Thomas Chalmers Sermons and Writings.* Last modified February 7, 2001. www.newble.co.uk/chalmers/quotes.html.

Newman, F. W. *Phases of Faith.* London: Trübner, 1870.

Nienkirchen, C. "Christian and Missionary Alliance." In *NIDPCM*, edited by Stanley M. Burgess and Eduard M. Van der Maas, 523–25. Rev. ed. Grand Rapids: Zondervan, 2003.

———. "Simpson, Albert Benjamin." In *NIDPCM*, edited by Stanley M. Burgess and Eduard M. Van der Maas, 1069–70. Rev. ed. Grand Rapids: Zondervan, 2003.

Oliphant, Mrs. Margaret. *The Life of Edward Irving, Minister of the National Scotch Church, London.* 2 vols. 2nd ed. London: Hurst & Blackett, 1862.

Oliver, W. H. *Prophets and Millennialists: The Uses of Biblical Prophecy in England from the 1790s to the 1840s.* Auckland: Auckland University Press, 1978.

"On Miraculous Powers in the Church." *TMW* 3 (1831) 206–25.

Orme, William. *Memoirs, Including Letters and Select Remains, of John Urquhart, Late of the University of St. Andrew's.* Vol. 2. Boston: Crocker & Brewster, 1828.

Parham, Charles Fox. *A Voice Crying in the Wilderness.* 2nd ed. Baxter Springs, KA: Apostolic Faith Bible College, 1910.

Partridge, Eric, and Jacqueline Simpson, eds. *A Dictionary of Historical Slang.* Penguin Reference Books. Harmondsworth, UK: Penguin, 1972.

Patterson, Mark Rayburn. "Designing the Last Days: Edward Irving, the Albury Circle, and the Theology of 'The Morning Watch.'" PhD diss., University of London, 2001.

Pearce, Joseph. *Life-Changing Evangelism.* London: Marshall, Morgan, & Scott, 1936.

Piggin, Stuart, and John Roxborogh. *The St. Andrews Seven: The Finest Flowering of Missionary Zeal in Scottish History.* Edinburgh: Banner of Truth Trust, 1985.

Pilkington, George. *The Unknown Tongues Discovered to be English, Spanish, and Latin.* London: Field & Bull, 1831.

Presbyterian Church, Office of the General Assembly, USA. "The Scots Confession." In *The Constitution of the Presbyterian Church: Part I, Book of Confessions,* by the Presbyterian Church, USA. Louisville: Geneva, 1996. http://www.creeds.net/reformed/Scots.

[Empson, William?]. "Pretended Miracles, Irving, Scott and Erskine." *Edinburgh Review* 53 (1831) 261–305.

"Prophets and Apostles." *TMW* 5 (1832) 332–38.

Reid, W. S. "Presbyterianism." In *The New International Dictionary of the Christian Church,* edited by J. D. Douglas, 800–802. 2nd ed. Grand Rapids: Zondervan, 1978.

Renwick, Alexander Macdonald. *The Story of the Scottish Reformation.* 2nd ed. London: InterVarsity, 1960.

Review of *Babylon and Infidelity Foredoomed of God,* by Edward Irving. *Baptist Magazine and Literary Review* 18 (1826) 317–20.

Review of "Expostulatory Letter to the Rev. Edward Irving," by William Orme. *Congregational Magazine,* July 1825.

Review of *For the Oracles of God: Four Orations. For Judgment to Come: An Argument, in Nine Parts,* by Edward Irving. *The Christian Spectator* 6 (1824) 150–67, 199–218.

Review of *For the Oracles of God: Four Orations. For Judgment to Come: An Argument, in Nine Parts,* by Edward Irving. *Westminster Review* 1 (1824) 29–30.

"The Rev. Mr. Irving's Orations." *Blackwood's Edinburgh Magazine* 13 (1823) 214.

———. "The Rev. Mr. Irving's Orations." *Blackwood's Edinburgh Magazine* 14 (1823) 145–62.

"Rev. of—Irving's *Orations,* etc." *The Christian Observer* 23 (1823) 490–502, 557–587.

Robeck, C. M., Jr. "Azusa Street Revival." In *NIDPCM,* edited by Stanley M. Burgess and Eduard M. Van der Maas, 344–50. Rev. ed. Grand Rapids: Zondervan, 2003.

Robinson, Henry Crabb. *Diary, Reminiscences, and Correspondence of Henry Crabb Robinson.* 3 vols. Edited by Thomas Sadler. London: Macmillan, 1869.

Root, Jean Christie. *Edward Irving: Man, Preacher, Prophet.* Boston: Sherman, French, & Co., 1912.

[Row, Walter?]. "Reply to the above [Letter from Christiania], and Defence of Mr. Irving." *GM* 5 (April 1830) 212–13.

———. Review of vol. 1 of *Sermons, Lectures, and Occasional Discourses,* by Edward Irving. *GM* 4 (April 1829) 181–83.

———. Review of vol. 1 of *Sermons, Lectures, and Occasional Discourses*, by Edward Irving. *GM* 4 (June 1829) 269–75.

———. Review of vol. 1 of *Sermons, Lectures, and Occasional Discourses*, by Edward Irving. *GM* 4 (August 1829) 368–74.

Roxborogh, John. "As at the Beginning in Britain: Michael Harper, Edward Irving, and the Catholic Apostolic Church." *Theological Renewal* 11 (1979) 17–23. Last modified August 2003. www.roxborogh.com/catholicapostolic.htm.

———. "The Charismatic Movement of 1830." Presentation at Charismatic Tea, General Assembly, Wellington, New Zealand, November 4, 1980. Last modified 2003. www.roxborogh.com/1830charismatics.htm.

Sandeen, Ernest Robert. *The Roots of Fundamentalism: British and American Millenarianism, 1800–1930.* Chicago: University of Chicago Press, 1970.

Schlossberg, Herbert. *The Silent Revolution and the Making of Victorian England.* Columbus: Ohio State University, 2000.

Scott, Walter. "The Journal of Sir Walter Scott: May 23, 1829." *Literature Network, Jalic Inc.* Last modified 2013. www.online-literature.com/walter_scott/journal-of-scott/39/.

"Spiritual Gifts and Demonical Possessions." *TMW* 5 (1832) 152–54.

Spurgeon, Charles H. *Commenting and Commentaries.* Lafayette, IN: Sovereign Grace, 2007.

Standish, Russell R., and Colin D. Standish. "The Trinitarian Bible Society." In *Modern Bible Translations Unmasked*, ch. 24. Rapidan, VA: Hartland 1993. http://www.sundaylaw.net/books/other/standish/bibletrans/mbtu24.htm.

Stanley, Arthur Penrhyn. *The Life and Correspondence of Thomas Arnold.* New York: Appleton, 1845.

Story, Robert H. *Memoir of the Life of the Rev. Robert Story.* London: Macmillan, 1862.

Strachan, Charles Gordon. *The Pentecostal Theology of Edward Irving.* 1973. Reprint, Peabody: Hendrickson, 1988.

Stunt, Timothy C. F. *From Awakening to Secession: Radical Evangelicals in Switzerland and Britain, 1815–1835.* Edinburgh: T. & T. Clark, 2000.

———. "'Trying the Spirits': The Case of the Gloucestershire Clergyman." *Journal of Ecclesiastical History* 39 (1988) 95–105.

Surtees, Virginia. *Jane Welsh Carlyle.* Salisbury: Russell, 1986.

Sutherland, Martin. "Preaching as Truth: The Religious Epistemology of Edward Irving." *Colloquium* 36 (2004) 3–19.

Synan, H. Vinson, ed. *Aspects of Pentecostal-Charismatic Origins.* Plainfield, NJ: Logos, 1975.

———, ed. *The Century of the Holy Spirit: 100 Years of Pentecostal and Charismatic Renewal, 1901–2001.* Nashville: Nelson, 2001.

———. "Classical Pentecostalism." In *NIDPCM*, edited by Stanley M. Burgess and Eduard M. Van der Maas, 553–55. Rev. ed. Grand Rapids: Zondervan, 2003.

———. *The Holiness-Pentecostal Tradition: Charismatic Movements in the Twentieth Century.* Grand Rapids: Eerdmans, 1997.

Torrance, Thomas F. *Scottish Theology: From John Knox to John McLeod Campbell.* Edinburgh: T. & T. Clark, 1996.

Trial of the Rev. Edward Irving M.A.: A Cento of Criticism. 4th ed. London: Brain, 1823.

Tudor, John. "Prophetic Aspect of the Church." *TMW* 3 (1831) 11–14.

Vereté, Mayir. "The Restoration of the Jews in English Protestant Thought, 1790–1840." *Middle Eastern Studies* 8 (1972) 3–50.

Vidler, Alexander Roper. *The Church in the Age of Revolution.* Pelican History of the Church 5. Harmondsworth, UK: Penguin, 1971.

Vreeland, Derek. "Edward Irving: Preacher, Prophet, and Charismatic Theologian." *Pneuma Review* 5 (2002). www.pneumafoundation.org/resources/articles/EIrving.pdf.

W. of Exeter. "On Christ's Human Nature." Letter to the editors dated February 1830 in *GM* 5 (July 1830) 292–94.

Warner, W. E. "Montgomery, Carrie Judd." In *NIDPCM*, edited by Stanley M. Burgess and Eduard M. Van der Maas, 904–6. Rev. ed. Grand Rapids: Zondervan, 2003.

Warr, Charles Laing. *The Presbyterian Tradition: A Scottish Layman's Handbook.* London: Maclehose, 1933.

Wesley, John. *The Works of John Wesley.* Edited by Thomas Jackson. 14 vols. 3rd ed. 1872. Reprint, Grand Rapids: Baker, 1991.

Westminster Confession of Faith and the Larger and Shorter Catechisms. 1646. Reprint, Inverness: Free Presbyterian, 1981.

Whitley, Henry Charles. *Blinded Eagle: An Introduction to the Life and Teaching of Edward Irving.* Chicago: Allenson, 1955.

Wilks, Washington. *Edward Irving: An Ecclesiastical and Literary Biography.* London: Freeman, 1854.

Williams-Wynn, Frances. *Diaries of a Lady of Quality from 1797 to 1844.* Edited by A. Hayward. 2nd ed. London: Longman, Roberts, & Green, 1864.

Wingfield, Theodosia A. Howard. *Letters and Papers of the Late Theodosia A. Viscountess Powerscourt.* Edited by Robert Daly. 5th ed. London: Seeley, 1845.

Wordsworth, William. "I Wandered Lonely as a Cloud." In *William Wordsworth*, edited by Harold Bloom, 54. Bloom's Biocritiques BBC Series. Broomall, PA: Chelsea House, 2003.

Wordsworth, William, and Dorothy Wordsworth. *The Later Years: Part 1, 1821–1828.* Vol. 3 of *The Letters of William and Dorothy Wordsworth.* Edited by Alan G. Hill. 2nd ed. Oxford, Clarendon, 1978.

Index

Made in the USA
Monee, IL
23 October 2020

45596276R00197